Christianity in Japan, 1971–90

Christianity in Japan, 1971–90

Successor to *The Japan Christian Yearbook*

compiled and edited by

Kumazawa Yoshinobu & David L. Swain

91-233

Kyo Bun Kwan (THE CHRISTIAN LITERATURE SOCIETY OF JAPAN)
TOKYO, JAPAN

Christianity in Japan, 1971-90 is the successor
to *The Japan Christian Yearbook* (1932–70)
and its predecessors since 1903.

Typeset at the Nanzan Institute for Religion and Culture, Nagoya, Japan
Printed in Japan

Library of Congress Cataloging-in-Publication Data applied for

ISBN 4-7642-7133-8

DISTRIBUTORS

Japan: Kyo Bun Kwan, 4–5–1 Ginza, Chuo-ku, Tokyo 104, Japan.
        TEL. (03) 3561–8446 / FAX: (03) 3535–5033

USA: Friendship Press Distribution Office, P.O. Box 37844,
        Cincinnati, Ohio 45222–0844, USA. TEL. (513) 948–8733

For out-of-country orders, write or call the nearest distributor about
pre-payment arrangements.

CONTENTS

List of Writers and Translators

Note: Writers' names are listed by Part and Chapter numbers. Japanese names are in the East Asian order: surname first, personal name(s) last.

Translators names (where applicable) are in italics, but see Translators list for identification.

Entries conclude with place of residence in parentheses.

Abbreviations most used below:

ELCA Evangelical Lutheran Church in America
KCCJ Korean Christian Church in Japan
NCCJ National Christian Council in Japan
NSKK Nippon Sei Kō Kai (Anglican Church in Japan)
UCC United Church of Christ (USA)
UCCJ United Church of Christ in Japan
UMC United Methodist Church

PART I

1. **James P. Colligan.** Maryknoll priest; Tokyo correspondent for Catholic News Service in the United States (Tokyo).
2. **Kanda Kenji.** UCCJ pastor; associate professor, School of Theology, Kwansei Gakuin (Nishinomiya). *Robert Mikio Fukada, tr.*
3. **Uda Susumu.** Pastor, Seibu Yanagizawa Christian Church (independent); professor, Tokyo Christian College (Tokyo). *Robert M. Terhune, tr.*
4. **Yamano Shigeko.** Director, NCCJ Center for Christian Response to Asian Issues (Tokyo).

   Katsuragawa Jun (on Korea). Staff, Japan Emergency Christian Conference on Korean Problems (Tokyo). *Aiko Carter, tr.*

   Takeuchi Kentarō (on China). Moderator, NCCJ General Assembly; pastor, NSKK Tokyo Holy Trinity Church (Tokyo). *Yamano Shigeko, tr.*

   Katō Minoru (on Taiwan). Pastor, UCCJ Katase Church (Kanagawa District). *Aiko Carter, tr.*

Akiyama Naoe (on the Philippines). Associate secretary, NCCJ Philippines Committee; teacher, Azabu Gakuen school (Tokyo). *Aiko Carter, tr.*

Sakamoto Yoshito (on Japan Overseas Christian Service). JOCS public relations director (Tokyo). *Aiko Carter, tr.*

Takami Toshihiro (on Asian Rural Institute). Chair, ARI Board of Trustees, and director emeritus, ARI (Nishi Nasuno, Tochigi Prefecture).

Hiroki Michiko (on Asian Women Workers' Center). General secretary, Asian Women Workers' Center (Tokyo). *Yamano Shigeko, tr.*

PART II

5. **Tsukada Osamu.** NSKK priest; professor, St. Paul's University (Rikkyō Daigaku) (Tokyo). *Henry French, tr.*

6. **Shōji Tsutomu.** Pastor, UCCJ Inagi Church; instructor, Tsurukawa Rural Seminary; chair, NCCJ Peace Committee (Tokyo). *David L. Swain, tr. (hereafter DLS).*

7. **Nakajima John Masaaki.** UCCJ pastor; general secretary, UCCJ (Tokyo).

8. **Nakajima John Masaaki.**

9. **Yasuda Haruo.** Pastor, UCCJ Takehara Church (Hiroshima Prefecture). *Robert Ramseyer, tr.*

10. **Watanabe Mine.** Former president, YWCA of Japan; member, NCCJ Executive Committee (Tokyo). *Margaret Warren, tr.*

11. **Lee Chong-il.** KCCJ pastor; director, Korean Christian Center (Osaka). *Robert Stieber, tr.*

12. **Matsuda Mizuho.** Director, Asian Women's Shelter HELP (House in Emergency of Love and Peace) (Tokyo). *Dan and Noriko Corl, trs.*

13. **Hoshino Masaoki.** Pastor, UCCJ Mitaka Church; lecturer, Tsurukawa Rural Seminary (Tokyo). *Armin Kroehler, tr.*

14. **Jan Swyngedouw, CICM.** Professor, Nanzan Institute for Religion and Culture (Nagoya).

PART III

15. **Koyanagi Nobuaki.** UCCJ pastor; staff, Kansai Laborers Evangelism Committee; member, Buraku Liberation Center committee (Osaka). *Carl Gabrielson, tr.*

16. **Kumazawa Yoshinobu.** Pastor, UCCJ Igusa Church; professor, Tokyo Union Theological Seminary (Tokyo). *George W. Gish, Jr., tr.*

17. **Saitō Takeshi.** Coordinator of Health Education, Life Planning Center; counselor, St. Luke's Hospital Nursing School (Tokyo). *Etsu Reid, tr.*

18. **Saitō Yukio.** Pastor, UCCJ Genpyō Church; director, Tokyo Inochi no Denwa (Tokyo). *Saul Stensvaag, tr.*

19. **Yuguchi Takashi.** Assistant director, Lutheran Hour (Tokyo). *DLS, tr.*

20. **Akiyama Norie.** Chair, Board of Directors, Christian Literature Center; president, Shinkyō Shuppansha (Protestant Publishing Co.) (Tokyo). *DLS, tr.*

21. **Takenaka Masao.** Chair, Asian Christian Art Association; professor, School of Theology, Dōshisha University (Kyoto).

22. **Takado Kaname.** Playwright; director, Kyo Bun Kwan (Christian Literature Society) (Tokyo). *Noah S. Brannen, tr.*

PART IV

23. **Douglas P. Mikell.** Missionary, appointed by Christian Church (Disciples of Christ) and Presbyterian Church (USA) to work with UCCJ, Tokyo District; managing editor, *The Japan Christian Quarterly* (Tokyo).

    Igarashi Yoshinobu. Managing director, Kirisuto Shinbunsha (Christ Weekly Publishers), and director of publications (Tokyo). *Joe Stroud, tr.*

    William F. Honaman. Missionary, Episcopal Church (USA); secretary to the Primate, NSKK (Tokyo).

    Henry French. Missionary, Japan Evangelical Lutheran Missionary Association of the ELCA; professor, Japan Lutheran College and Seminary (Tokyo).

    Leroy Seat. Missionary, Japan Mission of the Foreign Mission Board, Southern Baptist Convention; professor, Seinan Gakuin Seminary (Fukuoka).

    Glenn Gano. Missionary, American Baptist Foreign Mission Society; mission correspondent, ABFMS Japan Office (Tokyo).

    John McIntosh. Presbyterian Church in Canada missionary with KCCJ, pioneer outreach and church planting; also works with the Korean Christian Center (Osaka).

24. **Yamaguchi Akiko.** Former secretary for public relations, NCCJ. *DLS, tr.*

25. **Izuta Akira.** Pastor, Nerima Church, Japan Baptist Church Association; chair, Japan Evangelical Association (Tokyo). *Gary Carlson, tr.*

26. **Izuta Akira.** *Timothy Johnson, tr.*

27. **Matsumoto Saburō.** Priest, Kyoto Diocese, Japan Catholic Church; former Planning Bureau chief, Catholic National Committee (Kyoto). *Carl Gabrielson, tr.*

28. **Maejima Munetoshi.** UCCJ pastor; general secretary, NCCJ. *Aiko Carter, tr.*

TRANSLATORS

Note: Listed alphabetically, with translated chapter/section noted by Part and Chapter number(s).

Noah S. Brannen. Author, translator; professor (ret.), International Christian University (Tokyo). III-22.

Gary Carlson. Missionary, Evangelical Covenant Church (Isezaki, Gumma Prefecture). IV-25.

Aiko Carter. UCC missionary; secretary, NCCJ (Tokyo). I-4, sections on Korea, Taiwan, the Philippines, and JOCS; IV-28.

Dan and Noriko Corl. Dan teaches at Fukuoka Jo Gakuin College; Noriko has a special interest in Asian women in Japan (Fukuoka). II-12.

Henry French. Missionary, Japan Evangelical Lutheran Missionary Association of the ELCA; professor, Japan Lutheran College and Seminary (Tokyo). II-5.

Robert Mikio Fukada. UMC missionary; professor, School of Theology, Dōshisha University (Kyoto). I-2.

Carl Gabrielson. Missionary, Japan Evangelical Lutheran Missionary Association of the Evangelical Lutheran Church in America (Toyota, Aichi Prefecture). III-15, IV-27.

George W. Gish, Jr. United Methodist missionary with UCCJ, Tokyo District, Honda Kinen [Memorial] Church (Tokyo). III-16.

Timothy Johnson. Missionary, Evangelical Covenant Church; feature staff, *The Japan Christian Quarterly* (Niiza, Saitama Prefecture). IV-26.

Armin Kroehler. UCC missionary with UCCJ; board member, Tsurukawa Rural Seminary (Aizu Takada, Fukushima Prefecture). II-13.

Robert Ramseyer. Missionary, General Conference Mennonite Mission (Hiroshima). II-9.

Etsu Reid. United Methodist missionary (ret.) with UCCJ (Tokyo). III-17.

Saul Stensvaag. Missionary, Japan Evangelical Lutheran Missionary Association of the Evangelical Lutheran Church in America (Sapporo). III-18.

Robert Stieber. UCC missionary with UCCJ; staff, UCCJ Buraku Liberation Center (Osaka). II-11.

Joe Stroud. United Methodist missionary with UCCJ, Shikoku District (Matsuyama, Ehime Prefecture). IV-23, section by Igarashi Yoshinobu.

David L. Swain. UMC missionary with UCCJ; editor, *The Japan Christian Quarterly*. II-6; III-19, 20; IV-24.

Robert M. Terhune. UMC missionary with UCCJ, Tokyo District, East Sub-district (Tokyo). I-3.

Margaret Warren. UMC missionary with UCCJ; staff, YWCA of Japan (Tokyo). II-10.

Yamano Shigeko. Director, NCCJ-CCRAI (Tokyo). I-4, sections on China, and Asian Women Workers' Center.

The Japan Christian Yearbook Genealogy

Published annually, 1903–70 (except 1942–49, 1952, 1969).
The last volume (No. 58) was the combined 1969–70 edition.

Publishers:

1903–05	Japan Missionary Federation
1905–70	Kyo Bun Kwan (except 1912–15)

Name changes:

1903–05	*The Christian Movement in its Relation to the New Life in Japan*
1906–14	*The Christian Movement in Japan*
1915–20	*The Christian Movement in the Japanese Empire, Including Korea and Formosa*
1921–26	*The Christian Movement in Japan, Korea & Formosa*
1927–31	*Japan Mission Year Book: The Christian Movement in Japan & Formosa*
1932–70	*The Japan Christian Yearbook*
1991	*Christianity in Japan, 1971–90.*

Foreword

TWENTY YEARS MAY BE only a tiny stretch in Christian history or Japanese history. But the 1971–90 period is one-sixth of the modern era of Christianity in Japan since the Meiji Restoration of 1868, and nearly half of the postwar span since 1945. In Christian circles it has been a time of striking contrasts and tensions that give sharper focus to the picture of Christianity depicted by the articles in this book.

BIBLE SALES: THE BRIGHT SIDE

One of the most remarkable developments in recent decades is the continued sharp rise in sales of Bibles in Japan. Indeed, annual sales reported by the Japan Bible Society are astonishing (cf. Appendix).

In the remaining months of 1945 after World War II ended on August 15, only twenty-three Bibles were sold in Japan. During the next twenty-five years, aggregate sales of full Bibles and single Testaments rose rapidly to pass the half-million mark, and exceeded one million in thirteen of the twenty years under review. Average annual Bible sales (1,035,472) in the 1971–90 period were 2.5 times the late 1960s average of 400,000. For Bible sales to exceed the number of Christians each year is simply phenomenal.

Even larger numbers of single books of the Bible and other biblical supplies (tracts, tapes, maps, etc.) are distributed each year. When these are added to Bible sales, annual counts exceed the number of Christians by several times.[1] The overall sales/distribution figure topped 10 million for the first time in 1977, and hit an all-time peak of 11,227,317 in 1982. While single-sheet tracts make up the bulk of these large figures, the overall counts are still indicative of general public interest.

Above we have referred only to sales of the Japan Bible Society. The Japan Bible Publisher (Nihon Seisho Kankōkai), established by evangelical groups in 1965, was also busy publishing and distributing Bibles throughout the same period. Recently a number of major commercial publishers, such as

---

[1] At the much-disputed Christian Pavilion at Expo 70, sales of full Bibles and single Testaments were limited, but the enormous distribution of all biblical supplies at the Pavilion helped set a single-year record of 8.8 million in 1970.

Iwanami Shoten, Chūō Kōronsha, Chikuma Shobō, and Kōdansha, have also produced Bibles. At least as an indication of interest among the general public, the sale of Bibles and Bible portions portends a fairly optimistic future for Christianity in Japan.

CHURCH MEMBERSHIP: THE DARK SIDE

If baptisms matched Bible sales each year, the future of Christianity in Japan would be bright indeed. Unfortunately, the outlook for baptisms and committed Christians is much dimmer.

For the year 1970, the 1971 *Kirisutokyō nenkan* (Christian yearbook)[2] shows 722,942 Protestants and 371,148 Catholics, for a total of 1,094,090 Christians in Japan that year.[3] Even though the yearbook then included some heterodox groups not included now, Christians were a mere 1.06 percent of Japan's total population of 102,650,000.

The 1990 "Christian yearbook" shows for the year 1989 a Protestant count of 638,850[4] and a Catholic increase to 435,826; with 25,803 Orthodox Church members reported, the 1989 total Christian count is 1,074,676. Christian numbers had slipped during the twenty-year period to only 0.87 percent of the 1989 total population of 123,450,000. The overall Protestant-Catholic-Orthodox figure reported in the forthcoming 1991 yearbook for 1990 is 1,092,034, a gain of 15,358 over 1989. This edges the Christian portion of the total population up to 0.88 percent.

In the two-decade span (1970–89 figures) the number of Catholics rose by 64,678, while the Protestant count dropped by 84,092, yielding an overall decrease of 19,414 in Christian numbers. Catholic gains were more than wiped out by heavy Protestant losses. This period opened with an animated but enervating dispute over the Christian Pavilion at the 1970 World Exposition (Expo 70) in Osaka. While this internecine struggle among Protestants, especially in the United Church of Christ in Japan, was surely not the only reason for the severe shortfall in church members, it was undoubtedly one of the crucial factors.

---

[2] Each yearbook gives statistics for the previous year; so statistics for 1970 appear in the 1971 *Kirisutokyō nenkan*. This yearbook is published by the Kirisuto Shinbunsha (Christ Weekly Publisher) in Tokyo.

[3] Orthodox Christians are included in this figure, as are also Jehovah's Witnesses, Mormons, and the members of the Unification Association ("Moonies"). Due to uncertainties regarding statistical methods of the latter three heterodox groups, they are not included in later editions of the "Christian yearbook." For that reason, they are not included in "Members, Churches, Clergy: 1970–90" in the Appendix.

[4] This count does not include the heterodox groups mention in n. 3.

Looking again at the statistics, the 1990 Christian yearbook lists new baptisms for Protestant churches at 9,541; for Catholic churches, 10,179; and a total of 19,720 baptized in 1989. However, the total number of Christians in the 1990 yearbook (for 1989) is 23,432 below the total given in the 1989 yearbook (for 1988). This means, of course, that there were over twenty thousand "dropouts" in 1989 alone. (New figures for 1990 show an additional 3,651 dropouts.) These membership numbers paint a very dim picture for evangelism in contemporary Japan, especially on the Protestant side. For whatever reasons, an enormous barrier seems to block the road to church growth.

EVANGELISM: THE INTERPRETIVE TASK

This sharp bright/dark contrast actually makes our evangelistic task quite clear. On the one hand, anyone in Japan can easily acquire a Bible, and as we have seen, many do. A door-to-door survey asking "Do you have a Bible in your house?" would most likely prompt responses such as "Yes, there's one somewhere in the closet" or "On the bookshelf there is a Bible portion someone gave me long ago." It would not be surprising to find that one in every two or three homes has a Bible.

On the other hand, why do so few actually go to church and become Christians? The answer is suggested, I believe, in the account (Acts 8:26–40) of the Ethiopian official who was reading the book Isaiah while riding in his chariot, and Philip was led by the Spirit to ask him, "Do you understand what you are reading?" The man said, "How can I, unless someone guides me?" After hearing from Philip the good news of Jesus, the Ethiopian was baptized. For the millions of Japanese who have their own Bibles, "Do you understand what you read?" is the right question; and their replies may well be "Not unless someone guides me."

The evangelistic task is, then, to resolve this incongruent situation by fulfilling the interpretive task as Philip did for the Ethiopian. The interpretive role is woefully unfulfilled in our time. If contemporary Japanese could hear the Bible interpreted properly, the prospects for evangelization would become much brighter.

MATCHING TEXT AND CONTEXT

The twenty-eight articles gathered in this volume portray a variety of Christian efforts to deal with turbulent times in responsible ways. In a sense, they record positive attempts to interpret faith through many kinds of witness and

service. Yet the articles also cast into sharp relief the great difficulty of the interpretive task.

The task is made even more difficult by the legacy of bitter dispute over
the Christian Pavilion at Expo 70. After twenty years the ruptures in our
Christian community remain hard to heal, and the scars still smart. Still
worse, we remain burdened by polarized positions such as individual soul-
winning versus social salvation, the "gospel faction" versus the "social faction," and church growth versus human liberation. And allegiance to these
positions has rendered reconciliation very difficult.

These polarities are by no means unique to Japan, but here the positions
have become entrenched to the point of sterility. Living faith has become
fixed mindset, and thus converted into ideology. Church life is torn between
strong centripetal forces centering on faith and church, and equally strong
centrifugal forces reaching out from church to society. Harnessing and har-
monizing these two extremes into a healthy union is our primary task. Many
of the bitter struggles of the past twenty years can be seen, in retrospect, as
earnest gropings toward the way of resolution and reconciliation.

The history of the Christian church has often shown docetic tendencies to
reject and abandon its current context and, just as often, ebionite tendencies
to be so involved as to become buried in the present situation. But the same
history shows that it is faith in Jesus Christ, the truly constant and trustwor-
thy one, that overcomes these extremes. Far from abandoning history, this
faith stands firmly within it. Yet this faith is not overcome and buried by history; rather, it is the instrument of God's saving work in history. It is none
other than faith in the mission of God (*missio Dei*). In this faith, salvation is
not for the soul or the body alone; nor is the fullness of the gospel warped
by ideology.

To emphasize text (Biblical truth) at the cost of forsaking one's context
(social situation) is to fall into fruitless isolation. Likewise, to emphasize context while ignoring the text is to risk being utterly swamped by one's situation. Japanese Christianity over the past two decades has been groping, I
believe, for the proper matching of text with context in order to make clear
the way to the full humanity offered by the gospel. In other words, we have
been trying to carry out our interpretive task. How we do so in the days
ahead will determine the course of Christianity in Japan well into the twenty-
first century.

                                                    Kumazawa Yoshinobu

February 1991

Introduction

THIS BOOK IS the successor to *The Japan Christian Yearbook*, which was published annually from 1903 to 1970 with few exceptions (see box, p. xi). Key editorial roles for the *Yearbook* were taken in prewar years by the Japan Missionary Federation and the National Christian Council of Japan (1932–42) and in the postwar era by the National Christian Council in Japan (1957–70). The last volume was the combined 1969–70 edition, which adopted a "new policy" of offering "pertinent information and statistical data of both Catholic and Protestant churches."

As many articles in this book make clear, the Christian community in Japan in 1970 faced a crisis of confidence and cooperation, and it was extremely difficult to formulate editorial policies for dealing with the hotly debated issues. The National Christian Council also found itself unable to provide adequate editorial staff and funding for the *Yearbook*, and the Kyo Bun Kwan, while ready to continue publishing it, could not take over editorial duties. The NCCJ Executive Committee reluctantly discontinued the *Yearbook*.

Since 1970, however, overseas churches and libraries have repeatedly sent requests for current issues of the *Yearbook*, only to be told that it is no longer being published. Recognizing the need for a continually updated, reliable, and broadly ecumenical record of Christianity in Japan, the NCCJ Executive Committee on September 21, 1989, approved a proposal, made by members Nakajima John Masaaki and Takado Kaname, to compile a "twenty-year book" on the 1971–90 period — provided that adequate editorial funds could be secured. The Editorial Committee began meeting regularly, but it was spring 1990 before minimal funding was assured. The requested articles came in by autumn of that year, and translations were completed by January 1991.

EDITORIAL POLICY

The 1970 *Yearbook* announced a "new policy" of Catholic and Protestant coverage; this twenty-year book continues that policy and adds a more extensive reporting on evangelical churches and councils. It also offers, in Part I, a survey of the worldwide setting in which Japanese churches and Christians have carried out their common tasks of witness and service. It does not, however, include extensive statistical data (only basic church data in the Appendix), nor are there church directories as in past editions.

Christianity in Japan, 1971–90 is a history book — but not in the sense that the writers are dispassionate outside observers; they are all impassioned participants in the processes they describe and interpret.

The same can be said of the Editorial Committee; a different assortment of persons on the committee might have chosen a different approach to the 1971–90 period. Indeed, some important areas are not included, such as parish ministries, theological education, Christian schools, cooperative relations with mission boards and societies. Even so, this book is offered with considerable confidence that the issues treated are all high on the list of those that gave this period its distinctive character.

A glance at the List of Writers and Translators readily reveals that production of this volume was an extensive ecumenical undertaking. Writers of entire chapters or of portions number 40; translators of full chapters or parts, 20. Two of these 60 persons read all manuscripts for problems of fact, translation, and expression; and two others read selected chapters as requested by the editor. Beyond these 60, two veteran editors read selected chapters, and two experienced proofreaders went over all printouts for typographical and topographical errors. All together, 64 persons collaborated with the editor in producing the final text. Add in a gifted computer-compositor and the ever-helpful publisher, and the total is five and a half dozen.

Since the Kyo Bun Kwan also publishes *The Japan Christian Quarterly*, it is not surprising that seven persons currently on the *JCQ* staff, two former staff members, and three on the journal's backup group, the Publications Committee of the Fellowship of Christian Missionaries, make up one full dozen of the total.

As for mission board involvement in Japanese Christianity, it is worth noting that eight of the 40 writers and all but three of the 20 translators are missionaries (and another is a son of missionaries). In fact, no separate treatment of mission boards bespeaks a very positive thing: most mission personnel are deeply involved in the life and work of the churches, councils, and movements in Japan.

The common motivation among all these busy people was a sense of compelling need to fill the "twenty-year gap" since the last *Yearbook* appeared. The 1970s and 1980s were times of complex, far-reaching changes in the Christian churches, organizations, and movements in Japan. It is vital to have a broadly ecumenical outlook on the period's distinctive events and issues, not merely to counter parochial views but also to enhance wider cooperation. Moreover, the two-decade summing up is especially timely for North

American churches engaging in the "Japan study year" plans of the National Council of the Churches of Christ in the USA.

Although there is as yet no official endorsement of the idea, either by the NCCJ or the publisher, informal discussions have already begun focusing on the next volume — perhaps a "ten-year book" covering the 1990s and looking toward the twenty-first century. If this dream is to become reality, it will surely involve a similar, though perhaps even larger, gathering of volunteered talents from all sectors of Japan's Christian community. There is, we are convinced, both an inner compulsion among Christians in this country and an external challenge that together make this kind of periodic reporting necessary and fruitful for the mission of God here and throughout the world.

NOTES ON STYLE

It is expected that many readers will read this book selectively; some may never read all chapters. For that reason there is some repetition of explanations in text and footnotes. Suggested cross-references such as "cf. III-22" also appear occasionally.

With so many writers and half as many translators, the editors were faced with great variety in conceptual approach and literary style. We have tried to achieve general consistency in presentation, without losing the distinctive touch of each writer and translator. Several working standards merit brief explanation.

Capitals. A reference work of this kind inevitably includes many names of organizations, including commissions, committees, councils, and movements. These names are capitalized, as are names of radio and television programs.

The text also has numerous titles of themes of conferences and study groups — and these most often appear along with organizational names. To avoid filling our pages with capital letters, only the initial word and proper nouns in theme titles are capitalized.

Also, the Japanese language has no "capital letters." Titles of books and articles in romanized Japanese and in English equivalents are treated as themes are: capitals only for initial words and proper nouns.

East Asian names of persons. The East Asian order is followed for Japanese, Korean, and Chinese names: surname first, personal name(s) last. For this reason, no comma follows Japanese surnames in the List of Writers and Translators.

Abbreviations. A list of most-used abbreviations (acronyms) of organizational names is given at the beginning of the List of Writers and Translators;

a longer list appears in the Chronology. Otherwise, acronyms are given in parentheses on the initial appearance of organizational names for subsequent use.

Caveat on the Catholic Church. Although for convenience we regularly refer to the "Roman Catholic Church" in Japan, it is technically a misnomer, as the Japanese name is Nihon Katorikku Kyōkai, rendered "Catholic Church in Japan" in the *Kirisutokyō nenkan* (Christian yearbook). Let it suffice to say that "Catholic Church" and "Catholic" as used here always refer to the church affiliated with Rome (unless otherwise specified).

ACKNOWLEDGEMENTS

On behalf of the Editorial Committee, genuine appreciation is expressed to all writers and translators. Together they have done much to make the contemporary Christian minority in Japan, its struggles and hopes, better known to the larger Christian world.

The editor is particularly grateful to Nakajima John Masaaki and Douglas Mikell for their careful and critical reading of all chapters. Our best efforts would have been much poorer without their generous help.

Aiko Carter was especially helpful in confirming materials related to the National Christian Council in Japan and many related ecumenical matters (besides ably translating one chapter and several portions of another).

Frank Baldwin, chief editor and translator at Japan Translation Center, gave invaluable critiques of chapters in Parts I and II.

Sr. Cheryl Allam, one of the editors of *The Japan Christian Quarterly*, provided much helpful advice on Catholic matters. Betty Sisk Swain, also of the *JCQ* staff, critically commented on many chapters and helped rewrite some. Another *JCQ* staff member, Blanca F. Mikell, joined Betty Swain in proofreading of the computer-composed printouts prior to offset printing of the book.

The mere listing of writers and translators, and the brief mention of the above-named, fall woefully short of reflecting the many qualities necessary to the writing, translating, critical reading, copyediting, and proofreading of this long and complex text. Those qualities are the fruit, in every case, of years of dedicated use of God-given talents in comprehending and contributing to the very processes of witness and service recounted in this book.

David L. Swain

April 1, 1991

I
World Christian Trends

1

Roman Catholicism Since Vatican II

The Church in the World and in Japan

James P. Colligan

CHRISTIAN DENOMINATIONS in 1981 numbered 20,000, according to editor David B. Barrett in his preface to the unique reference book published by Oxford Press, *World Christian Encyclopedia: A Comparative Study of Churches and Religions in the Modern World*. Tabulated in twelve years of research until it was four times the estimate made at the start of the project in 1968, the count apparently troubled Barrett himself. "The proliferation of 20,000 denominations is sure to cause unfavorable comment. Some will see it as sectarianism run riot," he wrote.

But he saw another side to his statistics. "It is what we would expect when Christianity is being spread among some 8,990 peoples speaking 7,010 languages." He urged toleration for the beliefs of others, especially for all co-believers in Christ. Diversity, or divergence in faith and practice, is not divisiveness, he concluded.

However sectarianism is viewed, the Roman Catholic Church headquartered in the Vatican is one of these 20,000 denominations worldwide. It is the most centrally governed. It comprises all churches and persons in communion with the Holy See and the Church of Rome, including five major Eastern Catholic rites. In mid-1990 it is the largest in number of adherents, approaching 900 million. It is the most widely diffused among nations and cultures. It claims an unbroken line of direct descent from Jesus through his chosen Twelve Apostles and their successors, the pope and bishops. For these bishops it claims authority in matters of faith based on the Bible. The Roman Catholic Church (or simply "the Church" hereafter) advocates Christian unity, including denominational reunion when agreeable.

History aside, its leaders today are neither blind to the reality of diversity, nor hell-bent on damning those of a different persuasion, especially since the 1960s. It was then that its Vatican Council II expressed profound respect for the positive role played by major world religions in fostering spiritual, moral, and cultural values. In four sessions from October 11, 1962, through December 8, 1965, the Church took a conciliatory and respectful approach to establishing bilateral dialogue, and on occasion multilateral cooperation, aimed at mutual understanding with other Christians and other religions.

VATICAN II

Vatican Council II was an ecumenical council, that is, an assembly of Catholic bishops from around the world, with and under the presidency of the pope. It has supreme authority over the Church in matters pertaining to faith, morals, worship, and discipline. ("Ecumenical" in this context describes the global nature and supreme authority of the assembly, a meaning different from that ecumenism wherein the term refers to relationships with other Christians in the interest of unity.) The councils have played a significant role throughout Christian history. They represent attempts of the Church to mobilize itself in times of crisis for self-preservation, self-purification, and growth. As Vatican II documents were gradually promulgated and studied, the impact of this council resonated deeply and widely.

The entire work of the Council centered about the theme of the Church. No mere exercise in navel-gazing, this assembly of more than 2,800 bishop-participants from most nations produced sixteen documents that exhibit an awareness of the contemporary world. A pivotal document was the Dogmatic Constitution on the Church, commonly referred to as *Lumen Gentium*, the opening words of its original Latin text. "Christ," it begins, "is the light of all nations."

Contrary to the perception of rigid conformity suggested by the word "dogmatic," the document expresses a conciliatory and ecumenical tone more pastoral than professorial. Christocentric, biblical, and historical, it always faces the horizon of eternal salvation. *Lumen Gentium* offers an authoritative, descriptive, and some would say radically new overview of the Church's understanding of itself as the People of God.

Three additional constitutions and their accompanying documents deepen and broaden aspects of this theme under topics that include divine revelation, sacred liturgy, ecumenism, religious freedom, the apostolate of the laity, priestly formation, missionary activity, relationships with non-Christian religions, Christian education, and a distinct pastoral statement on the Church in the modern world. In the Council's aftermath, the Roman Curia was revamped and internationalized. The Curia contains the central administrative agencies that have authority granted by the pope. Further, the body of laws that apply to the organizational and disciplinary aspects of the Church was reworked. The New Code of Canon Law went into effect worldwide in November 1983.

Understandably then, this twenty-first ecumenical council in the Church's nearly 2,000-year history, interpreted in context with its predecessors yet firmly set in our own day, has exerted a dominant influence during the twenty-year period under consideration here. It stimulated radical changes in the thinking and attitudes of Catholics.

Sectarian Storms

There was nothing secret about the Council and its debates. Prominent non-Catholic observers attended by invitation. The world media gave it extensive coverage. Countless volumes have since been written on its inner workings and conclusions. Though widespread rejoicing and hopeful enthusiasm accompanied the promulgation of its documents, the Council did not landscape an ecclesiastical "United Garden of Eden" for twentieth-century Catholics. On the contrary, controversy over interpretations, turmoil in religious practices, and painful questioning in the hearts of the faithful were part of its predictable but less desirable outcome. The Bark of Peter in 1990 is in the midst of a stormy shakedown cruise after a spiritual refitting to meet modern needs.

Take the matter of sectarianism, with which this essay opened. At least two more groups have furthered fragmentation in the 1980s in the spotlight of media attention. One originated in Europe, the other in the United States. Archbishop Marcel Lefebvre of Econe, Switzerland, rejected Vatican II enactments as unacceptable. He was suspended from priestly functions by papal authority in 1976. He founded the Priestly Society of St. Pius X, with an eventual membership of several bishops, some three hundred priests, and tens of thousands of adherents in more than thirty countries. As prime mover of the first schism in nearly a hundred years, he rejected repeated attempts at reconciliation by the present pope. He incurred excommunication in 1988 when he illicitly ordained four men as bishops.

Father George A. Stallings, Catholic priest and an official of the Archdiocese of Washington, D.C., disclosed plans in June 1989 to form a black Catholic church over the objections of his archbishop. He announced that his Imani Temple African-American Catholic Congregation would address the cultural needs and aspirations of African-American people. The temple encompassed a few parish congregations. Stallings, a black, said the Temple would give black Catholics total control over their lives without domination by the "Euro-American white male hierarchy." The U.S. hierarchy, including black bishops, in July 1989 urged Stallings to return to the unity of the Church. They reminded the public that Pope John Paul II on a visit to the United States two years earlier had told the black Catholic community that "its vitality is a sign of hope for society." Stallings continues on his course.

Or take the matter of liturgical renewal, which played a part in both cases above. Recognizing the close relationship of religion with culture, and recognizing the educational role played by ritual worship and liturgical functions, Vatican Council II downgraded the universal and traditional use of the Latin language in precisely defined ceremonies like the Mass. It encouraged, rather, the use of the vernacular, permitting too a degree of experimentation in ritual accoutrements like vestments, music, and the architectural and decorative surroundings at ceremonies, as well as in female participation. In general, it placed emphasis on catholic unity in diversity rather than on universal conformity to a cultural mode now foreign to most Catholics, especially in the non-Western cultures of Asia and Africa.

The objections of Lefebvre and his followers extended to the inevitable loss of truly devotional prayer as they knew it in their European milieu — cultured, more elevated than sensual, artistic in the highest sense. Their loss was felt in displacement of the centuries-old Gregorian Chant by often saccharine popular hymns hastily written. It was felt in the substitution of teenage guitars for towering pipe organs. It was tangible in the disruption of stately Gothic structural lines by an altar and temporary chairs seemingly misplaced part way down the nave to bring the Mass closer to the people. The loss, too, of Latin, a language of precision that enabled a Catholic to worship comfortably in any church in the world, proved unacceptable despite the Council's intention to make worship more meaningful to the masses. Unacceptable not only to this educated archbishop but also to many Catholics of the working class whose spiritual growth from childhood was nourished by candles, incense, psalmody, and their own profound adoration of God to a suitably mysterious Latin-language accompaniment.

Stallings, on the other hand, even with the experimentation allowed by Vatican II's new guidelines, apparently could not find enough of the fervor and enthusiasm and the joyfully shouted praises of a ceremonial style often thought stereotypical of a devout congregation of black Christians.

Authority and its exercise calls for attention in cases like these. Authority to speak in the name of Jesus Christ is the perennial core of dispute since Paul confronted Peter on the question of Jewish converts. Or since the priest Arius of Alexandria was condemned by the first ecumenical council, Nicea I in 325, for denying the divinity of Christ.

Questioning Authority

Authority in the Church underwent serious inspection, perhaps introspection, during Vatican Council II and since, with the pope at the heart of the matter. One aspect was his relationship to the other bishops. A concept of "collegiality" evolved during discussions and in later documents, confirming the undeniable teaching authority of each bishop in his own diocese. An occasional theological opinion then and since leaned toward extending that authority to national or regional conferences of bishops acting independently of the pope, one assumption being that they understand better the ethnic and cultural mores of their people.

According to Church teaching based on the Bible, the pope has full and supreme authority over the universal Church. He is not merely first among equals. He is not simply the presiding officer of a council. He is the head, the Vicar of Christ. In an ecumenical council the bishops act together with the pope to formulate, clarify, and expound universal teachings. His authority, however, remains undiminished.

Bishops in their respective dioceses carry the burden of authority conferred by Christ in Church teaching. They are assisted by theologians, not subordinate to them. And geographical groupings of bishops are intended to assist their individual bishop-members in common problems, not usurp or dominate their role as shepherd. The lines of authority, clearly defined, are intended to assure fidelity to the essentials of Christ's teaching amid ethnic and cultural diversity, and throughout changing times. Mistakes will be made along the way, but not in essentials if approved by the pope.

Liberation theology. Meanwhile, prominent theologians like Hans Kung, Charles Curran, and Edward Schillebeeckx have been rebuffed and refuted, with much publicity. So have scholarly advocates of "liberation theology" when judged to be twisting the Gospel message into a quasi-political tract on social activism, or when thought to be bent on restructuring political and social entities in the name of an otherwise acceptable "preferential option for the poor." Liberation theology has made a contribution to interpreting the gospel message, which Church authority has acknowledged. In the process, some of its strongest advocates have veered into streams of opinion deemed unnavigable by official charts of Church teaching.

The debate over authority is not a new one. It is, however, exacerbated when theologians resort to modern media to diffuse their opinions, as though pleading for public opinion to back their position before presentation to the hierarchy. The official stance, put forth emphatically in late June 1990, contends that publicly expounding views contrary to official teaching has created a "climate of conflict" distressing to the faithful. The document is entitled "Instruction on the Ecclesial Vocation of the Theologian." Its source is the Congregation of the Doctrine of the Faith. The implied question it carries is this: Can such scholars then call themselves Catholic theologians? Indeed, due to public confrontations, a few prominent scholars have been banned from teaching in Catholic universities. The smoke is still rising from this latest cannonade.

Sex and celibacy. Authority and its exercise are at the core of issues pertaining to the role of the laity in the Church. Clericalism has long been a pejorative term, yet a reasonable biblical interpretation has Jesus Christ confer full authority on Peter and the Apostles. Vatican Council II produced a Decree on the Apostolate of the Laity even after extending them lengthy attention in *Lumen Gentium*. The documents strongly urged greater participation in areas of church life. Yet criticism recurs over moral strictures enacted by aging prelates, by childless clerics, by unmarried males. Negative reactions accompany Church teaching on divorce, birth control, abortion, homosexuality, and artificial means of conception — all of which have sexual import. Some of the blame, where blame is called for, can be laid to the sexual revolution in society at large, the inflated insistence on individual liberty and self-determination, the emphasis on lifestyle and comfort prevalent in many countries these past twenty years.

Sex inevitably plays a role in religion. Some Christian denominations recently have accepted the ordination of women to the priesthood, and even to the episcopacy. The Roman Catholic Church has not. Progress in ecumenism may have been seriously affected in the process. Dialogue with the Church of England, for example, was showing signs of mutual agreement in doctrine and authority until suddenly the chill of a new dissension was felt, even dividing Anglicans among themselves.

The value of a celibate priesthood came into question indirectly as Vatican Council II documents extolled the undeniable part played by marriage in God's plan. They described the Christian laity in glowing terms. "These faithful are by baptism made one body with Christ and are established among the People of God. They are in their own way made sharers in the priestly, prophetic, and kingly functions of Christ." Even the Decree on the Ministry and Life of Priests, while recounting the tradition and purposeful dedication of priestly continence in the Western or Latin Rite, acknowledged that celibacy is not a divinely stipulated requisite but a discipline defined by the Latin Church. Eastern Rite churches in union with Rome have always had a married clergy.

Thousands of priests in the past two decades saw in this a signal flare. Many began to suspect that Vatican Council II had taken a sledgehammer to their altar of sexual sacrifice. Before the altar became totally destroyed and they found themselves too old to reconsider, they opted out of their perpetual promise. Social and psychological restraints imposed by a continent single life, complicated further by the demands and discipline of priestly duties in service to so many, had less attraction now when expounded in terms of a common priesthood. Many thus seriously asked, "Why bother?" When Curia officials with papal approval granted increasing numbers of dispensations from the vow of celibacy, the stigma of disloyalty disappeared. Growing numbers of priests chose marriage and "laicization," with or without papal approval.

Shifting roles. Worldwide, the number of priests has dropped sharply. Aspirants to the priesthood (i.e., seminarians) have declined in number. The resulting shortage of clergy has reached proportions viewed as serious. A salutary side effect, meanwhile, is the increased involvement of laity to fill gaps in many areas of church life. In recent generations, priests increasingly shouldered administrative, educational, and welfare duties in addition to their particular charisms of conducting worship and preaching the gospel. Lay women and men now find an active place for themselves in the makeup of the Catholic community. The shortage of clergy to perform sacramental duties continues to be a major concern, however. An eventual solution may lie in motivated Catholic parents setting an example of Christian service, while encouraging their sons to become priests. Or it may lie in Church acceptance of a married clergy, which would reverse a centuries-old tradition. Or in ordaining women to the priesthood, heretofore judged unacceptable as contrary to Jesus' own example. One thing is certain: the priesthood of Christ will not disappear.

"Signs of the times" is a catch phrase utilized at Vatican II and since. It refers to contemporary events, trends, and developments as well as to the aspirations of people in various cultures and societies. The Church lives and functions in these, not in an abstract, ethereal world of its own. The signs of the times, then, call for prayerful observation as related to, even as witness to, the will of God in contemporary Church existence. The signs may be positive or negative. What meaning to Christians in Japan and their future, for example, has the 1990 ceremonial enthronement of the new emperor of Japan, a man explicitly described as a "priest-emperor" by government officials and advisers? What significance has the collapse of Communist ideology for Christians of Eastern Europe and the world? What is the will of God for the Church and its peoples in respect to advocacy of the emancipation of women?

The Papal Impact

The second factor of major impact on the Church today is the person of the present pope, John Paul II. He was elected Bishop of Rome on October 16, 1978, almost midway into our twenty-year period under review. The 263rd successor of Peter the Apostle, he is the first Polish pope in history. Marriage and a trip to the moon are among the few adventures he has not undertaken in a lifetime of experience. His forty-five or so pastoral trips to foreign countries might well equal a trip to the moon in mileage, as he seeks to personalize his papal role as universal pastor. These visits also kept him in trouble-shooting touch with post-Council problems. A highly talented linguist and more happily at home in a crowd than Paul VI, for example, he makes an effort to learn the basics of the vernacular of each country prior to his visit. He uses these basics effectively in greetings and speeches.

Born Karol Wojtyla in Wadowice, Poland, on May 18, 1920, he showed an early interest in poetry and theater arts. His studies stopped with World War II, when he went to work in a stone quarry and a chemical plant. He began studies for the priesthood in 1942 at a time when Nazi fascism obliged seminaries in occupied Poland to go underground. After the war he earned doctorates in Rome and Lublin in ethics and moral theology. Later, as Bishop of Cracow, he walked a risky line in resisting with his fellow bishops the efforts of the ruling Communist regime to impose atheism and secularism on the Polish people. He made recognized contributions to Vatican Council II. As pope his "Ostpolitik," the knowledgeable attention he paid in preaching and diplomacy to the Eastern-bloc nations, surely played a role in recent developments there. He narrowly escaped death in St. Peter's Square on May 13, 1981, when shot in an assassination attempt. Soon recovered from his wounds, he showed no sign of slowing the pace of his myriad travels, administrative duties, private and general audiences, writing, preaching, and praying.

John Paul II is tagged "ecclesiastical conservative" by observers in and out of the Church. Since elected, he has staunchly affirmed earlier instructions and decisions on moral teachings in general, including explosive issues like birth control, abortion, and divorce. He soon battened the hatches on dispensations from priestly celibacy. With authority to appoint bishops to sees around the world, he has consistently selected men with proven loyalty to a disciplined view of Christian life in all its moral and doctrinal dimensions.

Noisy protests by interested parties in and out of the Church have met some choices in personnel. His appointees to sees worldwide will serve as navigators for the near term in the post-Council voyage. "Progressives" judge the trend to be a betrayal of the spirit of the Council. Others see in it a necessary reefing of sails, in winds of change reaching dangerous velocities.

No ivory tower recluse unaware of winds and tides, however, John Paul II is a survivor of fascist and communist oppression and terrorist attack, a scholar of ethical behavior, an experienced pastor and professor, a world traveler with incomparable sources of information, a pleasant personality, a play-wright. He is captain of the Church, licensed by Christ. Loyal Catholics pay him allegiance.

Typical of his meetings with other Christians, perhaps, was that with a high-ranking delegation of the National Council of Christian Churches in the USA, April 10–14, 1989, for wide-ranging discussions on ecumenical, political, and social issues. He told the delegation that ecumenism will prog-ress if all "remain ever faithful to the Lord." The Reverend Patricia A. McClurg, president of the NCCC-USA, expressed gratitude for "the oppor-tunity to confess together what we share of the common apostolic faith," and to "pray that the day may be hastened when full communion among our sep-arate ecclesial communities may be realized."

Of wider scope was the October 27, 1986, gathering of religious leaders, including the pope, in Assisi, Italy. He called it "a coming together of a vast movement of reflection and prayer in which followers of every religious faith should feel themselves involved." Protestants, Catholics, Orthodox, Bud-dhists, Hindus, Shintoists, Muslims, Zoroastrians, and others were repre-sented.

JAPAN: INDIGENIZATION AND INTERNATIONALIZATION

John Paul II visited Japan, February 23–26, 1981. Thousands stood for hours in a rare Nagasaki snowfall to attend an outdoor papal Mass. Crowds thronged to see and hear him at the Hiroshima commemoration of the atomic bombing. But the visit received less fanfare than in other lands. The Church here is small, even minuscule numerically and in proportion to the total population. Annual statistics for 1989 count some 412,000 Catholics. Structurally it reflects Japanese organizational skills, with sixteen dioceses led by indigenous bishops who coordinate activities and pronouncements through an increasingly efficient headquarters in the capital. This episcopal conference is in turn an active element in the Federation of Asian Bishops Conferences (FABC). Neither continuing "Japanization" nor Asia-wide col-laboration awaited John Paul II's visit; Japan's dioceses have been transfer-ring to native Japanese clerics since 1927. Wartime and postwar developments hastened the process. The transfer was completed in 1973 when Naha, Okinawa, was made a diocese under a Japanese bishop following the death the previous year of its American apostolic administrator.

Close association with bishops of thirteen other Asian nations, notably since the FABC was established in 1970, has facilitated understanding of similar problems and prompted greater self-assurance and action on the part of the Japanese hierarchy. In a real sense, Japanization is less urgent when examining the thinking of bishops than internationalization. Prime Minister Nakasone Yasuhiro (1982–87) made "internationalization" a catchword in encouraging the citizenry to overcome their prejudice against imported goods. Presumed to be sincere, he meant his publicized campaign to alleviate trade tensions with Western nations. The internationalization necessary to bishops of any nation likewise reduces tensions. It is a breadth of vision that reaches panoramic scope in viewing moral issues, administrative procedures, and the Church's place among nations. Perhaps catholic is the better word here. Indigenization should never quarantine one ship in the fleet.

Foreign clergy still number nearly 900 men here, close to half the total.[1] But pastoral and administrative authority is entirely in the hands of Japanese bishops. Of course, a racial change in ranking prelates does not automatically and immediately effect an indigenization that converts details of worship and preaching and moral consciousness into forms compatible with ethnic sensitivities. (Nor does it necessarily effect the contextualization which follows indigenization, as some writers now distinguish.)

Liturgy and Evangelization

Much remains to be done even in the relatively simple matter of adapting liturgical practices to native Japanese modes without altering essentials, as in the Mass. What the Church is about, after all, is worship of the Eternal God in word and action, day and night. Vatican Council II documents include a Constitution on the Sacred Liturgy, which reads:

> Even in the liturgy, the Church has no wish to impose a rigid uniformity in matters which do not involve the faith or the good of the whole community. Rather she respects and fosters the spiritual adornments and gifts of the various races and peoples. Anything in their way of life that is not indissolubly bound up with superstition and error she studies with sympathy and, if possible, preserves intact. Sometimes in fact she admits such things into the liturgy itself, as long as they harmonize with its true and authentic spirit.

John Paul II's visit received credit from Japan's bishops for stimulating and encouraging in particular their evangelizing efforts. Following three years of planning and preparations, the first National Incentive Congress on Evange-

---

[1] This refers only to clergy; the larger number given for Catholics in "Members, Churches, Clergy" in the Appendix includes, besides native and foreign clergy, men and women in religious orders and societies. — Ed.

lization (NICE I), November 20–23, 1987, brought together 273 participants — bishops, priests, female and male religious and laity — representing all
sixteen dioceses. They discussed the overriding concerns of the Church in
Japan as they pertain to evangelization. The much publicized meeting helped
the Church to focus its efforts nationally, to reassess its organizational structure, to review the entire spectrum of its activities in education, in social welfare, in parish life, in clergy training. Committees and commissions of clergy
and laity are engaged now in implementing the NICE I suggestions under a
follow-up program that involves the bishops. NICE II is planned for a few
years hence.

Church and Society

The bishops have demonstrated a readiness also to express objections to the
Japanese government on issues of social and moral concern affecting all or
part of society — a faint cry in a packed coliseum, perhaps, given the size of
the local church, yet considered a duty nonetheless. The death of Emperor
Shōwa (Hirohito) in January 1989 elicited a letter to then-prime minister
Takeshita Noboru, asking caution lest constitutional guarantees of separation of religion and state be disregarded in the funeral rites. The Catholic
Council on Justice and Peace under the direction of a bishop has exercised
vigilance in collaboration with other Christian bodies over imperial succession and enthronement ceremonies held in November 1990. A
fingerprinting requirement that demeans Korean residents, discriminatory
practices involving the socially rejected Buraku people, the proliferation of
nuclear armaments, politically opportune visits of politicians to Yasukuni
Shrine, even human rights issues on the Indonesian island of Timor, all have
caught the council's attention. All have been addressed publicly.

Beyond issues of human rights and justice and peace, the most felicitous
effort in conjunction with other Christians was, fittingly, the publication of
a common Bible. More than eighteen years of Protestant-Catholic cooperation among biblical scholars and church leaders culminated in publication of
the New Japanese Common Bible Translation in September 1987 (cf. IV-
28). The involvement of the bishops with the Japan Bible Society dates back
to May 1969 after preliminary meetings of scholars. Episcopal participation
was stimulated by publication the previous year in London and Rome of the
"Guiding Principles for Interconfessional Cooperation in Translating the
Bible." Joint publishers were the United Bible Societies and the Vatican's Secretariat for the Promotion of Christian Unity. The Secretariat was opened
following Vatican Council II. Somehow symbolic of the outcome for Japanese Catholics was the willing acceptance of the unfamiliar Japanese rendering

of Jesus' name as long used by Protestants (Iesu, replacing the traditional Catholic form, Iezusu).

The bishops in February 1985 issued an instruction on the subject of ancestor veneration as understood and practiced in Japanese Buddhism, emphasizing respect rather than worship. Shinto rites, however, were not within the purview of their exposition. The degree to which ancestor "worship" with ethnic and nationalistic coloration keeps the nation wrapped in robes that repel a deeper religious permeation constitutes a permanent point of reference in Christian evangelization.

An instance of prayer life adopting and adapting to indigenous modes is evident in the scholarly study and practice of Zen Buddhist procedures in Christian meditation. Priest-practitioners have written books on the subject. They have utilized Zen methodology in conducting spiritual retreats. A mutual interchange of extended visits by Japanese Buddhist monks with their European Catholic counterparts in the others' monasteries has been realized. The bishops with their FABC confreres have written publicly and positively of the Asian contribution to prayer, "a richly developed prayer of the whole person in unity of body-psyche-spirit."

Consternation followed a January 2, 1990, letter from top-level Vatican authority to all bishops on "some aspects of Christian meditation." Unmistakably critical of Zen and Yoga concepts, this instruction (itself criticized as void of suitable consultation on the matter) was issued by the same Congregation for the Doctrine of the Faith that has reined in theologians. On Zen and Yoga concepts, it warned against erroneous notions of physical and psychological relationships to God in prayer. Resolution of this matter will occur when "the other side is heard," that is, when Asian bishops and scholars respectfully proffer dissenting arguments.

Conflict, Openness, and the Future

Might it not be better for the Church to acknowledge the important role played by public awareness, even in contentious issues? Is a "climate of conflict" in Church-related questions of international scope a greater obstacle to belief and practice than a resolution reached secretively by a perceived élite suspected of self-serving interests? At what point is expressed diversity of opinion perceived as disconnection, disloyalty, disobedience, disregard, disrespect? How does this differ, depending on intellectual sophistication and common-sense simplicity? With all its experience and the purposeful "openness" of its Vatican Council II, the Church, universally and locally, has still to settle on proven procedures when seeking solutions in the public forum.

A crystal-ball vision of tomorrow in any but general terms is justifiably suspect. But where the Church in Japan will steer in these often troublesome gusts and currents need not be feared. Countless challenges, some without precedent, will continue to summon courage, loyalty, dedication, patience, and wisdom — and unity also — from the broad stream of Church adherents in the wake of Vatican Council II. Twenty earlier councils summoned the same from our predecessors. In isolation, as if under a microscope, differences might be dealt with, one by one. The Christian faithful will be served, their faith defended as much by honest effort in diversity as by permanent solutions.

Too often in the past, however, the irritations of political and national and ethnic friction have turned pinpricks into major plagues, dividing entire races and nations in their Christian convictions. The Church in China is a proximate example. Meanwhile, all of the above appears to bypass the lonely grief and ecstatic joy of the individual creature, Christian and other, bishop and mother, who is immersed in sin and hatred, alienation and pain, doubt and denial, oppression and suffering, rebirth and thanksgiving and *nirvana*-like fulfillment, reaching out for God. A guided accommodation based on the mutual understanding of East and West and North and South, as represented in the Church — and in the Sign of the Cross — is essential to unity. The Church and the faithful in turn will then present a salutary example to those outside, and this is the essence of evangelization.

2

World Ecumenism

Kanda Kenji

CHANGES OF UNPRECEDENTED scale and kind during the 1971–90 period have forced the Christian churches to see history in radically different terms. Attempts to cope responsibly with an ever-changing world have compelled the churches toward self-renewal. The ecumenical movements embodied in the World Council of Churches and the Christian Conference of Asia, in undertaking the tasks of renewal, have sought greater unity among themselves and greater solidarity in their common witness.

The challenges of renewal, unity, and witness have also confronted the churches in Japan. To see how the Japanese churches have tried to meet these challenges, we need to place their efforts within a critical review of the larger ecumenical scene. Our review shall focus on four key issues: ecumenical assemblies and actions; faith and order issues; mission and dialogue; and justice and peace. Then we shall conclude with a word on future tasks and prospects.

ECUMENICAL ASSEMBLIES AND ACTION

When the World Council of Churches (WCC) was founded in 1948, the United Church of Christ in Japan (UCCJ) and the Nippon Sei Kō Kai (NSKK; Anglican Church in Japan) became full members as churches, and the National Christian Council in Japan (NCCJ)[1] joined as a council. The Korean Christian Church in Japan (KCCJ) became an associate member in 1962, followed in 1973 by the Orthodox Church in Japan as a full member. The Japan Evangelical Lutheran Church (JELC), the Japan Baptist Conven-

---

[1] When formed in 1948 the name was "National Christian Council of Japan," but it was changed to "in Japan" in 1985. To avoid confusion, "National Christian Council in Japan" is used consistently herein. — Ed.

tion, and the Japan Baptist Union are members of the NCCJ, and thus have indirect ties to the WCC.

The East Asia Christian Conference (EACC), organized in 1959, was renamed the Christian Conference of Asia (CCA) in 1973. The UCCJ, KCCJ, NSKK, and the NCCJ are members of the CCA. The two Baptist groups and JELC[2] are related to the CCA through the NCCJ.

WCC Assemblies

As shown in table 2.1, the WCC General Assembly was convened twice during the 1971–90 period: the Fifth (1978) in Nairobi, the Sixth (1983) in Vancouver. The Seventh General Assembly is scheduled to be held in Canberra in 1991. The Nairobi assembly, with the theme "Jesus Christ frees and unites," emphasized the struggle against racism and the importance of dialogue with non-Christian religions. This assembly had five Japanese delegates: three from the UCCJ, one from the NSKK, and one from the Orthodox Church. One representative each from the KCCJ and the NCCJ also attended.

The Nairobi assembly elected Okuda Michiko (UCCJ) to the WCC Central Committee, but she soon resigned because of her husband's illness. D. T. Niles of India was elected one of four WCC presidents and served till his death in midterm, when Chō (Takeda) Kiyoko of the UCCJ replaced him. Recognition of these two women in WCC circles was an inspiration to Christian women in Japan. The ecumenical journal *Fukuin to sekai* (The gospel and the world) carried a report on the Nairobi assembly in its April 1976 issue, as did the 1977 *Kirisutokyō nenkan* (Christian yearbook).[3] There was no report in book form for the Nairobi assembly as there had been for the Third (New Delhi, India; 1961) and the Fourth (Uppsala, Sweden; 1968) general assemblies.

The Vancouver assembly met in July 1983 under the thematic banner "Jesus Christ — the life of the world." The central issues were environmental destruction, the North-South poverty gap, and political oppression throughout the world. Extended discussions sought to discern how Jesus Christ is indeed "the life of the world" in the midst of critical situations.

At this assembly there were three UCCJ delegates, two from the NSKK, one from the Orthodox Church, along with two KCCJ representatives and one from the NCCJ. Kawabata Junshirō (UCCJ), a layman, was made a member of the WCC Central Committee. Reports of this assembly appeared in "The gospel and the world" (December 1983, January 1984) and in the

---

[2] JELC was a member of the CCA till 1984.
[3] The English equivalents of the journal and yearbook titles are used throughout this article. — Ed.

TABLE 2.1

ECUMENICAL ASSEMBLIES AND CONFERENCES SINCE 1970

World Council of Churches

General Assemblies:

5th:	1978	Nairobi, Kenya
6th:	1983	Vancouver, Canada
7th:	1991	Canberra, Australia

Faith and Order Conferences:

1971	Louvain, Belgium
1974	Accra, Ghana
1978	Bangalore, India
1982	Lima, Peru
1985	Stavanger, Norway
1989	Budapest, Hungary

Mission Conferences:

1973	Bangkok, Thailand
1980	Melbourne, Australia
1989	San Antonio, USA

Justice and Peace Conferences:

1974	Sankt Pölten, Austria
1985	Tōzansō, Japan
1986	Glion, Switzerland
1988	Glion, Switzerland
1990	Seoul, Korea

Christian Conference of Asia

General Assemblies:

5th:	1973	Singapore
6th:	1977	Penang, Malaysia
7th:	1981	Bangalore, India
8th:	1985	Seoul, Korea
9th:	1990	Manila, Philippines

Mission Conferences:

URM:	1978	Auckland, New Zealand
	1979	Singapore
	1989	Cipanas, Indonesia

1984 "Christian yearbook." The WCC's preparatory study book, *Jesus Christ — the Life of the World*, was published in Japanese translation by Shinkyō Shuppansha (Protestant Publishing House).

CCA Assemblies

In contrast to the WCC's two assemblies in the twenty-year period, the Christian Conference of Asia convened its general assembly five times. The CCA Fifth General Assembly, meeting in Singapore in 1973 with the theme

"Christian participation in the Asian struggle," explored the challenges of common witness among suffering Asian peoples. This assembly, opened under the EACC label, restructured the organization and renamed it the Christian Conference of Asia. Of the eight delegates from Japan, Nakajima John Masaaki, then NCCJ general secretary, was elected to the CCA General Committee. There was no published report of this assembly.

"Jesus Christ in the suffering and hope of Asia" was the theme of the CCA Sixth General Assembly held in 1977 in Penang, Malaysia, with four NCCJ delegates and one each from the UCCJ, NSKK, and KCCJ. John Nakajima was chosen as one of the four CCA presidents, and Mrs. Sekiya Ayako was elected to the General Committee. "The gospel and the world" put out a pre-assembly issue in May 1977, and the 1978 "Christian yearbook" carried reports by delegates. The Kyo Bun Kwan in 1980 published a volume of assembly discussions under the title *Okore, hikari kiyuru to mo — Ajia no kunan no naka de* (Express your anger, even if the light is extinguished — amid the sufferings of Asia).

The CCA Seventh General Assembly met in Bangalore in May 1981 with the theme "Living with the people in Christ." It was the first time in Asia that "people" was made the central focus; this, of course, reflected the rise of Minjung (people) theology in South Korea during the 1970s. Of seven participants from Japan, Shōji Tsutomu, then NCCJ general secretary, was elected to the General Committee. "The gospel and the world" (September 1981) carried delegates' reports.

A specific contribution was made by Japanese delegates to the CCA Eighth General Assembly held in Seoul in 1985: a resolution (approved) that the Japanese government drop its required fingerprinting of long-term foreign residents in Japan. The theme was "Jesus Christ sets us free to serve." NCCJ General Secretary Maejima Munetoshi led an eight-member delegation, and he was elected to the General Committee. Detailed reports appeared in "The gospel and the world" (October 1985) and in *Ajia tsūshin* (Asia newsletter; November 1985) issued by the NCCJ's Center for Christian Response to Asian Issues (CCRAI).

The most recent CCA General Assembly, the Ninth, met in Manila in June 1990 with the theme "Christ our peace: building a just society." Eight Japanese delegates participated; Yawata Akihiko, executive secretary of the NCCJ, was made a member of the General Committee, while Maejima Munetoshi, NCCJ general secretary, was elected honorary treasurer to work with the four CCA presidents. Bishop John Samuel of Pakistan was elected general secretary, replacing Park Sang-jung of Korea. The possibility of the (Roman Catholic) Federation of Asian Bishops' Conference affiliating with the CCA was discussed at this assembly.

From this deliberately abbreviated rundown of the ecumenical organizational setting, we now turn to more substantive matters.

FAITH AND ORDER

The first World Conference on Faith and Order was held in 1927 in
Lausanne, Switzerland; the second in 1937 in Edinburgh, Scotland; the
third in 1952 in Lund, Sweden; and the fourth in 1963 in Montreal, Canada.
While there has been no "world conference" as such since Montreal, the
World Council of Churches has held six general meetings on faith and order
in the past twenty years: 1971 in Louvain, Belgium; 1974 in Accra, Ghana;
1978 in Bangalore, India; 1982 in Lima, Peru; 1985 in Stavanger, Norway;
and 1989 in Budapest, Hungary.

From Japan, Professor Maeda Gorō (Mukyōkai, or "nonchurch" movement) attended the Louvain meeting; Professor Ogawa Keiji (UCCJ) participated in the Bangalore and Lima meetings; Pastor Imahashi Akira joined the
Stavanger and Budapest meetings. At Bangalore in 1978, Professor Ogawa reported on the UCCJ position regarding the Yasukuni Shrine issue (cf. II-5).

The most significant fruit of all these faith and order meetings is the "Lima
Document" titled *Baptism, Eucharist, and Ministry* (or BEM Document).
This historic statement represented not only an evolving ecumenical consen-
sus among Protestants; it included the views of Roman Catholics as well.
The document was approved by the 1983 WCC General Assembly in Van-
couver.

The Accra meeting in 1974 had produced a forerunner document called
"One Baptism, One Eucharist, and a Mutually Recognized Ministry," which
was circulated to churches worldwide for critical response. None came from
any responsible church body (just one from a Roman Catholic priest speaking for himself). Interest in the subject was at a low ebb in the mid-1970s.
The Accra materials were not translated or otherwise introduced into Japan
at the time.

The Lima Document of 1982, however, was translated and published in
1985 by the UCCJ Board of Publications[4] in response to widespread interest.
This publication was the cooperative product of the NCCJ Faith and Order
Commission and the Roman Catholic Church's Ecumenism Committee (cf.
IV-28). It also included the "Lima Liturgy" and the earlier Accra materials,
with detailed commentaries and interpretation. Breaching conventional wisdom that ecumenical books do not sell well, this one has gone through three

---

[4] The Japanese title is *Senrei, seisan, shokumu — kyōkai no mieru itchi o mezashite* (Baptism,
eucharist, ministry — seeking a visible church unity).

printings. It is intriguing that, in this turbulent period, a book on basic matters of faith attracted so much attention.

The Lima Document was extensively studied and discussed at the national, district, and local levels. The East Subdistrict of the UCCJ's Tokyo District, for example, compiled a written response in December 1985 after careful deliberation. Catholic and Orthodox churches waited to see what worldwide response would be. Official responses were sent to the WCC by the Nippon Sei Kō Kai and the UCCJ. The NSKK response, dated November 1985, affirmed the document's appeal for visible unity in terms of the following points: (a) it is an expression of the church's historically transmitted faith; (b) it values denominational traditions, yet allows for mutual supplementing of each denomination's shortcomings; (c) it provides useful directions for revitalization in liturgy, education, ethics, spiritual life, and witness; and (d) it indicates the need for continued study.

In its March 1986 response, the United Church of Christ in Japan also positively appraised the document's formative process and directions, yet raised some questions from its perspective as a younger church, and a united one, in a missionary situation. For instance, there was no mention of possible baptism of the mentally disabled. It did not deal with participation of the non-baptized in the eucharist. And treatment of the place of the Word in worship seemed inadequate. The UCCJ critique focused particularly on ministry: "The document's concept of ministry definitely lacks a perspective on the needs of missional outreach through pioneer ministries of the laity and especially women. The document is essentially conservative." The UCCJ statement then goes beyond criticism to suggest "promotion of ecumenical dialogue with churches throughout the world." In this dialogue "the UCCJ should be able, as an Asian, young, minority church, to make a constructive contribution to the traditional, historical, well-organized churches of the world."

In connection with the Lima Document, the UCCJ Research Institute on the Mission of the Church published its study results on the eucharist in 1987. Reflecting the UCCJ's development as a union of many denominations, this book offered insights on children's participation in communion services, the mentally disabled, and the non-baptized. Meanwhile, the general assembly of the Japan Evangelical Lutheran Church, though not responding officially to the document, in 1986 approved participation by children in communion services.

The "Lima Liturgy" has also received much attention in Japan. The ecumenical journal *Reihai to ongaku* (Worship and music) in 1984 devoted an entire issue (#43) to it; and the liturgy has been used experimentally on various occasions, though interest in formal liturgy is generally low in Japanese

Protestantism. The UCCJ Twenty-third General Assembly (1984) dealt with a draft of revised rites that expressed new understandings of worship, baptism, and the eucharist. More time will be required, however, for acceptance of new liturgical practices by the nonliturgical churches in Japan.

In 1986 the Anglican communion (NSKK) issued a new Book of Prayer that abandoned the *bungotai* (old literary style) in favor of more contemporary colloquial Japanese. In 1989 the NSKK Press published a detailed discussion of the ecumenical perspective reflected in the new Book of Prayer, with the title *Sei Kō Kai no reihai to kitōsho* (Worship in the Sei Kō Kai and the Book of Prayer).

A new Book of Worship was adopted in 1982 by the general assembly of the Japan Evangelical Lutheran Church. It too embodies a broader ecumenical approach in its order of worship.

The place of music in worship has also received attention. With the founding of the Center for Worship Resources in the WCC Department of Life and Renewal, calls went out for the contextualization of music in worship by incorporating local music. In Asia the first conference on this theme was held in Manila in 1987 under CCA auspices. It produced a collection called *Asian Songs of Worship*, which includes some Japanese and Okinawan hymns. In 1990 the CCA and the Asian Institute for Liturgy and Music jointly published a new CCA hymnal titled *Sound the Bamboo*. But the Western influence on church music in Japan is so overwhelming that much time will lapse before indigenous creativity will find expression in worship music.

MISSION AND DIALOGUE

Key Conferences

In 1961, the WCC General Assembly meeting in New Delhi approved a merger with the International Missionary Council to form the WCC Commission on World Mission and Evangelism. Since then, four conferences have been held, the first being held in Mexico City in 1963. The next, and the first in the period under review here, was the Bangkok meeting (1972/73) on the theme "Salvation today"—with heated discussions on whether the salvation of the gospel concerns only the individual soul or extends also to the broader sociohistorical context. This heated debate seems to have produced cracks in the ecumenical movement itself.

The National Christian Council in Japan followed up the Bangkok debate with a four-day conference in 1971, with specific reference to Japan. The 1972 "Christian yearbook" included two articles on the subject, while "The gospel and the world" (April 1973) ran reports by seven participants in the Bangkok meeting. The churches in Japan had just gone through a tumultuous season of dispute over the Christian Pavilion at the 1970 World Exposition in Osaka (cf. II-8) and were therefore keenly alert to critical, even radical, rethinking of basic issues of mission and salvation.

The 1980 conference on mission, held in Melbourne, considered the theme "Your kingdom come." Again, the understanding of the Kingdom of God as good news for the poor and of the centrality of this perspective for mission today were hotly debated. The NCCJ had sponsored a preparatory conference on "Your kingdom come — mission in the 1980s," and "The gospel and the world" journal produced a preparatory issue (June 1980) on the this theme as well as a follow-up issue with reports (August 1980). Reports by four Melbourne participants were included in the 1981 "Christian yearbook."

An important regional preparation for Melbourne was the Singapore conference in 1979, sponsored by the CCA Mission and Service Department. Of the four Japanese participants, Shinmi Hiroshi, then general secretary of the Japan Bible Society, led the Bible study sessions.[5]

The WCC Conference on Mission held in 1989 at San Antonio — the tenth such conference since the first in Edinburgh in 1910 — took the theme "Your will be done — mission in Christ's way." In preparation for this conference, the NCCJ held a mission consultation in fall 1987 on "Seeking to work together in the Lord" to discern where and how Christ is at work in the world today. The San Antonio conference brought greater clarity to problems of environmental destruction and to minority peoples and their cultures. Japanese participants presented a critique of Japan's Alien Registration Law and reported on the life and witness of Korean residents as a vital part of today's mission. Reports were carried in the *Kirisuto shinbun* (Christ Weekly) newspaper and in "The gospel and the world" journal (September 1989).

Shortly after the San Antonio conference, evangelical groups convened the Second Lausanne World Evangelism Congress (July 11–20, 1989) in Manila (cf. I-3). The CCA Mission Conference was held in Indonesia in September that year on the theme "The mission of God in the context of the struggle and suffering of Asian peoples." Many Japanese Christians participated in study meetings held prior to this conference on the Asian context, with important results reported in "The gospel and the world" and in CCRAI's "Asian newsletter." The CCA-prepared Bible study was made available to these study meetings in Japanese translation.

---

[5] Soon after landing at Narita on his return from Singapore, Shinmi died of heart failure at age 56. — Ed.

Missional Priority of the Asian Context

Having recounted the many world and regional conferences and Japanese participation in them, let us now see some of the important fruits the rethinking of mission has had for the Japanese churches.

Certainly the unity of the church and cooperation in mission have been promoted as top priorities in order to overcome the colonial legacy of Western missions. It is vitally important for the churches in Japan to continue efforts to realize unity and cooperation in mission, though this need not exclude Western participation. The Mission Consultation held in March 1982 with church representatives from Japan, Canada, and the United States, for example, confirmed the necessity of adapting mission to the Asian context.

This emphasis was exactly what the United Church of Christ in Japan had in mind when it issued its "Confession of Responsibility During World War II" in 1967. The confession broke down the walls of residual wartime hostility so that the healing work of forgiveness and reconciliation could begin. Mission agreements were made between the UCCJ and the Presbyterian Church in the Republic of Korea (PROK), the Presbyterian Church of Korea (PCK), and the Methodist Church in Korea immediately after the confession was issued. A consultation in 1980 examined these agreements in detail. Then the UCCJ in 1984 produced its Basic Understanding of Mission in the World, which reaffirmed the priority of the Asian context in forming its mission strategy.

The Korean Christian Church in Japan and the Presbyterian Church of Canada redefined their longstanding relationship in a series of negotiations (1962, 1971, 1984) so as to reflect the centrality of mission as articulated in the WCC Third General Assembly in 1961.

Dialogue with Others

Dialogue with other religions has proved to be ecumenically necessary and useful in the Japanese context. This critical aspect of mission has undergone sustained research and reflection at the world level in the International Missionary Council from the 1950s and in subsequent conferences in Beirut (1970), Colombo (1974), and the WCC Fifth General Assembly (1975).

The subject has become a familiar one among Japanese Christians since the founding of the NCC Center for the Study of Religions in Kyoto in the 1960s. The Center has conducted various programs for interreligious dialogue since the 1970s. One of the most important of these is the annual seminar for study of other religions such as the Tendai, Sōtō sect of Zen, Pure Land, and Shingon traditions in Buddhism, as well as the Izumo Grand Shrine of State Shinto, and Tenrikyō among the "new religions". The Center continues to play a vital role not only in fostering cooperation with other religions but also in enriching ecumenical understanding among Christian churches.

Another unique case involves dialogue that led to cooperative efforts for human rights. In 1982 a coalition called the Religious Council for Solidarity in Dealing with the Dōwa [Assimilation] Problem [6] was formed to work for the liberation of the oppressed Buraku people (cf. II-11).

PEACE AND JUSTICE

The focus of the churches' sense of social responsibility in the past twenty years has been on peace and justice issues. Here I shall touch first on the human rights of minorities; then on peace and reunification of the Korean peninsula; and finally on issues raised at the WCC Conference on Justice, Peace, and the Integrity of Creation in March 1990.

Human Rights of Minorities

The WCC consultation held at Sankt Pölten in 1974 issued a statement on human rights that was approved later by the Nairobi general assembly in 1978. One of the major concerns of both meetings was apartheid in South Africa. The WCC had established its Committee on Programmes to Combat Racism (PCR) in 1970, and Dr. Lee In-ha of the KCCJ had become vice-chairperson of the PCR in 1973. Human rights in Asian situations were increasingly emphasized by the CCA Urban Rural Mission (URM) from the mid-1970s. The CCA-URM conference in Auckland, New Zealand, in 1978 offered three definitions of minority groups:

1. People who are forced to leave their normal residential settings within their native land; examples are the Aborigines in Australia, the Maoris in New Zealand, the mountain tribes in Thailand, and the Ainu in Japan.

2. People who are forced out of their native country by colonial and other policies, and who maintain temporary residence in a foreign land; examples are the Chinese in Indonesia, the Tamils in Sri Lanka, and the Koreans in Japan.

3. People who are branded as inherently different and thus suffer discrimination within their own country; examples are the Dalit people in India and the Buraku people in Japan.

Japan obviously is involved in each of the three categories, and the churches in Japan are beginning, however slowly, to acknowledge and deal with the problems. It is important to see that from the mid-1980s ecumenical

[6] Dōwa Mondai ni Torikumu Shūkyō Kyōdan Rentai Kaigi (Dōshūren).

solidarity has greatly strengthened the struggle against the Alien Registration Law and its fingerprinting requirement aimed especially at Koreans (though all foreigners are affected). International solidarity also helps. The CCA General Assembly in Seoul (1985) passed a resolution calling on the Japanese government to drop the fingerprinting rule, and in May 1986 a joint WCC-CCA team visited Japan to inquire into discrimination cases.

In another area of human rights, the WCC held a conference in Berlin in June 1974 on "Sexual issues in the 1970s" and one on "Man and woman in community: the unity of the church and the renewal of community" held in September 1985 in Prague. Isshiki Yoshiko (UCCJ) was an active woman participant in these conferences devoted to eliminating sexual discrimination.

The WCC General Assembly in Nairobi (1978) took up issues of disabled persons as part of the church's mission. The NCCJ's Task Force for Disabled Persons and the Churches compiled its findings in *Kami no kazoku — shōgaisha to kyōkai* (God's family — Disabled persons and the churches) in 1981.

Peace and Korean Unification

Concern for peace in Northeast Asia cannot ignore the question of peace and unity on the Korean peninsula. The international conference sponsored by the WCC International Affairs Commission in October 1984 in Tōzansō, Japan, dealt specifically with this subregion, seeking to initiate processes that would bring about peace and justice. That the conference was held in Japan suggests the expectations placed on Japanese Christians, who since the early 1970s had actively supported the democratization movement in South Korea.

The work of the Tōzansō conference led to the first visit by WCC officials to North Korea. International Affairs staff Ninan Koshy and E. Weingultner visited various churches there in November 1985. The WCC International Affairs Commission held a consultation on peace and the reunification of Korea in September 1986 in Glion, Switzerland, with delegates from both Koreas attending for the first time since division of the peninsula in 1945. Shōji Tsutomu attended from the Japan NCC. Further consultations on peace and unification of the Korean peninsula were held in Glion in November 1988 and December 1990. NCCJ General Secretary Maejima Munetoshi attended both meetings.

These WCC initiatives stimulated a visit to North Korea in June 1987 by an NCCJ-sponsored delegation of three persons: Professor Sumiya Mikio, UCCJ General Secretary Nakajima John Masaaki, and NCCJ General Secretary Maejima Munetoshi. Their report appeared in the May 1988 issue of "Asia newsletter" (Japanese) and the NCCJ's English *Japan Christian Activity News*. Four North Korean Christians returned the visit in September

1989, and the meeting with them included, besides the host Japanese, Korean residents in Japan as well as Christians from South Korea. This groundbreaking venture was reported in "Asia newsletter" (January 1990). Division of the Korean peninsula was one tragic result of Japanese colonial rule from 1910 to 1945. The Japanese churches have an inescapable responsibility to be active in ecumenical international efforts to restore peace and unity to the peninsula. We can say that it is a penitential act for the Japanese church.

Justice, Peace, and the Integrity of Creation

With the Berlin wall falling and Germany destined to be reunited, the urgency of unity for the two Koreas was intensified. At just such a time, in March 1990, the WCC called together people from around the world for its consultation in Seoul on "Justice, Peace, and the Integrity of Creation" (JPIC). This conference had, to some extent, a determinative effect on the future direction of the ecumenical movement. Its roots go back to the 1983 Vancouver assembly, then through a series of consultations at denominational and regional levels. Among these was the Consultation on Peace in Asia and the Pacific, jointly sponsored in March 1989 by the NCCJ and the National Council of Christian Churches in the USA (NCCC-USA).

The significance of the JPIC consultation lay in its emphases on the seriousness of environmental pollution and destruction as a global concern, and on the connection of environmental problems with the prolonged processes of militarization of societies, and then on how the arms race and destruction of nature are both tied into the tortuous record of injustice in the world. Above all, it stressed our stewardship for creation in all areas of peace and justice.

The idea of the integrity of creation surfaced first in the WCC Project Preparation Committee in 1970, but it underwent concrete and productive development first in the Bucharest meeting in 1974 on "Christian hope and the uncertain future: development of science and technology for humanity" and then in the Boston meeting in 1979 on "Faith, science, and the future." Thirteen Japanese participated in the latter, which was an especially important conference. "The gospel and the world" devoted an issue to it in November 1979. From Japan, a scientist deeply involved in environmental problems and a Buddhist philosopher shared their perspectives, as part of the larger discussion among Christians and persons of other religious backgrounds.

At the JPIC meeting in Seoul, Japan's twenty participants included two representatives from Risshō Kōseikai.[7] The NCCJ held a post-conference

---

[7] A large Buddhist organization founded in 1938, Risshō Kōseikai is a faith-oriented fellowship dedicated to personal enlightenment, perfection of society, and world peace, especially through its offshoot, the Niwano Peace Foundation. — Ed.

meeting to hear reports, and "The gospel and the world" carried an extensive report and analysis of the Seoul meeting. Prior to the consultation, preparatory materials went to various church offices and groups to arouse serious interest. In the Kansai area, an ecumenical group undertook translation of the pre-consultation materials for publication in "The gospel and the world" and in "Asia newsletter." Many local meetings were held to discuss these materials and the consultation plans.

In the past, international conferences and ecumenical meetings have had little or no preparatory or follow-up activity outside the conference site. The content and aftereffects therefore depended heavily on the individual participants and seldom reached local, or even national, church levels. The JPIC meeting, surrounded before and aft by a variety of local and national activities, may have altered somewhat this trend in ecumenical circles.

PROSPECTS AND TASKS

We have tried to portray the life of the churches in Japan in connection with work of the World Council of Churches and the Christian Conference of Asia. The picture is a historical spectrum of membership in ecumenical organizations, participation in assemblies and conferences, wrestling with basic issues of faith and order, striving to promote mission and dialogue, and struggling to be responsibly engaged in peace and justice issues. It is natural now to ask what tasks and prospects all this effort has left for the Japanese churches today and tomorrow. My own response concentrates on four points.

Responsible Membership

The first and always basic task is to strengthen our sense of responsibility and self-awareness as members of ecumenical bodies. Whether full or associate members of the NCCJ (or like bodies), a clear consciousness of being a responsible part of the ecumenical movement has often been lacking in Japanese churches. Certainly we witnessed much change in this respect in the 1970s as more individuals and even churches tackled Asian problems seriously. Yet there is still a strong tendency to be self-contained and self-protective. For the sake of the churches' own integrity, this tendency must be transformed.

Active Sharing

The second task, which flows from responsible self-awareness as constituent bodies in the ecumenical movement, is active participation in sharing. Here "sharing" includes all kinds of material and personnel resources.

Considering the Japanese Christian community's small size, it has contributed a fair number of full-time staff persons to ecumenical agencies: Buma Kentarō (Rev.), Church World Service (1971–74); Arai Toshitsugu (Rev.), WCC Life and Renewal (1983–); Yamashita Masaichi, Church Cooperation Cambodia Project (1987–); Kim Yon (Rev.), Women's Issues and Theological Education (1988–89).

Japanese persons who have served as CCA executive secretaries include: Arai Toshitsugu, Education (1977–81); Ueda Jintarō, Service and Development (1981–85); Matsuda Mizuho, Women' Issues (1981–85); Ōtsu Ken'ichi (Rev.), Service and Development (1985–). Kurata Masahiko served as CCA project staff for Urban Rural Mission (1981–82).

Financial contributions have been made through the NCCJ to the WCC for mutual church aid, refugees, and world service. The main channel for contributing to work in Asia and Africa has been CCA Service and Development. Too, the CCA Urban Rural Mission was provided with office space in Tokyo in the 1970s, and since 1988 the CCA head office has been located in Osaka.

These limited contributions are important, yet much more is expected of the churches in Japan. There is no question about the pressing responsibilities placed upon us.

Ecumenical Communications

The third task has to do with conveying ideas and sharing concerns. Throughout this article I have indicated the resources we have in this country for ecumenical sharing—*Kirisuto shinbun* (Christ Weekly), *Kirisutokyō nenkan* (Christian yearbook), *Fukuin to sekai* (The gospel and the world), *Ajia tsūshin* (Asia newsletter), and *Reihai to ongaku* (Worship and music). The crucial question is how extensively these resources reach local congregations.

The Lima Document stands out as an exception. Otherwise, ecumenical publications are rarely promoted in Japan. WCC and CCA assembly reports other than for the CCA Penang assembly were never published in Japanese. No doubt financial limitations inhibit publishing in Japanese translation. Even so, something must be done to make ecumenical materials more readily available in Japanese. We also need more local study and discussion of ecumenical issues and conference materials, such as preceded the JPIC meeting in 1990. Materials and meetings are, of course, the tools of the basic ecumenical networks that need to be developed at the local, district, and national levels if we want an ecumenical movement capable of shouldering its many responsibilities.

Substance and Direction

The fourth and final suggestion concerns the content of our contribution. Individual Japanese have made significant contributions to the substance and directions of ecumenical activity, but such has been rare. Collective contributions include only the resolution on discontinuing the Alien Registration Law and some input on peace and reunification of the Korean peninsula.

In considering the future of the ecumenical movement and its relevance for Japanese churches, we must see the need to witness together with the Catholic and the evangelical churches. We have one exciting example in the long history of Catholic-Protestant cooperation in the Kamagasaki Christian Association for serving day-laborers in Osaka (cf. III-15). The movement against the Alien Registration Law is ecumenical in nature; and Catholic, evangelical, and NCCJ-related churches came together in a coalition to oppose the Daijōsai rite in autumn 1990 (cf. II-5).

Nor must we neglect religious dialogue. Complex and crucial issues such as comparative religious studies, mutual development of spirituality and its daily practice, human rights, peace, and environmental protection could all benefit from more extensive interreligious dialogue, especially if based on stronger ecumenical cooperation among Christians.

3

International Evangelicalism

Uda Susumu

SINCE WORLD WAR II, evangelical movements have attracted attention throughout Christendom. To discuss these movements I shall first explain what is meant by the term "evangelicals," with reference to their beliefs, activities, and their unique ethos.

In the Japanese Christian context, the term "evangelicals" is often regarded as synonymous with "fundamentalists," which carries with it the negative nuances stemming from Elmer T. Clark's[1] prewar analysis of fundamentalism as a reactionary, irrational form of religion unable to keep pace with modern industrial society. A recent study by Dean Kelly[2] of the National Council of Churches of Christ in the USA indicates that Clark's evaluation is less influential today in the United States and elsewhere.

Negative attitudes once led to the rather widespread expectation that evangelicalism would eventually become extinct. But in the postwar era it has made a remarkable surge and spread to many countries around the world. Some observers see American evangelicals as a third vital force, distinct from both mainline Protestantism and Roman Catholicism. In Europe, the National Evangelical Anglican Congress within the Church of England and the surge of "Evangelikaler" (Conference of Confessing Fellowships) in Germany, among others, attest to growing evangelical strength. The rising prominence and influence of evangelicals in Japan has also been documented.[3]

[1] E. T. Clark, *Small Sects in America*, 1937.
[2] Dean Kelly, *Why Conservative Churches Are Growing — A study in sociology of religion*, 1972.
[3] *Japanese Evangelicals — Looking toward the twenty-first century*, Japan Evangelical Association, 1989.

WHAT ARE EVANGELICALS?

The advance of evangelicalism since the 1970s has been accompanied by a serious identity problem among evangelicals.[4] They have been likened to small inlaid chips of glass, tile, and marble that make up a mosaic or kaleidoscopic pattern. To be sure, they may have roots in the extensive spectrum of Protestantism – Lutheran, Reformed, Presbyterian, Anglican, Baptist, Wesleyan, Methodist, Holiness, Brethren, Pentecostal, or any of the many independent churches. The black Protestant church in these traditions has its own unique characteristics. There have been and still are ample opportunities for great diversity among evangelicals. Even so, a basic common nature and sense of unity has characterized the dynamic, historic Christian community known as evangelical.

What, then, constitutes this basic common nature and sense of unity? Neither space nor the purpose of this essay allows a detailed answer, so it must suffice to say that evangelicals trace their heritage directly from the original apostolic faith through the orthodox faith of the ancient church, the sixteenth-century Protestant Reformation and the ensuing Protestant orthodoxy, the modern pietist and revivalist movements, to specific events such as the 1846 Evangelical Alliance, the Lausanne International Congress on World Evangelization in 1974, and its 1989 sequel in Manila. Their distinguishing label comes from the Greek *evangelion* for "gospel," and the evangelicals find their ultimate starting point in the apostolic gospel and lifestyle and the passion for mission (Phil 3:7–8; I Cor 9:16). They lay claim to ancient orthodoxy as crystallized in the "ecumenical creeds": in all places (catholicity), at all times (universality), and believed by all (conformity of agreement).

In professing Protestantism, evangelicals have espoused three great tenets: (a) the sole authority of the Bible, (b) justification by faith, and (c) the church as the fellowship of believers. Although the legitimacy of seventeenth-century Protestant orthodoxy is questioned today, evangelicals regard it as the systematization of historical Christianity and promote its vigorous continuation.

In evangelicalism's modern development, two other movements were important. One was the spiritual reform movements in the Lutheran and Reformed churches during the seventeenth and eighteenth centuries; the other, the nineteenth-century revival movements and the pietist movement in general, as found, for instance, in the Holiness and Pentecostal churches. Emphases on individual conversion and rebirth, disciplined living, and spiritual

[4] Bernard Ramm, *The Evangelical Heritage*, 1973; Carl Henry, *Evangelicals in Search of Identity*, 1976.

training of the Christian as a spiritually changed person, along with a vision of mission outreach, are all noteworthy traits of evangelicals.

A commitment to the concept of the "free church," a spontaneous gathering of believers with common beliefs and goals, is another distinctive feature of the evangelical tradition. Historically developed in early American society, the churches of this tradition have preserved a unique Christian mentality and community ethos.

The blending of the characteristics outlined above has yielded the mosaic that is the evangelical church of today. The basic pattern was anticipated in the 1846 gathering in London of 800 representatives of 50 denominations around the world to form the Evangelical Alliance. The flourishing liberal churches of the time were viewed as "extreme," and the evangelicals felt the need for conformity and cooperation among themselves for the goal of world evangelism. The nine articles adopted by the new alliance were developed as the standard articles of faith that undergird the faith of many evangelicals today.[5]

The 1974 Lausanne Congress is a present-day version of the 1846 Evangelical Alliance, and its official "Covenant" is a contemporary witness to evangelical faith and mission awareness.

BROAD-STROKE DIFFERENTIATIONS

North American Subcultures

Generally speaking, Japanese evangelicals have been strongly influenced by their North American counterparts, so an overview of the American situation will facilitate an understanding of the Japanese scene. Robert Webber has discovered fourteen subcultures in North American evangelicalism; these are briefly indicated in table 3.1.

International Groupings

On the international level, six schools of thought were proposed at the Theological Conference of the World Evangelical Fellowship in 1975 by Peter Beyerhaus of Tubingen University. Here a similar grouping is presented.

Separatist fundamentalism. This school of thought is the direct offspring of the controversy between fundamentalism and modernism that occurred primarily in the United States in the first quarter of this century. Emphasis is on complete separation from liberal Christianity and secularism. The World Christian Fundamentalists Association, founded in 1919, and the

[5] P. Schaff, *Creeds of Christendom*, vol. 3.

TABLE 3.1

FOURTEEN AMERICAN EVANGELICAL SUBCULTURES

Legend: Subculture Designation
a = specific features
b = representative organizations
c = representative publications
d = representative personalities

---

1. Fundamentalist Evangelicalism

a. Personal and ecclesiastical separationism; biblicalism
b. Bob Jones University; American Council of Christian Churches
c. *Sword of the Lord*

2. Dispensational Evangelicalism

a. Dispensational hermeneutics; pre-Tributionalism and pre-Millenialism
b. Dallas Seminary; Moody Bible Institute; Moody Press
c. *Moody Monthly*

3. Conservative Evangelicalism

a. Cooperative; inclusive of all evangelical groups; broad theological base
b. Wheaton College; Trinity Evangelical Divinity School; Gordon-Conwell Seminary; National Association of Evangelicals; Zondervan Corporation
c. *Christianity Today*
d. Billy Graham

4. Nondenominational Evangelicalism

a. Unity of the church; restoration of New Testament Christianity
b. Milligan College

5. Reformed Evangelicalism

a. Calvinism (some with decidedly Puritan flavor); covenant theology and hermeneutics
b. Covenant College; Calvin College and Seminary; Westminster Seminary; Reformed Seminary
d. Francis Schaeffer

International Council of Churches, formed by Carl MacIntyre and others, are prime examples of this movement.

Open fundamentalism. This school of thought is based on the dispensational hermeneutics first proposed by John Derby of England and then

TABLE 3.1 — Continued

___

6. Anabaptist Evangelicalism
  a. Discipleship; poverty; peacemaking and pacifism
  b. Goshen College; Reba Place Fellowship
  d. John Howard Yoder

7. Wesleyan Evangelicalism
  a. Arminianism; sanctification
  b. Asbury College and Seminary; Seattle Pacific University

8. Holiness Evangelicalism
  a. The work of grace
  b. Lee College; Nazarene Church

9. Pentecostal Evangelicalism
  a. Gift of tongues
  b. Church of God; Assembly of God

10. Charismatic Evangelicalism
  a. Gifts of the Holy Spirit
  b. Oral Roberts University; Melodyland School of Theology

11. Black Evangelicalism
  a. Black consciousness
  b. National Association of Black Evangelicals

12. Progressive Evangelicalism
  a. Openness toward critical scholarship and ecumenical relations
  b. Fuller Seminary

13. Radical Evangelicalism
  a. Moral, social, and political consciousness
  c. *Sojourners, The Other Side, Wittenburg Door*

14. Mainline Evangelicalism
  a. Historical consciousness (at least back to the Reformation)
  b. Movements within major denominations (Anglican, Baptist, Lutheran, Methodist, Presbyterian)

___

Source: Robert Webber, *Common Roots: A Call to Maturity,* 1978.

___

widely propagated by the Scofield Reference Bible. While not as militant or judgmental as the separatists, their basic creedal stance is the same. Purity in lifestyle is stressed; liberalism is denounced. Hal Lindsey, author of *The Late Great Planet Earth*, exemplifies this group.

Post-fundamentalist evangelicalism. This approach, which first emerged after World War II, is more catholic and modern; it avoids tendencies toward isolationism, anti-intellectualism, and other-worldliness. Examples in North America are the National Association of Evangelicals (est. 1922); the journal *Christianity Today*, started in 1956 with Carl Henry as editor and now a leading organ of evangelicals; Youth for Christ, Campus Christian Crusade, and other interdenominational evangelical movements.

Confessional evangelicalism. This stance is found in historic churches traditionally preserving a standard confession of faith and liturgy, such as the Lutheran, Presbyterian-Reformed, Anglican, and Mennonite churches. These historic communions often contrast with modern evangelical groups born and nurtured in North America with respect to expressions of piety in observing the Lord's Day, the role of education in Christian life, the work ethic, and political and economic issues.

Progressive evangelicalism. Though basically grounded in historic evangelical faith, this school exhibits several distinguishing features: (a) Higher criticism of the Bible is accepted, and biblical infallibility is ascribed not to the biblical text itself, but to the Bible's salvific power, which effectively leads people into a personal relationship with the Lord Jesus Christ. This view might be called "functional fundamentalism." (b) Great value is placed on the continuing experience of sanctification in everyday life after conversion. (c) Dispensationalism's negative apocalyptic view of history is rejected. (d) Serious consideration is given social, political, and economic ethics. (e) Dialogue with ecumenical churches and with other religions is valued. (f) Broad interaction with various sciences is promoted.

Charismatic movement. This represents a modern version of the Pentecostal movement that developed in the Baptist and Holiness churches in North America early in this century, and is thus a new religious phenomenon. It has spread rapidly since the 1960s.

New Brands

During the 1970s there appeared a very progressive movement called "Young Evangelicals" and "Worldly Evangelism," which advocated an evangelical social gospel. More recently, two other groups have emerged: liberal evangelicals within evangelical churches, and evangelical liberals within ecumenical denominations. These groups have been concerned with four crucial issues: (a) neo-orthodox theology as articulated by Karl Barth and others; (b) self-criticism of failed attempts to ascend to God by existential and anthropological methods, but also criticism of other-worldly faith's failure (exposed by contextual theology) to interact with the real world; (c) efforts to harmonize evangelical stress on biblical authority with critical historical study of the Bible; and (d) an overlapping of evangelicals' awakened interest in "wholistic" mission and liberals' revived concern for the traditional commitment to the salvation of each individual soul. The last of these trends cannot yet be found in evangelical churches as such.

THE LAUSANNE WORLD MISSION MOVEMENT

In the aftermath of World War II, evangelicals embraced anew the faith and vision pioneered a century earlier by the Evangelical Alliance, with a rededication to world mission. The rejuvenated evangelical movement reached another historic apex in the Lausanne International Congress on World Evangelization in 1974. It initiated a process that found further expression in the Second Lausanne Congress held in Manila in 1989.

Lausanne 1974

The Lausanne International Congress on World Evangelization convened July 16–25, 1974, under the theme "Let the earth hear his voice." Billy Graham chaired the gathering of over 3,000 evangelicals from more than 150 countries. Recognized by the mass media as well as the World Council of Churches as a momentous event, this congress had four main objectives: (a) to present to the churches of the world a clear and compelling Bible-centered mission; (b) to challenge the churches to take responsibility for the unfulfilled task of world evangelization; (c) to explore the relationship of mission and social responsibility in terms of biblical faith in a wholistic way; and (d) to promote fellowship and union among evangelicals worldwide.

The Lausanne Covenant issued by the congress has become the contemporary guideline of faith and mission for evangelicals. That it was a covenant rather than a declaration testifies to the sense of unity expressed as a resolve to carry out a common calling. Of the Covenant's fifteen paragraphs, the first three reiterate the historic doctrines of the triune God, God's will for human salvation, and the full authority and power of the Bible, and the human-divine Jesus Christ as the only savior of the world.

The document's first section is devoid of the humanistic, utilitarian concepts found in many recent statements on mission. It stresses, rather, God himself and his eternal will as the source and power of all things. The fourth section defines evangelism:

> To evangelize is to spread the good news that Jesus Christ died for our sins and was raised from the dead according to the Scriptures, and that as

the reigning Lord he now offers the forgiveness of sins and the liberating gift of the Spirit to all who repent and believe.

Within this orthodox context, the "presence" of Christ and "dialogue" with ecumenical communions were discussed.

The Covenant's key section, the fifth, highlights "the Christian's social responsibility." While the sociopolitical reforms central to missional liberation affirmed by the WCC conference held in Bangkok (1972–73) clearly influenced this section, the emerging ethical awareness among evangelicals, especially in the United States, was also operative.

The sixth section defines the church as the people of God and their relation with the world. The seventh and eighth call for mission cooperation and genuine unity among God's people, while exhorting churches to deploy missionaries so as to meet needs of the new era, to live simply and to help the poor. The ninth cites the urgency of world evangelism, noting that over two-thirds of the world's population (2.7 billion in 1974) had as yet no opportunity for exposure to the gospel.

Section ten discusses the relation of evangelism to culture; eleven deals with leadership needs for church growth; twelve and thirteen portray the spiritual battle of Christians against secularism and other errors. The document concludes with proclamation of the Holy Spirit as evangelism's real power (section fourteen) and affirms the eschatological doctrine of Christ's second coming (fifteen).

Clearly the Lausanne Congress marked the beginning of a wave of evangelical vitality that has led to sizable church growth.

Manila 1989

The Second Lausanne World Evangelism Congress was conveved July 11–20, 1989, in Manila with the theme "Proclaim the Gospel until the Second Coming of Christ." Compared with the first congress, there was a notable increase in the numbers of participants and countries represented. Of some 4,000 participants from 173 countries, about one hundred were from the Communist bloc, including 61 ministers and laypersons from the Soviet Union. Others came from lands suffering war and famine. About 130 Japanese attended. Over twenty percent of all participants were women; nearly sixty percent were under age forty-five. Another marked contrast was the large number of charismatics present. Much attention focused on observers from the Roman Catholic Church, the Greek Orthodox Church, the Russian Orthodox Church, and the World Council of Churches.

The Manila Declaration, updating the earlier Lausanne Covenant, stressed "the whole gospel, the whole church, the whole world," reflecting ideas of the drafting committee's chairman, British evangelical leader John Stott. The declaration's focal point is the urgency of mobilizing all churches to convey the inexhaustible gospel to the entire world in a wholistic[6] sense.

The whole gospel. The declaration first tackles people's desperate situation. Because of sin, all human relationships—with God, nature, other people, oneself—are impaired and cannot be restored by one's own strength. Persons suffering such broken relationships must see that Christ's gospel is indeed "good news," the answer to the human needs of body and soul. The declaration then reiterates the matchless nature of Jesus Christ as both God and man.

Strict caution is urged against current religious syncretism, even while encouraging understanding of other religions. Traditional imperatives for evangelism are stressed alongside social responsibility in the document's wholistic perspective. The road of incarnational mission, it says, must involve the contextual realization of the gospel in our time.

The whole church. The declaration confirms the belief that mission is empowered by God's Spirit, the very point made at the Oslo Consultation on the Holy Spirit (1985) in relation to a topic of current missional concern called "power evangelism." The focus is on mission that recognizes the miraculous work of the Holy Spirit ("signs and wonders" in the New Testament) that accompanies evangelistic activity and pits the power of God's Spirit against that of evil spirits ("power encounter"). This, it declares, is the core of evangelism.

Turning to church structures and missional context, the church visitation model (bringing in veteran leaders from outside) is rejected in favor of local churches mobilizing all their own potential. Though serious theological differences remain, possibilities of cooperation with the Roman Catholic Church as well as the Greek and Russian Orthodox churches are considered, particularly in areas such as Bible translation, theology, ethics, social service, and political action. Efforts to influence the WCC stand on biblical concepts of mission constitute the limits of suggested cooperation with that body.

The whole world. The declaration also deals with the impact of "modernization," including science and technology, secularization, and urbanization, on the present world missionary situation. It also considers anticipated problems of the twenty-first century, when a projected fifty percent of the world's population will be living in cities or countries "closed to the gospel." New coun-

---

[6] This term is used increasingly in church circles to mean "inclusive, all-embracing," and as such is slightly different from the philosophical term "holistic," from "holism," a theory that the universe, and especially all living beings, are correctly seen in terms of interacting wholes that are more than the mere sum of elementary particles.—Ed.

countermeasures for recruitment, training, and deployment of missionary forces will be needed.

In all, twenty-one topics were addressed in 425 seminar groups. The full report is still awaited. The fruits of the gathering will be reflected in the Third Japan Congress on Evangelism planned for 1991.

THE CHARISMATIC MOVEMENT AND EVANGELICALS

One worldwide renewal movement that is crossing denominational and theological lines is the charismatic movement. Directly rooted in nineteenth-century American society, the movement has three main sources:

1. John Wesley's emphasis on two different and distinct religious experiences — conversion, as new birth through the Holy Spirit, and the experience of being filled with the Holy Spirit. The latter is called the "baptism of the Holy Spirit" in the contemporary Holiness movement and has come to be regarded as an extraordinary experience.

2. The heightened emotional response accompanying the revivals of Charles Finney (1795–1875) led to acceptance of a variety of emotional expressions, the absence of which was taken to inhibit revival.

3. The Holiness method of interpreting the Bible by sections linked the baptism of the Holy Spirit to the gifts of the Holy Spirit, particularly the gift of spiritual healing.

In this context, Pentecostalism regards speaking in tongues as a sign of the baptism of the Holy Spirit. The connection was first made when groups of people began speaking in tongues at Charles Parham's Bible School in Topeka, Kansas, in 1901, and again at the Los Angeles Azusa Street Revival Meeting in 1916, where the key figure was black evangelist William Seymour, of Holiness background. The charismatic movement currently being discussed is a modern version born in like manner in the 1960s. It is generally called Neo-Pentecostalism.

America in the 1960s, it should be remembered, was caught up in the Vietnam War and antiwar movements, a period of mounting violence with assassinations of famous figures. It was a decade of great flux and contrast: declining morals and noncommittal, along with highly committed movements for women's liberation and black power, not to mention the "death of God" theology, secularism, hippies and the drug scene, Jeanne Dixon (prophesied President Kennedy's assassination), astrology, occult religion, and Satan worship. In Christendom, there were the epochal reforms and experiments of Vatican Council II, along with the Jesus movement, and among the established churches a sense of losing ground. It was a time of confusion, instability, and searching. Or, as Richard Quebedeaux pointed out, a time when the irrational, the ecstatic, the mysterious, the extraordinary, the therapeutic, the gloom-dispelling experience all had peculiar appeal.[7]

Contemporary charismatics do, in fact, have deep relationships with evangelicals, and evangelicals definitely embrace some emphases of the charismatic movement. Areas that do not overlap, however, make it clear that the charismatic movement is a new religious phenomenon with its own distinctive features. Indeed, Quebedeaux reports that among American charismatics, only half believe in the inerrancy and authority of the Bible, though roughly sixty percent profess a biblical view of salvation. He finds that views of Christ and Satan among charismatics do not coincide with evangelical doctrine.

The charismatic movement received much attention at the Second Lausanne Congress in Manila, which took a mediating position: it rejected charismatic extremes, but advised against being so cautious as to lose faith in the Holy Spirit's power. Evangelicals in Japan are expected to engage in serious consideration of the Holy Spirit in the years ahead.

---

[7] Richard Quebedeaux, *The New Charismatics II*, 1983.

4

Asian Churches and Projects

Compiled by Yamano Shigeko

AT THE VERY BASE of our ecumenical relations with Asian churches lies the Japanese churches' deep sense of war responsibility. This sense of responsibility extends back to prewar times when churches in Japan cooperated in the colonization of Taiwan and Korea and the invasion of China, the Philippines, and other Asian lands. It also includes the churches' submission to government policies of Shinto shrine worship.

In the postwar era we could not resume church life or restore Asian ecumenical relations without first acknowledging and confessing our war-related sins. Korea, China, Taiwan, and the Philippines, and the churches in these lands, had suffered most and longest under the Japanese empire. Renewal of ecumenical relations had to begin with churches in these four lands. As the following reports show, the groundwork for renewed relations was laid in the 1950s and 1960s.

The restoration of ecumenical relations with Asian churches has been more than an accessory to normal church life in Japan; these relations have been essential to our self-understanding and life as Christians. During the 1970s our Asian colleagues' struggles for democracy opened our eyes to the meaning and value not only of democracy but also of human rights. Then in the 1980s their critique of Japan's economic invasion of their countries sharpened and expanded our sense of justice. From the shared struggles for human rights and justice we have learned some basic things about the meaning of Christian conversion, and thus gained a new vision for mission.

Although vision exceeds practice, the reports presented here indicate the directions taken in ecumenical church relations and in practical projects. The overall record, while modest in scope and achievement, is a testimony to God's grace and guidance in difficult times.

ECUMENICAL CHURCH RELATIONS IN ASIA

The four reports in this section were prepared by the following persons: on Korea, Katsuragawa Jun; on China, Takeuchi Kentarō; on Taiwan, Katō Minoru; on the Philippines, Akiyama Naoe. (See the List of Writers and Translators for further information.)

Churches in South And North Korea

The first official postwar contact by the National Christian Council in Japan[1] (NCCJ) with Christians on the Korean peninsula took place in May 1962 when three NCCJ representatives, including NCCJ Moderator Mutō Ken, visited churches in South Korea. This visit was limited to expressing good will; the time was not yet ripe for developing fellowship and dialogue. Soon after Japan and South Korea signed a treaty for normalization of relations on September 25, 1965, the Rev. Ōmura Isamu, moderator of the United Church of Christ in Japan (UCCJ), attended the general assemblies of the Presbyterian Church in the Republic of Korea (PROK) and the Presbyterian Church of Korea (PCK). Before very tense audiences, Ōmura confessed the sin of the Japanese church in supporting Japan's thirty-five-year colonial rule of the entire Korean peninsula. This confession relieved the tension and created an opportunity to break through the wall that had separated the churches of Japan and Korea. From this time, the UCCJ entered into cooperative covenants with the PROK, the PCK, and the Korean Methodist Church.

The National Christian Council in Japan sent Yuasa Kyōzō and three other lay representatives to South Korea in March 1966 to establish formal relationships with the Korean churches. Not until the 1970s, however, were substantive forms of cooperation begun. South Korea fell under dictatorial rule when General Park Chung-hee took power in the 1971 presidential election and declared martial law in October 1972. Even though democratic movements were harshly suppressed, the Korean Urban Industrial Mission (UIM) courageously opposed the dictatorial administration. Begun in the late 1960s as a more conservative pastoral ministry, UIM changed its orientation in the 1970s in response to the people's suffering, and it became a leading force for democratization. On Easter Sunday in 1973 the Rev. Park Hyung-kyu and other UIM leaders were arrested for distributing leaflets that were critical of the Park regime.

Such was the setting of the first Japan–South Korea Church Consultation held in Seoul by the National Christian Councils of both countries in 1973.

---

[1] When formed in 1948 the name was "National Christian Council of Japan," but this was changed to "in Japan" in 1985. To avoid confusion "in Japan" is used consistently herein. — Ed.

The evolving fellowship between churches in Japan and Korea could no longer ignore the role Korean churches were playing in the democratization of Korea. Nor could the two sides ignore regressive acts by the Japanese government to revise school textbooks so as to obscure Japan's wartime oppression. This was the focus of the 1982 Japan–South Korea Church Consultation. Successive consultations have continued to examine and evaluate the Japanese churches' responsibility in the postwar era.

In the early 1980s attention turned to Japan's Alien Registration Law, which required foreigners to carry at all times an Alien Registration card bearing the holder's fingerprint. The card and fingerprinting rule was directed principally at Korean residents of Japan, by far the largest group of non-Japanese in the country. The NCCJ Committee on Human Rights of Foreign Residents collaborated with the Korean NCC's Human Rights Committee for Korean Residents in Japan in opposing this law. The Ecumenical Youth Council in Korea and the NCCJ Youth Council have promoted fellowship through personnel exchanges by groups and local churches. Collegial relations and dialogue have grown between churches in both lands.

The Japan Emergency Christian Conference on Korean Problems and the Liaison Christian Council between Korea and Japan were organized in 1974 to build solidarity in the struggle for democracy in Korea. The Liaison Christian Council, which included members of the Roman Catholic Church in Japan and of the Korean Christian Church in Japan, actively involved citizens in meetings to pray for the struggling Korean people. In 1980 when Chun Do-hwan (Park's successor as dictator) brutally suppressed an uprising in Kwangju in southwestern Korea, protest actions in both countries were well coordinated by the NCCs in Japan and Korea.

Since the Chun regime was checked by pressure from the people's democratization movement in 1987, the situation in South Korea has changed dramatically, with the reunification of the Korean peninsula becoming a primary issue alongside democratization. The Korean churches have advanced the cause of reunification with the understanding that without democracy there can be no reunification, and democracy is not complete without reunification. Public discussion of reunification had been taboo under the Chun regime.

The Ecumenical Consultation on Peace and Justice in Northeast Asia was held from October 29 to November 2, 1984, at the YMCA Tōzansō center in Gotemba, Japan, sponsored by the NCCJ with the cooperation of the World Council of Churches' International Affairs Commission. Focusing on peace and reunification in Korea, the participants agreed to seek resolution of the Korean problem through cooperative and united efforts of churches at the world level.

Accordingly, two WCC staff members visited North Korea in 1985, and in 1986 Christians from North and South Korea met — for the first time since division of their country — at a WCC-sponsored seminar in Glion, Switzerland, and partook of the Lord's Supper together. In 1987 Sumiya Mikio, Nakajima John Masaaki, and Maejima Munetoshi were sent by the NCCJ to North Korea for visits with Christian leaders and government officials there.[2] The three NCCJ representatives confessed the churches' sins of wartime collusion and also their complicity in the postwar division of the Korean peninsula. Their expressed desires for peace and unity were warmly received.

In February 1988 the National Council of Churches in Korea issued its "Declaration of the Churches of Korea on National Reunification and Peace," confessing the churches' failure to overcome the division of the peninsula and proclaiming 1995 — fifty years after liberation from Japan — as the "Jubilee Year" for reconciliation. In April 1988 the International Christian Consultation on Peace and Justice in Korea was held in Inchon, South Korea; the participants fully supported the "Declaration of the Churches of Korea" and renewed the appeals of the Tōzansō and Glion meetings.

A symposium on "Japan and the peaceful reunification of the Korean Peninsula" was held in October 1988 in Tokyo, though no representative from North Korea was able to attend this time. The following month the second Glion meeting was held, and Christians of North and South Korea attended. Four North Korean Christians visited Japan from September 28 to October 5, 1989, and thirteen church representatives from South Korea joined in meetings sponsored by the Japanese hosts. Five delegates from North Korea visited Japan, July 10–13, 1990, at the invitation of the Korean Christian Church in Japan for meetings in Tokyo on peace and reunification of the Korean peninsula. The agreement approved by this gathering was titled "Advancing toward the Jubilee Year of Peace and Reunification of South and North Korea."

On September 30, 1990, South Korea established diplomatic relations with the Soviet Union at the United Nations headquarters in New York City, and talks are now under way for normalization of Japan–North Korea diplomatic relations. The journey toward reunification of the Korean peninsula is approaching a crucial juncture. While the governments of North and South Korea have held talks, communications and personal contacts between the peoples north and south are still quite limited. In this stand-off

---

[2] In terms of breaking new ground for further contacts between Christians north and south, the meeting with government officials was extremely important. (Private communication with a team member. — Ed.)

situation, the pioneer initiatives taken by ecumenical agencies to build relationships among the churches of North and South Korea have been markedly successful. The fellowship nurtured by the NCCJ with Christians in both parts of the Korean peninsula has far-reaching historical significance.

The China Christian Council

China made a new start in 1949 as the People's Republic of China. The churches at the time did not appear to change drastically, at least on the surface; but they did take new steps toward independence from their "mother churches" in order to cope with the new national situation. The basic principles in the process of realignment were "self-propagation, self-government, and self-support," popularly called the Three Self Principles. The determination to build up their own churches was very strong, though church unity — an ideal since the 1920s — was not yet achieved.

The storm of the Cultural Revolution (1966–76) was a severe blow to the Chinese churches. All church buildings were seized and used as schools, hospitals, or apartments. Christian books were thrown away, and mission activities were banned. But Christians met for worship in their homes and kept their faith. The strength of their devotion during the Cultural Revolution is evident in the rapid growth of churches after that trying time ended.

Restoration of the churches got under way between 1976 and 1979. In 1980 a number of church buildings in major cities were returned to their congregations, and worship services were resumed. About this time the China Christian Council (CCC) was organized to work for unity among the churches. The CCC took clear positions on matters inside and outside of China.

In 1983 the CCC sent an official invitation to the National Christian Council in Japan, expressing its desire for CCC–NCCJ relations and inviting the NCCJ to visit the restored churches. In response, the NCCJ dispatched an eleven-person team that included Nakamichi Yoshio, bishop of the Nippon Sei Kō Kai, and Shōji Tsutomu, general secretary of the NCCJ.

In 1984 the NCCJ hosted ten church leaders, including Bishop K. H. Ting and Li Shou-pao, general secretary of the Chinese YMCA, on an exchange visit to Japanese churches in various cities. This marked the opening of formal relations between the two councils. In a joint statement, the NCCJ acknowledged the wartime responsibility of Japanese churches and its intention to respect the Three Self Principles of the CCC. It also expressed its hope of deepening mutual understanding and enlarging areas of mutual cooperation in mission. The CCC expressed its respect for the mission activities of the Japanese churches, particularly in peacemaking, and its hope for strengthened cooperation for world peace and the well-being of all peoples.

It is widely known that the base for mission in China is the YMCA and that the Three Self Principles were born out of the YMCA and YWCA. The Japan YMCA has long had good relations with the Chinese YMCA, maintaining various forms of exchange even during the Cultural Revolution. Many Chinese YMCA staff personnel have visited Japan and taken part in training programs. The close relations between the YMCAs in China and Japan developed independently of the CCC–NCCJ relationship.

Since establishing relations in 1984, the NCCJ has sent three teams to China to foster fellowship. In July 1990 the NCCJ's Center for Christian Response to Asian Issues (CCRAI) sent to China a group that included Takeuchi Kentarō, NCCJ moderator; Yamano Shigeko, executive director of CCRAI; and Professor Kumazawa Yoshinobu of Tokyo Union Theological Seminary. In many cities they participated in discussions of theological development and education, and those present experienced a new level of fellowship.

The China Christian Council took the initiative in forming the Amity Foundation to promote the work of nation-building, especially in the areas of education, welfare, and medicine. The NCCJ decided to cooperate with the Foundation's work in line with the Three Self Principles. In 1987 the NCCJ sent a Japanese-language teacher in response to the Foundation's request. With the cooperation of the Japan Overseas Christian Medical Cooperative Service (see below), it sent a medical doctor to help with a short-term course.

The Japan Bible Society has made, and continues to make, financial contributions to the Amity Printing operation in Nanking (founded by Amity Foundation) for its building and printing equipment. Nationwide Japanese contributions have exceeded one million yen.

One primary task of CCC is the training of ministers for the rapidly growing congregations throughout China. There are presently thirteen seminaries, but more ministers are urgently needed than they can turn out. The CCC has the NCCJ's cooperation in this area. The CCC is an enormous experiment in church unity, though it is still very young. The contemporary church in China is also young. Toward them, the Japanese churches feel a great responsibility for having cooperated with Japan's imperialist wars and its actual invasion of the Chinese continent. Thus the churches in Japan feel they should cooperate actively with the CCC's mission to Chinese society.

China has a large place in peacemaking not only in East Asia but also in the whole world. The mission of the Chinese churches has great bearing on the mission of all Asian churches. The churches in Japan should make every effort to deepen mutual relations and cooperation.

Churches In Taiwan

With a history of complex denominational backgrounds, the overall Christian community in Taiwan is about three percent of the total population, with three roughly equal groups: the Roman Catholic Church, the Presbyterian Church, and other Protestant and evangelical groups.[3] In 1969 these three groups formed the Ecumenical Cooperative Committee for mutual consultation.

On the occasion of its centennial celebration in 1965, the Presbyterian Church in Taiwan (PCT) issued a courageous appeal concerning church autonomy and democratic government based on evangelical faith. The church won the people's trust but, for the same reason, suffered harsh repression by the government. This church then faced a difficult phase of its history. On Easter Sunday in 1970 the PCT had to withdraw from membership in the World Council of Churches,[4] but in December of that year it issued a statement that the future of Taiwan should be decided by all people who resided in Taiwan.[5] In November 1975 the church formally protested government confiscation of Taiwanese-language Bibles.[6] In August 1977, in its "Human Rights Declaration," the PCT demanded that the government take effective measures for establishing a new and independent Nation of Taiwan. And in April 1980 the General Assembly of the PCT approved a resolution on resuming membership in the World Council of Churches. A few days later, the Rev. Kao Chun-ming, general secretary of the PCT, was arrested on charges of insurgency and sentenced to seven years' imprisonment.[7] His appointment as general secretary was continued throughout his prison term (he was released in 1984) and after.

Churches in Japan reacted to the travail of the PCT in two diametrically different ways: one group sought to learn about and actively participate in

[3] The oldest is the Presbyterian Church in Taiwan, whose members are mostly native Taiwanese; the Catholic and other Protestant churches developed in Taiwan after the Communists took over in China in 1949, their members being largely mainland Chinese who migrated to Taiwan and their descendants. — Ed.

[4] The WCC, like many other government and nongovernmental agencies, recognized the People's Republic of China — a position the Republic of China (Taiwan) rejected. — Ed.

[5] Native Taiwanese are an overwhelming majority in Taiwan. — Ed.

[6] A much earlier derivative of one Chinese dialect, Taiwanese is not readily understood by mainland Chinese immigrants. — Ed.

[7] The specific charge against Kao was harboring a political fugitive; the man was a dissident in a troubled spiritual condition whom Kao counseled for three days — a legitimate act of pastoral care — and then recommended that the man turn himself in to government authorities, which he did. — Ed.

the Taiwanese church's struggle; the other avoided the issue by interpreting troubles faced by churches in Taiwan as political matters in which the church in Japan had no part.

The United Church of Christ in Japan had entered into an agreement with the Presbyterian Church in Taiwan in 1963, but there was no specific cooperative activity throughout the 1960s and 1970s. The UCCJ had undertaken its own organizational reform in 1968 and from the following year was embroiled in dispute. In 1980, however, the UCCJ engaged in self-evaluation — reflecting upon its ignorance of realities in Taiwan — and made a new agreement with the PCT. Soon after Kao's arrest the UCCJ formed its Taiwan Issues Committee, which mobilized support for Kao and an imprisoned lay elder named Lin When-chen. The present writer, a UCCJ minister, in 1972 went to study at Taiwan Theological College in Taipei, and from 1974 to 1984 he served as a UCCJ missionary by PCT invitation at the Tan Shui College of Business Administration. In that capacity he was able to serve as a channel of updated and accurate information.

In the 1980s UCCJ missionaries to Taiwan increased to nine persons. The Asia Gospel Mission, based in Kyoto, has sent six missionaries to Taiwan. The Evangelical Alliance Mission (TEAM) has sent two; the Japan Holiness Church, the Japan Church of Jesus Christ, and the Immanuel General Mission have each sent one or two. The Christian Brotherhood in 1980 established an agreement with the PCT, to which it has sent short-term missionaries. The Church of Christ in Japan opened fellowship at the general assembly level with the PCT in 1985.

Japan Overseas Christian Medical Cooperative Service sent Horita Hisako, a specialist in education of mentally disabled children (1980–84), and from 1985 she has served as UCCJ missionary-pastor of the Taipei Bible and Prayer Church. Dr. Wakai Susumu went to Chang Hua Christian Medical Hospital in 1981; Onodera Yoshinao, to a deaf mission in 1983.

Through the Northeast Asian Theological Education Association a number of Japanese professors have contributed to theological education in Taiwan. These include Watanabe Nobuo (Japan Church of Christ Theological Seminary), Tokuzen Yoshikazu (Japan Evangelical Lutheran Seminary), Mizuno Makoto (Aoyama Gakuin Junior College), and Kumazawa Yoshinobu (Tokyo Union Theological Seminary). Theological contributions have also been made by Takahashi Saburō and Sekine Masao of the non-church movement, and by Tōge Katsuya and Matsutani Yoshiaki of the Church of Christ.

Resources on Taiwan include four books published by the Kyo Bun Kwan, one each by Kishimoto Yōichi and Kaino Nobuo of the UCCJ Taiwan

Issues Committee; the UCCJ's *Taiwan kyōkai tsūshin* (Taiwan church news-letter); and NCCJ-CCRAI's *Ajia tsūshin* (Asia newsletter).

Churches in the Philippines

Prior to the 1970s, Christian fellowship between Japan and the Philippines was carried on through youth work camps, women's conferences, and urban industrial mission meetings. These were organized by various ecumenical agencies, including the International Missionary Council, the East Asian Christian Conference and its successor since 1973, the Christian Conference of Asia, and the National Christian Council in Japan.

The country fell under harsh autocratic rule when President Marcos de-clared martial law in 1972. Under neocolonial dominance by multinational corporations of Japan and the United States, the gap between rich and poor grew wider, with increasing human rights violations. The people in the Phil-ippines suffered much; at the same time, their movements for democracy be-came more powerful.

The Philippine churches, the Catholic Basic Christian Communities (BCC), the National Council of Churches in the Philippines (NCCP), and the NCCP's largest member body, the United Church of Christ in the Phil-ippines (UCCP) have, as a missional responsibility, stood with the suffering people in their struggles. Church-to-church relationships were established by the Nippon Sei Kō Kai (Japan Anglican Church) with the Philippine Angli-can Church and the Philippine Independent Church; by the Japan Baptist Union with the Philippine Baptist Church; and by the United Church of Christ in Japan with the United Church of Christ in the Philippines.

In the late 1970s, Kawasaki Steel Corporation built a sintering[8] plant on Mindanao Island, in effect exporting pollution to the Philippines. This was opposed by organized movements as a matter of human rights. In the early 1980s excessive use of toxic chemicals on banana plantations and by the ba-nana exporters were protested by workers trying to improve their working conditions. And campaigns against sex tours to the Philippines were con-ducted by churches and citizens' groups.

After the assassination of Benigno Aquino in August 1983, labor organi-zations, women's groups, and peace movements began focusing on a wider range of human rights issues concerning US military bases, nuclear power plants, government developmental aid, and migrant workers.

Against this background, the Regional Conference on Human Rights Is-sues of the Philippines was held in Tokyo in 1979, sponsored by the Resource Center for Philippine Concerns (RCPC) based in Hong Kong.

---

[8] Sintering causes agglomeration of metal by heating, but without melting. — Ed.

Spurred by this meeting, the Japan Coalition for Philippine Concerns (JCPC) was initiated by Protestants and Catholics who had attended the conference. In 1983 an international solidarity conference held in New York City established the Ecumenical Partnership for International Concerns (EPIC) to be based in Manila, and it maintained a relation with JCPC in Tokyo. Following up these initiatives by Protestant and Catholic churches, the RCPC office moved from Hong Kong to Tokyo. Through these developments, grass-roots fellowship and cooperation grew between movements in Japan and the Philippines.

To coordinate activities among churches, the first Japan–Philippine NCC Mission Cooperation Consultation was held in 1983 at a time of distorted political and economic relations between the two countries. The second such consultation was held in 1986, and the third in 1989, to find cooperative mission strategies that could cope with issues such as Japan's economic invasion of the Philippines, exporting of pollution, militarization of societies, the impact of US military bases, and problems of migrants workers.

A spin-off of JCPC activities was the 1986 formation of the Japan Committee for Negros Campaign (JCNC) to promote church and citizen support groups for the self-reliance of people on Negros Island, where acute poverty and starvation are exacerbated by low-intensity warfare.[9]

Meanwhile, an alternative trade group was organized to connect consumers in Japan with people in Negros. This experimental project for solidarity with "Third World people" has been carefully watched by the international community. Likewise, the evolving network of ecumenical relations among Protestant and Catholic groups, eliciting response and involvement by citizens' groups, has also drawn widespread attention.

Political power in the Philippines has shifted from Ferdinand Marcos to Corazon Aquino, who had massive popular support in the beginning. As it turns out, however, no real change in the people's lives and living conditions has occurred. The people's own involvement in dealing with their situation must be encouraged more than ever.

[9] Low-intensity warfare, also called low-intensity conflict, is a comprehensive counter-insurgency strategy implemented on social, political, economic, and psychological levels; applied most widely by the United States in Central Anerica, but also in the Philippines, with minimal use of US forces by aiding and training indigenous "surrogate forces" (right-wing vigilante groups), which also have support from "private" sources such as CAUSA (political arm of the Unification Association) and the World Anti-Communist League (WACL). Cf. Reynaldo Ty y Racaza, "A global perspective on low-intensity conflict: total war at the grass-roots level,(170 NCCP-HRD Occasional Papers 1987–3 (National Council of Churches in the Philippines, Human Rights Desk). – Ed.

CHRISTIAN PROJECTS IN ASIA

Beyond church-to-church relations, our aim has been "living together," which required that we do something practical, or our efforts would be hollow. The ecumenical projects reported below may seem small compared with the needs, but they are genuine expressions of reknitted ties based on reconciliation and thus are part of our shared ecumenical mission. Reporters for the first three projects are, in order: Sakamoto Yoshito, on JOCS; Takami Toshihiro, on Asian Rural Institute; Hiroki Michiko, on Asian Women Workers' Center; the remaining four were prepared by the compiler. (See the list of Writers and Translators.)

Japan Overseas Christian Medical Cooperative Service

Japan Overseas Christian Medical Cooperative Service (JOCS) was formed in 1960 by the Japan Christian Medical Association as one way to follow Jesus' commandment: "Love one another as I have loved you" (John 15:12). Since then, JOCS has sent doctors, nurses, public health workers, and nutritionists to areas where medical services are scarce. Sharing the peoples' problems and treating their pains, they have focused on local cooperation and resources for improving health conditions in these areas.

The first JOCS worker was Dr. Umeyama Takeshi, who went to the Immanuel Hospital in Bandung, Indonesia, in 1961. In the same year two nurses went to Nepal, and Dr. Iwamura Noboru arrived there in 1962. By 1970 fifteen workers—doctors and nurses—had gone to Indonesia, Nepal, Taiwan, Nigeria, and India. During this decade the work of JOCS became well known in Japan through Dr. Iwamura's speaking at various meetings and also through the fund-raising movement to collect used postage stamps.

In 1970 Nara Tsunegorō, a former career YMCA worker, became the general secretary of JOCS, supported by an able staff. The first Bangkok Conference was held in 1971 by the JOCS Board of Directors to review the first decade and seek guiding perspectives for the next.

In the 1970s nutritionists and public health nurses were added to the JOCS list of workers overseas. This expansion was influenced by the World Health Organization's (WHO) stress on the importance of primary health care. Community health programs, while no longer widely practiced in Japan, were seen as vital in parts of Asia where many tuberculosis and leprosy patients needed professional care.

In the 1980s, JOCS formed an inquiry commission to evaluate basic policies and reorganize programs to meet needs in a changing world. The second Bangkok Conference met in 1982 to assess the previous twenty years and to set directions for the future. Besides the conference report, JOCS also issued a statement on "Requests for medical cooperation in developing countries."

JOCS is not a funding agency; it sends neither money nor materials. Its policy is to cooperate in the sending and training of medical personnel to be leaders. This policy seeks to avoid the growing dependency on aid from others by discovering and utilizing resourceful personnel in each specific situation and by introducing techniques that are useful and supportable in local communities. One way of implementing this policy is to provide scholarships for Christian medical workers to obtain further training in Japan and other countries. Since the scholarship program was begun in 1959, forty-three recipient students have pursued their studies in nine countries.

In the transition from the 1970s to the 1980s, medical mission policy also changed, as Indonesia, Thailand, and Taiwan would no longer admit foreign medical doctors and nurses. Thus JOCS began concentrating its efforts in Southwest Asian countries such as Pakistan, Nepal, and Bangladesh. Many problems are now encountered. It is difficult to obtain medical missionary status in many Asian countries. More and more nations have public health policies for training their own medical personnel. And the public health situation in many places remains desperate: not enough hospitals, medicines, medical equipment and supplies, personnel, and funds. The necessary conditions for raising the level of public health are still very poor in a number of Asian countries.

Currently there are 10 workers — 4 doctors, one nurse, 4 public health workers, and one nursing teacher — serving in Bangladesh, Nepal, Cambodia, and Indonesia. Since its beginning, JOCS has sent a total of 38 persons to nine countries. These persons included 16 medical doctors, 7 nurses, 9 public health workers, 2 nutritionists, one nursing teacher, and one social worker for disabled children.

Asian Rural Institute

Asian Rural Institute, founded in 1973, is an ecumenical, interfaith, intercultural, interracial, self-training ground for rural community leaders. ARI's motto is: "That we may live together." Its stated purpose is:

> To nurture and train in the love of Jesus Christ
> rural community leaders, both men and women, to facilitate
> self-development of Third World people
> at the grass-roots level in order to achieve the building of a
> just and peaceful society in which each can live to the fullest potential,
> free to work together, sharing resources and abilities with neighbors
> for their common good.

As of today, ARI has over 650 graduates at work in forty countries in the Third World. The training emphases are work-oriented, participatory, and self-supporting in food for self-reliance so that we may identify ourselves with the life of people at the grass-roots levels of many societies.

The entire training program is based on our concept of FOODLIFE. We believe that Food and Life, as understood in the Bible as well as in the practice of our daily life, cannot be separated one from the other. Food – produced jointly by the workings of the things of nature and the workings of human beings – sustains and enriches Life when appropriately produced, processed, stored, and shared. Sharing Food is sharing Life.

Thus all activities at ARI are centered around, based upon, and aimed at the practice and realization of FOODLIFE. The practice of organic farming methods at ARI is a means to achieve a more satisfactory FOODLIFE at ARI as well as in the Third World and elsewhere through the influence of ARI graduates and their colleagues.

The natural and social environment of ARI have been slowly but steadily improving. Working together as a wholistic community of human beings and nature, we maintain a high self-sufficiency in food. About ninety percent of the food we eat in our dining hall, Koinonia House, comes from our farm of about two hectares (five acres). In the process of working and learning together to produce, store, and share foods among ourselves, keeping in mind the needs of future generations, our God-given senses are developed and enriched so that we appreciate progressively the ongoing work of creation.

With eighteen years of accumulated experience since its founding, the Asian Rural Institute is keenly aware, as it steps into the 1990s and in anticipation of the twenty-first century, of the enormous challenges for its future service and mission. Some of these challenges are:

1. To evaluate, reflect, and plan effectively the activities at ARI with our graduates and their colleagues in the Third World as a step toward sharing our experiences and learning with others.

2. To do the same things (as in item 1) with various groups of concerned people in communities in Japan, with some of whom we already have working relations.

3. To strengthen the ARI curriculum with subjects such as "A just society for women and men," "Spirituality in rural life," and "Appropriate technology."

4. To strengthen our commitment and to continue working and identifying ourselves with people of the grass roots – a term often overused and abused in recent years.

5. To identify ourselves clearly as an ecumenical Christian community par-

ticipating in God's mission (*missio Dei*) to bring the whole creation into Shalom.

6. To upgrade the ARI staff and improve the selection of participants.

7. To build a stabler, stronger financial network so as to strengthen and sustain ARI.

Asian Women Workers' Center

From the late 1960s until the early 1970s an export-oriented industrial policy took hold in Asia as countries opened their doors to foreign capital. This policy had serious effects on many young women who left the countryside to seek work in urban centers. These female workers were offered to foreign capital as a hard-working, obedient, and cheap labor force. Many problems developed out of this situation, both at the workplace and in the personal lives of the women.

In the mid-1970s the Christian Conference of Asia's Urban Rural Mission (CCA-URM) decided to tackle this problem as one of human rights violation. At the time Shiozawa Miyoko, now director of the Asian Women Workers' Center, was asked to become an organizer for CCA-URM, working specifically on women's labor issues. After several years of this work, the Committee for Asian Women (CAW) was established in 1981. Two years later, the Asian Women Workers' Center was founded.

While women workers in Asia were being exploited by transnational corporations (TNCs), Japanese workers came to realize that Japan had become headquarters to many TNCs. The Asian Women Workers' Center was formed to support CAW in coping with Japan's new regional role in Asia.

Information services. To inform the public about Asian women workers, the Center publishes a quarterly newsletter titled *Ajia no nakama* (Asian friends), which ran to thirty issues by the end of 1990. Resource-study materials in Japanese are produced for examining topical issues of Asian women workers. An English newsletter, "Resource Materials on Women's Labor in Japan," is issued twice a year.

From 1986 the Center undertook projects in translation, surveys, and publications so as to provide basic resources on women workers' issues in Japan and the rest of Asia. Responding to requests from women's labor organizations, universities, and local governments, the Center does outreach work through lectures and information services to raise consciousness concerning the issues.

Group activities. The Center promotes direct exchanges among Asian women workers. Once a year women workers or labor organizers are invited to Japan for a symposium. Visits are made to local labor unions to give Asian guests and host Japanese workers an opportunity for small-group discussions and information exchange.

Since 1987 the Center has held annual study tours to other Asian countries — thus far to Thailand, Malaysia, Korea, and the Philippines. A study tour affords a chance to learn about the life and labor of Asian people and to see firsthand the impact of the Japanese government and the TNCs on Asian communities. Participants can realize their responsibility to fellow Asians when they understand the repressive economic and political conditions faced by women workers and women's organizations. After a study tour, participants often become more involved in the activities of the Center.

The Center works to promote solidarity between Japanese labor unions and workers elsewhere in Asia. In May 1988 the All-Japan Federation of Metal Workers asked the Center to coordinate their study tour to Thailand and Hong Kong. The Federation at the time was trying to organize labor unions in small- and medium-sized companies in the heavy metal and machinery industries. In June 1989 the Center coordinated a study tour to the Philippines for the women's section of the Osaka Municipal Government Workers Union.

The Center also sends delegates to international conferences sponsored by the CCA's Committee for Asian Women and by other women's organizations. It helps arrange training programs in Japan to promote mutual understanding among Asian women labor activists.

Protests and vigilance. Responding to requests from Asian groups, the Center mobilizes its members to write protest letters and raise funds. It has protested unfair labor practices by G. S. Steel in Thailand, by Asia Swany and Pico Products in South Korea, by ARE (Asia Rare Earth) Company in Malaysia, and by Polytechs Company in Sri Lanka. The unfair arrest of the chairperson of the Korea Women Workers Association and mass arrests in Malaysia under the Internal Security Act also drew protests from the Center.

As a member of the group called People's Action Network to Monitor Japanese TNCs, the Center joined other groups in drawing up regulatory standards to be promoted among Japanese companies operating overseas. It is involved in a number of similar networking activities.

Training in translation. A monthly study group was formed by the Center to foster translating skills. English-language materials on women's concerns are translated into Japanese. The objective is to train volunteer translators to help the Center.

In the past several years the number of Japanese companies with overseas operations has increased, as has the number of Asian migrant workers in Japan. This rapidly changing scene makes solidarity between Japanese workers and their Asian counterparts more important, especially as the labor union situation in Japan is also changing rapidly. As expectations toward the Center and its role grow, it will continue to promote mutual understanding and support among workers here and abroad.

The School For International Experiences In Asia

This school has since 1979 specialized in sending young people every year to various Asian countries—in principle, one person at a time to one country. Many young persons have gone out under its bold motto, "To change Japanese society in 100 years." In 1990, the school's twelfth year, six trainees were dispersed to the Philippines, Malaysia, India, Indonesia, and Thailand to spend periods ranging from three weeks to two months. With the help of host contact groups, they live in homes and study according to their individual programs.

The school has no "graduation ceremony." Trainees work at many different places after their return to Japan. Examples include jobs in a day-laborers' community, a welfare institution, a medical facility, a company, as well as school teacher and church pastor. Their work styles also vary.

Participants are usually motivated to probe serious questions such as "What do we mean by 'Live together'?", "How can Japanese churches build solidarity with other Asian Churches?" and "What future goals should the Japanese churches have?" The personal probing deepens their understanding and leads to witness and action that, little by little, will help transform Japanese churches and society.

The school is managed by ecumenical leaders in the Kansai (Osaka–Kobe) area; former trainees serve as the organization's secretaries. Advisers include Koyanagi Nobuaki (cf. III-15), Maejima Munetoshi (IV-28), and Murakami Kimihiko. Dr. Iwamura Noboru of JOCS was the school's first principal. Funds are raised annually for the school's activities.

The PHD Foundation

Dr. Iwamura Noboru, who was awarded the Rotary Prize in 1981, proposed the founding of the PHD Foundation for promoting Peace, Health, and Human Development. Since 1982 it has received six groups of trainees from other Asian countries. Staying with Japanese families, they study farming or fishing, ways to improve the quality of life, and the self-reliant development of villages. They also search for ways of living together in Asia. The PHD Foundation is not a specifically Christian organization; it is a citizens' organization. But it is Christian in background and spirit and in working for exchange among people at the grass-roots level. Funding is by membership fees. The present moderator is Imai Shizuo (adviser to Kobe YMCA), and the secretary is the Rev. Kusachi Ken'ichi. PHD issues an occasional newsletter.

Asian Health Institute

Established in 1980 by the Asian Health Study Foundation, the Asian Health Institute (AHI) has as its aim the training of leaders among community health workers. Its motto is "Sharing for self-help."

In the 1979–90 period, 291 trainees participated in courses offered in Japan. Another 601 trainees participated in courses conducted in India, Nepal, Indonesia, Cambodia, South Korea, and the Philippines, with assistance from local contact groups in all places. Special attention is given to issue-based consultation, studies of Oriental medicine, and community health care. Visiting former trainees in their workplaces is also part of the program.

Another important aim of AHI is to encourage better understanding of Asia among the Japanese. This is considered useful as a challenge to the increasingly dehumanized Japanese society, a stimulus to Japanese people to reconsider their lifestyles, and an eye-opener to Japanese as to how they are causing damage to other Asian societies. The methods for this activity are: study tours to other Asian countries, fellowship meetings with AHI trainees, lectures in schools and communities, and providing information in AHI's newsletters, "Asian health" and "Asian children."

The understand-Asia emphasis is consciously linked to fund-raising, as an expression of the founding spirit of "people-to-people" interaction. Committees for recruiting members and soliciting funds are closely coordinated. The present chairperson of the board is Dr. Nakamura Michitarō (honorary chairperson of the Prefectural Physicians Association). The director is Dr. Kawahara Hiromi (head of Aichi International Hospital). AHI has 6,000 supporting members.

Center for Christian Response to Asian Issues

At its July 1981 meeting the executive board of the National Christian Council in Japan passed a resolution to form a preparatory committee for the "Center for Christian Response to Asian Issues" (CCRAI), and the Center was officially approved by the NCCJ General Assembly in March 1982. Ecumenical leaders at the time shared the will and hope to form a documentation center, in the belief that solidarity with Christians in Korea, Taiwan, and the Philippines was crucially important for the mission of the churches in Japan. This belief stemmed from many experiences in the 1970s. The plan also had the understanding and support of the Christian Conference of Asia (CCA), the main forum of the ecumenical movement in Asia. The theme of the NCCJ Twenty-eighth General Assembly that approved the CCRAI plan was "Christ stands with the least."

The principles agreed on by CCRAI's founders were as follows:

1. CCRAI is to question Japan's overwhelming presence in Asian countries, and its political, economic, and cultural dominance so evident since 1965 and especially throughout the 1970s.

2. CCRAI is to help the churches in Japan — which thus far have focused more on Western churches and theology — become aware of their common responsibilities and tasks in Asia.

3. CCRAI is to promote understanding between Japanese churches and other Asian churches, giving much attention to Japan's war responsibility and to the churches' own failure to resist government policies of aggressive war.

4. CCRAI is to focus on the realities of Asian countries undergoing drastic change due to developmental polices that involve oppression and exploitation of farmers, workers, the urban poor, and minority groups by élite classes; focus is to be also on Christians who stand on the side of marginalized and suffering peoples who are struggling to recover their human dignity.

In the early 1980s Japan was one of the few Asian nations where freedom of speech, including publication, was guaranteed. CCRAI was expected to produce and disseminate materials on behalf of colleagues in other less-free countries. The following publications are expressions of this purpose of CCRAI.

Ajia tsūshin (Asia newsletter). Monthly analysis and interpretation of Asian situations; focus on Asian peoples' voices. Audience: churches, Christian schools, individuals.

Asian Issues. Occasional topical studies in booklet format. Some examples are: *Tashika na koe o kike — Kaigai dekasegi no Ajiajin no josei no shōgen* (Listen to authentic voices — Testimonies of Asian women migrant workers); *Ajia no kodomotachi* (Children of Asia); *Kusa no ne no majiwari — kyōkai to shimin no kōryū* (Grass-roots fellowship — church encounters with citizens); and *Gekidō no Firipin kara* (From the tumultous Philippines).

Japan Militarism Monitor. Bimonthly English news service on Japan's militarization and militarism; news clippings and background analysis.

Documentation series. Occasional English resource materials on critical issues and tasks of Japanese Christians. Examples are: *Textbook issues* (dealing with government revision of school texts), and *Hirohito and his legacy*, a special issue of the *Japan Militarism Monitor* (#34, Feb. 19, 1989) on Japan's emperor system.

CCRAI also has conducted seminars and workshops, such as a beginner's guide to practical study of Asia (1985–86), a series of workshops on mission tasks (1988–90), and occasional lecture/solidarity meetings. It cooperates in related programs of the parent NCCJ bodies and with other ecumenical agencies. CCRAI's governing board consists of representatives of the NCCJ member churches and organizations. Its main income source is membership fees, with supplementary income from donations and publication sales. CCRAI's financial accounts are separate from those of the NCCJ.

CCRAI's "tasks ahead" derive principally from the fact that churches and Christian bodies related to the NCCJ all have more and more direct involvements in Asian countries. Information on Asian situations is increasingly available through citizens' movements, and much of this information is specialized. CCRAI's operational environment has changed considerably; it is no longer the unique source for general information it was in the early 1980s.

Even so, understanding of, and involvement in, Asian issues by the Japanese churches is still limited and fragmentary. Often the piecemeal information does not add up to a coherent perspective of mission for the churches and for individual Christians. Moreover, new issues continue to emerge and impinge upon our lives, such as Asian migrant workers, official development aid (ODA), transnational corporations, and more. These issues, and new ones yet to come, will require careful analysis translated into visible and durable solidarity relationships. It is essential for CCRAI to pursue its mission of collecting information, doing analysis and investigation, and promoting cooperative study and action on particular large-scale issues that affect the lives of Asian peoples in profound ways.

II
Christians in Turbulent Japanese Society

5

Yasukuni Shrine and the Emperor System

Tsukada Osamu

IN 1869, THE SECOND YEAR of the Meiji Emperor's reign, a Shinto shrine named Shōkonsha was built in Tokyo to enshrine the spirits of those killed in the civil war that resulted in the Meiji Restoration of 1868. In 1879 it was renamed Yasukuni Shrine and reorganized as the government's special shrine for all who would die for the state in any war. Fallen soldiers and sailors in Japan's subsequent foreign wars of aggression were enshrined as deities of the shrine. During World War II, thousands of young men went off to war shouting, "Long live His Majesty the Emperor!" and "Let's meet again at Yasukuni Shrine!"

Except for the Grand Ise Shrines, where Japan's legendary founder, the sun goddess Amaterasu, was enshrined, only Yasukuni Shrine received imperial visits.[1] For bereaved families of the military war dead, therefore, having relatives enshrined by Yasukuni Shrine was considered a great honor. As the citadel of moral and spiritual support for Japan's imperialist wars, Yasukuni Shrine and the Emperor of Japan became inseparable.

Following Japan's defeat in World War II in 1945, the Allied Occupation headquarters dismantled State Shinto.[2] Yasukuni was disestablished as a state-run, state-financed shrine; its officials registered it as a "private" shrine under the new Religious Corporations Act. In September 1951, Japan signed both the San Francisco Peace Treaty with the United States and the Japan–US Security Treaty. When these treaties became effective in April 1952, Japan fully

---

[1] The Japanese term *sanpai* means "go to worship at" a shrine; here the simpler English word "visit" is used. — Ed.

[2] "State Shinto, a political creation that had its beginning in the Meiji period [1868-1912], may be understood as a combination of Shrine Shinto and the Shinto of the Imperial House." Ueda Kenji in *Japanese Religion: A survey by the Agency for Cultural Affairs* (Tokyo: Kodansha International Ltd., 1972), p. 30. — Ed.

regained its independence. Almost immediately, moves to reunite shrine and emperor appeared.

TOWARD REINSTATING YASUKUNI SHRINE

On May 2, 1952, a government-sponsored memorial service for Japan's 2.4 million military casualties was attended by the late Shōwa Emperor (Hirohito) and Empress. In October of that year, the imperial couple made their first postwar visit to Yasukuni Shrine. In November the Japan Bereaved Families' Public Welfare League (founded in 1947) called for the national government to fund memorial rites for the war dead held at Yasukuni Shrine. The movement to maintain Yasukuni Shrine with public funds was launched. But this was not an isolated launching; a number of critical political initiatives were also under way.

One crucial event was the abrupt shift in US occupation policy when the Korean War broke out in 1950: having first promoted a neutral, unarmed Japan, the United States now turned Japan into an advanced base in the strategy to contain communism. On July 8, Allied Supreme Commander Douglas MacArthur ordered Japan to establish the National Police Reserve (forerunner of today's Self-Defense Forces). In concert with this action, the Ministry of Education announced its desire to have the Hinomaru (rising-sun flag) displayed and the *Kimigayo*[3] (imperial anthem) sung on national holidays — these were the banner and battle hymn of the recent wars. The Ministry's efforts to revive patriotism were accompanied by a steady buildup of the "self-defense forces." And the movement to reinstate Yasukuni Shrine to its state-funded role became more animated, especially under the aegis of the Japan Association for the Bereaved Families of the War Dead (Nihon Izoku Kai; incorporated in 1953).

In 1953 the Japanese government collected from the Pacific war zones the remains of its war dead, among which were those of unknown persons and those whose families could not be located. For these the government in 1959 erected the National Tomb of the War Dead in Chidorigafuchi Park, located in Tokyo's Kudan section (where Yasukuni Shrine is also located). The emperor and empress attended the inaugural memorial service for the 80,000 unknown and unclaimed war dead memorialized there. This nonreligious tomb in a public park can legitimately be regarded as a state-sponsored memorial for all the nation's war dead.

Even so, the Bereaved Families' association persisted in calling for state maintenance of Yasukuni Shrine, and it had the backing of the ruling Liberal

---

[3] The lyrics of *Kimigayo* exalt the emperor of Japan. — Tr.

Democratic Party (LDP) in its campaign. In 1967 an LDP subcommittee prepared a "Yasukuni Bill" for submission to the National Diet (parliament) — prompting protests from religious circles, particularly Christians. The United Church of Christ in Japan (UCCJ), which issued its "Confession of Responsibility During World War II" on Easter Sunday, 1967, formed a special committee on the Yasukuni problem. The (Presbyterian) Church of Christ and the Japan Baptist Convention were among groups that soon followed suit, and late in 1967 the National Christian Council in Japan formed its special committee. In March 1968 the NCCJ General Assembly issued a statement opposing the Yasukuni Bill. The National Catholic Committee in 1968 gave permission to the Catholic laypersons' association to collect signatures opposing nationalization of Yasukuni Shrine.

Transportation Minister Nakasone Yasuhiro countered with a speech in favor of state maintenance of Yasukuni Shrine, and the shrine's officials announced their readiness "to renounce our status as a religious corporation the moment the bill is passed." Religious, political, and civic groups again erupted in protest.

The Yasukuni Bill Goes to the Diet

Despite the public outcry, the Liberal Democratic Party introduced the Yasukuni Bill in the Diet on June 30, 1969, with 244 of its members backing the proposed legislation. Its stated objectives were to provide for ceremonial functions that would "express a sense of veneration for the spirits of the war dead who had sacrificed themselves for the nation's interests, remember their outstanding virtue, offer them solace, extol their meritorious deeds, and immortalize their great achievements."

Given the shrine's history and imperial linkage, protest activities sprang up all over Japan. The opposition parties — Clean Government Party, Socialist Party, Democratic Socialist Party, and Communist Party — all issued protest statements. The Christian anti-Yasukuni movement staged sit-down demonstrations, hunger strikes, protest rallies and marches, and expanded its signature campaign. By the end of July 1969, the nationwide campaign by many religious groups for signatures on a petition opposing state administration of Yasukuni Shrine had garnered 3,772,218 names.

The United Church of Christ in Japan, having long wrestled with this issue, issued its opposition statement immediately. The statement's gist was as follows: the proposed bill is unconstitutional as it violates both Article 20, which guarantees religious freedom, and Article 89, which prohibits disbursement of public funds to religious organizations; the government's claim that Yasukuni Shrine is not a religious organization is itself an intrusion in religious affairs, violating the constitutional principle of separation of religion and state; and the bill violates democratic freedoms of religion, thought, conscience, assembly, and association. Without Yasukuni's prewar and wartime record, these arguments might have seemed excessive; given that record, they made sense to many citizens.

In July 1969, on the eve of the period under review here, the Liaison Committee on the Yasukuni Problem, the National Christian Council, the All-Japan Association of Buddhists, and the Religious Federation of Japan (mostly "new religions") issued a joint statement against the Yasukuni officials' statement regarding "Renunciation of [Yasukuni's] Status Under the Religious Corporation Act." The statement made seven points:

1. The Liberal Democratic Party claims that "the people favor state maintenance of Yasukuni Shrine"; but "public enshrinement" is a specific religious act and thus contravenes the constitution.

2. The victims of the war also included civilians; therefore, to single out military casualties this way is a violation of the spirit of our Peace Constitution.

3. The government's assertion that Yasukuni Shrine is not a religion takes the same line of religious interference and suppression of thought that characterized the years of nationalism and militarism.

4. Yasukuni Shrine's statement of readiness to abandon its status as a legal religious corporation is merely an attempt to escape censure for its part in this conjoining of the government with a particular religion, which violates the principle of separation between state and religion.

5. The bill exploits people's feelings toward the spirits of the war dead.

6. The war dead should be memorialized in keeping with the spirit of the Constitution, and Yasukuni Shrine should stay out of governmental affairs.

7. We appeal to the public to oppose the bill for the sake of peace and democracy in Japan.

Ultimately the bill was stalled and tabled in the Diet; on August 5, 1969, it was declared null and avoid. The Liberal Democratic Party made four other attempts — in 1970, 1971, 1972, and 1973 — to push the bill through the Diet (where the LDP has enjoyed a consistent postwar majority status); each time the bill wound up null and void. The ruling party subsequently turned to extra-legislative attempts to give the shrine national status (more on this later). Meanwhile, the opposition movement was expanding to include groups in Sect Shinto[4] as well as large religious bodies such as Risshō Kōseikai and Perfect Liberty Kyōdan.

---

[4] The term "Sect Shinto" referred in prewar days to thirteen groups formed in the nineteenth century (there are more now); it was a government term applied to Shinto groups officially regarded as "religious," and thus distinguished them from the legally "nonreligious" State Shinto. On State Shinto, see n. 1 above. — Ed.

Moreover, surviving families of Christians who had been enshrined as "deities" of Yasukuni Shrine, by the state or by shrine officials, had formed their own Association of Bereaved Christian Families. On August 15, 1975, they issued a resolution based on the Constitution's renunciation of war. This resolution repudiated formal Yasukuni visits by the emperor, who bore responsibility for the war; denounced unilateral state acts to memorialize Christians; and rejected claims by the much larger Japan Association for Bereaved Families of the War Dead that Yasukuni Shrine is a sacred place for all of Japan's war dead. The resolution also expressed the Christian association's determination to develop, in cooperation with Asian neighbors, a new movement that would transcend ethnic and religious boundaries. It concluded with a warning to all political parties not to exploit the problems of bereaved families for partisan interests.

Key Issues of Yasukuni Shrine

Although the Yasukuni Bill has been abandoned (at least for the time being), it has cast into sharp relief the issues felt keenly by supporters and opponents alike. Some of these issues are constitutional; others are religious. The key issues are as follows.

The Shrine's religious status. Yasukuni Shrine officially attributes its origin to the imperial will of the Emperor Meiji to assure a "peaceful nation,"[5] and the shrine therefore has the character of an "imperial shrine." It exists primarily to enshrine the spirits of the "heroic war dead" who sacrificed themselves for the sake of Japan, "the land of the gods." It is a religious institution grounded in Shinto. It follows, then, that under the principle of separation of religion and state, it would be unconstitutional for the state to maintain the shrine. It is to get around this that the government seeks to remove Yasukuni Shrine from its legal status as a religious corporation and establish it as a nonreligious institution. But would the artificial removal of the shrine from religious corporation status really change it into a nonreligious institution? In prewar days we Japanese were told, "State Shinto is not a religion; for us Japanese it surpasses religion"—then we were forced to worship at Shinto shrines.

Who are the "heroic war dead"? It is only natural for a people to honor those who die for their country. The Yasukuni connection, however, is not quite so simple. In the expression "heroic war dead" the implicit standard of judgment is loyalty to the emperor. The ideology that glorifies self-sacrifice for national interests translates easily into the idea that to die for the nation

[5] The Chinese characters for Yasukuni can be translated "peaceful country."—Tr.

is to die for the emperor, and that this is the highest virtue. Such thinking is grounded in a national ethic which presupposes that "public" always takes priority over personal matters.[6] The criterion is loyalty to the emperor, and thus the state determines both public morality and human values. Under such an ideology the danger of marked infringements upon human rights, especially freedom of conscience, is very great.

Remembering the heroic dead. The practice of remembering the noble virtues of the war dead, offering solace to their spirits, and extolling their meritorious deeds is dear to the hearts of many Japanese people. This, however, is a religious sentiment and practice rooted in the ancient Shinto tradition of appeasing the spirits of the dead and praying to ancestral gods for the peace and prosperity of the nation. To compel all Japanese people to follow this particular practice is to deny their freedom of religion.

What price dissent? What becomes of those persons who do not participate in the ritual veneration and glorification of the war dead? From Meiji times on, the state compelled the Japanese people to visit shrines and persistently demanded that they sacrifice all for the sake of the state. Those who failed to obey this "national morality," or "national religion," were labeled "non-citizens." The Yasukuni Bill is fraught with the danger of reviving this prewar nightmare. The bill's excessive esteem for the "heroic war dead" raises many legal and moral issues. By centering spiritual values and meaning on the spirits of the war dead, then tying spiritual and religious values to national sovereignty, the bill runs the danger, in due course, of absolutizing the Japanese state, which, in turn, easily leads to the exclusion of other peoples and nations. The end result could well be the jettisoning of the Constitution's express goal of a "peaceful nation."

The way back to State Shinto. As many people have pointed out, the Yasukuni Bill opens the way for a return to State Shinto. The government wants to provide state support for Yasukuni Shrine and to remove the shrine from the jurisdiction of the Religious Corporations Act. Shrine officials are more than willing to accommodate by surrendering their legal status as a religious corporation. For the government even to discuss the rights and wrongs of such a move is to trample underfoot the principle of separation of state and religion and presents a serious challenge to the preservation of religious freedom.

[6] In Japan's traditional hierarchy, the term *ōyake*, nowadays rendered "public," referred primarily to the emperor. Cf. Nishikawa Shigeru, "The Daijōsai, the Constitution, and Christian faith," *The Japan Christian Quarterly*, 56/3, Summer 1990, pp. 140–41. — Ed.

State control of religion. A further danger lurks in the government's easygoing attitude toward religious organizations. The mentality that proposes exempting Yasukuni Shrine from the Religious Corporations Act could easily mastermind a return to the Japanese government's unceasing attempts, begun early in Meiji times, to gain state control over religion.

The movement to nationalize Yasukuni Shrine has exposed a fundamental disposition in Japanese society that was dominant before and during the war, but has been dormant for most of the postwar period. To put it bluntly, the democratic Constitution reportedly "forced upon Japan by MacArthur's staff" in the late 1940s began coming apart in the 1970s. The chief unraveling agent was the LDP's nationalization bill—defeated five times, to be sure, but that was hardly the end of the matter.

Abandoning legislative processes, the LDP adopted tactics for reshaping public opinion: a series of official visits to Yasukuni Shrine by public figures, presented as "routine" and needing no justification.

State Visits to Yasukuni Shrine

New measures to win state support for Yasukuni Shrine opened with visits by the prime ministers and Cabinet ministers. Next came imperial visits, accompanied by "educational" activities for promoting reverence for the emperor. The Liberal Democratic Party then unfolded a nationwide campaign to get city councils and prefectural assemblies to pass resolutions urging official Yasukuni visits by the emperor and prime minister. Supportive activities included Shinto ceremonies sponsored by local municipalities, use of public monies for these ceremonies, and fees paid for *tamagushi*[7] to honor fallen war heroes for their glorious deeds.

Prime Minister Miki Takeo made the first postwar visit to Yasukuni Shrine, but did so as a "private citizen." This visit took place on August 15, 1975, when a government-sponsored service of national mourning was held. At this service, a ceremonial wooden tablet first inscribed "Emblem of the War Dead" was rewritten to read "To the Spirits of the Fallen Heroes." Miki's shrine visit and the memorial ceremony helped redefine August 15; what had been a day for memorializing the war's end now became a day for honoring the nation's "fallen heroes."

Once begun, Yasukuni visits by prime ministers and Cabinet ministers escalated in scope and gravity. Prime Minister Fukuda Takeo first went to the shrine on April 2, 1978, accompanied by three Cabinet ministers, and again on August 15 with the Cabinet's chief secretary and vice-secretary. Fukuda signed the shrine registry as "Prime Minister of the Cabinet." Next came

[7] Offerings of sprigs or branches of a sacred tree to Shinto deities. —Tr.

Prime Minister Ōhira Masayoshi, a Christian who was severely criticized by fellow Christians, even though he visited the shrine as an individual citizen. When the next prime minister, Suzuki Zenkō, made his Yasukuni visit in 1982, he took along nineteen Cabinet ministers.

The most forthright challenge came from Nakasone Yasuhiro who became prime minister and visited Yasukuni Shrine on April 21, 1983, signing the registry as "Cabinet Prime Minister Nakasone Yasuhiro." He declared his subsequent visit on August 15 an "official visit." He then ordered the Chief Cabinet Secretary to demonstrate that official visits to Yasukuni Shrine are not unconstitutional. On November 14, 1983, the LDP Subcommittee on the Yasukuni Issue obliged by making public its opinion that official shrine visits do not violate the constitution. On August 15, 1985, Nakasone broke all precedents and led his entire Cabinet on an official visit to Yasukuni Shrine.

The opposition movement, of course, regards these visits as clearly unconstitutional, and more, as phased steps toward reconstructing Japan as a quasi-religious state grounded in State Shinto and placed under imperial rule. The opposition has had only limited success thus far in blocking the incremental reinstatement of Yasukuni Shrine's former official status. Indeed, Nakasone's success led him to claim that he had "closed the books on postwar politics."

Nakasone's official Yasukuni visits and his bravado regarding postwar politics stirred up bitter war memories in Asian countries once victimized by Japanese aggression. The peoples of Asia have not forgotten the suffering and tragedy they experienced at the hands of the war dead whose "outstanding virtue" and "meritorious deeds" many Japanese people want to recall and exalt. It is thus quite understandable that, on August 15, 1985, the Taiwan Presbyterian Church conveyed its misgivings over the issue to the United Church of Christ in Japan. It was also natural for the Korean National Council of Churches to communicate its uneasiness over official Yasukuni Shrine visits at the same time. The LDP elders were forced to put Yasukuni visits on diplomatic hold for a while.

REVIVING THE IMPERIAL SYSTEM

Since Yasukuni Shrine is an "imperial shrine," reverence for the emperor can hardly be separated from state support of the shrine. The more the emperor is revered, the more justifiable it is to extol those sacrificed in his name for the nation. Their actions become the most virtuous, their deaths the most patriotic. Beyond official Yasukuni visits by specific prime ministers, the goal was to make "imperial shrine visits" an annual event. Petitions calling for official visits, passed and promoted by local assemblies, gave this movement a broader grass-roots base.

Imperial Rites

In 1976 a ceremony celebrating the fiftieth year of Emperor Hirohito's reign was held at a large hall beside the imperial palace grounds. Outside, voices of criticism and opposition arose from several quarters. This outcry of protest was by no means strange, for the ceremony completely ignored the basic difference between the prewar and postwar emperor systems—the fundamental shift from divine emperor to human emperor. The ceremony also ignored the emperor's responsibility for the war. Taking into consideration contemporary moves to reestablish Yasukuni Shrine, we have certainly not been amiss in discerning a movement to reshape public opinion so as to revive the prewar imperial system with its divine emperor.

Our reading of the situation is clearly supported by the Ministry of Education's administration of the educational system. In 1977 the Education Ministry mandated *Kimigayo* as the national anthem in the New Course of Study for Elementary and Middle Schools.[8] In June 1979 the government promulgated and put into effect a law stipulating that the entire duration of an emperor's reign be designated by one era name.[9] The Japanese people would, accordingly, understand themselves as living in, and thus identify themselves with, a specific emperor's reign.

Government administration of the educational system has actively aimed at fostering reverence for the emperor. The Ministry of Education's power to authorize textbooks has been consistently used to carry out a policy of not allowing public schools to address the history of Japan's aggression against Asian countries in World War II. This policy goes hand in hand with the Yasukuni bill's history-revising aims of reestablishing Yasukuni Shrine and praising the war dead. It is only natural that public controversy over the ideology-driven textbook revision should evoke severe criticism from neighboring Asian countries, as it did in 1982, when certain revised portions of the textbooks in question had to be restored to accord with reality.

Ceremonial commemoration in 1986 of the sixtieth year of the Shōwa Emperor's reign drew attention to "X-day,"[10] the imminent succession of a new emperor, and thus to the various Shinto rites and ceremonies that would mark the succession. Specific questions were raised about funeral rites for the aging emperor and enthronement rites for his successor; whether the rites

[8] *Kimigayo* has no legal standing as "national anthem," despite its customary use. — Ed.

[9] In premodern times, imperial era names were sometimes changed on propitious occasions during an emperor's reign. The late Emperor Hirohito's reign (1926–89) is called Shōwa; the present Emperor's era is Heisei (1989–). — Ed.

[10] This term is a media expression, not an official one; it was widely used in autumn 1989 to refer to the impending death of the then-ill Shōwa Emperor and to problems of the imperial succession to follow. — Tr.

would be state ceremonies or private rites of the Imperial House; and whether the expenses incurred would be covered by public funds. The problem of how much official recognition should be given the ceremonies was also raised.

The funeral rite for Emperor Hirohito in 1989 and the Great Food Offering Ceremony[11] in autumn 1990 to conclude the accession to the throne of Emperor Akihito were both performed according to Imperial House traditions, as there are no stipulations in postwar constitutional law for these occasions. The "imperial traditions," however, involve prewar Shinto assumptions about the new emperor's assuming "divinity." While the ruling party's intentions of returning to prewar values and practices were openly displayed, most Japanese appear to have accepted these events without questioning the overt reversion to "imperial traditions."[12] Despite generally mild reactions among the public, there is no doubt that the government wanted Japan's emperor to appear once again as "divine."

Challenges in the Courts

While the Liberal Democratic Party was suffering setbacks in pushing its Yasukuni Bill and, changing tactics, enjoying limited success in getting prime ministers and Cabinet members to visit Yasukuni Shrine officially, the Association to Express Gratitude to the Spirits of the War Dead mounted a drive to gain ten million signatures on a petition that claimed official Yasukuni visits by state officers and state guests were not unconstitutional. Meanwhile, the LDP had its loyalists in local assemblies pass similar resolutions in rapid succession. In September 1980, for example, the Yamaguchi Prefectural Assembly became the twenty-fourth prefectural assembly (of a total of 47) to pass a petition promoting official Shrine visits, after the opposition parties had walked out of a losing debate. In 1981, LDP supporters in the Diet

[11] The Great Food Offering (Daijōsai) has roots in ancient harvest festivals. The imperial rite, observed annually in antiquity, is now used only as the major concluding ritual in a new emperor's accession to the throne. Ritually prepared food is received by the emperor and offered by him to the ancestral spirits and national *kami* (gods) as a thanksgiving for harvests and preservation of the nation. Through this ritual act, the new emperor enters into an ancient mythic history in which he joins the succession of emperors and becomes the sacred living *kami*, who represents the people before the *kami* of heaven and earth, and within whom the entire welfare of the people is enfolded. – Tr.

[12] The "imperial traditions" are not all ancient; many were manufactured late in the nineteenth century to support the Meiji "restoration" of imperial rule. Cf. Helen Hardacre, *Shinto and the State, 1868–1988* (Princeton University Press, 1989). For more extensive discussion of religious aspects of imperial traditions, see the special issue of the *Japanese Journal of Religious Studies*, 17/2–3, June-September 1990, on "The emperor system and religion in Japan." – Ed.

formed an association for group visits to Yasukuni Shrine, choosing February 11, National Founding Day,[13] to carry out their plan.

On the whole, however, the ruling party has benefitted more from challenges in the courts. The issue has been joined mainly in lawsuits on the constitutionality of local shrines dedicated to the war dead and on questions of the separation of government and religion. In a number of municipalities, lawsuits have been initiated involving (a) government payment of fees for offering *tamagushi* at shrines dedicated to the war dead, (b) contributions to shrines paid from public funds, and (c) the use of public funds in relocating monuments to the war dead and in festivals for consolation of the war dead. Judgments in lower courts have generally held that these actions were unconstitutional in that they violated the constitutional principle of the separation of state and religion.[14]

One such case arose from payment by Tsu City to Shinto priests who conducted a traditional Shinto groundbreaking ceremony.[15] The Supreme Court in 1977 reversed the "unconstitutional" verdicts of lower courts, ruling that the intent of the ceremony was "general" in nature and that its "effect" did not lead to the support or promotion of a particular religion. The traditionally religious (Shinto) rite was held to be merely a "custom" now, so the groundbreaking ceremony for the city's gymnasium was judged constitutional. In a similar suit, the Osaka High Court, ruling on an appeal, upheld the constitutionality of the Minoo City's Monument to the War Dead and its Festival for the Consolation of the Spirits of the War Dead.

This doctrine of "intent" and "effect" has subsequently led many to accept the expenditure of public funds for Shinto ceremonial activities. This doctrine implicitly views these ceremonies as "public" events. Hence, it is pregnant with grave problems.

The cumulative weight of these legal judgments has heavily influenced the debate on the enthronement rites held for the new emperor as well as controversy over use of public funds for these ceremonies. In due time this line

[13] Traditionally this day celebrates the divine origin of the Japanese nation; it refers to legendary Emperor Jinmu's accession to the throne. — Ed.

[14] The pro-Yasukuni forces suffered a stunning setback on January 10, 1991, when "a resolution by the Iwate Prefectural Assembly calling for the emperor and Cabinet ministers to pay official visits to Yasukuni Shrine was ruled unconstitutional by the Sendai High Court." (*The Japan Times*, January 11, 1991.) The Iwate government has since decided to appeal the decision to the Supreme Court. — Ed.

[15] The Japanese term is *jichinsai*, the ceremony for purifying a building site prior to construction. It is performed by Shinto priests, and in this case public funds were used to pay for the priests' services at the construction site for a municipal gymnasium in Tsu City, Aichi Prefecture. Cf. David Reid, "Separation of Religion and State: How Japanese religions line up," *The Japan Christian Quarterly*, 56/4, Fall 1990, pp. 214. — Ed.

of judicial reasoning will certainly affect the issue of the constitutionality of official visits to Yasukuni Shrine.

Controversy over Yasukuni Shrine and the emperor system clearly involves more than proper relations between religion and government. At stake are the larger issues of democracy, human rights, freedom, and peace at home and abroad. Christian contributions to this controversy have definitely been conspicuous, but far from sufficient.

Two immediate tasks lie before us. One, we must further widen the supportive circle of solidarity within Japan. Two, we must, however belatedly, learn to see these issues from the perspective of our Asian neighbors. A negative example of this need lies in the fact that it was our Asian neighbors, not ourselves, who forced reversals in Nakasone's official Shrine visits and in the textbook controversy. We have little difficulty in seeing ourselves as the victims of the government's ill-conceived designs; even more must we see the issues, and indeed ourselves, through the eyes of our Asian neighbors who, much more than we, are victims of the uses and abuses of power in and by Japan.

6

Christians and Peacemaking

Shōji Tsutomu

CHRISTIAN PEACEMAKERS in any country usually cooperate closely with peacemakers of other faiths and ideologies. This is especially true of Christian peacemakers in Japan, for they are only a tiny minority of the entire Christian community—itself but a tiny minority of the total Japanese population. Alone and separate, Christians in Japan can do little for peace. But strengthened by prayer and worship in their churches, Christians then go out to make vital contributions to the larger citizens' peace movement.

Christians do more than simply add a little weight to what others are already doing. They share a unique understanding of peace based on their faith. For example, Christians have given to the struggle against nationalization of Yasukuni Shrine a distinctive ethical definition of religious freedom and the human rights of minorities. Too, by following biblical imperatives and confessing their own wartime responsibility, Christians have deepened the larger peace movement's understanding of Japan's wartime aggression. Moreover, peace activists here, as elsewhere, sometimes suffer burnout; Christians can then offer an inner peace and hope sustained by faith.

Since Christians, like everybody else, are subject to ideological differences and division, the split since 1963 in Japan's antinuclear movement along lines taken by the Socialist and Communist political parties has been reflected in the Christian peace movement as well.[1] At times, though, Christian peacemakers have been able to affect some reconciliation at the national and grassroots levels. Sekiya Ayako, former president of the YWCA in Japan and

---

[1] On this split, see Yutaka Shishido, "Christian peace activities in postwar Japan," in *Called to Be Peacemakers*, edited by Suguru Matsuki and David L. Swain (Tokyo: Japan Ecumenical Books, 1989), distributed in North America by Friendship Press. —Ed.

chairperson of the National Christian Council in Japan's Nuclear Problems Committee, has given outstanding leadership in such reconciliation.[2]

The Christian minority, as the "light of the world" and the "salt of the earth," has a special role as catalyst in the peace movement. As is suggested by the following survey, lack of wisdom and courage has often kept the churches from fulfilling this role. Indeed, in the four postwar decades, many churches may have done little more than help maintain the status quo. And yet, God has led some of these very churches to confess their wartime responsibility and has given many a vision of shalom in which all good things are shared with our neighbors in Asia and around the world. Above all, God has enabled many to commit themselves to realizing this shalom vision.

THE ROOTS OF POSTWAR PEACEMAKING

The peace movement was born partly out of bitter wartime experiences. Fifteen years of war (1931–45) in Asia and the Pacific cost over two million Japanese lives and at least 20 million lives in other lands. War left the country exhausted and in ruins. Except for a few farmers, hunger was a daily experience; the disabled, unemployed, orphans, and prostitutes were seen everywhere. The people had had enough of war.

There was also the sheer joy of the peace that came with defeat. Since the late nineteenth century the Japanese empire had relentlessly pursued the goals of national wealth, military might, and territorial expansion. For the people this had meant wholesale denial of human rights and sacrifice of life itself, along with total subjection of education, culture, and even spiritual life to absolute state control. All life and liberty were at the disposal of the state and its emperor. For the people, defeat in 1945 meant liberation from this long nightmare.

Hence peace meant far more than the absence of war; it meant a new opportunity for democracy and human rights. Japan's new postwar Constitution (1947) was founded firmly on three cornerstones: peace, democracy, and human rights. Because conservatives soon mounted efforts to revise this Constitution, the peace movement was all the more committed to preserving it. The course of this conflict from the late 1940s through the 1960s needs to be reviewed briefly before turning to the 1970s and 1980s.

[2] On Sekiya's personal peace pilgrimage, see her autobiographical essay "Our Call to Peacemaking," in *Ibid.* — Ed.

The Peace Constitution

Soon after the Korean War erupted in June 1950, the United States abruptly reversed its policy of promoting the democratization of Japan. The US offered Japan a peace treaty in September 1951, but it came at the price of a "mutual security treaty" that programmed Japan for rearmament and incorporation into the victor's Far East strategy.

Popular support for the new Peace Constitution derived partly from the desire to restore friendly relations with all nations against whom Japan had waged aggressive war. That is, popular sentiment favored "multilateral treaties" with all former belligerents, not just a single two-party peace settlement with the United States. This aspiration was expressed in the new Constitution's preamble:

> We, the Japanese people, desire peace for all time . . . and we have determined to preserve our security and existence, trusting in the justice and faith of the peace-loving peoples of the world. We desire to occupy an honored place in an international society striving for the preservation of peace, and the banishment of tyranny and slavery, oppression and intolerance for all time from the earth. We recognize that all peoples of the world have the right to live in peace, free from fear and want.

The Constitution's principal item in support of this declaration is Article 9, which reads as follows:

> ARTICLE 9. Aspiring sincerely to an international peace based on justice and order, the Japanese people forever renounce war as a sovereign right of the nation and the threat or use of force as a means of settling international disputes.
>
> In order to accomplish the aim of the preceding paragraph, land, sea, and air forces, as well as other war potential, will never be maintained. The right of belligerency of the state will not be recognized.

These are more than idealistic wishes; they express a people's firm determination forged from the tragedies of all-out war. "Trusting in the justice and faith of peace-loving peoples" took concrete form in the commitment to multiple treaties with all nations — an early postwar attempt to transcend the Cold War order shaped by the American and Soviet powers.

While this commitment found expression in a nationwide citizens' movement, it proved inadequate to restrain the government's power to conclude the peace and security treaties with the United States.[3] Worse still, the government had readily complied with General Douglas MacArthur's order

---

[3] Signed on September 8, 1951, the two treaties became effective on April 28, 1952. — Ed.

(July 8, 1950) to establish the National Police Reserves, forerunner of today's Self-Defense Forces.

The Christian Peace Association

On New Year's Day of 1951, General MacArthur publicly called for peace treaty negotiations with Japan—and simultaneously for Japan's rearmament. In February 1951 some Protestant leaders gathered in Tokyo to oppose the rearmament policies that threatened the peace and democracy so recently won, and in April they formed the Christian Peace Association (CPA). For them the new Constitution was not merely the product of political processes; it was "a precious gift from God to be cherished." Besides protesting rearmament and calling for multiple peace treaties, CPA also opposed reinstated police powers, supported victims of union-busting forces, and promoted antiwar and antinuclear efforts in many localities.

Thus far CPA resembled other citizen peace groups. But there was one significant difference: recognition and confession of personal wartime guilt, especially toward neighboring Asian peoples. The association's inaugural statement said: "During World War II we Christians not only sinned against the gospel of peace but also failed to commit ourselves wholly to working for peace, and we deeply repent these sins." This repentance refers not merely to the Christian churches' failure to criticize the wars of aggression but also to the many ways Christians actually cooperated with the war effort, which imposed great sacrifices upon the peoples of Asia and elsewhere in the world.

The association took the lead in forming a five-person ecumenical team that visited China in 1957 to find out how Christians had fared since the Communist revolution (1949) and to apologize for Japan's wartime atrocities against the Chinese. At a time of mounting threats to peace, these Christians saw the need to atone for past sins before they could turn anew to the tasks of peacemaking. Members of this team were warmly received by leaders of the Chinese churches.

The Rise and Falter of the Peace Movement

On March 1, 1954, the United States conducted its largest-ever hydrogen bomb test at Bikini Atoll in the mid-Pacific. Radioactive fallout from this test fell on a distant Japanese tuna-fishing vessel, contaminating twenty-three crewmen, one of whom died six months later. Alarmed women in Tokyo's Suginami district started an antinuclear signature campaign in April that quickly spread nationwide, collecting 18 million signatures by November. By August 6, "Hiroshima Day," of the following year, when the first World Conference Against Atomic and Hydrogen Bombs opened, the campaign had garnered 34 million signatures — more than half of Japan's registered voters at the time. Members of CPA and many other Christians were active in this campaign.

From 1955 the peace movement in Japan continued to grow, drawing its strength partly from the "victim consciousness" of the only people ever to experience atomic horror. "No more Hiroshimas!" naturally included the strong desire to avoid a second time. But that is only one aspect of the appeal. "No more Hiroshimas!" also warns that another nuclear holocaust would threaten all peoples and all living things on earth, even the future possibility of life itself. The appeal cries out from experience that nuclear weapons must never be used for any reason; indeed, there is only one acceptable option — abolish them all. The appeal insists that the very existence of the "ultimate weapon" outlaws all wars. With Cold War fever fueling the mounting US–Soviet nuclear arms race, people in the world's only atomic-bombed land felt compelled, on behalf of all peoples, to signal a resounding "No!" to nuclear weapons.

The first World Conference Against Atomic and Hydrogen Bombs in August 1955, with 30,000 Japanese participants joined by 54 persons from twelve foreign countries, was followed by annual world rallies held alternately in Hiroshima and Nagasaki. But factional disputes in the early 1960s over whether to oppose "all nuclear tests" or only those of rival political camps split the entire peace community in 1963. While the peace movement survived this split, it was considerably weakened.

Meanwhile, the US–Japan Security Treaty of 1951 came up for renewal and revision in 1960. Starting in 1959, the peace movement tried to block extension of the treaty because it would boost Japanese rearmament and further integrate Japan's Self-Defense Forces into US Cold War strategy. Still worse, all this violated the basic principles of the Peace Constitution. But the ruling party, with an overwhelming legislative majority, was able to push the new treaty through the Diet, and the peace movement slumped into stagnation.

The movement came to life quickly, however, when Japan went beyond mere rearmament to play a new role in supplying safe bases, mainly in Okinawa, from which US Forces in 1965 began the relentless bombings of North Vietnam. The Japanese campaign against the US war in Vietnam was by no means simply anti-American. Rather it represented profound revulsion at the thought of the Japanese government once again collaborating in aggressive war against fellow Asians. Japan did not, of course, send any troops to Vietnam; but it provided vital bases and supplies for that war — and in the process Japan reaped huge profits from US procurement programs. It galled conscientious Japanese to realize that profits from the sufferings of fellow Asians fueled the engines of Japan's high-growth economy.

The collective conscience of the Christian Peace Association was also quickened. In March it sent to the United States a five-person team, headed by Omura Isamu, then moderator of the United Church of Christ in Japan (UCCJ), to plead for a cessation of hostilities. Traveling to several major cities, the team encountered varied response; but leaders of the National Council of the Churches of Christ in the USA set up a special inquiry commission for peace in Vietnam, an important precedent of Christians transcending national interests for the sake of peace.

With peace at stake, and Japan's international relations expanding, the UCCJ took account of itself. On Easter Day in 1967, its "Confession of Responsibility During World War II" was issued over the name of then moderator Suzuki Masahisa. The church could not with integrity appeal for peace now, it was felt, until it had atoned for sins in wars of the past. This classical act of Christian fidelity opened the way for restored relations with churches in Korea and Taiwan (former colonies), with whom covenants of cooperation were soon sealed.

THE NATIONAL CHRISTIAN COUNCIL:
PEACE FORUM IN THE 1970S AND 1980S

As the Vietnam War wound down in the early 1970s, the Christian Peace Association became largely inactive, except for some members who continued efforts on behalf of the Hiroshima and Nagasaki atomic bomb victims. But antiwar efforts were now modulated into new concern for relations with Asian peoples, and the National Christian Council in Japan (NCCJ) became the forum for new interactions with Asian churches, especially in South Korea and the Philippines. These concerns were incorporated into a broadened peace strategy with networks for joint study and action. The NCCJ worked closely with the International Affairs section of the Christian Conference of Asia (CCA) to sponsor international conferences on peace and related issues in the Asia-Pacific region.

Struggles on the Home Front

The end of hostilities in Vietnam led, ironically, to renewed efforts by the Japanese government to revise the war-renouncing Constitution, not by legislative procedure but by political "interpretation,"[4] so as to permit further buildup of the Self-Defense Forces. As defeat left the United States unable to maintain Asian hegemony alone, it pressed further military buildups on its

---

[4] Cf. Ohtori Kurino, "Observations of a peace researcher," in *Called to Be Peacemakers* (see n. 1 above). — Ed.

Asian allies, particularly Japan. In the Japan–US defense guidelines[5] adopted in 1978, Japan went beyond the "defense-only defense" stance thus far claimed to be consistent with the Peace Constitution; its Self-Defense Forces became, in effect, fully integrated into the command structure of US global strategy. Joint military exercises escalated in number and scale, and US command, control, communications, and intelligence (C^3I) facilities — the "software" of nuclear war — multiplied throughout Japan.

Also in 1978, the National Christian Council formed a new Peace Committee to give focused attention to the new phase of Japan's militarization. This was the year of the United Nations General Assembly's first Special Session on Disarmament.

Field studies and networking. The NCCJ Peace Committee first concentrated on linking Christians already active in peacemaking. Nationwide conferences, local field trips, and long-distance caravans were conducted with broad participation from groups such as those opposing military bases in Okinawa as well as Yokosuka and Atsugi in the Tokyo area, Hiroshima Christians' opposing nuclear arms, and NCCJ-related organizations such as the national YWCA, the Japan Woman's Christian Temperance Union, and the Fellowship of Reconciliation.

In March 1985 some thirty participants, from Okinawa in the south to Hokkaido in the north, assembled near Tokyo for the first nationwide peace conference. The second such gathering, held in Yokohama in August 1986, made on-site observations of US and Japanese military facilities in Yokosuka, Zama, Atsugi, and Zushi — all on metropolitan Tokyo's southern perimeter. Participants were startled to find how many key C^3I facilities Japan had allowed the US to install so close to the nation's capital. The conference also prepared and hand-delivered to the US naval command in Yokosuka a letter opposing the introduction of nuclear arms into Yokosuka Bay, in contravention of Japan's "Three Non-nuclear Principles."[6]

In late July 1987 twenty persons joined a ten-day Peace Caravan from Tokyo to Aomori Prefecture and back. Spending time along the way with church groups in Fukushima, Hachinohe, and Misawa, and at a large lay-clergy retreat of the UCCJ Ōu District at Lake Towada, with citizens' groups in Hachinohe and Misawa, and with farming and fishing folk in Aomori's Rokkasho village, the caravan paid special attention to the US airbase in Misawa (with its advanced C^3I facilities) and to Japan's new nuclear fuel

---

[5] Strategic and tactical implementations of the Japan–US Security Treaty; these guidelines are not publicized. — Ed.

[6] The Three Non-nuclear Principles forbid the "production, possession, or introduction into Japan" of nuclear weapons. — Ed.

processing facilities (which will produce plutonium when completed) in the Rokkasho area. On the way home the caravan stopped in Sendai for a three-day NCCJ-sponsored peace conference early in August on the theme "Peace as a missional task today." This caravan-conference event did much to deepen our common awareness of military and nuclear problems and our solidarity as Christian peacemakers.

Again in August 1988 the NCCJ Peace Committee conducted a study caravan along Tokyo's perimeter and into four adjoining prefectures — Kanagawa, Saitama, Ibaraki, and Chiba — to observe the top-level command facilities of US Forces in the Far East as well as some Self-Defense Forces installations. Topping off previous study programs, this one afforded a comprehensive perspective of Japan's place in US global nuclear strategy.

Peace education and protest. Parallel to the above activities, the NCCJ Peace Committee has sponsored numerous seminars and lectures, issued many peace statements, sent protest letters, and prepared materials on peace education and worship for use by churches and other Christian groups. In March 1982 the committee gained the NCCJ General Assembly's approval for a "Peace Appeal" that called for Japan's return to the war-renouncing Article 9 of the Constitution as the proper path to peace, for solidarity in combatting discrimination in Japan and in Asia, and for the churches to overcome the false worship of power in today's world. This appeal was addressed to churches throughout Japan.

A peace appeal approved by the March 1985 NCCJ General Assembly addressed the escalating arms race and the militarization of nation, society, and public opinion; it called the churches to prayer, dialogue, and cooperative action to reverse these trends.

In March 1988 the Peace Committee brought before the NCCJ General Assembly a peace appeal (approved) that noted the relaxation of tensions in Europe (represented by signing of the US–USSR treaty on reduction of intermediate-range nuclear arms), then criticized Japan for continued designation of the Soviet Union as its enemy and persistent increasing of its military budget until it had become the third largest in the world.[7] The churches were called to intensify their efforts for disarmament.

Cooperation with other groups. From its beginning the NCCJ Peace Committee had cooperated with the Justice and Peace Council of the Catholic Church in Japan to hold joint prayer meetings, seminars, and advocacy marches. Most recently, on August 26, 1990, a joint peace assembly was held

---

[7] Besides the substantial annual budget increases, the near doubling of yen over dollar values in the 1987–88 period helped to catapult Japan's military budget into this high rank. — Ed.

in the Catholic church in Yokosuka to oppose homeporting there of two US naval vessels that are fitted for nuclear-tipped Tomahawk cruise missiles. The committee has also joined various citizens' groups in peace meetings and rallies and in presenting protest letters to the US naval command in Yokosuka and the US Embassy in Tokyo, as well as to Japan's Ministry of Foreign Affairs and the Defense Agency.

Cooperation with other religious groups has been another important avenue of peacemaking. In June 1982, Sekiya Ayako, then vice moderator of the NCCJ General Assembly, served as head of a religious delegation (37 Christians, 24 Buddhists, 11 Tenrikyō adherents, and 4 Shintoists) that delivered a peace appeal with 200,000 signatures to the United Nations as its Second Special Session on Disarmament opened. This delegation then toured the United States to meet with a wide variety of religious groups.

Japan and Asia

Efforts by churches in Japan to atone for their wartime responsibilities and to renew their Asian connections have enabled the National Christian Council member bodies to develop deeper ties with Asian churches (cf. I-4).

Since the first consultation of the Japan and South Korea NCCs, held in Seoul in June 1973, churches in the two countries have almost every year held joint conferences, usually on some variation of the theme "Peace in Northeast Asia." Summer 1982 was an especially critical time. Japan's Ministry of Education was trying to purge school history textbooks of all references to Japanese atrocities against peoples of its wartime colonies; the sufferings of Asian peoples were being ignored, as revised texts sought to beautify Japan's past wars. The NCCs of Japan and South Korea sent a joint letter of protest to the Japanese government. In November at a joint consultation in Tokyo both NCCs committed themselves to making fair and accurate assessments of Japan's colonial and wartime record, promoting free development of life and culture among Asian peoples, and opposing resurgent militarism in Japan.

In June 1987 three representatives of the National Christian Council in Japan made a formal visit to the North Korean Christian Association. Then in September 1989 twenty church representatives from both North and South Korea were invited to Tokyo for a consultation with Japanese colleagues to consider how Christians might contribute to peaceful reunification of the Korean peninsula.

Parallel overtures were made toward the Philippine churches. The NCCJ in September 1978 invited the general secretary of the NCC in the Philippines, along with Filipino lawyers and activists involved in peace and human rights issues, to a Japan–Philippines consultation in Tokyo. Soon afterward the NCCJ formed its Philippines Committee, which has promoted many exchanges between churches and Christians of the two countries.

Formal relations with the China Christian Council (CCC) were opened when ten representatives of the NCCJ visited China in September–October of 1983, and ten CCC delegates came to Japan the following year. The 1983 Japan–China interchurch communiqué clearly affirmed the Japanese side's confession of wartime responsibility and the common desire of churches in both countries for peace. The Chinese churches especially appreciated the critical attitude taken by Japanese churches toward the textbook revision scandal as well as their vigorous opposition to militarism in Japan.

The initiative in restoring relations with churches in Taiwan was taken by the United Church of Christ in Japan, which led to closer relations between the NCCJ and Taiwanese churches. The NCCJ lent strong support to the church leaders in Taiwan when they suffered suppression by the Taiwanese government in 1980.

Through the Christian Conference of Asia the NCCJ-related churches have fellowship with churches in sixteen Asian lands. From all these associations the Japanese churches have learned a vital lesson: the Japanese, in their headlong rush to catch up with the advanced countries of Europe and North America, have ignored the misery and suffering they caused to their fellow Asians. Indeed, they did not even try to assess the impact their successes had on the rest of Asia. The Japanese people have been much too ignorant of and irresponsible toward Asian peoples, and Japanese Christians are no exception.

Based on this self-appraisal, the NCCJ in March 1982 founded its Center for Christian Response to Asian Issues (CCRAI). Its aims are to help Japanese Christians understand the churches and peoples of Asian lands; to develop solidarity with Asians who, despite great hardship, struggle for human rights and democracy; and thus to contribute to peace in Asia. To this end CCRAI has prepared numerous pamphlets and books, sponsored seminars and lectures, and conducted various Asian study tours.

Japan and North America

Japan's position within US global strategy makes it imperative that Japanese peacemakers work hand in hand with their North American colleagues. This priority, long recognized by churches on both sides, has found concrete expression in various projects jointly sponsored by the NCCJ and the NCCC-USA.

The Okinawa Christian Council (OCC) joined these two bodies in an April 1980 church consultation on problems of US military bases in Okinawa — and found the reality to be, rather, "Okinawa within a huge US base." Accordingly, discussions focused on moving beyond US-supported "ministry to US personnel" to cooperative Japan–US church efforts for dealing with the base problem in the context of larger issues of peace, disarmament, and human rights. One concrete form of cooperation envisioned by this consultation is the Peace Center founded in 1983 in the Okinawa Christian Center in Ginowan City, Okinawa. The Peace Center has both Japanese and American staff persons.

The NCCs of Japan, Canada, and the United States in March 1983 held a consultation on cooperative mission, which stressed the need for reshaping missional patterns to let the voices of all Asia be heard and heeded. Redefinition of missional tasks must, the participants said, recognize that economic and military powers of advanced nations, and particularly of the United States and Japan, pose serious threats to the impoverished peoples of Asia. Churches must overcome their indifference to suffering and oppression if they would be faithful to Christ and his death on the cross for all peoples. These convictions in time affected a shift in the missional agenda of some NCC-related churches in North America and Japan.

Another US–Canada–Japan consultation was held in April 1984 in Kyoto and Osaka to consider discrimination against ethnic and other minorities. It was a natural follow-up to the perspective taken in the previous meeting.

A sense of mounting crisis in the Asia-Pacific region marked the Peace Consultation on Japan–US Military Cooperation in Asia and the Pacific held near Tokyo in late March 1989. Although Cold War tensions were subsiding in Europe, East Asia was experiencing intensified military buildups. The NCCJ and NCCC-USA jointly sponsored this large gathering of 80 participants, including 20 from the United States, 5 from South Korea, 3 from the Philippines, and one each from Canada and the Christian Conference of Asia.

The Soviet Union was in fact reducing its naval forces in the region, although this was assessed as a rationalization of forces, not a step in the direction of disarmament. Meanwhile, the United States was beefing up its nuclear capabilities in the area. In August 1988 it had, as noted earlier, homeported at Yokosuka Naval Base two warships fitted with the Navy's newest pride, the Tomahawk cruise missile.[8] Port calls by nuclear-capable US submarines were increasing. Joint US–Japan military exercises were expanding in scale. Indeed, the largest exercise in recent history, called PACEX, would soon take place in September, with forces from Japan, South Korea, the Philippines, Canada, and Australia joining. PACEX included air and sea drills in the Sea of Okhotsk, provocatively close to the Soviet Union. We have also already noted the many C^3I facilities introduced into Japan about this time. Japan too

---

[8] The Tomahawk missile can be fitted with a conventional or nuclear warhead, though the missile in each case looks the same; potential victims of its use or of accidents can only safely assume the nuclear option. – Ed.

went against the disarmament trends seen elsewhere in the world, steadily acquiring advanced capabilities supplementary to US strategy in the region. The government's controversial defense policies cast a chilling shadow across society, reminiscent of wartime military arrogance.

This consultation, then, had an urgent agenda: to inform the churches, particularly in the United States, of these trends; to develop the communications and cooperation necessary to reversing them; and to initiate alternatives for peace and justice in our region. The overall task was by no means easy, as the issues addressed by the consultation show: nuclear weapons and strategies, related political and economic forces, military bases, environmental destruction, US and Japanese complicity in low-intensity warfare in the Philippines and elsewhere, and, not least, the churches' role in promoting peace and justice.

In its final statement the consultation called for a complete ban on nuclear tests, implementation of the Nuclear Non-Proliferation Treaty, respect for the non-nuclear positions of Japan and the Philippines, respect for the South Korean people's free choice on deployment of nuclear arms in their country, removal of Japan from US nuclear strategy, and cancellation of PACEX. The statement also called for giving preference to human rights of people living near military bases, and for thorough, extensive, and publicly reported investigations of low-intensity warfare. The churches in particular were called to confession of their sins of submitting to state power instead of standing up for those who suffer and are oppressed, and to work for world security systems that liberate all oppressed peoples.

Following the consultation, representatives of the NCCJ and the NCCC-USA joined in delivering statements to the US Embassy and the Japanese Foreign Ministry, urging respect for Japan's Three Non-Nuclear Principles and for cessation of PACEX plans.

SEEING BEYOND THE PRESENT CRISIS

Recalling the atmosphere surrounding the Peace Consultation of March 1989, the trends toward disarmament at the time of writing in autumn 1990 are astonishing. In October the two Germanys reunited, essentially putting NATO and the Warsaw Pact out of business, and the rest of Europe is now groping toward demilitarized security arrangements. East Germany's denuclearization move sets a precedent in Europe, one that can be expected to affect West Germany in due course.

US–Soviet relations are being relaxed even in Asia. In September 1990 the US Commander in the Pacific made a friendly call at Vladivostok port and joined his Soviet counterpart in a no-war pledge. It is hard to believe that

PACEX took place only one year ago. Clearly, mutual security and disarmament are the course for Asia today. Put differently, events are proving that the multiple-peace-treaty stance we have advocated throughout the postwar era is the right choice after all.

Now we must take care that the Middle East situation not negate world trends toward disarmament. The Japanese government sticks doggedly to its demand for Soviet return of the northern islands[9] and, out of distrust of the USSR, presses on with its military buildup. Even though Japan's defense budget increase for 1991 was lowered to four percent, the growth is still sizable. Then, when Iraq seized Kuwait, Japan went beyond the expected financial aid to the US effort by attempting (though unsuccessfully) to send Self-Defense Forces to the Middle East in clear contravention of the Peace Constitution. Some of the ruling party élite seemed to have thought that the time was at last ripe for revising the Constitution; this naturally caused consternation among Asians who remember World War II.

This is, of course, precisely the time when Japan must hold fast to its constitutional peace principle, assess the Middle East turmoil in the context of world disarmament trends, and work to find a peaceful solution to the conflict there. Japan has had no territorial designs in the Middle East, nor has it had any share in the massive arms exports to that region. It has, rather, sought good relations with all Middle East countries. Japan should focus on diplomatic efforts through the United Nations, exerting efforts to restrain precipitous US actions while insisting upon Iraqi withdrawal from Kuwait. Japan was not party to deciding on US actions in the Middle East and is not therefore obliged to pay for them; rather, it should devote its resources to assisting needy countries in the region and providing medical supplies and other aid to refugees, as well as help shoulder the costs of any UN-arranged peacekeeping operations.

Over the years I have learned from dialogue with brothers and sisters in the United States that what many Americans want from Japan is not servile adherence to US military strategy; they would prefer, rather, that we pursue our own peace principle in ways that will promote world order. Far beyond merely protecting our Peace Constitution at home, now is the time to devote every effort to making it the principle of world peace. This is the cause we must pursue in the United Nations, not counting the costs.

In its September 20, 1990, meeting the NCCJ Executive Committee approved a statement that captures this very point: "With faith in Jesus Christ

[9] Three small islands and one small island group off the northeast coast of Hokkaido that were seized by Soviet forces in the waning days of World War II; the USSR has maintained that the case is closed, while Japan refuses to discuss a peace treaty with the Soviet Union until the islands are returned. — Ed.

who gave himself for the smallest and weakest, we must work for a peace that liberates oppressed peoples." We are citizens of a country whose strength causes great anxiety among the peoples of Asia, but as Christians we believe that what God wills is a peace founded on justice for powerless peoples.

7

Campus Protests Inaugurate the 1970s

Nakajima John Masaaki

RADICAL STUDENT PROTEST[1] against Japan's establishment was ignited in 1968 at the University of Tokyo's medical school, and the flames soon spread like wildfire to over a hundred other campuses. Christian schools were not exempt. The June 28, 1969, issue of the *Kyōdan shinpō* (biweekly news of the United Church of Christ in Japan) gave a five-point rundown of five Christian universities and two theological schools, all related to the UCCJ. The seven schools were: Tōhoku Gakuin, Meiji Gakuin, Aoyama Gakuin, Kantō Gakuin, Kwansei Gakuin, Dōshisha School of Theology, and Tokyo Union Theological Seminary (TUTS). The situation at these campuses in mid-1969 was as follows:

Origin of dispute. Objections to tuition rise (Tōhoku, Kwansei); opposition to an earlier 1960 official school notice[2] (Aoyama); demands for rebuilding a burned-down dormitory (Kantō), for curricular reform (Dōshisha); reaction to pro-school students who tore down a protesting students' signboard (Meiji); and opposition to Yasukuni Shrine, to public laws for universities, and to a proposed Christian pavilion at the 1970 World Exposition (TUTS).

Forms of protest. Barricading of campus buildings (Tōhoku, Meiji, Aoyama, Kantō) or of entire campus (Kwansei); student hunger strike (Tōhoku, TUTS); and formation of a student protest committee (Dōshisha).

Christian students' actions. YMCA students supported arrested protesters in court trials (Tōhoku); Student Christian Association held a "Conference

---

[1] The Japanese term is literally "struggle"; herein "protest" is the usual alternative. — Ed.
[2] See item 3 in final section, "Some Observations." — Ed.

on the Common Protest" (Aoyama); Christian students organized the "Christian Struggle Alliance"[3] (Meiji, Kantō), and also barricaded the theological building (Kantō, Kwansei) or campus chapel (Meiji).

School authorities' reactions. Board of trustees, chancellor, and faculty remained flexible, open to reforms (Kantō); faculty members mediated between students and school authorities (Tōhoku); faculty undertook study of school problems (Dōshisha); efforts made to hold discussions with students (TUTS); Board of Trustees and chancellor indecisive, faculties of literature, law, theology issued critical view of previous school notice (Aoyama); school authorities called in riot police to break students' barricade ((Meiji, Kwansei).

Situation as of mid-1969. Court case dragged on (Tōhoku); classes resumed (Meiji); students' barricade broken by riot police, school imposed lockout of protesting students, classes resumed (Aoyama); theology, technology and other buildings still barricaded (Kantō); all-campus lockout by school, all classes cancelled (Kwansei); theology building still barricaded (Dōshisha); discussions continued (TUTS).

SOME GENERAL CHARACTERISTICS

The recorded commentaries of some perceptive observers provide insights into the general characteristics of this time of turmoil.

The campus disputes that swept the nation in 1968 were not just a university problem, or even just a Japan problem; they were part of a worldwide phenomenon. The campus protests were inextricably a part of the contemporary revolt against the alienation of human beings caused by the establishment's excessive control and rationalization of society. (*Meiji Gakuin hyakunen shi* [Centennial history of Meiji Gakuin], 1977, p. 503.)

A well-known lecturer recently spoke of reactions to economic affluence and discontent with educational decline as essential causes of the current campus turmoil. Educators themselves seem to have abandoned idealism for open indulgence in materialism. The students have sensed a curious contradiction in the coexistence of social affluence along with political distrust, and they have sounded the alarm. Should we not listen carefully to the "anguished groaning" of these young people who seek personal renewal through the overcoming of established ideologies and stubborn systems? (Letter to the editor by a 48-year-old merchant, in *Shinto no tomo* [Friend of the laity], Feb. 1969.)

---

[3] "Tōsō Kirisutosha Dōmei," abbreviated as "Tōkidō."

The complex university problems stem from various roots. For one thing, the university administrative systems are antiquated and ill-suited to rapid expansion. The universities have adopted popular programs but failed to adapt to social changes. Stubborn adherence to old traditions has thrown universities of all advanced societies into crisis. Moreover, distrust of politics arises from the feeling of being subject to political powers beyond our reach. While our economic prosperity has risen to make Japan third in world GNP ranking, our sense of alienation and spiritual void has intensified. Young people feel burdened with pressures to achieve and personal insecurity. As we search for the background causes of this crisis, we must face a fundamental question: Will the universities, which are falling apart around us today, be able to recover their role as functioning communities again? (Yamaoka Kikuo, professor at Waseda University and a UCCJ layman, in a symposium reported in *Shinto no tomo* [Friend of the laity], Feb. 1969, p. 17)

The initial cause of a dispute could be almost anything—tuition raises, torn-down signboards, burned-down dormitories—but the students very quickly sought and found deeper issues in basic school policies and administrative procedures. School administrators, and often faculty members, just as readily found something wrong with the protesting students, though their reactions were not always as probing. One college professor in the heat of dispute confidently remarked: "No matter how fast they pitch the ball to us, we only have to throw it back very, very slowly."

The students usually insisted upon "public collective bargaining sessions" (*taishū dankō*), by which they meant that all responsible administrative staff must assemble in front of the entire student body to answer direct, probing questions. Seldom did school administrations accede to this demand. The students' mounting frustration usually erupted into violent action, or *gebaruto* (from the German *Gewalt*, or "power"). In barricading campus gates or clashing with riot police, students used a three-foot bamboo stick called *geba-bō* ("power-staff").

Administration refusals to get involved in student-style collective bargaining were not without reason. Meiji Gakuin's chancellor once wrote of the definition of "collective bargaining" taken for granted by students:

The students set the terms of the session; the highest university authority is obliged to appear at a place and time set by them, and is allowed to reply only with "yes" or "no." If he tries to say more, or what he says is not pleasing to the students, they seize the microphone and shout their demands over and over for extended periods. (Takao Toshikazu, ed., *Kirisutokyō-shugi daigaku no shi to saisei* [The death and resurrection of Christian universities], 1969, p. 172)

Student protests took many forms: class strikes, hunger strikes, barricades,[4] extended confinement of school representatives for cross-examination, and other actions of varying duration. At most schools, the barricades were forcibly removed with the help of riot police, a number of students were arrested, and then classes were resumed. Thus order was restored to the campuses.

But there were other reasons for the eventual defeat of student power. From the outset, student bodies were often divided. On the right were powerful student groups, usually male cheerleaders and athletes, who defended the school administration. And the left was usually divided between the Minsei[5] group adhering to the Japan Communist Party line, which adopted a protest strategy of orderly negotiation with authorities, and the "new left" coalition of three radical sects, known as Zenkyōtō,[6] which led sympathetic students in violent attacks on the "establishment." In between were the majority — nonsectarian, nonpolitical, noncommittal, but potential recruits for the left.

At first Zenkyōtō exercised hegemony over these competing groups (though only by a slight majority on some campuses) and could persuade many students to engage in strikes and barricades. As the protest struggles wore on, Zenkyōtō's power dissipated; and friction between its radical sects escalated into intramural violence called *uchi-geba*. In time, Zenkyōtō lost the support of most students.

In response to the protest actions, some schools introduced mild democratic reforms, such as limited participation by the student body in decision-making. But in most cases, campuses returned to the same old peace and order. The National Diet (parliament) in 1969 enacted legislation to give greater administrative power to university chancellors and more control to the Minister of Education. In the end, academic communities found themselves subject to greater outside control and supervision.

A SPECIFIC CASE

Each campus dispute had its own specifics, but the similarities among Japanese universities in the 1960s and 1970s were striking. Indeed, one can follow the course of events in any one of a hundred schools and discern the issues that students and administrations grappled with in all of them. Here we shall

---

[4] Desks, chairs, and the like were use to build barricades to deny entry to individual buildings or to blockade the whole campus. — Ed.

[5] "Minsei" stands for Nihon Minshu Seinen Dōmei, or Democratic Youth League of Japan.

[6] Zenkyōtō is short for Zengaku Kyōdō Tōsō Kaigi, or All-Campus Joint Struggle Committee.

look at Meiji Gakuin's case, for no specific reason other than availability of ample materials.

From April 1968 students at Meiji Gakuin had sensed mounting administrative pressures on their autonomous activities. Then, in October the student council erected a huge signboard (of twelve plywood boards) appealing for participation in the International Antiwar Day on October 12. The administration considered the display of the signboard "disorderly" and requested its removal. But on October 8 it was violently destroyed by members of the cheerleading club and the athletic association, while an officer of the Student Liaison Office watched and grinned, without trying to stop or even warn against use of violence. Student indignation exploded, for this was taken as a suppressive maneuver by the school administration, an action akin to the use of riot police in suppressing citizens' movements.

Immediately some 1,300 students assembled in protest, but no responsible administrative staff or faculty member showed up (the Students Liaison Office person slipped away under protection of the athletes). The gathered students called for a public bargaining session, which they saw as right and necessary. "Individual students have no power to challenge school authority," said one student. "The students must act as a whole if they are to deal with the campus situation." (Takao, 179)

A meeting of school authorities and the student body was scheduled for 2:30 P.M. on October 15. The school saw this meeting as an enlarged Roundtable Discussion, a regular once-a-month faculty-student meeting held since 1960. When about fifty faculty members appeared and were told that it was to be a collective bargaining session, they retreated on the ground that free discussion could not be guaranteed. About 9:30 P.M., the chancellor and department heads, along with forty other teachers, entered the room to read a statement that criticized as "regrettable" both the students' refusal to remove their signboard as requested and the violent destruction of it by other students.

The assembled students were not interested in the statement; they wanted a collective bargaining session. In rejecting their demand, the chancellor declared flatly that he could not agree to "collective bargaining" because it obliged school authorities to stand on an equal level with students. The school's representatives said no more, and once it was clear that communications had broken down completely, the students finally dismissed the school authorities at four o'clock the next morning.

Of the 1,300 students who had gathered at noon the previous day, 353 remained to discuss their next step. A simple majority of 176 (with some abstentions) voted to occupy and barricade the Main Hall immediately. One student explained the move as follows:

For the first time in Meiji Gakuin's history of ninety-odd years, student power on campus rose up and affirmed the reality of the student as the subject of university autonomy. In a radical action — the barricade — we showed the whole student body our ideal vision of the university, as well as our willingness to mobilize student power to realize this vision. In this sense, the barricade at Main Hall was very significant. (Takao, 180)

This first barricade was abandoned nineteen hours later, after lengthy student council discussions in which the Minsei group argued, successfully, for dropping the barricade in favor of mass participation in a general strike set for October 21. Leaders of the impromptu barricade acknowledged their inability to persuade and organize others for effective public action. But their radical action had served to awaken other students with little previous concern for the issues.

Student demands for collective bargaining were repeated; so were school refusals. Barricades were also repeated, as were occasional student-school discussions — all to no avail. Sporadic violence occurred, with minor injuries on both sides.

At the heart of student criticism lay the charge that the university functioned to produce effective, obedient workers for Japan's capitalist system. Within that system the universities themselves followed the same logic, constructing large buildings on small campuses to churn out as many workers as possible for the corporations. The students felt they were being treated as marketable commodities. Thus they believed it was necessary to dissolve the present system in order to create a true academic community.

A scheduled collective bargaining session on December 3 was ignored by the school: no responsible persons were on campus that day, and no note of explanation came, although the school had promised on November 28 to make every effort to have all faculty members present. Many members of the Student Christian Association then formed the Christian Struggle Alliance[7] and set up a barricade of the campus chapel. Three large signs were posted outside, which read as follows:

STRUGGLE DECLARATION

Today this chapel stands as the symbol of Meiji Gakuin's loss of its founding Christian spirit. Worship services have become only a means for maintaining the school's power structure. We cannot ask for participation in this decaying instrument of control. We declare, rather, its destruction and the death of its spirit. At the same time, we aspire to the renewal of the church

[7] See n. 3.

today and intend to realize in our own bodies the gospel of the cross, redeemed by Jesus' precious blood. — December 9, 1968.

AN OPEN INQUIRY

1. What is the theological foundation of a Christian university? How is it expressed concretely?

2. While extolling its founding Christian spirit, why does the school reject collective bargaining, our only opportunity for "dialogue"?

3. Why is a Christian university unwilling to take the first step toward a solution of the dispute by responding to our nine-point request?

4. Why is use of the chapel not permitted for other than Christian activities?

5. Why can chapel worship not be observed in forms of worship planned independently by students? — December 9, 1968.

WHY DID WE BARRICADE THE CHAPEL?

Today at Meiji Gakuin a serious struggle to regain autonomy is under way. From this process has come the chapel barricade as a matter of principle on which we stake our existence as students. As our very humanity comes from an encounter with God, so we intend to resist all powers that deny God, and we look for God's presence in the turmoil of today's world.

This chapel is held up as a symbol of the "founding Christian spirit" of the "Christian" Meiji Gakuin. But what is the Christianity to which Meiji Gakuin's authorities lay claim? The presence of the chapel and of required courses on Christianity are claimed as evidence that the school is Christian.

Chapel services have degenerated into a mere means of maintaining the school's authority. Moreover, our struggle process has revealed problems among school administrators no less serious than the perversion of chapel services. This has generated a complete distrust of Christianity. The school authorities cannot escape heavy responsibility for this situation.

We have therefore staked our faith on challenging school authority, and with pain in our hearts have barricaded the chapel. By treating the chapel as merely a material thing to be barricaded and camped in, we testify before the school authorities and the student body that Meiji Gakuin and its worship services are symbols of the absence and neglect of human dignity. We hope a true Christian community among all students will be created out of the present turmoil.

Our challenge is not confined to Meiji Gakuin. We ask all churches in Japan what their mission is in today's turbulent society. God is not to be found in this fine, solemn chapel. He is to be encountered in the life, work, and fellowship of people. Our actions should not be taken as political opportunism, but as a struggle in which we risk our lives to probe the very meaning of life.

This barricade is the cross borne by some Christians who study here at Meiji Gakuin. "If any man would come after me, let him deny himself and take up his cross and follow me." — Mark 8:34 (Takao, 169)

Early in February the chancellor sent to each student's home a letter titled "Collective bargaining: why it must be rejected." After many explanations of his views, often repetitive, he turned to two basic demands of the students: the right of collective bargaining, and the insistence that school representatives appear for questioning at times and places designated by the students. He then addressed these two points:

If the school administration agreed to these two items, then the students could press any unreasonable demand at any time and thereby control the school. Therefore I strongly reject collective bargaining.

Let me make myself perfectly clear. I do not believe, as some do, that the university can claim that the campus is off-limits, that it is exempt from police action to quell riots. It is all too easy to think, when the campus is taken over by violent groups who think they are the prime protectors of academic freedom and university autonomy, that we should immediately call in the riot police. If we do so, then when the police leave and another barricade is erected, we will have to call in the riot police again. In the process, the campus will be devastated. We should not rely on others; we must first do what we can by ourselves. God helps those who help themselves.

What is required now is to speak out against the barricade, and to renew our determination to oppose the campus blockades. (Takao, 173)

On February 8, 1969, at the request of the chairman of the Board of Trustees, the president, and the chancellor, the riot police were called in and all barricades were forcibly removed. Two students were arrested. The entire student body was locked out of the campus; and entrance examinations were held behind guarded doors. In March the graduation ceremony was held[8] with little hindrance, and classes for the spring term began in April. Thus ended the first round.

The dispute, however, continued. Meiji Gakuin's centennial history lists various incidents up to March 1974: repeated barricades, repeated use of riot police, repeated lockouts. But fewer and fewer students participated in radical, violent actions. The centennial history explains:

The deep scars of dispute remain. Though the campus was eventually restored to normalcy, it was not because the school administration adopted

---

[8] Japan's academic year begins in April and ends in March. — Ed.

a positive strategy. Rather, student activists turned from campus affairs to larger sociopolitical issues, and they could no longer win the support of the students at large. This contributed to eventual normalization. Also, sectarian conflict on campus shifted from the simple competition between the Minsei group and the "new left" radicals to a fiercer, more complex antagonism among the radical groups that ended in violent intramural battles. This alienated students in general from the radical sects. (*Meiji Gakuin hyakunen shi*, 510)

In Meiji Gakuin's centennial history, the overall process is summed up as follows:

The original point of the dispute was university autonomy, with particular focus on student autonomy, and university reform was needed to assure that autonomy. As the dispute dragged on, however, the protesters forgot this central point and jumped from one issue to another. All this kept the administration busy adjusting to new situations. So as not to waste all the effort already expended, Chancellor Wada tried to initiate work on university reform, and he hoped something positive would emerge from the all-department Faculty Committee on University Reform. Even so, practically nothing was done. One crucial negative factor was the dissolution of the student council, which deprived the school administration of its partner in discussion. That aside, we have learned a vital lesson: we cannot expect anything fruitful to come out of "collective bargaining."

In the early stages of the dispute, the students had made practical demands: revision of various rules concerning students, restructuring of the Student Liaison Office, establishment of a class system, formation of a conciliar organization of students and professors, and so on. None of these has yet been discussed with the students. In instruction methods, a number of improvements in scheduling and curriculum have been put into practice already. These innovations resulted from teachers' self-evaluation spurred by their own experiences in the dispute. To promote cohesive classes by grade, freshman camps for each department have been introduced. (*Ibid.*, 518)

SOME OBSERVATIONS

1. Wherever and however disputes began, the students were quick to ferret out the root issues and causes. At no other time in recent history have students put so much energy into collective thinking and discussion to reach consensus in their analysis of society's defects as they did in these few years.

2. The nature of Christianity experienced by students in the Christian

schools was radically exposed. The student leader who wrote the signboard messages displayed in front of Meiji Gakuin's chapel is the same person who is quoted several times in this essay. He was a baptized, committed 21-year-old Christian. Living on campus with other students during the dispute, he conducted daily worship services inside the barricades. He and his fellow protesters were deadly serious. Their critique of campus Christianity was on target.

3. From another prominent Christian school, Aoyama Gakuin, a theology professor explained the situation in the July 28, 1969, issue of the *Kyōdan shinpō*. At the height of the 1960 protest against the Japan–U.S. Security Treaty, the school administration issued an official notice prohibiting the following: (a) political activities on campus, (b) participation in Zengakuren (nationwide leftist student organization), and (c) interference in classes and other school work. These bans were explained as being in line with the school's Christian spirit. At the height of the 1968 dispute, when challenged not only by students but also by many professors, the administration suddenly withdrew this official notice. Thus the questions arose: What is the nature of that Christianity once identified with the notice? What happened to Christianity on campus when the notice was withdrawn?

4. The school authorities seldom responded directly to such penetrating questions. As the quoted chancellor's letter shows, no clear reply to the students' query was made; it only notes how ill-behaved the student activists were, and insists that order be restored. Meiji Gakuin's centennial history devotes 24 of its 694 pages to the campus dispute. The course of events is fairly well described, but apart from a general summary of student aspirations, there is no indication what the school thought the issue was. Nor does it say how the school responded.

5. The frustrated students were eventually driven into a corner and so turned to the use of force. In response to a reporter's questions, the aforementioned theology professor said: "I'm not in favor of using violence. But when the students asked repeatedly about the meaning of the official notice and were completely ignored because they did not represent the recognized student council, where else could they turn? It was like inviting them to use *gebaruto* (*Gewalt*)."

6. This, however, is precisely where the student activists failed. The use of violence could not win the support of the majority of students, nor the sympathy of the public watching the course of events. In the progression from frustration to violence to factional splits, people lost track of the serious questions originally raised. When it all ended, a rare opportunity for the reform of Japan's higher education system and of society in general had been lost.

7. Overall, it is difficult to judge whether there was more gain or loss.

Some helpful innovations were made, but more means of institutional control were introduced. The theological departments of two Christian schools, Aoyama Gakuin and Kantō Gakuin, were forced to close down, partly because many of their professors sympathized with the students against the school authorities. Perhaps this generation must yield to the next before the net results can be appraised.

8

The Church in Dispute over Expo 70

Controversy in the United Church of Christ in Japan

Nakajima John Masaaki

AT THE WORLD EXPOSITION in Montreal in 1967,[1] Catholic, Protestant, and Orthodox Christians joined for the first time in erecting a Christian Pavilion. This achievement deeply impressed Japanese Christians, inspiring them to plan for a Christian Pavilion at the 1970 World Exposition (popularly, Expo 70) to be held in Osaka. The following brief outline is taken from a booklet entitled "Eyes and Hands: The Discovery of Humanity—the Christian Pavilion at Expo 70, Osaka, Japan," published in October 1970 by the Committee for the Christian Pavilion.

THE CHRISTIAN PAVILION PROJECT

"Discussions concerning the project to erect a Christian Pavilion at the Japan World Exposition in Osaka began early in 1967 within the National Christian Council in Japan (NCCJ), to which belong the major Protestant bodies of Japan. These talks began at the Japan Consultation on Mission in Unity, held in March under NCCJ sponsorship." In the following year, discussions in the NCCJ Executive Committee culminated in formal approval of the plan by the NCCJ General Assembly in March 1968, including the decision to seek the ecumenical cooperation of the Roman Catholic Church.

In Osaka itself, on April 20, the executive committee of the Osaka Christian Council (OCC) took up the question of participation in Expo 70 and

[1] The World Exposition was resumed after World War II in 1958 in Brussels.

appointed a ten-member study committee. In an extraordinary meeting on September 4, the OCC's General Assembly decided to participate.

The Japan Catholic Church was approached by both NCCJ and OCC representatives. At its extraordinary meeting in January 1968, the Japan Catholic Bishops' Conference gave its approval to the project for a common Christian Pavilion at Expo 70. In explaining its decision, the Bishops' Conference pointed out that this first World Exposition on Asian soil, with millions of visitors expected, offered a unique opportunity to present "the message of Christianity and its role in modern society, and [that] the ecumenical movement in Japan would be greatly strengthened." Meanwhile, overtures were made in Rome for Vatican City to participate, and "in December 1968, Pope Paul VI gave his approval to this form of participation [i.e., joint sponsorship of the Christian Pavilion]."

Accordingly, "on March 29, 1968, the Central Committee for the Christian Pavilion at Expo 70 was established, with Anglican Bishop Yashiro Hinsuke as president, and Catholic Archbishop Taguchi Yoshigorō, NCCJ Chairman Ōmura Isamu, Mr. Igarashi Takeo," and some other Christian leaders as vice-presidents. In addition to the 38-member central committee, there were also a 19-member executive committee, a 14-member theme commission, and a 19-member financial committee. Mr. Nishimura Jirō was appointed general secretary, with Fr. Hayashi Atsushi as his assistant. The general secretariat was located in the Osaka Christian Center; two branch offices were opened in Tokyo, one at the NCCJ, the other at the National Catholic Committee.

Eyes and Hands for a Theme

"The theme commission set to work without delay. It was jointly chaired by professors Kitamori Kazoh of Tokyo Union Theological Seminary and Yanase Mutsuo of Sophia University. Professors Kumazawa Yoshinobu (TUTS) and Hoshino Eiichi (University of Tokyo), and Mr. Saitō Kazumichi from Nara served as secretaries. After three months of earnest deliberation, the theme was formulated: 'Eyes and hands: the discovery of humanity', with two subthemes, 'Harmony through reconciliation' and 'Progress through creation'. In the midst of displays of human achievement and progress at Expo, the Christian Pavilion should be, as it were, the Eyes which, in the light of the Christian faith, discover human dignity and destiny . . . which are so easily overlooked due to people's absorption in technical progress and economic prosperity; and it should symbolize the Hands of the church, praying for and serving humanity in the spirit of the Gospel of Christ."

The Christian Pavilion was situated on a 1,034-square-meter plot and

was surrounded by foreign and Japanese pavilions. From an entrance sym-
bolizing Faith, Hope, and Love, visitors were led downstairs to the exhibition
hall, where a photographic display depicted the daily life of people in
Japan with so many problems, conflicts, and pain. Several sculptures were
placed alongside a wall covered with three large sixteenthth-century tapes-
tries by Raphael, loaned by the Vatican. The upstairs hall, conceived as a
"holy space" of "holy emptiness," was the scene of many happenings: daily
prayers for peace, Catholic and Protestant Sunday services, rich musical programs (with the largest bamboo-pipe organ in Japan), and theatrical perfor-
mances.

"Toward the end of 1968," the sponsoring group's booklet continues, "a
movement opposing the Christian Pavilion project at Expo began and took
more and more vehement forms." This movement had close ties with the
general student unrest and reflected various social and political issues hotly
debated at the time. Opponents contended that Expo was being staged as a
celebration of Japan's socioeconomic success, and under such circumstances
"the Christian Pavilion . . . could not give valuable witness to Christ and his
Gospel." This movement flared up among students of Christian schools in
the Osaka–Kyoto district, then spread to other cities, particularly Tokyo, and
"gave rise to discussions and divisions within several local churches, especially
in the United Church of Christ in Japan." The Central Committee for the
Christian Pavilion, therefore, on June 20, 1969, issued a statement titled
"Fundamental Views on Participation in Expo 70."

This statement stressed that "the theme of the Christian Pavilion was the
rediscovery, in the midst of the general interest in enterprise and production,
of the real human values and of the need, in the midst of Japan's economic
expansion, to seek out Japan's neighbors; the theme, moreover, showed the
desire to become the serving hands for this great work." Participation in the
project did not mean "approval of Expo in every aspect," it said, adding that
"disapproval of every aspect and non-participation could not be our attitude
either. Because we believe that, notwithstanding numerous grave problems,
Christ is present in Expo, we decided to participate in it. To give witness to
the saving presence of Christ is the unique role of the Christian Pavilion, and
to cooperate for its fulfillment is the right ecumenical attitude."

Participation and Payments

During Expo's six-month period (March 14 – September 13), visitors to the
Christian Pavilion numbered 2,324,679, or 3.62 percent of all visitors to
Expo (64,217,000). Nearly 4 million Bible booklets or tracts were distrib-
uted, with 17,391 books (including full Bibles) sold. "In the midst of Expo,

the Christian Pavilion, by its exhibits, daily prayers, and other programs, gave witness to the merciful presence of our Lord and Savior."

The final financial statement, issued by General Secretary Nishimura on August 20, 1970, showed a total expenditure of 153.5 million yen, including construction costs of 89.5 million yen. The Vatican had contributed 25 million yen; the Japan Catholic Church, 35 million; the World Council of Churches, around 35 million; and Protestants in Japan, 36 million — which fell short of the latter's 48-million-yen goal. The pavilion committee was left with a 14-million-yen deficit. Nishimura contributed 5 million yen (proceeds from the sale of his personal real estate) and made up the remaining deficit of 9 million yen by taking out a loan, which he promised to pay back annually. Later his Christian friends formed a group to join in bearing this loan.

DISPUTE EXPLODES IN THE CHURCH

In the early stage, no one anticipated this plan was a time bomb that would explode and shatter the whole Christian community in Japan, especially the United Church of Christ in Japan (UCCJ), or "Kyōdan."[2] Some other churches had disputes and disturbances, but none so bitter or prolonged as the UCCJ. This essay therefore focuses on the UCCJ so as to reflect the full scope of the issue. In the preface of an unpublished study undertaken by the UCCJ Research Institute on the Mission of the Church, the author says:

> The "Expo Christian Pavilion issue" began with questions originally raised at the UCCJ Fifteenth General Assembly held in October 1968 to assess the pros and cons of its decision to participate in the NCCJ-sponsored pavilion. But it evolved into a movement that directed basic questions to the UCCJ itself and its churches. Everything was questioned: the timing (1970), the site where Expo took place, the concrete relations between the church and the state, the church's war responsibility, the circumstances of the UCCJ formation in 1941, its representative system of commissions and committees, its mode of examining ministerial candidates, its relations with theological seminaries, the norms and realities of the UCCJ as a church and of its districts, its missiology and ecclesiology, and so on.

[2] The Japanese name is Nihon Kirisuto Kyōdan, and its members find the last term a convenient everyday name. It means "religious organization" (and not specifically "church"); the acronym "UCCJ" is used herein to avoid confusion with other groups, both Christian and non-Christian, that also use the term. — Ed.

Assembly Actions and Reactions

The Fifteenth General Assembly (1968) of the United Church of Christ in Japan had a loaded agenda. It settled a controversy over the "Confession of Responsibility During World War II" (issued over the name of the UCCJ moderator on Easter Sunday in 1967); approved major structural changes in the UCCJ that had been in preparation for several years; approved a proposal for union with the United Church of Christ in Okinawa[3]; and voted to establish a home for elderly victims of the Hiroshima atomic bombing. Each of these items involved lengthy—often heated— deliberation and a difficult decision. Compared with these matters, Bill #47 calling for "participation in building a Christian Pavilion at Expo 70 and cooperation in the fund-raising campaign" attracted little attention at first.

On the fourth and last day, the assembly's fourth section reported its consideration of this bill by simply saying no one opposed it. When the chair called for final discussion, one delegate rose to express his doubts about the bill. He gave as his reasons: the UCCJ should concentrate on building the home for elderly A-bomb victims; the claim that the Christian Pavilion is "evangelism" is dubious; and the critical problem in 1970 is the renewal of the Japan–US Security Treaty, which will be obscured by the Osaka festivities. No one else spoke. The bill was put to a vote and, to everyone's surprise, was defeated.

The pavilion project's key supporters, who had taken for granted the bill's passage with little objection, rose one after another to plead for reconsideration. They argued that the assembly's fourth section unanimously supported the bill; the NCCJ had decided to participate; and as an NCCJ member body, the UCCJ was obliged to support the plan.

Following a lunch recess, a new bill (#55)—initiated by none other than the moderator himself and signed by sixteen other delegates—was introduced. Now the bill read: "The General Assembly agrees that the Christian Pavilion be established in Expo 70 under the initiative of the National Christian Council and supports its promotion activities." By changing the wording, Bill #55 was made to look different from defeated Bill #47. This time the delegates were sympathetic and gave the proposal a majority vote.

The compromise, instead of calming down feelings, stirred up controversy, which then spread nationwide to the UCCJ's fifteen districts, but especially the three districts (Hyogo, Osaka, and Kyoto) in the Kansai area where Expo 70 would take place.

Osaka District Assembly, meeting in December 1968, unanimously agreed to ask the Christian Pavilion planners to include the showing of "the prophetic documentary film on the atomic bomb" (reported to be in the posses-

[3] Okinawa Kirisuto Kyōdan.

sion of the government's Ministry of Education). This request was repeated at the May 1968 District Assembly, as no response had come from the pavilion planners. The Extraordinary District Assembly scheduled for July to settle the Expo issue had to be called off due to the harsh demands made by the young people who virtually controlled the floor with their demands for responsible answers from those in positions of authority, throwing the assembly into chaotic disorder.

Three successive district assembles scheduled between September and November followed a similar course. The last one lacked a quorum because 101 delegates, who could not tolerate the young people's violent attitude, boycotted the meeting—and this too became the target of harsh criticism. Among the Osaka delegates, supporters and opponents of the Christian Pavilion may well have been almost equally divided. But, because the planned assemblies were all disrupted, a formal split of Osaka District Assembly never occurred.

The Hyogo District Assembly was held in February, May, and July of 1969. District Moderator Nakamura Toshi's report at the September UCCJ Executive Council meeting may be quoted here because it summarizes the anti-Pavilion point of view.

> Hyogo District at its Extraordinary Assembly in July passed a resolution opposing participation in the Christian Pavilion at Expo, and it requests the UCCJ to convene an Extraordinary General Assembly to reconsider the matter, for the following reasons: (a) there is danger that Expo 70 may obscure the importance of the 1970 Japan–US Security Treaty issue; (b) Expo 70 puts undue pressure on local governments and disrupts people's lives by causing environmental pollution and other hazards; (c) participation in Expo is contrary to directions taken in the UCCJ's Fundamental Policy on Mission, its Confession of Responsibility During World War II, its opposition to the nationalization of Yasukuni Shrine, and so on; and (d) the UCCJ should put its effort, rather, into raising funds for the anti-Yasukuni struggle and the home for elderly A-bomb victims in Hiroshima.

Kyoto District's experience was similar to Osaka's; several assemblies were convened, only to be adjourned due to disruption. Some other district assemblies dealt with the issue, and many of them requested that an extraordinary session of the UCCJ General Assembly be convened.

An Extraordinary Assembly

On the national level, a twenty-hour discussion meeting was held from 1:30 P.M. on September 1 till 8:00 A.M. the following day (nicknamed the "9.1–2 Meeting") between ten members of the standing committee of the UCCJ Executive Council and about 150 opponents of the Christian Pavilion. This marathon session took place in the Kyo Bun Kwan (Christian Literature Society) building in Tokyo's downtown Ginza section. Six of the standing committee members were also on the Christian Pavilion's central committee. Each of them was subjected to much rancor and yelling. When their response ran contrary to the questioners' expectations, they were called all sorts of names. TUTS professor Kitamori Kazoh, theme commission chairman, was struck twice on the cheek. Finally, UCCJ Moderator Ii Kiyoshi, after consulting the standing committee members, declared that he would call an Extraordinary General Assembly for the purpose of reconsidering Bill #55 passed by the Fifteenth General Assembly.

Later, Moderator Ii explained his motivation in reaching this decision. During the first half of the September 1–2 meeting, he believed in political maneuvering, as moderator, as a way of reaching mutual compromise. In a sense, he took refuge in the committee system without exposing his own views and without taking full responsibility for his own opinion and actions. But the marathon meeting changed him. He realized that he could not be true to his Christian conviction unless he spoke and acted openly and squarely before God and people. The Christian Pavilion issue had placed the UCCJ at a critical junction; a general assembly was needed. Many people denounced the anti-Expo group's attitude and behavior, but it was a mistake to focus solely on outward matters and evade the real issues being raised. The September 1–2 meeting had been very useful in bringing out the real issues. (Moderator Ii expressed this view in his report to the Sixteenth General Assembly.)

Three bills were prepared by three different groups in the Executive Council for presentation at the Sixteenth Extraordinary General Assembly held November 25–26, 1969, at a church in Tokyo. They were: Bill #3, "to nullify Bill #55 of the Fifteenth General Assembly and to reconsider the issue"; Bill #4, "to reconfirm Bill #55, but not make it binding on churches, districts, clergy, and laity of the UCCJ"; and Bill #5, "to oppose construction of the Christian Pavilion at Expo 70."

The February 1970 issue of *Shinto no tomo* "Friend of the laity" reported on this general assembly as follows:

> During the opening worship, the group of anti-Expo students and clergy intruded into the assembly room. Following worship, Moderator Ii gave his report. Immediately after that, the students occupied the space directly below the moderator's chair and proceeded to control the floor. The General Assembly was turned into a discussion meeting. For two days, no deliberations on prepared bills took place. The assembly was closed on the evening of the second scheduled day with Moderator's Ii's final remark and silent prayer . . . .

The Executive Council's official statement on this assembly was issued later, as follows: "The Sixteenth General Assembly was properly convened at 11:00 A.M. on November 25. The moderator gave his report, and during the question-and-answer period the assembly was turned into a general discussion meeting by including participant-observers. Without resuming deliberations, the General Assembly was adjourned by the moderator at 6:05 P.M. on November 26."

Appraisals of this meeting vary widely. Some rate it highly as a meeting which exposed the UCCJ as lifeless and empty. Others applaud the right motives but denounce the bad methods used in the session. Still others question even the motives in such a crazy performance. Surely this event will be discussed in UCCJ circles for some time to come.

Polarized Positions

One highlight of the assembly was the controversy between Moderator Ii and TUTS associate professor Kumazawa Yoshinobu, secretary of the Christian Pavilion's theme commission, who courageously expressed his convictions quietly and logically amidst the students' furious uproar. Kumazawa's argument was based on his conviction that Christ is present in this world, no matter how sinful the situation is. He acknowledged the problematic nature of Expo, but insisted Christ is there. The church, therefore, must also be there to witness to him. While Expo points only to human success, the Christian Pavilion must be the eyes and hands pointing out humanity's true nature. Moreover, whether to participate in Expo is not a life-and-death matter for the church; it is a relative matter of how witness is done, and many kinds of witness are needed. Some may want to be in Expo, and some may want to stay out. But to claim that staying out is the only choice for Christians is too legalistic. A moderator should preside over a meeting, not take sides. But the moderator is acting like a referee who takes one team's side.

To this Moderator Ii countered: One good act of a Christian during wartime may seem beautiful; but it cannot be fully commended, because the war itself is evil. To get inside the Expo 70 project is to become captive to iniquity. The church should be critical of Expo from the outside. During the past war, the churches felt they were witnessing to Christ by surviving the ordeal, but in fact they survived because they cooperated with the war effort. So the church failed in its mission then. Admittedly there needs to be a variety of witness, but in witnessing we must be willing to risk our lives. Expo is like a cancer; if left alone, it will corrupt the very roots of life. That is why this issue concerns our very existence. Ii said that, as moderator, he followed the example of his immediate predecessor, Suzuki Masahisa (who issued the 1967 Confession of War Responsibility). The UCCJ moderator is not supposed to be neutral; he is supposed to act like a team's top pitcher and throw the ball properly at the right time.

The two positions represented by Kumazawa and Ii became further polarized as the dispute wore on. On the whole, the UCCJ developed Ii's line of argument and tried to listen to the inner voices of conscience of the clamoring anti-Expo group, however irritating their attitudes and actions. In every decision-making body of the UCCJ, seats were given to these "problem-posers," even though they had no vote or legal right to be there. The UCCJ leaders felt that these people, despite — or even through — their very rude behavior, were raising critical issues for the church, for its relations to the state, for its missiology, for its ecclesiology. Thus, by accepting them as partners in the life and mission of the church, the United Church of Christ in Japan gradually began to restore its normal functions.

On the other hand, there were people who were greatly aggravated by the attitudes and arguments of these young anti-Expo people and could not tolerate their presence. For them, the councils of the UCCJ had been invaded by brutish, disorderly rascals. As long as they remained, there was no hope for the normalization of church life. Out of this conviction they formed the Federation of Evangelical Churches of the UCCJ,[4] with the goal of establishing a church solidly based on the UCCJ Confession of Faith by purging the church of evil elements.

After several failed attempts, the Seventeenth General Assembly of the UCCJ was finally convened November 20–23, 1973, at a hotel in the Hakone mountains south of Tokyo. Following heated discussions, the assembly was able to elect its moderator and vice-moderator, though not the Executive Council members. A year later, the Eighteenth General Assembly was held December 10–13, 1974, in the same place. Among other things, this assembly approved by majority vote a resolution "to admit the Fifteenth General Assembly's mistake in voting for the 'Bill concerning the Christian Pavilion in Expo 70.'" When this news reached former general secretary Nishimura of the Christian Pavilion committee, who had retired and taken up poultry farming in the mountains of Wakayama Prefecture, he served notice of his withdrawal from membership in the UCCJ.

SPREADING WILDFIRE

The dispute over Expo 70 was only the beginning of the wildfire that swept over the United Church of Christ in Japan. Sparks jumped quickly to ignite controversies in various areas of UCCJ life, three of which we examine

---

[4] Kyōdan Fukuinshugi Kyōkai Rengō.

below. The overall process could be likened to "the fiery ordeal which comes upon you to prove you" (1 Peter 4:12).

Tokyo Union Theological Seminary

Immediately after the September 1–2 meeting, the faculty of Tokyo Union Theological Seminary (TUTS) issued its own statement on September 3 (nicknamed the "9.3 Statement"), censuring the UCCJ pastors who did nothing when Professor Kitamori was struck at the meeting, "regardless of whether one supports Expo or not." This censure triggered the TUTS students' anger. For them the issue of support/rejection of Expo was most important, and the faculty did not make clear its stand on this issue. The students demanded withdrawal of the faculty statement. Their requests for general meetings to discuss the matter were not met. Finally, the students barricaded the campus. All efforts to restore dialogue between students and faculty failed. On March 11, 1970, the seminary called in the riot police to remove the barricades, and classes were resumed on March 17, though many students refused to register. Consequently, about seventy students left the seminary; three involved in the barricades were arrested and indicted.

The Eighteenth UCCJ General Assembly passed a resolution censuring the TUTS faculty who called in riot police to settle the campus dispute. The TUTS faculty and board of trustees then, in effect, severed official relations with the UCCJ leadership by refusing to accept four UCCJ-appointed members on the board of trustees and by not allowing its president and members to participate in various UCCJ meetings and functions. This aborted relationship continues to this day of writing in 1990. A negotiation committee formed by the UCCJ Executive Council was finally accepted by the TUTS faculty, and negotiations to restore the relationship got under way in early 1990.

Tokyo District Problems

The Expo issue was first taken up by the Tokyo District at its Forty-fifth District Assembly in May 1969 in the form of a request, like that made by Osaka District, for the Christian Pavilion to include showings of "the prophetic film on the atomic bomb." When it was revealed, as happened in Osaka, that in fact the film was not available, the delegates felt that the Christian Pavilion organizers were somehow insincere. The outcome was a total rejection of the Christian Pavilion project. When this assembly was adjourned due to lack of a quorum, concerned delegates began campaigning to gather enough delegates (133) to call for an extraordinary session of the district assembly.

The district's executive committee met on September 26 to discuss the convening of an extraordinary session. Despite a promise by district officers that observers would be invited to this meeting, the latter were never called in. The observers lost their patience and broke into the room where the executive committee was in session. The meeting then lasted until the next morning, when the moderator promised to accord the right of "participant-observer" to one person for each group represented, with no limit on the number of observers.

The participant-observers came to the next meeting of the district executive committee, scheduled for October 7, only to be informed that the meeting had been cancelled. In the meantime, all three district officers had submitted their resignations on the ground that they had erred in promising to give problem-posers the privilege of participant-observer. From this point the issue shifted from its original focus on Expo 70 to the question of the trust relationship between UCCJ leaders and the problem-posers.

The Forty-sixth Tokyo District Assembly was held November 19–20, 1969, at Yamate Church. The first issue was whether the session could begin with the presence, among the hundred or so problem-posers, of some ten persons wearing helmets (the common headgear of protesting students at the time). This question was put to a vote, and 151 of the 220 delegates present agreed to begin with the helmeted students present. The host church, however, was resolutely against the inclusion of these students, and so the district assembly adjourned without taking any official actions.

The Forty-seventh, and to this day the last, Tokyo District Assembly was convened on May 25, 1971, at the same church. Arriving delegates were stunned to find a huge barricade built at the stairs to the front entrance. It had a narrow 70-centimeter (27.5-inch) passageway allowing one person at a time to enter, and about thirty stout young men standing guard. As though to satisfy the expectations of the district assembly organizers, about twenty helmeted young people came at around 9:00 A.M. and, upon seeing these preparations, launched a bamboo-stick attack on the church barricade and its protectors. When mediating efforts by older pastors failed, someone called the police, who came to pull the would-be mediators out of the melee. In the process, several persons were injured.

Since a report had been submitted to the police, three persons were arrested and indicted (one of the three later killed himself; another suffered a mental disorder). The Tokyo Christians' Group to Save the Victims (Tokyo Kirisutosha Kyūenkai) was formed to support the defendants in their court trials. This group remains active to this day, while Tokyo District remains stalemated.

Many attempts were made to reconvene the district assembly. On July 15, 1975, the district executive committee sent out an official letter, signed by its appointed representative, turning over all its functions to the chairpersons of the district's six subdistricts. These six chairpersons decided to handle district functions through a six-member management committee, and they set up a Committee for Reconvening the District Assembly, composed of three members each from the six subdistricts. At almost every meeting of the latter committee, the question of whether to admit participant-observers was discussed, with opinions about equally divided. Members of the district executive committee were expected to come and engage in dialogue with the problem-posers, but they seldom came. The meetings seemed so fruitless that in March 1979 the North Subdistrict (Kita Shiku) withdrew all three of its members from the Reconvening Committee.

Since 1986 several efforts have been made by the six subdistricts to hold consultations for discussing UCCJ affairs. These efforts led to the first Reconvening Committee with full participation being held in October 1989. It was hoped that the first Tokyo District Assembly in nineteen years could be convened so as to elect and send delegates to the UCCJ General Assembly in November 1990.[5]

Ministerial Qualification Examinations

The nature of ministry was another area of basic questioning during the past two decades. The United Church of Christ in Japan administers two examinations annually for ministerial candidates. The examination for those wishing to become licensed preachers (*hokyōshi*; or "probational pastors") is conducted in the spring, mostly for candidates recently graduated from seminary,[6] though this examination is also offered in the autumn when the examination for ordained pastors (*seikyōshi*) is conducted. Licensed preachers must wait two years before they are eligible to take the ordination examination, and they cannot administer the sacraments until they pass this examination.

The origin of the dispute over ministerial examinations is explained in the comprehensive document prepared for the Seventeenth UCCJ General Assembly (November 1973), as follows:

> The current dispute began with the spring 1969 examination, when Kwansei Gakuin's School of Theology cancelled its recommendations — required by the UCCJ qualifying committee — for its graduate-candidates

---

[5] The Forty-eighth Extraordinary Session of Tokyo District, representing 338 churches, was convened on September 23 and October 10, 1990, but was unable to elect delegates to the UCCJ General Assembly scheduled for November 13–15, 1990. — Ed.

[6] The Japanese academic year begins in April and ends, with graduation ceremonies, in March. — Ed.

who had engaged in campus protests. The subsequent autumn examination was disrupted by persons protesting the school's action. The autumn examination was conducted by mail, instead. . . . Heated arguments over the introduction of riot police by Tokyo Union Theological Seminary in 1970 further complicated the matter. [Some TUTS graduate-candidates openly declared in the *Kyōdan shinpō* that they would boycott the examination in protest against TUTS and the UCCJ Ministerial Qualifications Committee.] The spring examination was suspended while the committee made an effort to discuss matters with related persons, including Kwansei Gakuin faculty members.

Gradually it became clear that the issues raised — the criteria of ministerial qualification, interpretation of the Confession of Faith, the twofold ordination system, criteria for authorizing theological schools — were too weighty for the committee to handle by itself. Having consulted various related organs, the committee now turned to the UCCJ Executive Council for a final decision. When the Executive Council failed to take a clear stand on the issue, the committee cancelled the autumn examination again, and all seven committee members resigned.

Each of the weighty issues mentioned above, long taken for granted, was now radically questioned. And there were no ready-made answers. Of course, they were all fundamental issues that needed to be discussed thoroughly so that there could be some basic agreement in the church. But many people, including some UCCJ leaders, felt it was more important to get on with the examinations in order to produce new pastors.

A new committee replaced the one that resigned en bloc, and conducted ministerial examinations from autumn 1971 to 1973. But it too had to suspend the examinations due to strong protests by the candidates, some district persons, and others. The rationale was that it was more important to deal with the fundamental issues being raised than to administer easy examinations. It took the rise and fall of two committees before examinations could be resumed three years later in autumn 1976, and only then because the committee promised to tackle the basic issues while carrying out the examinations.

In practice, however, it was virtually impossible for the committee to find extra time for dealing with weighty issues while also conducting qualification examinations for about eighty candidates twice a year. Moreover, the issues went far beyond the committee's mandate. So a liaison committee was set up in 1984 to coordinate deliberations among the Ministerial Qualification Committee, the Committee on Ministry, and the Faith and Order Committee.

This work continues. The examinations are given regularly. But there still are some eligible candidates who, in protest against the UCCJ for failing, in their view, to confront the issues sincerely, refuse to take the examinations. These persons are called the "refusers" (*kyohisha*), and the UCCJ takes them seriously enough to invite them to be regular participants in the above-mentioned liaison committee.

9
Environmental Issues

Yasuda Haruo

ENVIRONMENTAL PROBLEMS CAN be classified according to the geographical extent of their consequences: local, transnational, and global. We can also distinguish between chronic destruction of nature and acute industrial pollution. And it is important to note that large-scale destruction can turn local populations into refugees.

LOCAL DESTRUCTION OF THE NATURAL ENVIRONMENT

The term "local destruction" does not mean that a problem occurs in only one locality. Minamata Disease, for example, is not confined to Kumamoto; it is found also in Niigata and as far away as Canada and Indonesia. Here "local" means that the destructive effects tend to remain within a clearly defined area. With urbanization and modernization, however, even problems that are initially local can quickly become transnational or even global. For example, the impact of resort development in Japan, particularly golf course construction, has spread to Indonesia and Malaysia; and pollution of the atmosphere, arising from many local sources, has become a nationwide concern in many industrialized countries.

There is also a personal sense of "local." Even though human survival is not immediately threatened, places where human beings can come into contact with the world of nature are rapidly disappearing. And the human body is increasingly subjected to a variety of poisons.

Uncontrolled Development

For the past twenty years urban developers have treated the natural world as if it were utterly without value, devouring large areas for housing, ski resorts, roads for tourism, airports. In reaction, citizens' movements to protect nature have arisen in Japan, with some moderate successes. The sanctuary movement, for example, has been able to protect the shore of Nitonai Lake in Hokkaido (1981), a corner of Kiyosato Highlands in Nagano (1983), and the Yaezu Tidelands in Chiba (1984). The Tenjin Cape in Wakayama came under the National Trust movement in 1987, and the Shiretoko National Park in Hokkaido saw the birth of the 26,000-strong Landlords for the Preservation of Nature. Unfortunately these are exceptions to the uncontrolled destruction of forests, the pollution of marshes, lakes, rivers, and streams, and the filling in of coastlines.

Successful opposition to construction of the New Ishigakijima Airport in the Ryukyu Islands (includes Okinawa) is of great significance for us today. Building this airport would have destroyed the northern hemisphere's largest collection of Shiraho coral. Since the Ryukyu Islands were returned to Japan in 1972, natural destruction there has proceeded apace; already 90 percent of the coral reefs are gone. Blocking this airport project was a kind of last ditch stand for people concerned about preserving not only a very rare coral but Okinawa's overall environment as well.

Resort development, particularly golf courses, is one area of uncontrolled development that has received close scrutiny since the Diet passed a resort law in 1987. The law's ostensible objective was to provide leisure facilities for the public. The actual result, however, was many golf courses built by felling natural forests, taking tillable land from farmers, and in effect creating vast wastelands. Golf courses are difficult to maintain in Japan's prevalent warm, humid climate; so herbicides are used in quantities far larger than for agriculture. This causes serious contamination of the surface water runoff from golf courses. If resort development continues at present planned levels, the water in many areas of Japan will be poisoned. Some localities have tried to neutralize this poisoning with charcoal. But the charcoal is obtained by the wholesale felling of forests in Singapore and Thailand, aggravating their deforestation problems.[1] When forests are cleared for golf courses, the resulting rise in carbon dioxide levels contributes to global warming.

Industrial Pollution

Industrial pollution in Japan is gradually shifting from outlying areas to metropolitan centers. Minamata Disease (organic mercury poisoning) is well

---

[1] In another case, in 1988 nearly three hundred farm families in Indonesia were forcibly removed from their lands in the interests of tourism controlled by Japan-related firms. They responded with a "Return to the Land" movement; when farmers lose their farmlands, they turn to clearing tropical rain forests for new land. This shows the linkage between golf courses and rain forest destruction.

known worldwide; now cadmium and dioxin poisoning are also increasing. Various kinds of high technology pollution are also attracting attention. Atmospheric pollution is not as serious as it was during Japan's period of rapid economic growth, but in the Tokyo area the level of airborn nitrous oxides is returning to the levels of ten years ago.

Minamata Disease was first discovered in the area of Minamata Bay in Kumamoto Prefecture among people who had eaten fish containing alkyl mercury compounds in the 1953–58 period. It is a classic example of industrial pollution during Japan's heyday of rapid growth. Victims of the disease lose feeling in their hands and feet, are unable to walk, their tongues become numb so that they are unable to taste, their limbs shake, they are subject to seizures, and they are unable to feed themselves or use a toilet by themselves. All of this was general knowledge, but it was 1988 before the Supreme Court finally handed down a verdict against the Chisso Corporation, which had discharged mercury-laden waste into the bay.

In 1975 a Native Canadian in Ontario was diagnosed as having Minamata Disease, induced by waste materials from upstream chemical and pulp factories. Residents near Jakarta Bay in Indonesia are also said to have symptoms of Minamata Disease.

Cadmium, a heavy metal found in wastes from electroplating and cement factories, can cause bones to crack so that even a cough can fracture ribs. A district court in 1971 and a higher court in 1972 ruled in favor of the plaintiffs in a case of cadmium poisoning.

Cases of "Yokkaichi asthma," named after an industrial city near Nagoya, also began to appear during the high-growth period. Similarly, lung problems among children living along major transportation routes as well as bronchial asthma and lung cancer have become relatively common.

Dioxins are some of the most poisonous substances known, and they retain their toxicity indefinitely. Dioxin contamination is still detected at factory sites in America where defoliants were manufactured for the Vietnam War. In Japan, dioxins are found in herbicides and in the residue of incinerators used for the disposal of plastic materials. In 1985 the Ministry of Health and Welfare set up a special committee to study this problem.

PCB (from "polychlorinated biphenyl") is the organic chlorine compound that caused the Kanemi Oil poisoning incident in 1972, which led the Japanese government to ban PCB manufacture. Thousands of tons of PCB remain to be disposed of, however. In 1985 at a testing facility in Takasago in Hyogo Prefecture, tests were begun on the burning of PCB, though it is feared that this process may yield dioxins.

Arsenic is used in the production of agricultural chemicals, paint, rodent poisons, chemicals for tanning leather, preservatives, and glass. As of 1988,

160 people had been diagnosed as having arsenic poisoning. Of these, 66 have died.

Because high technology uses only small quantities of energy, it was assumed that its industrial applications would be relatively pollution-free. But this was an illusion. Chemicals used in making integrated circuits are strongly carcinogenic and pollute the soil and ground water—a serious problem already in Taishi, Hyogo Prefecture. Moreover, the fluorinated hydrocarbons used to clean integrated circuits destroy the ozone layer, exacerbating a major world problem.

Trash disposal has recently become a major problem in Japan. Trash has traditionally been used for coastal landfill, but now few places are left for landfill. Government authorities have projected plans for filling in valleys, but this has led to confrontation with local residents who fear pollution. The Phoenix Project for waterfront development by filling in much of Tokyo Bay has aroused fears of a new outbreak of Minamata Disease.

Disposal of dry-cell batteries has attracted much attention since 1988, because heat and bacteria can change the mercury in dry cells into highly toxic organic mercury. An immediate solution is imperative. As fluorescent bulbs also contain mercury, their disposal poses a similar problem.

Pollution is not limited to industrial pollutants. Dangers lurk also inside buildings and homes. Heaters and gas appliances can produce carbon monoxide and nitrous oxides. Organic solvents used in building maintenance can be poisonous. Asbestos used in building materials, electrical appliances, and automobile parts can cause asbestosis and lung cancer. Harmful electromagnetic waves from electrical appliances are further reason for concern, as are potentially carcinogenous preservatives, dyes, and mold preventatives in food.

TRANSNATIONAL ENVIRONMENTAL DESTRUCTION

The worldwide expansion of Japanese industry has spawned international disputes over the transnational destruction of nature. Here too the issues involve both natural and industrial damage.

Destruction of Nature

Destruction of tropical rain forests has attracted much attention, and rightly so. A tropical rain forest literally provides everything (food, clothing, shelter) for those who depend on it; its uncontrolled destruction turns them into refugees.

Because Japan imports 51 percent of the unfinished logs traded on the international market, the people of Malaysia and other Asian countries as well as environmental groups accuse Japanese commercial lumbering interests of destroying Asia's tropical rain forests. Moreover, the cultivation of shrimp for export to Japan involves the cutting of coastal mangrove trees. Japan's link to rain forest destruction extends beyond lumbering to the dinner table. At a recent summit on reducing carbon dioxide in the atmosphere, there was a sharp contrast between American footdragging and stress by Germany and other European countries on rain forest destruction as a major hindrance to reduction of atmospheric carbon dioxide. Japan, sometimes called "the forest-eating insect," is caught between the developing countries and the European community.

Fishing grounds have received less attention than tropical forests, but their destruction is also a serious issue. Japanese trawlers have almost completely depleted the fish in coastal waters of the Philippines, Indonesia, and some other Asia-Pacific countries, leaving the sea bottom looking like a glistening desert. As with the rain-forest peoples, the sea-dependent peoples have also become refugees in their own countries.

Industrial Pollution

As the Japanese public has become increasingly critical of industrial pollution, the corporations have transferred production plants abroad, making pollution in other countries as bad as, or worse than, pollution at home. The Asahi Glass plant in Thailand has dumped large quantities of mercury into the Chao Phrayo River, and Furukawa Mining's copper refinery on Leyte Island in the Philippines has become a major polluter.

In one of Japan's worst overseas incidents, three thousand people mounted a demonstration in Pahang[2] against the dumping of radioactive waste materials by a joint company financed by Mitsubishi Chemical. The waste included radioactive thorium with a half-life of fourteen billion years. Local people said that they did not want a Hiroshima in their own backyard and called on the company to move its plant to Japan.

In 1980 a treaty was negotiated to stop the dumping of waste materials in the seas. This treaty absolutely forbids the dumping of mercury and cadmium and designates limited areas for dumping PCB. Limitations on radioactive wastes, however, were not included—a callous ignoring of the wishes of people living in areas, such as the South Pacific, where dumping is actually done.

GLOBAL ENVIRONMENTAL DESTRUCTION

Since the early 1970s environmental problems have become global in scale, affecting places far removed from point of origin. The destruction of the

---

[2] A state on the SE Malay peninsula.

ozone layer, acid rain, global warming, and radioactive pollution are primary examples.

Ozone is produced by the action of ultraviolet light on oxygen in the atmosphere. Destruction of the ozone layer has harmful effects on the human body; is harmful to forests, agricultural crops, and fishing grounds; and leads to global warming. Thus finding a substitute for the ozone-destroying fluorinated hydrocarbons is imperative.

In 1974 the Kantō area (surrounding Tokyo) was subjected to highly toxic acid rain, and over fifty thousand people complained of eye and throat pain. By 1983 atmospheric pollution was so bad in the Kantō area that acid rain fell on Niigata Prefecture (on the opposite side of the main island). Rapid industrialization in China and South Korea, which are upwind from Japan, has resulted in high concentration of sulfurous oxides over Japan and a sharp increase in acid rain.

Global warming is widely expected to produce flooding, desertification, drought in agricultural areas, drastic reduction of forest lands, and a rise in sea level. Increased carbon dioxide in the atmosphere is seen as the major cause of this greenhouse effect, and as long as fossil fuels continue to be used at present levels, global temperatures are expected to rise further.

Having experienced the Hiroshima and Nagasaki bombings in 1945 and fallout from the Bikini tests in 1954 (cf.II-6), the Japanese people are keenly aware of nuclear radioactive damage. In the past this awareness has focused primarily on movements against nuclear weapons. Awareness of radioactive pollution as an environmental issue has come from more recent reports about mutations in fish and clover around nuclear power plants. Public anxiety was heightened by accidents at Three Mile Island in the USA and Tsuruga at home. In these cases, however, radioactive contamination was localized.

The Chernobyl accident in 1986 changed all this. Pronuclear attempts to portray radioactive pollution as merely a local concern were now undermined by the fact that radioactive pollution had transcended national boundaries on a large scale. The global effects of this accident were clear to all. Struggles against new and existing nuclear power plants, the movement to block construction of a nuclear fuel reprocessing plant at Rokkasho village, and movements against building sites for radioactive waste disposal are increasingly seen as concerns of all human beings, with import for all of creation.

Although nuclear power plants pose a global threat, they impact local communities directly through emission of radioactive materials and heat into the atmosphere and through effusions of waste materials into streams and underground aquifers. Discrimination against workers from outcaste communities (assigning them to dangerous jobs) and the health of employees of subcontracting firms who work at the plants are also involved. The presence of nuclear power plants divides local communities and destroys human relationships—another form of their oppressiveness.

During the 1970–90 period, public interest in environmental problems rose sharply. There is scarcely a day when the press does not take up some environmental issue. Even the government and big business, often considered major culprits in environmental destruction, have begun to talk about the environment and its protection. Even so, it remains doubtful that government and industry really see the environment as an important issue.

At the Tokyo conference on "Preservation of the Earth and the Environment" sponsored by the government and the United Nations Environmental Plan in September 1989, an appeal was made for reduced use of fossil fuels and greater reliance on renewable energy sources. The government merely pointed out that nuclear generators do not produce carbon dioxide. A citizens' group complained that the conference had ignored local problems entirely. Still, growing interest in environmental issues is a hopeful sign, even if government and industry attempts to lead environmental protection movements do little more than remind us of their responsibility for nuclear power plants and their role in opposing and delaying local struggles.

Also, isolating environmental issues from other social issues raises human rights issues. The victims of the Kanemi Oil poisoning incident, for example, were rejected as if they had a contagious disease. Residents of communities affected by Minamata Disease were often considered unfit as marital partners. Perhaps the fact that nuclear technology began with the development of nuclear weapons in an atmosphere of hatred between nations, races, and peoples is enough to remind us that environmental issues must not be considered apart from healthy human relationships.

THE CHRISTIAN RESPONSE

Christians in Japan have generally shown little interest in environmental issues. Even when perceived as a social issue, the environment has not been viewed as related to the core of Christian faith. Moreover, concern has usually been shown by individuals, not churches. Japanese Christians have, of course, long focused on the nuclear issue, and it was from this common ground that some Christians first began to work together on broader environmental issues. Among local citizens' groups, which include Christians, concerns tend to be quite limited in scope; the wider range of pollution issues—such as dioxin poisoning, discarded dry-cell batteries, high technology, waste disposal sites, and the interior environment of buildings—have hardly been addressed yet. Even so, it is worthwhile to survey what has been done in Christian circles.

Practical Projects

The YMCA has been an active promoter of direct involvement with nature. Its activities include the operation of an outdoor observation center (Nobeyama Highlands Center), natural salt-making (Suginami YMCA), and working in agricultural fields (Meguro YMCA). These activities have all played a part in the founding of new environmental groups.

In 1983 the Nippon Sei Kō Kai (NSKK) established a sanctuary in one corner of the Kiyosato Highlands in Nagano Prefecture. Here wildlife is protected and direct contact with nature is encouraged. A Kiyosato ecology camp was begun in 1985, an environmental educational forum in fall 1987, and a nature school in summer 1988. These projects go beyond helping people draw closer to nature by including activities such as charcoal-making that directly engage people with natural resources.

Resistance to Destruction of Nature

In 1974 a real estate developer proposed turning the Tenjin Cape area in Tanabe, Wakayama Prefecture, into a resort for the wealthy. When local people became aware of the proposal they immediately began circulating petitions in opposition. After overcoming a great many obstacles, a citizens' group was finally able to buy up the area in 1987. This was a major success for the National Trust movement. The Christian who led the movement did so because he understood it to be a battle of faith in the Lord of creation. But this community now faces a new challenge in the proposal to develop Tanabe Bay as a marine resort.

The Okinawa District of the United Church of Christ in Japan (UCCJ) saw the preservation of Shiraho coral as a mission issue and passed a resolution to this effect in 1987. The location of the New Ishigakijima Airport[3] has now been changed, but the new location also involves a coral reef, and thus a new opposition campaign was begun.

Christian involvement in opposition to the unrestricted development of golf courses and other resort facilities only became apparent in 1989 when the issue was finally seen as a life-and-death matter for a Christian in Yakoda in Aomori Prefecture who was in danger of being driven off his land; when Christians on the Hachiro Lagoon saw their drinking water in danger; and when a Roman Catholic priest in Nagano saw that all of these issues are a matter of encountering the living God through life-giving soil and water.

Organic farming is gradually coming to be seen as a testimony to a faith that cares for life in contrast to an agriculture that produces food contaminated with chemicals. For Christians this is more than just a matter of

[3] On the small island of Ishigakijima near Taiwan.

producing foods that promote health. It is closely linked to a lifestyle which says that all living creatures need to live on this planet together. (Asian Rural Institute is a good example of this basic view. Cf. I-4.) Some groups, upon finding out that nuclear wastes threaten their own existence, have come to see that their own problems cannot be separated from global environmental concerns.

The movement for protection of access to beaches and shore lands maintains that rights to resources such as shellfish, seaweed, and driftwood, as well as swimming and fishing rights, belong to everyone. This position was first declared publicly in a movement led by a Christian pastor in Takasago, Hyogo Prefecture, to indict those who were responsible for water pollution. An international symposium in 1983 was a direct result of this movement. Later he became convinced that environmental pollution stems from modern civilization based on Christianity, and he left the pastorate. Many other pastors, however, have been active leaders in environmental movements while continuing their pastoral ministries. In 1990 the moderator of the UCCJ's Ōu District led a protest against a meeting held ostensibly to promote more productive oceans but actually intended to take fishing rights away from the local people.

In 1985 a national convention of local citizens' groups met in Matsue, Shimane Prefecture, and issued a proclamation on waterfront cities and towns. The convention also called for a conference to deal with the pollution of the Shinji and Nakaumi lakes in Matsue. Local pastors have made significant contributions to all of these movements.

Resistance to Industrial Pollution

Christians in the Japan Evangelical Lutheran Church (JELC) took on the issue of PCB poisoning as a battle of faith, seeing that nationalism and materialism were making human life a commodity and destroying creation. The Japan Baptist Convention's committee on pollution has also been actively involved in this concern. Victims of arsenic poisoning at Toroku in Kyushu have been greatly encouraged by the active involvement of Roman Catholics.

The plan for geographical redistribution of Japanese industries in the 1970s brought rapid growth to the cement industry. One of the world's largest cement plants was built in Mine, Yamaguchi Prefecture, in 1974. Its 230-meter-high chimney spewed cement powder over a large area. A Christian pastor played an active role in the antipollution council formed to deal with the problem. Cadmium in the cement powder entered the bodies of victims and ate away their bones in an extremely painful process. The sight of these suffering people was one of the primary reasons for the organization of this antipollution movement.

Although acid rain is a global problem, Christian opposition to thermo-electric power plants has not been rooted in recognition of its global scope. Christian opposition has come rather from more localized issues of industrial pollution. In 1970 a 5-million-kilowatt thermoelectric power plant was pro-posed for Chōshi in Chiba Prefecture. At that time the world's largest ther-mal power plant was the Yokosuka power plant with a capacity of 2.6 million kilowatts. The proposed new plant's daily consumption of fuel would have been twenty thousand tons of fuel oil and thousands of tons of sulfur dioxide gas—two to three times that of the Yokkaichi petroleum complex. It would have used twenty million tons of water to cool the reactor daily, raising the temperature of as much water as fills the entire Tone River (Tokyo area) by six to seven degrees Celsius, water that would then have been discharged into the sea to destroy fishing grounds.

When local fishermen and farmers learned of these plans, they demon-strated on a scale never seen before and were able to prevent the construction of the plant. A local NSKK priest was a leader in this movement, and the na-ture and style of the movement was shaped by his own Christian character and lifestyle. The fact that acid rain caused by thermoelectric power plants is no longer a major problem in Japan is largely due to this Chōshi movement.

Resistance to Transnational and Global Destruction

The "One Green Tree Movement" has been active in gathering petitions op-posing the destruction of tropical rain forests in Malaysia and Sarawak and in raising funds to protect the forests. These activities also have direct rele-vance to the problem of global warming. A number of churches have been active in this movement.

As noted above, Christian involvement in movements against nuclear power plants has been relatively strong. A number of UCCJ districts have formed committees to work on the nuclear power issue. Kanagawa District organized such a committee in 1981; West Chūgoku District, in 1982; and the Ōu district in 1990 organized a special committee to deal with the pro-posed nuclear fuel recycling plant.[4] Many districts and congregations have organized lectures, on-site studies, film-showings, demonstrations, petition drives, legal actions, and various other forms of study and protest. In January 1985 the social concerns committee for the southern part of the UCCJ's Ōu District sent a letter to the governor of Aomori Prefecture to oppose the

---

[4] This neutral-sounding term masks the reality that the Rokkasho plant would produce plutonium from spent uranium rods, eventually making Japan independent of external sources of radioactive materials. — Ed.

building of the Rokkasho nuclear facilities. This action launched the movement opposing the plant.

In 1980 a group in which Roman Catholics played a leading role learned of plans to dump drums of low-level radioactive waste materials from Japanese nuclear power plants into the South Pacific. Their opposition soon developed into a nationwide drive against the proposal. Petitions for international distribution were prepared in Hiroshima, and an appeal was sent to Roman Catholic justice and peace commissions/councils in the South Pacific and around the world, asking that they appeal to the Japanese government to abandon the project. The Science and Technology Agency of the Japanese government replied that, while it was not prepared to abandon the project, it would defer its implementation. As a result, a storage facility for these radioactive materials has now been planned for Rokkasho village — an ironic twist that links the fate of this village with the people of the South Pacific.

Christians have also been active in opposing construction of facilities for disposal of radioactive waste materials at Horonobe in Hokkaido, at Ningyo Pass in Okayama Prefecture, and at Tojo in Hiroshima Prefecture. Likewise they have actively opposed the operation of nuclear power plants such as those in Tomari, Hokkaido, a second reactor in Shimane, and plants in Maki, Kashiwazaki, and Hamaoka, and the construction of new plants at Kaminoseki in Yamaguchi Prefecture and on the Hioki River in Wakayama Prefecture. The UCCJ districts of Kanagawa and Osaka have been active in opposing the transport of nuclear fuels on public highways.

Additional areas of Christian activity are opposition to changes in laws regulating nuclear reactors, to construction of nuclear power plants in South Korea, to air transport of plutonium, to trial operation of the Ikata power plant, to importing plutonium, as well as support of laws to eliminate nuclear power plants, and fund-raising to aid the Chernobyl victims.

In addition to local and district activities, statements have been issued at the national level: by the National Christian Council in Japan, on the nuclear issue (1985); by the UCCJ General Assembly, on the Japanese government's nuclear policies (1986); and by the Japan Baptist Convention's environmental pollution committee, on Chernobyl immediately following the accident (1986).

A peace seminar sponsored by the Japan Evangelical Lutheran Church (JELC) in March 1990, with the theme "The earth is groaning now," passed a resolution questioning Japan's use of unprecedented quantities of energy and calling for the coexistence of all of creation. This was in preparation for the World Conference on Justice, Peace, and the Integrity of Creation (JPIC), to be convened in Seoul, March 6–12, by the World Council of Churches.

Since 1986 the annual Conference on Religion and Peace, which brings together representatives of many religions, has issued appeals to the general public, local government bodies, the Japanese government, and the world's nuclear powers. In its second appeal (1987) it called for reexamination of the manipulation of peace for environmental destruction, the spread of damage from radioactivity, and affluent lifestyles in which material interests reign supreme. In its third appeal (1989) it called for a fresh look at the consumer civilization built on the sacrifice of developing countries and for adoption of a lifestyle built on a symbiotic relationship with all of life.

INTELLECTUAL RESPONSES

Since the most important factor in confronting environmental issues is one's consciousness of the problem, there is very little difference between Christians and non-Christians on these issues. Christians have stimulated non-Christians, and the reverse has also been true. Here we briefly note some shared shifts in perspective.

Responses from Fields other than Theology

In sociology, a developmental model that stresses development based on a nation's own internal needs and resources has become prominent in contrast to the assumption of traditional modernization theory that nations will follow some general model. In this internal model, people and regional groups work in ways adapted to the ecology of their region and base their development on their own cultural traditions, adopting from others what fits their own needs.

Economics as a scholarly discipline has also become quite critical of development aid that destroys the environment and health of recipient peoples, especially in the Third World. Scholars in this field have called for reassessment of the uncritical pursuit of affluence.

The history of science has begun to reflect critically on the modern Western use of the slogan "knowledge is power" in the pursuit of happiness. Modern civilization has been built on human rule over nature, but in the process God has been left out of the picture and God's judgment has been forgotten. In this field, dialogue with theology is an urgent need.

The situation is similar in technology. Past levels of energy consumption are no longer viable. Development of an energy-saving technology and change in individual lifestyles are both urgently needed, while working to construct a new ethical system for technology.

In philosophy, putting humanity at the center of everything has led to the myth of objectivity and the death of God. Modern society has veered sharply toward aimless hedonism, giving free rein to human desires. Recoiling from this excess, individuals have discovered that at the root of their own selfhood there is an "other" to which we are bound in responsibility for suffering, wherever we live.

In a sense, these new understandings are all brought together in the idea of entropy[5] — the law that says energy flows from a higher to a lower temperature, eventually dissipating. One clear implication of this is that industries, which consume so much energy, must take responsibility for their own waste products, not foist them off on society to spend additional energy for disposal.

Ecology, a discipline directly concerned with the environment, questions modernity's appetite to make the natural world its own possession. While it does not call for a restrictive asceticism, it does calls for the liberation of nature from human oppression and at the same time for liberation of nature within human beings — the human nature that shares the chemistry of the earth's climate and seas.

Theological Responses

As Japan's rapid growth began to reveal its own bankruptcy in the early 1970s, theology began to question modernity and the technological civilization it has spawned. This critique arises not only from industrial pollution and the destruction of nature but also from the reduction of our labors to mere toil in the service of profit and the loss of our own selfhood.

Since about 1983 theology has focused on ecology, creation, and bioethics. Chernobyl transformed the environmental crisis into a crisis of civilization, and the present age was called the age of catastrophe, the end of civilization. God's activity in providing blessings through agriculture was placed alongside God's activity in salvation. Ecological concern for the present and future of the universe, our only habitat, has grown. The beginnings of these changes go back to the 1960s.

In 1967 the American historian Lynn White, in response to the US lecture tour of Buddhist scholar D. T. Suzuki, published "The historical origins of the present ecological crisis" in the journal *Science*. White called into question Western thought patterns and caused a major stir not only among American but also South Korean, Japanese, and German thinkers. In 1972, Suh Namdong of South Korea published a paper titled "Ecological ethics" in the Japanese journal *Daigaku Kirisutosha* (University Christian).[6] He predicted that

[5] The Entropy Study Society in Japan was formed in 1984.

[6] Organ of the Christian Scholars Fellowship, a nationwide Christian university teachers organization, related to the Student Department of the National Committee of YMCAs in Japan. — Ed.

in the near future there will be a climactic ecological end-time that will bring the entire human race together in unity. He dealt not only with issues of economics, justice, and quality of life, but also with the Christian linear view of history and the meaning of a female deity. He said that while the church in the West waits for the last days, the church in the East emphasizes the restoration of creation and the sacramental quality of nature. He included not just living things but all of creation as an organic whole. His essay constituted his personal response to the World Council of Churches' early call for the World Conference on Justice, Peace, and the Integrity of Creation scheduled for 1990.

In Germany, G. Liedke responded to White's thesis with a new interpretation of the creation story. His treatise, along with his related statement on reconciliation with nature, was translated into Japanese and led to the formation of a study group on Nature, Science, Technology, and Human Beings by the Tomisaka Christian Center in Tokyo. This group, formed in 1987, organized an interdisciplinary program for natural scientists, legal scholars, social scientists, and theologians. The group has discussed the broad range of issues considered in this essay, especially in terms of fundamental conceptual shifts in theology and other fields.[7]

RETROSPECT AND PROSPECT

Retrospect

The World Exposition held in Osaka in 1970 was viewed as a sort of final report on Japan's period of rapid economic growth (cf. II-8). Its exhibits seemed to promise a future without limitations, even though the suffering of the victims of Minamata Disease and cadmium poisoning were already well known. While their suffering cast a dim shadow over Japan's evident prosperity, the exposition was an occasion for most people to extol the dawn of a new world in which they could freely use the unlimited electric power expected to flow from nuclear power plants.

---

[7] Some titles of the themes taken up by this group are:

"The structure and present state of science, technology, and faith"

"The history of antipollution movements in postwar Japan and local residents' movements"

"Nuclear power plants and human beings"

"Paradigm shifts in the history of theology and the church"

"Ecology: theology and Buddhism"

"Creation and lordship over the earth: relation to New Year's festivals"

"The current state of bioethics"

"Barth's theory of creation: a new look at the theory of providence"

"Report on the World Convocation on Justice, Peace, and the Integrity of Creation"

"The theory of internal development and the Christian understanding of nature"

Soon the oil shock cast some temporary doubt on the prospects of this life-style, but subsequent economic recovery left the population drunk with a new surge of prosperity. The 1986 science exposition followed by an economic summit conference in Japan in April that year further strengthened this sense of euphoria.

News of the Chernobyl accident reached Japan while the economic summit was in session. It came as a sort of final warning from God to the so-called advanced nations, including Japan, and to all who would follow in their wake — indeed, to all people who believed that human beings could rule as independent autocrats over the created world.

By 1990 "environment" had become an in-word in Japan, yet no one seemed interested in probing the issue in depth. Concern for the environment has not kept people from climbing on the bandwagon of unlimited resort development. The situation, however, has now reached the point where the fate of the environment can no longer be dismissed as a momentary fad.

Until recently the Christian churches had, as noted earlier, shown little interest in environmental issues; now they are calling into question an exclusive focus on the human aspect of creation and are beginning to talk of the importance of human coexistence with nature. Christians are taking a new look at the creation of heaven and earth with which the biblical story begins. The environmental crisis calls into question the very foundation of theology and the church, and urgently demands an answer.

In February 1988 three thousand people from all over Japan gathered to protest the test run of the Ikata nuclear reactor. One woman who had been instrumental in organizing the protest said, "I was living a very satisfied and happy life until I suddenly realized that I was actually standing on a precipice. I hugged my two children closely and cried in anguish." Her words express more than fear of the nuclear threat to our lives. Her anguished cry laments the perverted path taken by the advanced nations, including Japan, and by Christians who follow that path toward the fatal precipice. There is an eerie warning for all of us in the story of the cat, afflicted with Minamata Disease, that reared up on its hind legs and plunged into the sea.

Prospects

In examining the past we must turn away from the mythological dualities of subjectivity and objectivity, mind and matter, nature and history, time and space, natural science and psychological sciences. Only then can we begin to see the future whole, and thus come within range of the possible. Otherwise, ones-sided vision may yield technological dreams that turn into human nightmares.

Japan, for example, is planning a rail line on which trains powered by linear motors will operate at very high speeds by the year 2001. This technology, however, is very closely tied to nuclear power generation. Far from holding promise of a bright future, this new technology threatens to propel our future toward a violent end.

Our lives are further threatened by the development of altered forms of living beings produced through genetic engineering. The human race has no experience whatsoever in this area, where an error may bring irreparable harm.

Further study is also needed on the impact computers have on society. Already we can see that the rapid introduction of computers has led to grave losses in human emotions and in the sense of the passage of time. There are also many other aspects that need to be studied.

The church must take care that Jesus' words "Take no thought of tomorrow" not lead us into irresponsible self-indulgence that is nothing but rejection of our responsibility for the present. If we are indifferent to the gradual snuffing out of life around us, we shall one day see our own lives snuffed out as well.

Paul's words in his letter to the Romans (8:19–21) have special relevance for us today. "All of creation waits with eager longing for God to reveal his sons. For creation was condemned to lose its purpose . . . but creation itself would one day be set free from its slavery to decay and would share the glorious freedom of the children of God." Surely today is the time that waits with longing for the appearance of God's children. We also need, however, to remember the words of Frank Chikane: "It is important to emphasize that *kairos* is not only a time of blessing. It is also a time of judgment. If we waste our opportunities, hope will turn into a time of judgment, and we will live in fear of death as we face the destruction of all of God's creation."[8]

---

[8] From his keynote address to the World Convocation on Justice, Peace, and the Integrity of Creation, March 6–12, 1989, Seoul, Korea.

10

Women's Issues

Watanabe Mine

REMARKABLE CHANGES IN WOMEN'S consciousness and the women's liberation movement have taken place in the last twenty years. The history of oppression of women around the world is long; yet the energy of women — held down so completely, but now activated by worldwide political, economic, and social changes — has finally burst forth in powerful waves felt around the world. The United Nations Decade for Women (1975–85) was a major product of these waves. Raising its banner of "Equality, Development, and Peace," the UN Decade for Women had far-reaching influence on many grassroots movements, which in turn provided women with a framework within which to act. All this has had a great impact on the women's movement in Japan.

To prepare for the opening of the Decade for Women in 1975, Japanese women with different political views and values banded together. Fifty women's organizations joined to create the International Women's Year Liaison Committee, and proceeded to examine the conditions and problems of women all across Japan. The Japan Woman's Christian Temperance Union (JWCTU), the YWCA of Japan, the National Christian Council in Japan (NCCJ) Women's Committee, and the Association of Roman Catholic Women's Groups were all members of this Liaison Committee. And all now participate in the "Liaison Committee for Carrying Out the Resolutions Made During the Women's Year."[1]

In connection with the three UN-sponsored International Women's Conferences held in Mexico City, Copenhagen, and Nairobi, Japan's Liaison Committee sponsored a conference in Japan. Many women's organizations and labor unions joined forces to create the base for a Japan-oriented non-

---

[1] This is a 1986 change from the committee's original name.

governmental plan of action to raise the status of women in Japan. It is significant that in our conservative and patriarchal society, women from such diverse backgrounds were able to link arms in this endeavor.

Among resolutions passed at the Japan Conference was one on peace that called for complete disarmament, the abolition of nuclear weapons, and the preservation of Japan's peace constitution. In 1979, after the treaty to abolish discrimination against women was passed by the United Nations, the Japan Liaison Committee lobbied for its ratification by the Japanese government and for the revision of Japanese laws to comply with this treaty.

Looking back over the UN Decade for Women and how it influenced women's movements in Japan, two generalizations might be made:

1. Of the three objectives (equality, development, and peace), a positive step was taken toward equality. A widening of thought to include development and peace issues in the women's movement, however, was not forthcoming.

2. Women in Japan have not yet come to the understanding that the fundamental human rights of *all* women around the world must be guaranteed. On this matter, their view is still very narrow. But the Liaison Committee's report does emphasize the responsibility of Japanese women to stand in solidarity with other women ensnared in international disputes and those suffering from hunger in developing countries.[2]

One distinctive trend of the last twenty years is the rise of many different citizens' movements, not only those related to women, and women have played a significant role in this overall trend.

THE ROLE OF CHRISTIAN WOMEN

Since Christians are less than one percent of Japan's population, and two-thirds of these Christians are women, "Christian women" here refers to only a tiny minority. Being rooted, however, in the source of wisdom and truth, these Christian women have spoken out and acted on basic issues so often overlooked by others. They have been on the cutting edge, ahead of their time, and have therefore led the way for many more women.

This movement did not arise initially from within the church. In the early 1970s, Christian women found themselves compelled by their faith to become involved in a number of issues in society, particularly peace and human rights issues. Involvement aroused their consciousness so that they became aware of their own situation as women, in church as well as society. From all

[2] *Rentai to kōdō — Kokusai Fujin Nen Renraku Kai no kiroku* (Report of the International Year of the Woman Liaison Committee — solidarity and action).

this was born an interest in women's liberation and feminist theology. A general description of that development follows.

INVOLVEMENT IN SOCIAL CONCERNS

Peace, Nuclear Energy, and the Environment

The 1970s and 1980s were a time when concerns for peace and nuclear weapons expanded to include nuclear power plants and pollution. These common concerns then expanded further to encompass the whole environment and the integrity of creation.

In 1963, at the YWCA World Council in Denmark, delegates of the YWCA of Japan caused quite a stir when they expressed doubts about the rosy outlook for peace based on the deterrent power of nuclear weapons. Their statement read: "Nuclear power has become so great that it far exceeds the reaches of human action and intelligence. The power to control this gigantic energy source exists only as individual persons come to an understanding of what nuclear power really is."

This strong antinuclear position was further strengthened at the Japan YWCA's National Convention in 1970: "Our modern scientific and technological civilization has mistakenly sought progress in terms of power, speed, and convenience. It appears to be headed toward a denial of *all* of life, including humanity. When we speak of 'antinuclear', we see 'nuclear' as a symbol for this misdirected modern civilization, and we must choose life, not death."[3]

It would be an overstatement to say that in 1970 all members of the YWCA were knowledgeable about the true nature of nuclear energy. Rather, the intuition and insight of a core group led them to choose this special emphasis. It was the first step of a journey in which all of the members eventually embraced the antinuclear stance. One concrete example of how this happened is the "Pilgrimage to Hiroshima."

Junior and senior high schools began taking study trips to Hiroshima and Nagasaki in the mid-1970s. One of the most influential of these is sponsored by the YWCA of Japan—the "Pilgrimage to Hiroshima" series begun in 1971.[4] Participants in this pilgrimage—Christians and non-Christians, Japanese and non-Japanese—have been confronted and enlightened by a number of issues: the realities of nuclear power, the present state of civilization,

[3] *Mizu to kaze to hikari o — Nihon YWCA 80-nen* (Water, wind, and light—The 80-year history of the YWCA of Japan), YWCA of Japan.
[4] *Hiroshima o kangaeru tabi* (Pilgrimage to Hiroshima), YWCA of Japan, Pilgrimage to Hiroshima Planning Committee Report.

the recent history of Japan as aggressor, foreign atomic-bomb victims (*hibakusha*), human rights, discrimination, and the environment.

The YWCA's antinuclear stance encountered many difficulties at first, but in time it came to be understood as something related closely to everyday life, leading to "a reassessment of lifestyle and an emphasis on organic farming and natural foods" that spread throughout the membership. This movement had natural ties with many citizens' groups that became popular in the late 1970s, and it is now attracting other Christian women's groups.

Prostitution

Japan is a feudal society where for centuries men have completely dominated women and controlled sexual relations. Since the Meiji Restoration (1868), Christian women's groups, especially in the JWCTU and the Salvation Army, have formed the core of the movement against prostitution. Over time the prostitution business has changed, but Christians holding fast to the principles of respect for life and liberation have continued to anticipate the successive shifts and confront this issue boldly.

In 1973, at the Japan–Korea Consultation in Seoul, Korean Church Women United issued an appeal that something be done about Japanese men using their economic power to turn Korean women into "sex slaves." Responding to this, the JWCTU called on all churches and organizations related to the NCCJ Women's Committee to join in a campaign aimed at exposing and halting the sexual exploitation of South Korean women by money-laden Japanese male tourists. The campaign widely distributed this appeal with supporting documents, especially targeting the Japan Association of Travel Agents and the Ministry of Transport, calling on them to stop the sex tours. These actions had repercussions in the general public, and voices from Korea, Taiwan, the Philippines, and Thailand joined in. Consequently, some changes were made, including some revision of laws governing the tourist business.

Sex tourism declined slightly because of this, but in the early 1980s the problem of Asian women migrant workers emerged (cf. II-12). The JWCTU responded quickly and appropriately to this problem by establishing the Asian Women's Shelter HELP (House in Emergency of Love and Peace), which was opened in 1986 to commemorate the 100th anniversary of the founding of the Japan WCTU. Christian women throughout the country support and assist in this facility that offers refuge, legal advice, contact with relatives, and many other services.[5]

---

[5] *Nihon Kirisutokyō Fujin Kyōfūkai hyakunen shi* (Centennial history of the Japan Woman's Christian Temperance Union), Japan WCTU.

The Roman Catholic Church in Japan organized the Task Force for Asia, and women religious who participated in its experiential educational opportunities became painfully aware of the problems of Asian women migrant workers. They now have a program similar to HELP, making the movement truly ecumenical.

Korean Residents in Japan

As this issue is treated elsewhere (II-11), here women's concerns and contributions can be highlighted.

The National Federation of Kyōdan (UCCJ) Women's Societies in 1973 formed a study group on the Japan–Korea issue. In addition to seminars held jointly with the Women's Association of the Korean Christian Church in Japan (KCCJ), the Federation has published a number of small pamphlets and engaged in other consciousness-raising activities.

The KCCJ Women's Association, as a member of the NCCJ Women's Committee, relates to women of other NCCJ member bodies to share burdens and work for the elimination of discrimination and prejudice. It is impossible to describe fully the pain that all first-generation Koreans in Japan have had to endure; but Korean women must suffer additional pain in strongly Confucian homes and society simply because they are women. To preserve the stories of these first-generation mothers, the KCCJ Women's Association published six collections of the mothers' stories, between 1975 and 1978. In 1985, the original tapes were again used to produce an anthology of their testimonies. This same group is now pouring new enthusiasm into a study program for young women of the third generation, to enable them to discover their Korean roots and think about what it means to live as Koreans in Japan.

The JWCTU and YWCA are also related to this issue on a nationwide scale. Christians are being called to challenge Japanese society's scant toleration for ethnic diversity, its limiting of choice to "assimilation or expulsion." Because prejudice is fostered at a very early age, women have a special responsibility in this area.

The Nakaya Trial

While the court case of Nakaya Yasuko had no overt gender-specific aspects, it was a politically significant trial involving a Christian woman married to a member of the Self-Defense Forces (SDF) who in 1968 was killed in an accident while on duty. As a Christian, she chose to have a Christian memorial service for him, as she sought to comprehend his untimely death in terms of her faith. In 1972, however, the local SDF support group informed her that it intended to enshrine her husband's spirit in the prefecture's "nation-protecting shrine" (a prefectural version of the nation's Yasukuni Shrine for venerating the war dead. Cf. II-5). She explained her Christian belief clearly and rejected the proposal.

The SDF group, however, obtained permission from her husband's father and enshrined his spirit anyway. The widow had no choice but to bring suit against the state and the SDF, claiming infringement of her freedom of religious expression. The ensuing court battle, fought by Mrs. Nakaya with the support of her church's pastor and lay members as well as Christians and non-Christians throughout the nation, dragged on for fifteen years.

This story of an ordinary widow who objected to state interference in her private life, especially in her feelings about her deceased husband, may appear insignificant on the surface. But it is about someone's basic human rights and dignity being trampled underfoot by powerful public institutions, and thus it had a great impact on other women. Those who supported Mrs. Nakaya became aware, through this experience, of the awesome powers of the state, traditional patriarchy, the emperor system, and Yasukuni Shrine.[6]

Mrs. Nakaya won her case in the lower court and also in the high court, only to lose finally in the Supreme Court in 1988. All was not lost, however, because many people were deeply moved, especially by Mrs. Nakaya's testimony at the Supreme Court trial, to take a stand themselves on the many related problems that still remain.

ECUMENICAL ACTIVITIES OF CHRISTIAN WOMEN

Inspired by feminist theology in Europe and the United States, Japanese women have probed for the relevance this movement has for Japan and have begun to establish networks with women at home and abroad.

The Women Doing Theology Group

In June 1984, about twenty women with an interest in theology met to form this group. They were clergy and lay, Roman Catholic and Protestant, church and nonchurch Christians. The meeting's chairperson described their objective as follows: "We want to create something new—something that is not imported but comes out of the Japanese context, something from the viewpoint of women who have been excluded from traditional theology, something that takes women's experience seriously."

Meeting once every three months, the group began by sharing personal stories—stories of oppression and of racial and gender discrimination. Before

[6] *Josei to Shingaku no Kai kiroku* (Women Doing Theology report), NCCJ Women's Committee.

long they were taking up such topics as women in the Early Church and the writings of women in the Middle Ages, the Renaissance, and the Reformation. While retracing history, they examined scripture by historical-critical methods. One of them commented, "Discovering women's long-hidden thoughts was like finding the lost coin. I was overjoyed, and felt a new and vibrant strength."[7]

The women have also held annual overnight seminars as well as special meetings with guests from abroad. The themes of the seminars are as follows: "Women in the church" (1985), with presentations about day laborers in Kamagasaki, sex tourism and prostitution in Okinawa, and Taiwanese living in Japan; "Women living in Asia" (1986); and "Feminist theology—Yesterday and today" (1987).

The Bible study leader at one retreat suggested that theology may be understood as the simple act of each person reading the Bible and reflecting on its meaning for herself; thus, when women of faith talk together, they are doing theology. From the perspective of traditional theology, the task is to "rethink theology." Another participant said of the issues facing Christian women in Japan: "Within Japan's discriminatory society, we women are subjected to discrimination; but if we look beyond Japan, we see that Japanese women also exploit women in the Third World. We have a responsibility to view our own liberation in relation to the liberation of our sisters in the Third World. This is not only a women's issue. Women and men must cooperate to bring about change."

Summing up her impressions after the meeting, one participant with an international background wrote that in this seminar she had felt something that she had never felt before. "It was an atmosphere of complete openness. I think each participant saw herself as a perpetrator who needed both to liberate and be liberated."[8]

Japan–Korea Women's Theological Consultations

The Women Doing Theology seminar in 1987 had as its main speaker Sook Ja-chung, a minister from Korea who is active in feminist theology. As a result of this seminar, a joint seminar was planned with the Korean Women's Theology Conference, of which Ms. Sook is a member.

---

[7] Kawase Iseko, "Ushinawareta koin o mitsuketara—Josei Shingaku no Kai no konnichi made" (If we find the lost coin—a review of the Women Doing Theology Group), *Fukuin to sekai* (The gospel and the world), May 1988.

[8] Reports of seminars sponsored by the Women Doing Theology Group: No.1, *Sorezore no kotoba de* (Each in her own words); No.2, *Ajia ni ikiru watashi* (My life in Asia); No.3, *Josei shingaku no kino, kyō* (Feminist theology, yesterday and today); NCCJ Women's Committee.

In January 1988, seven women from Japan attended the first joint seminar in Seoul, with women from Korea, Burma, the United States, Canada, and Germany. There were about forty women in all. Letty Russell, then visiting Korea, was the main speaker. Dr. Russell's opening address, "The feminist touch: Authority and spirituality," was followed by presentations on "Spirituality and unification" and "Spirituality and woman" by a Korean and a Japanese participant, respectively. Through these presentations and the discussions that followed, participants shared each other's pain. They experienced a common sisterhood through mutual forgiveness of sin and reconciliation.[9]

The second Japan–Korea Women's Theological Consultation was held the next year in Tokyo. More than sixty women, including eleven from Korea, gathered to consider the theme "Women, peace, and life." The purpose of the consultation was to share in fellowship, worship, and Bible interpretation through the shared experiences of Koreans, Japanese, and Korean residents in Japan.[10] In 1990 the group met in Kwang-ju, Korea, with the theme "Northeast Asia, peace, and women's theology."

Church Women and Gender Discrimination

Recognizing how few women generally hold leadership positions in the United Church of Christ in Japan (UCCJ), some women clergy in the Women Doing Theology Group met in late 1987 to prepare for effecting change at the Twenty-fifth UCCJ General Assembly scheduled for November 1988. The ground of their concern was evident in women's low representation at the Twenty-fourth UCCJ General Assembly (1986): only one woman among 148 clergy delegates, and only 30 women among 148 lay delegates. The UCCJ Executive Committee membership had 14 male clergy, but no female clergy, and only 2 of 13 lay members were women.

The women clergy's caucus laid plans to organize a church women's consultation and invited women—most of whom were clergy and directors of Christian education with some formal seminary training—to become involved. About one hundred women responded, including ten women from other denominations. A committee of volunteers then spent six months making careful preparations, which included six newsletters, for a September gathering at the National Women's Education Center near Tokyo. Seventy women attended to consider the theme "The church is alive because of

---

[9] *Nikkan Gōdō Seminā kiroku—reisei to feminizumu* (Japan–Korea Women's Theological Consultation report—spirituality and feminism), NCCJ Women's Committee.

[10] *Nihon, Zainichi, Kankoku Kirisutosha Josei Fōramu kiroku: josei, heiwa, inochi—gendai o ikiru* (Japan–Korea Christian Women's Theological Forum report: women, peace, life—living in the present age), NCCJ Women's Committee.

women—What changes do we want in the church?" Discussion focused on clarifying goals and determining how to get more women involved in decision-making processes at the local church, district, and national levels. At the same time, they talked about basic changes that would take place naturally when long-silent women began to speak out.[11]

From this meeting came a proposal to work toward the establishment of a committee on gender discrimination issues. This proposal was presented and approved at the Twenty-fifth UCCJ General Assembly (1988). Almost immediately the new committee began activities aimed at making church members aware of the need to abolish all forms of gender discrimination. An initial tactic was to form district networks of persons already working on this issue. The committee also began publishing a newsletter called *Josei to jinken* (Women and human rights). Current areas of concern and action are women clergy, qualifications for general assembly delegates, and Asian women migrant workers.

These efforts have shown some positive results. The number of women clergy delegates for the Twenty-sixth UCCJ General Assembly (1990) has increased by four, the women lay delegates by five. The number of women on the Executive Committee has increased by two (one clergy and one lay).[12]

The Church Women's Consultation in 1989, under the theme "Renewal of the church—Women and the emperor system," assessed the extent to which the emperor system is embedded in Japanese society. The UCCJ Committee on Gender Discrimination Issues held its first national-level meeting following this consultation.[13]

ACTIVITIES WITHIN DENOMINATIONS

The National Federation of Kyōdan (UCCJ) Women's Societies

Any consideration of women's efforts toward autonomy and independence within Japanese church structures cannot ignore the work of the National Federation of UCCJ Women's Societies.

Formation. When it was proposed to not include a "women's" category in the Commission on Mission when the UCCJ reorganized (1968), women of the church objected. After considerable debate, it was decided to set up an

---

[11] *Onna no kotoba shū, 1* (A collection of women's statements, #1), NCCJ Women's Committee.

[12] *Josei to jinken* (Women and human rights), UCCJ Committee on Gender Discrimination Issues, No. 1.

[13] *Onna no kotoba shū, 2* (A collection of women's statements, #2), NCCJ Women's Committee.

autonomous women's group related to, but not an integral part of, the church's structure. This proposal was approved by the 1968 UCCJ General Assembly. The Federation was organized in June 1969, and all UCCJ districts except the Kyushu District voted to affiliate. (Kyushu District relates to the Federation through its own Commission on Mission.)

Being an autonomous organization within the UCCJ, the Federation was able to maintain some distance from the confusion that struck the UCCJ in 1970 (cf. II-8), and in fact it was strengthened internally.

Organizational characteristics. The Federation has four distinguishing organizational features:

1. Structural autonomy. Central Committee members are elected, not appointed by the UCCJ; they are associate members (nonvoting) of the UCCJ Commission on Mission.

2. Financial autonomy. Funded by independent contributions, the Federation receives no financial support from the UCCJ, nor does it have a system of apportionments.

3. Corporate identity. Belonging to the Federation means women are more than individual women who are members of local churches; they are a church women's group within the whole church; clergy women become members of the Federation the same as lay women.

4. Part of God's church. The Federation is not "autonomous" in the sense of being self-guided; its main guidance comes through study of the Bible as the basic standard of the whole church.

The national level. The Central Committee meets every two years to decide on the theme and priorities for the next biennium. Representative themes are "Church women as peacemakers," "Advancing the gospel," and "Living today in God's time."

The Central Committee sets up special committees as needed, and the work of these committees is widely circulated to districts, local churches, and individuals in many different forms. There are special committees for such issues as: movements in the world church, Japan–Korea relations, revision of school textbooks, and problems faced by women pastors and by ministers' wives.

Notable accomplishments. One project, two anniversary conventions, and a Bible study program merit mention here.

* Rainbow Haven. A seminar of women's society officers in 1966 proposed that a home for retired clergy women and widows of clergy be built, and this proposal was adopted at the first meeting of the newly formed Federation's Central Committee. Supported by prayers and funds from all over the country, the facility was completed in 1973 at Tateyama in Chiba

Prefecture, east of Tokyo. Despite many difficulties, a chapel and facilities for small retreats have been added to enable fellowship between retreat participants and residents, as well as carry out mission work in the area.

　* Anniversary National Conventions. On its tenth (1979) and twentieth (1989) anniversaries, the Federation held national conventions with about 2,000 women participating each time. Preparations were started a year in advance for the two-day conferences managed entirely by women. The 1979 convention theme was "Advancing the gospel — Born anew by the Word of God," based on I Peter; the 1989 theme was "Living today in God's time," based on I Thessalonians. In the communion services, the participants were deeply moved by the sense of community they experienced in the name of the Lord.

　Some plenary time was devoted to "Speaking my mind," presentations by sixteen women whose essays had been selected from those submitted a year earlier. Matching these essays on issues faced by church women with the themes of small study groups reveals church women's interests and how these interests change. In 1979, the study group topics were: church, evangelism, our women's group, passing on the faith, problems of aging, society and welfare, society and politics, and education. In comparison, the 1989 topics were: church, evangelism, aging, Bible study, human rights, discrimination, education, and nuclear energy and peace. Although the women's response to issues of human rights, discrimination, nuclear energy and peace has not been overly enthusiastic, they have acknowledged that these issues cannot be avoided.[14,15]

　* Study of the Bible as Canon. From the outset, the Federation has made "listening to Scripture" its basis, but at first there was not much emphasis on interpretation. Since the 1979 convention when Bible study stressed the biblical canon as "a model for faith and life," this has become a priority of the national movement. In various regions, study of the Bible as canon has been intentionally introduced. In 1988, the Canonical Bible Study Committee was established. Some of the activities of this committee include monthly Bible study meetings open to the public, studying the Bible one book at a time, publishing study results as texts for small Bible study groups, and a biennial nationwide Bible study meeting. "We must live and be guided by the Bible as the canon, in a concrete sense," the committee urges. "We believe that Jesus Christ will surely lead us in this endeavor."

---

　[14] *Zenkoku Kyōdan Fujinkai Rengō shōshi* (A short history of the National Federation of Kyōdan [UCCJ] Women's Societies).

　[15] *Nijusshū-nen Zenkoku Shūkai hōkoku: Kami no toki o ima ikiru* (Twentieth Anniversary National Convention report: Living today in God's time), National Federation of UCCJ Women's Societies.

Bible study methods used by church women's groups have undergone changes. The trend is for passive listening to pastors' exposition to be replaced by personal engagement in independent Bible study. An exclusive devotion to study of the Bible as canon, however, has aroused criticism throughout the country, and critics urge that a variety of Bible study methods be employed. It is unclear where this discussion will lead, and there has been little dialogue between the Federation and others such as the Women Doing Theology Group. It is hoped that the issue will be effectively addressed in the near future.

Other Protestant Churches

Compared with the UCCJ, other Protestant denominations are very small in numbers, but it is said that two-thirds of their members are women. While denominational structures vary somewhat, male leadership among clergy and laity is predominant in all. During the past twenty years, however, changes have been made in some denominations.

The Nippon Sei Kō Kai (NSKK). At its General Synod in 1977, the NSKK (Anglican communion) passed a resolution to eliminate the word "male" in the requirements for deacons, thus opening the way for female deacons. The first woman deacon was ordained in 1978, and now, thirteen years later, there are four.

After defeat in the two previous synods, a resolution for a committee to study "the ordination of women to the orders of priest and bishop" was finally passed in 1990. The committee will be composed of men and women, of known supporters and opponents. This was truly a "happening" for a synod that seated no women, since no diocese had elected a woman delegate. While a positive conclusion is not guaranteed, the synod's action is seen as a big gain for those favoring the ordination of women not only as deacons but also as priests. In a companion resolution, the synod mandated that several women shall be appointed to all committees at the provincial level.

The Korean Christian Church in Japan (KCCJ). Yielding to internal and external pressures (the Presbyterian Church of Canada to which it is closely related began ordaining women), the KCCJ ordained its first woman minister in 1983. At present the KCCJ has two women clergy.

The Roman Catholic Church

As the Roman Catholic Church is a worldwide organization, it is a bit difficult to identify in it trends peculiar to Japan. It can be said, however, that consciousness was raised among Catholic women religious in the 1980s, and study groups have been held to develop and demonstrate the leadership of women in the church. A few Catholic sisters are now preaching and leading Bible study.

The role of women in the Task Force for Asia,[16] in the Asian Meeting of Religious [women's orders] (AMOR), and in the Asian Partnership for Human Development (APHD) is significant. Women religious feel that working cooperatively on committees with male priests is an important challenge today. In 1987 a proposal "to include women equally in administrative planning" was made at the church's first National Incentive Congress of Evangelization (NICE I; cf. I-1), and since then a committee on women and the church has been established in the Tokyo Diocese.

In summary, there is a movement among women to expose the oppression and pain of their sisters around the world. Through this consciousness-raising process, women are becoming more sensitive to discrimination and pain, and are beginning to develop ways to stand by and walk with these suffering persons. This trend is evident both inside and outside the church. It is evident in the movements for reforming church structures. Even so, many who hear the calls for change remain conservatively content with the traditional roles of women.

In these days when the least of God's creatures are trampled upon, and not only human life but all life is endangered, the fundamental question facing all Christian women is: How shall we answer the call of our Creator God, the source of all life?

---

[16] *Ibid.*, p. 7.

11

Churches and Minorities in a Warped Society

Lee Chong-il

MUCH TIME HAS PASSED since Japanese churches began to express an interest in minorities. Yet that interest has focused on minorities mainly as objects of evangelism, not on the discrimination they face in daily life.

Organized church involvement in minority issues dates from June 1972, when the National Christian Council in Japan (NCCJ) held a conference on "Human rights issues of foreign residents of Japan." That meeting played an important part in the ensuing Japanese ecumenical involvement in minority problems. Then, in May 1974, the General Assembly of the Korean Christian Church in Japan (KCCJ) sponsored an international conference on "Minority problems and mission strategy," with eighty overseas participants. Representing Japanese minorities were one Ainu person, two persons from the Buraku group (see below), and twelve resident-Koreans. This conference did much to inform the churches of the world about the existence of minorities in Japan.

One major result of this international gathering was its clarification of "minorities," namely, that number should not be the basic criterion. Minorities are people who — numerical minority or not — are powerless, are oppressed, are made to suffer, are deprived of their basic human rights. They are a social group that, for historical, cultural, or economic reasons, is oppressed and subjected to prejudice and discrimination.

By this definition, Buraku persons, Ainu persons, Okinawans, resident-Koreans, resident-Chinese, resident-Taiwanese, resident-Southeast Asians, foreign migrant workers, and others are minorities in Japanese society. This article focuses on the first four of these groups, outlining each minority situation and then indicating church response.

THE BURAKU PEOPLE

Minority by Political Fiat

For over two centuries before Japan's modern society came into existence, the Tokugawa rulers set aside segregated communities called Burakumin.[1] These people were not a minority based on racial or ethnic differences, but one deliberately created by political decision. Putting them at the lowest level of society and calling them *eta* ("great filth") and *hinin* ("nonhuman") enabled the feudal government to deflect the peasant discontent that periodically erupted in revolts. But even in the modern society developed by the Meiji government from 1868, Buraku people were subjected to deliberate manipulation and discrimination. The liberation movement mounted by these people has brought about significant changes since then, but this minority group remains the object of callous discrimination even today.

After Japan's defeat in World War II, the National Levelers' Association (founded in 1922) resumed its activities, and the National Committee for Buraku Liberation was formed in Kyoto, February 19–20, 1946. The Association in 1955 changed its name to Buraku Liberation League. There are reportedly 4,594 discriminated-against areas with a total population of 1,163,372; but these figures (1985 report) are incomplete and reflect the complexity of the problem.

For the year 1982 the Ministry of Justice officially recorded discriminatory incidents in the following areas of life: marriage, 196; employment, 174; neighborhood and other social settings, 50; spoken remarks, 543; graffiti, 189; letters, 80; other kinds, 86 — a total of 1,318 incidents. Another major issue, noted primarily in Buddhist organizations, is that of assigning discriminatory posthumous names. The number of grave markers with such names has reached 2,254. This practice not only extends cruelty to Buraku people into the afterlife; it also exacerbates bigotry in this life. The Buraku Liberation League stands at the helm of current activities aimed at eliminating all forms of discrimination.

One major activity is the struggle to overcome the "Discriminatory Sayama Trial." On May 1, 1963, a high school girl in Sayama City near Tokyo was kidnapped and murdered. To restore waning respect for police authority, Ishikawa Kazuo (24), from a Buraku area, was arrested, forced to make a confession, tried and sentenced to life imprisonment. However, Ishikawa's persistent claims of innocence, citizens' campaigns for a fair trial, school boy-

---

[1] Tokugawa society had four formal classes: samurai, farmers, artisans, and merchants (in descending order). Strictly speaking, the Buraku group was "outside and below" this hierarchy of classes. There were others "outside" but not "below," such as Buddhist and Shinto priests, Confucian scholars, and "above all," the imperial household. — Ed.

cott protests by 100,000 Buraku area children, countless resolutions by town and city councils, protests by academicians and opinion leaders, and other efforts to deal with the notorious "Sayama Incident" have coalesced into a major struggle that continues to this day.

The infamous "comprehensive Buraku lists" of the addresses of Buraku area persons—purchased by some two hundred business firms and universities—is another key issue. The lists are closely connected with depriving Buraku persons of chances for employment, advancement, and marriage.

The Buraku Liberation League has vigorously pressured national government agencies to institute legal guarantees that would eliminate the root causes of discrimination. As a result, the Japanese government in August 1965 formed the Integration Policy Deliberation Committee within the Prime Ministers' Office. Later that year, this committee issued a report that stated: "Resolution of the integration problem is a national responsibility and also an issue that concerns all citizens." Since 1969 new special laws and integration programs have made available to Buraku people large sums of money, and the Buraku liberation movement has made some significant progress.

The Japanese Government, however, has no intention of enacting permanent legislation for Buraku liberation, and only two years remain until the last of the special laws expires. The Buraku Liberation League since 1985 has therefore called on government, labor unions, religious groups, and others to work for the passage of the proposed "Fundamental Law for Buraku Liberation," a goal not yet realized. This struggle is supported by efforts to develop international solidarity in the antidiscrimination movement.

From Self-criticism to Social Action

A voluntary group of Christians had formed the Consultation of Christians for Buraku Liberation back in 1962—a decade before the NCCJ conference of 1972 signalled church involvement. It was in the mid-1970s, however, that the churches really became aware of the Buraku problem. A discriminatory remark by the pastor of an Osaka church in 1974 became the occasion in May 1975 for the Buraku Liberation League to confront the Japanese Christian community with details of its discriminatory nature. In August of that year, the United Church of Christ in Japan (UCCJ) formed its Special Committee on the Problem of Buraku Discrimination. Similar initiatives were taken by the National Christian Council in Japan (1977), the Nippon Sei Kō Kai (1979), the Japan Baptist Convention (1981), and the Catholic Justice and Peace Council. The Buraku Liberation Center established in Osaka by the UCCJ in 1981, with a full-time director, represented a major commitment to the issue.

Efforts by the Christian churches to deal with the problem of Buraku discrimination were triggered by discriminatory incidents within the Christian community itself, particularly spoken remarks and written statements. Some lay in the past, such as comments by Kagawa Toyohiko (1888–1960) in his 654-page book *Hinmin shinri no kenkyū* (A study of the psychology of the poor).[2] Others are more recent, such as the statement by a senior Christian scholar — "No doubt I would hesitate to have my daughter marry someone from a Buraku community." First these errors were brought to light, and efforts at redress were made. The Sayama Trial struggle and support for the proposed Buraku Liberation Law came later. Then came expanded activities such as research seminars, study meetings, and newsletters to encourage broader participation in the Buraku liberation movement.

In 1983 the NCCJ Buraku Discrimination Committee published *Ibara no kanmuri* (Crown of thorns) as an integration-education text for junior and senior high school students. The UCCJ Buraku Liberation Center has continuing contacts with the World Council of Churches's Programme to Combat Racism and with India's Dalit liberation movement against caste discrimination. Through these contacts, it seeks to develop a Buraku liberation movement within the wider context of struggles against discrimination throughout the world.

THE AINU

Identity and the Right to Exist

"Ainu" means "people" — it is what they call themselves. Among the various ethnic groups inhabiting the Japanese islands, the Ainu are the most ancient. They call the land they live on "Ainu Moshiri"; the term "Hokkaido"[3] was applied to that land in 1869 by the Meiji Government. Ainu Moshiri became Japanese territory just 120 years ago when "assimilation policies" were instituted. In 1871 the Meiji government promulgated a Family Registration Law requiring the Ainu to forfeit their native names and adopt Japanese-style names. Officially referred to as "former aborigines," the Ainu were incorporated into the family register system.

Discrimination toward the Ainu people, however, did not disappear. It was strengthened. Besides names and language, the Ainu's manners, customs, and lifestyle — all deeply connected with their religious faith — were also

[2] A good recent biography of Kagawa is Robert Schildgen's *Toyohiko Kagawa: Apostle of Love and Social Justice* (Berkeley, California: Centenary Books, 1988). — Ed.

[3] Hokkaido, the now anglicized form of Hokkaidō, means "north sea circuit," signifying — by the suffix *dō* (road, route, circuit) — a northern island territory under central government control. — Ed.

suppressed. Japanese colonists occupied the good lands, yet forbade the Ainu to fish in the rivers and hunt in the mountains. The sudden influx of settlers and the diseases they brought destroyed the Ainu basis of livelihood, reducing them to severe poverty.

According to the 1986 Utari [Compatriot] Livelihood Survey, 24,380 Ainu were living in Hokkaido, among whom the ratio of welfare recipients was six times the national average. The Ainu high-school matriculation rate was 78.4 percent (national average, 94.2 percent); the college matriculation rate, 8.1 percent (national average, 30.2 percent). Speaking of poverty in her childhood, one Ainu said, "I never had a lunch to take to school." On the present situation, she commented: "Besides low matriculation rates, even those who do advance to the next educational level usually dropout due to the pressure of discrimination."

Under Japanese occupation and education policies, the Ainu were indoctrinated in the imperial ideology — the same as that used to embue the Japanese populace with prejudice toward the Ainu people. Some still deeply rooted prejudices are: "the Ainu are hairy," "they have no concept of numbers" and ". . . no understanding of hygiene", "the Ainu are a vanishing ethnic group," and (from a dean of Hokkaido University's economics department) "it is permissible to eliminate the Ainu people because they are not needed in Hokkaido's economic development."

The opportunity for the Ainu people to preserve their ethnic identity and to undertake activities in the political (land rights) and cultural (human rights) areas came with Japan's defeat in 1945. On February 24, 1946, Ainu compatriots gathered in Shizunai town and established the Hokkaido Ainu Association, a legally incorporated body, which was reorganized and renamed the Hokkaido Utari Association in 1961.

One of the events marking the centennial anniversary of Hokkaido's colonization was the publication of *Ainu minzoku shi* (Annals of the Ainu), which repeated the "vanishing ethnic group" bias. Because photographs of Chikappu Mieko were used in the book without permission, she filed suit in May 1985 for infringement of portrait rights. Her purpose in the lawsuit was to protect her ethnic dignity and to sound a strong "No!" against the idea that assimilation had been completed. On September 20, 1988, she won a de facto victory in the form of a court-ordered compromise.

Prior to 1983, 1,004 Ainu skeletons had been "collected" by Hokkaido University's medical department for use as research specimens. Many of them were obtained by trickery and grave robbery. Discussions between the Hokkaido Utari Association and the University of Hokkaido over return of the skeletons reached a settlement in 1983, and some have been returned. A crypt for them was built in 1984.

Since May 1984 the Utari Association has campaigned for passage of the proposed "Ainu shinpō" (New Ainu Law) to guarantee Ainu rights. The new law would protect and promote Ainu culture and education. In 1989, compulsory expropriation of land for the Nibutani Dam (in the Nibutani section of Hiratori township) precipitated an Ainu movement claiming rights to that land and seeking its return. The movement stemmed from the understanding that "the land problem basically determines the people's right to exist."

The Practice of Repentance

Christian concern for Ainu issues was transformed into action in the 1980s. The process began in 1980 with the UCCJ Hokkai District's invitation to Tokuhei Narita (then managing director of the Hokkaido Utari Association) to give a lecture at its All-Hokkaido Pastors Seminar so that the ministers could learn directly about the Ainu issue. In 1981, Christian churches helped to send Ainu representatives to the International Conference on Land and Peoples held in Indonesia by the Christian Conference of Asia's Urban Rural Mission (CCA-URM), and to the General Assembly of the World Council of Indigenous Peoples held in Australia. The NCCJ has since developed contacts with Ainu in the Kantō Utari Association and similar groups in Tokyo.

In 1985 the UCCJ Hokkai District, in repentance for its past violations of Ainu rights, sought forgiveness from both God and neighbor. It also established a Committee on the Ainu People to support the restoration of Ainu rights and to promote the district's own active involvement. Christian churches have given support to such causes as Chikappu Mieko's portrait rights' lawsuit, the New Ainu Law, and resistance to expropriation of Ainu land in Nibutani. To help educate church members about the issues, UCCJ Hokkai District's Committee on the Ainu People produced a year-long series of articles called "The Ainu People and Japanese History," which appeared in the church school teachers' magazine *Kyōshi no tomo* (Teacher's friend), from the April 1989 issue.

To promote education for persons of Ainu background, develop leaders, and encourage contacts between minorities, the Ainu Scholarship Committee was established in 1988. Committee members are from the NCCJ International Solidarity Committee, the NCCJ Women's Committee, the Association of Discriminated-Against Minorities, the Nippon Sei Kō Kai, and UCCJ Hokkai District's Committee on the Ainu People. In addition to continued scholarship grants, the committee will encourage Christian schools to enroll Ainu children.

RESIDENT-KOREANS

Fighting Institutionalized Discrimination

From the Japanese annexation of Korea in 1910 until Japan's defeat in 1945, Korea was a Japanese colony. Owing to loss of land under Japan's colonial policies, emigration due to labor recruitment, forcible labor conscription, and other factors, many Koreans had no choice but to move to Japan. By 1945, about 2.3 million Koreans were living in Japan. Many returned to their homeland after World War II, but some 600,000 remained in Japan. The approximately 680,000 Koreans living in Japan today[4] are those persons and their descendants (the latter are now the majority). According to 1987 statistics, resident-Koreans accounted for 76.2 percent of all foreigners registered in Japan.

The discrimination faced by Koreans in Japanese society can be broadly divided into two categories. One is institutionalized discrimination, best symbolized by the Alien Registration Law (ARL). On May 2, 1947, the day before Japan's democratic constitution went into effect, this law was issued as the emperor's final imperial ordinance under the old constitution. In 1952, as the Allied Occupation of Japan came to an end, the ARL was revised and fingerprinting was made mandatory. Ethnic schools and ethnic education in Japanese schools were banned by a 1965 notification from the Ministry of Education. Moreover, nearly all local governments have a nationality clause that excludes non-Japanese from teaching positions in public schools.

Discriminatory practices in society at large — in employment, school admission, private housing, and many other areas — are widespread. It is well known that a minority group member who graduates from a prestigious school, even with an excellent academic record, need not bother to apply for a civil service position. The same person will also be shut out of large- and middle-size companies. It is, of course, the prejudicial attitudes of the Japanese majority that support legal and social discrimination. Stereotypes that Koreans are "unclean," "cunning," "servile," "violent," and "have a low level of culture" are passed from generation to generation.

With the advent of the 1970s, second-generation Koreans who were born and educated in Japan, took a central role in opposing various kinds of discrimination. This grass-roots effort by Koreans themselves to secure their human rights grew into a large movement through solidarity with concerned Japanese. The movement had its beginnings in opposition to revision of the immigration and emigration laws around 1970, and also in the successful

---

[4] Resident-Koreans are generally divided by pro-North Korea and pro-South Korea orientations.

legal struggle to reverse the decision of the Hitachi company that had hired Park Jong-suk (he had used a Japanese name to apply), discovered his Korean identity, and then fired him. In 1974 actions to end discrimination in public housing admission policies in Kanagawa, Osaka, Hyogo, Kyoto and other prefectures with large resident-Korean populations quickly won an end to those policies. Further forms of discrimination have surfaced — in admissions at Otemae Women's Junior College (1974), in employment at the Nihon Telephone and Telegraph Corporation (1977), in private housing in the Ikuno district of Osaka (1977), and others — and have been eliminated.

The International Covenants on Human Rights were ratified in 1979, and equal access to public housing was assured. In 1981 the Convention on Refugees was ratified. These led, in 1982, to the inclusion of resident-Koreans in most social security benefits from which they had been excluded by nationality clauses. Within a few years after the September 1980 fingerprinting refusal by Han Jong-suk of Tokyo, demands for a complete revision of the Alien Registration Law developed into a nationwide decade-long struggle to assure basic human rights for foreigners with permanent resident status.

During that period, approximately 18,000 persons refused or postponed the fingerprinting required under the Alien Registration Law. Resolutions demanding basic changes in the law and its fingerprinting requirement have been passed by 1,083 city councils; 8 million signatures in favor of these changes have been collected; and 50 court cases have been fought over the basic unfairness of fingerprinting and the ARL.

Another issue demanding attention, both inside Japan and as a diplomatic matter between South Korea and Japan, is the status of third-generation resident-South Koreans under the 1965 Japan–ROK normalization treaty. Further issues to be faced in the future include institutional guarantees for ethnic education, stable legal status, elimination of the nationality clauses that block equal employment opportunities at the municipal government level, compensation for postwar losses, and efforts to reconcile the divided pro-South Korea and pro-North Korea communities in Japan.

Source and Center of Solidarity

The Korean Christian Church in Japan (KCCJ) is crucial to any consideration of the wider Christian involvement in resident-Korean issues. The early 1970s campaign against adverse changes in the Immigration and Emigration Control Law[5] began with a KCCJ resolution and appeal, then developed into a major churchwide movement.

The International Christian Solidarity Committee, formed with several

---

[5] This is the basic law; the ARL is its instrument of control. — Ed.

thousand persons at its founding rally in the Kansai, played a major role in later Christian involvement in resident-Korean issues. The international network developed by Christians to support Park Jong-suk's legal struggle against Hitachi spawned a boycott of Hitachi products by Christians in the United States and other countries, and this had strong repercussions in Japanese society. In 1971 the KCCJ planned its Korean Christian Center (opened in 1983) in Osaka's district where the largest concentration of Koreans live. Then, in 1974, the KCCJ Research and Action Institute for Koreans In Japan (RAIK) was founded in Tokyo. The KCCJ and RAIK have played leading roles in the movement to secure basic human rights for Koreans living in Japan.

Entering the 1980s, the movement to abolish two requirements of the Alien Registration Law — fingerprinting and possession of one's registration certificate at all times — gained nationwide ecumenical support and was able to put its case forcefully to Japanese society. This support first solidified regionally in the Kansai Christian Liaison Committee on the ARL Problem, formed in November 1984, and the Kansai Council of Representatives Concerned with the ARL Issue, formed in May 1985, and then nationally in the NCCJ Committee on the ARL Issue in 1987. This organization served as the nucleus for Christian involvement in demands for a basic revision of the Alien Registration Law and other issues related to resident-Koreans's legal status. International meetings to promote global solidarity were sponsored by Christian groups in 1985 and 1990.

OKINAWA

Sacrificial Settlements

For the past four centuries, the history of Okinawa has been one of discrimination and plunder. The former Kingdom of the Ryukyus, which includes the island of Okinawa, enjoyed great prosperity to the end of the 1500s through trade with China and other countries to the south. In 1609, the samurai warlords of Kyushu's Shimazu clan invaded the Ryukyu Islands to expand its own territory and take over Okinawa's profitable trade with China. With this, the merciless plunder and demeaning of Okinawa had begun.

In 1879 the Ryukyu Islands became Okinawa Prefecture under the Meiji government's policy of abolishing clans and converting feudal domains into prefectures through military force. This is called the "First Ryukyu Settlement." For the Okinawans it was merely a Meiji continuation of samurai-style discrimination and pillage. The Meiji imperialist policies of military expansion imposed many kinds of sacrifice on the Okinawan people. Not until 1909, some twenty years later than in the other prefectures, did the people of Okinawa acquire the rights and duties of political participation through election of a prefectural assembly. Eleven more years passed before full political rights, as enjoyed in Japan proper, were finally extended to Okinawa in 1920.

In 1940 Okinawa's rich cultural traditions came under attack, beginning with elimination of the Okinawan dialect — precisely the same tactic used in Hokkaido, Taiwan, and Korea to convert colonized peoples into loyal subjects of the emperor. Late in World War II over 100,000 Okinawans died when their prefecture was used as a shield for the Japanese mainland. By sacrificing Okinawa and turning it over to American domination, Japan gained freedom for the main islands when the San Francisco Peace Treaty took effect on April 28, 1952. This was the "Second Ryukyu Settlement." In unilaterally giving Okinawa over to foreign rule, the basic human rights and freedom of the Okinawans were callously ignored.

The US military appropriated 22 percent of the land on Okinawa's main island, creating a situation often summed up as: "Military bases do not exist in Okinawa; Okinawa exists in the midst of military bases." Although Okinawa reverted to Japan[6] on May 15, 1972, the American bases still lie at the root of human rights problems in Okinawa. Reversion was the "Third Ryukyu Settlement," another one forcibly implemented from the top without due consideration of the Okinawan people's wishes.

Okinawa's population is about 1.4 million. Another estimated 150,000 Okinawans live in the Kyoto–Osaka–Kobe region, of whom about 40,000 are concentrated in Osaka's Taishō ward — the result of a large migration over the last fifty to sixty years. Okinawans with financial means have tended to congregate in Tokyo, while those in the Kansai area generally have come as migrant laborers, singly or through group recruitment. Okinawans in Taishō ward have formed the "Gajumaru Club" (named for a strong Okinawan tree that stays green year-round). In 1974, a youth committed suicide out of despair induced by repeated incidents of employment discrimination. This death shocked Okinawan young people in mainland Japan, and it was the impetus for the Gajumaru Club.

Second-generation residents on the mainland face the loss of their language, culture, and customs due to Japan's assimilation policies. Discrimination and prejudice continue in such areas as marriage, employment, and housing. In Okinawa itself, movements are now underway to buy back land gobbled up by mainland Japanese capital and to oppose American military

[6] Technically Okinawa had remained Japanese territory under US administration; in 1972 it reverted to Japanese administration. — Ed.

use of land for the twenty years since reversion. Widely viewed as the primary regional bastion of opposition to the emperor system, Okinawa mounted a vigorous struggle to prevent the emperor's attendance at a national athletic meet held in Okinawa in 1987. Mass "human chain" rallies to encircle the U.S. air base at Kadena were held in June of 1987 and 1990.

Reassessment for Reconciliation

On February 25, 1969, the United Church of Christ in Okinawa and the United Church of Christ in Japan merged in a new union. Seminars were held in 1970 and 1971 to study continuing problems faced in Okinawa, and during preparations for the third seminar to be held in 1972 (the year of reversion), a major question was raised, primarily by young people, that caused the seminar to be cancelled. They asked: "Are the churches, pastors, and lay persons in Okinawa and on the main islands really concerned about the political and social problems clearly visible in Okinawa, and are they involved as if these were their own problems? . . . It seems, rather, that the merger — much like the Japanese and American agreement on 'reversion'—aims at justifying rather than rectifying the oppression we Okinawans suffer daily because of the military bases."

In response, the UCCJ Social Concerns Committee proposed in 1977 that the union of the two churches be reassessed. A bill to encourage this was debated from the Twentieth through the Twenty-second UCCJ general assemblies (1978–82). At the Twenty-third General Assembly in 1984, it was agreed to explore this issue as part of the church's overall mission, and a special committee was formed for that purpose.

Union required no structural changes of the Japan denomination; the Okinawa denomination made all the necessary adjustments. The merger was, in reality, an absorption of the Okinawan church by its Japanese partner — a key point in the reassessment process. To become a true union, a number of readjustments must be made. Areas already under consideration include the union's confession of faith, approved history, anniversary date, and official name.

Reassessing the union of the two bodies is more than an internal issue; it also involves reassessing the broader relationship between Okinawa and mainland Japan. And that, in turn, exposes the attitudes and predispositions of Japanese churches toward Okinawa. The deeper meaning of the process lies in dealing honestly with the mainland churches' part in the discrimination historically forced on Okinawa so that the union can move on to a reconciled relationship and a redemptive future.

MISSIONAL CONTEXT FOR THE FUTURE

Each of the four minorities treated above has a different history, different strengths and weaknesses, and a different contemporary situation. They also have much in common because they all suffer unfair treatment, denial of human dignity, and human rights violations. The structural discrimination inherent in Japanese society excludes these minorities from the mainstream of society, allowing them only a marginalized existence.

For years this situation has been excused with "let sleeping dogs lie" and "given time, discrimination will disappear naturally." Yet, closer examination of structural discrimination makes it clear that without carrying out social changes designed to eliminate those structures, the restoration to full humanity of both the discriminator and the discriminated-against cannot be achieved. This is the unmistakable lesson of the antidiscrimination struggles of recent decades.

Even so, the structures by which the majority suppresses the minorities in Japanese society remain firmly rooted. The myth of the Japanese as "a racially pure ethnic group" continues to flourish. The series of derogatory remarks coming from public leaders, beginning with that by former prime minister Nakasone Yasuhiro in 1986, show just how low ethnic awareness is in Japanese society. Public education that transmutes the popular notion of "Japan has no minorities" into a sanctioned stereotype is still standard. A society that does not take care of its minorities is, in fact, a sick society. A healthy Japanese society would accept the minorities in its midst, assure their equality, and promote an atmosphere in which all can live together.

The past twenty years of Christian ecumenical involvement with minorities has been an unparalleled experience in this country, one that is now having a positive effect on the church's calling, its mission, and its understanding of the gospel. Of particular importance is the focus on developing a broader understanding of living in equality, and then rooting that understanding firmly in the church. From this comes the challenge for the church to confront the value system of Japanese society. Indeed, this challenge helps shape the fundamental context for the mission of the church in Japanese society. Finally, for the effective and sustained pursuit of this mission, it is essential to recruit, train, and support persons who are committed to carrying out its tasks.

12

Asian Migrant Workers

Matsuda Mizuho

THE FOREIGN MIGRANT WORKER is a pawn on the international chessboard of labor supply and demand; in Japan, the migrant worker is also subject to strict state control. The economic disparity between Japan and the rest of Asia induces a large exodus of laborers from the poor nations. Japan's labor shortage, particularly of unskilled labor, serves as a powerful incentive for receiving them. Unscrupulous labor brokers capitalize on the disparity with little concern for injury and insult to the migrant worker.

Japan has consistently refused to grant working-visa status to unskilled laborers. Except for Korean conscripts forcibly brought to Japan before and during World War II and postwar Korean stowaways seeking work, there were few foreign laborers in Japan until the 1970s. In the late seventies, however, an influx of Asian women migrants began. The immigration bureau's current estimate (1990) is 100,000 migrants, both men and women, overstaying their visas and illegally working in Japan. Migrant support groups put the estimate at over 200,000. Recent reports and declarations by local government agencies and various support groups speak of the need to "live together." The fact that persons of different cultures, religions, languages, and races are rapidly increasing in Japan makes the search for ways of living together an urgent priority.

Statements such as "Whether we boil or fry them before eating them is entirely at our discretion," made in reference to resident foreigners by a Justice Ministry bureaucrat, raise serious questions. Has there been no change in Japan's traditional attitude of controlling foreigners? Are institutional xenophobia and social discrimination against foreigners still strong? Working with women migrant workers (as the present writer does) reveals that Japan's system of controlling foreigners—using them when convenient and forcibly deporting them when no longer needed—has not changed essentially since World War II.

In Japan, nationality legitimizes discrimination. Even the Constitution's provisions for basic rights are viewed as being for "all nationals" (i.e., the Japanese). Guarantees of basic human rights tend to be narrowly interpreted as applying only to Japanese. Only after concerned citizens took specific actions were the basic rights of access to medical care and welfare services granted to infirm or indigent foreigners. Parochial interpretations of the Constitution and narrow application of worker's compensation benefits are but two indications that government agencies function not to prevent but to preserve discrimination against foreign laborers. Official policies for excluding different people are buttressed by a social mentality that demands assimilation and conformity.

The issue of Asian migrant workers is inextricably bound to the unresolved issues of prewar Korean conscripts and the legal status of their descendants—the largest group of foreigners living in Japan. Controlled and manipulated to suit the interests of the Japanese state and people, the right of these foreign laborers to their own way of life is thwarted by pressures to assimilate and "Japanize."

STATISTICS AND TRENDS

The newly revised Immigration Control Act and Law in Recognition of Refugee Status went into effect June 1, 1990. It includes penalties for employers of illegal foreign workers and provisions for issuing work certificates to qualified legal workers. It gives the Justice Minister expanded discretionary powers to determine eligibility and length of stay for certain visa categories. As before revision, however, there are no provisions for granting visa status to unskilled laborers.In early April 1990, in anticipation of the revised law, large numbers of undocumented workers began appearing at immigration offices, volunteering themselves for deportation to avoid feared penalties. They were acting on a misunderstanding based on a mistranslation in an English-language newspaper (which the immigration authorities were unusually slow in correcting). The new penalties, it turned out, apply to the employers and labor brokers. But some 20,000 Asian and African workers, mostly men, had already left Japan.

Since work visas are not issued to unskilled migrant laborers, it is estimated that from 100,000 to 200,000 migrants are currently overstaying their tourist, student, or cultural visas. With no legal status, few dare complain to authorities about untreated job-related injuries, unpaid wages, or forced prostitution. They know that instead of receiving help in recovering their rights, they are more likely to be deported. Their vulnerability leads them to go into hiding, thereby exposing themselves to further exploitation and abuse. This makes it difficult to determine the actual numbers involved and the extent of the problem.

From around 1970, Japanese began traveling overseas in great numbers. Statistics for 1970 show that foreigners entering Japan outnumbered Japanese going abroad by 775,061 to 663,467. This flow was reversed the following year, and the ratio has continued to widen: 1989 figures show that 2,985,764 foreigners entered Japan (23.7 percent increase over 1988), while an astounding 9,662,752 Japanese travelled abroad (14.7 percent increase over the previous year). Among foreign entrants, men outnumbered women (1,816,061 to 1,169,703), except in the 15–24 age range, where women numerically exceeded men (194,929 to 123,419).

Of those entering Japan in 1989, 1,791,652 (60 percent) came from other Asian countries, a 29.2 percent increase over the previous year. The increase in Korean and Taiwanese entrants was particularly striking. Holders of visas as tourists, language school teachers, and trainees increased, while those with language student or entertainer visas decreased.

Running Afoul of the Law

It is difficult to grasp accurately the state of Asian migrant workers in Japan because of their shadowy existence, but annual statistics on violations of immigration law may indicate trends. In 1970, there were 1,651 prosecutions of immigration law violations. Illegal entry was the major cause for deportation, and 74.2 percent of these involved Korean stowaways. From 1970 to 1974, only 320 cases of working visa violations were prosecuted, and subsequent annual cases hovered around 250. During the 1970s, 80 percent of the prosecutions involved women. Taiwanese women were most numerous, followed by women from Chile, the Philippines, the USA, and Columbia.

In 1979 there was a dramatic increase to 667 cases due to relaxation of foreign travel restrictions in Taiwan. Taiwanese women entering Japan with tourist visas and working as hostesses in bars and cabarets accounted for 80 percent of the prosecuted violations.

At the same time, there was a proliferation of recruiters and promotion syndicates throughout Asia, luring women with job promises and sending them to Japan under tourist guise, then reaping profits by turning them over to labor-short employers. Such trafficking in women became increasingly well organized, providing passports and visas (sometimes forged) and cut-rate airline tickets, and dispersing points of entry into Japan away from the larger cities. Of the above 667 cases, 658 (98.7 percent) were women on tourist visas, and 70 percent worked in the entertainment/sex industry. Japanese gangsters are thought to have been involved in 43 percent of these violations.

Asian migrant workers continued to arrive in ever-increasing numbers during the 1980s, and prosecuted cases of men migrants outnumbered women in 1988 for the first time. (Table 12.1) Several factors account for this: attraction of Japan's strong yen; economic slump in the Middle East, usually a prime source of jobs for male workers; declining employment opportunities in migrants' native countries; and labor shortages in certain medium and small businesses and industries in Japan.

TABLE 12.1

IMMIGRATION LAW VIOLATORS BY GENDER

Gender	1984	1985	1986	1987	1988	1989
Violations total	6,380	7,653	10,573	14,129	17,854	22,626
Male	1,213	1,644	3,325	5,636	10,725	15,201
Female	5,617	6,009	7,248	8,493	7,129	7,425
Percentage:						
Male	17.8	21.5	31.4	39.9	60.1	67.2
Female	82.2	78.5	68.6	60.1	39.9	32.8
Numerical increase over previous year:						
Male	111	431	1,681	2,311	5,089	4,476
Female	1,951	392	1,239	1,245	-1,364	296
Percentage increase over previous year:						
Male	10.1	35.5	102.3	69.5	90.3	41.7
Female	53.2	7.0	20.6	17.2	-16.1	4.2

Source: Ministry of Justice, Immigration Control Bureau: 1989 Exit/ Entry Statistics on Foreigners and Japanese (*Heisei gannenchū ni okeru gaikokujin oyobi Nihonjin no shutsu-nyūkokusha tōkei ni tsuite*). 1990.

Even though men now outnumber women in terms of violations, the number of women entering Japan still rises annually, albeit at a slower rate. In fact, undetected women overstaying their visas probably still outnumber men in that category. Besides factors already mentioned, two others are at work: transnational brokers and promoter rings trafficking in women are usually better organized than those dealing with men; and women with no skills or education can readily find work in Japan's entertainment/sex industry.

Statistics released by the Justice Ministry in April 1990 indicate that there were 22,626 deportees in 1989, a 26.6 percent increase over 1988. Of these, 15,912 were working in violation of visa terms while also overstaying their visas, with another 696 working in violation of visa terms while their visas were still vaild. (Table 12.2)

By nationality, Filipinos were the most numerous at 3,740, though this was a decrease of 1,600 from 1988, owing probably to stricter scrutiny of

TABLE 12.2

FOREIGNERS' VISA VIOLATIONS BY YEAR

Offense	1984	1985	1986	1987	1988	1989
Illegal entry	513	460	597	542	616	2,349
Illegal landing	100	123	124	134	149	258
Overstay of visa term	5,569	6,592	9,215	12,792	15,970	19,105
(and working illegally)	4,426	5,411	7,782	10,935	13,475	15,912
Working illegally	357	218	349	372	839	696
Violations of penalties	291	260	288	289	280	218
Totals	6,830	7,653	10,573	14,129	17,854	22,626

N.B. Numbers represent persons apprehended by Immigration authorities

Source: Ministry of Justice, Immigration Control Bureau: 1989 Exit/ Entry Statistics on Foreigners and Japanese (*Heisei gannenchū ni okeru gaikokujin oyobi Nihonjin no shutsu-nyūkokusha tōkei ni tsuite*). 1990.

applications for entertainer visas from July 1988. Seven countries—the Philippines, Pakistan, South Korea, Bangladesh, Malaysia, Thailand, and China—accounted for 96 percent of the total number of undocumented workers deported in 1989. (Table 12.3) The number of nationalities, however, rose to 39, another increase over the 1988 level.

By occupation, construction and factory workers accounted for 87 percent of the men deportees, while 67 percent of the deported women had worked as hostesses in bars and clubs. (Table 12.4)

Work localities for men have expanded beyond the earlier concentration in the greater Tokyo metropolitan area. Dispersion had already become the pattern for women, but significant regional variations in women's relative concentrations by nationality point to distinct broker and promotion networks based in different countries. Both trends confirm that migrant labor-trafficking organizations are spreading throughout Japan.

TABLE 12.3

DEPORTED UNDOCUMENTED WORKERS BY NATIONALITY

Philippines	3,740	Malaysia	1,865
Pakistan	3,170	Thailand	1,144
Bangladesh	2,277	China	588
South Korea	3,129	Other	695

Source: Ministry of Justice, Immigration Control Bureau: 1989 Exit/Entry Statistics on Foreigners and Japanese (*Heisei gannenchū ni okeru gaikokujin oyobi Nihonjin no shutsu-nyūkokusha tōkei ni tsuite*). 1990.

TABLE 12.4

UNDOCUMENTED MIGRANTS WORKERS BY OCCUPATION

Male			*Female*
Construction	5,581	Hostess	3,225
Factory worker	5,581	Factory worker	323
Odd jobs	575	Odd jobs	276
Store clerk	227	Prostitute	178
Other	712	Housekeeper	156
		Stripper	156
		Store clerk	138
		Other	365

Source: Ministry of Justice, Immigration Control Bureau: 1989 Exit/Entry Statistics on Foreigners and Japanese (*Heisei gannenchū ni okeru gaikokujin oyobi Nihonjin no shutsu-nyūkokusha tōkei ni tsuite*). 1990.

Language Students and Industrial Trainees

In addition to migrants who enter as tourists and overstay their visas in order to work, recent years witness to the problems of legitimate visa holders who come to work, or are forced to work, under difficult conditions. Especially noticable is the rising influx of a de facto labor force under the guise of Japanese language school students and industrial trainees.

In 1988 there were more than 35,000 students working while attending Japanese language schools. (Most of the language schools are privately operated and may be opened without a license; current moves are being made toward self-regulation and government licensing.) In 1989, this number declined by 48.2 percent to 18,183, due in part to new and stricter guidelines for issuing such visas. Students need a legal guarantor to enroll, and often the guarantor is the migrant's employer. By law, such students are allowed to work twenty hours a week; but frequently language study is only a facade, and students are obliged to work long hours at low wages. Since 1987, when obtaining an entertainer visa became more difficult, the number of Filipino women applying to language schools has burgeoned, with bar and cabaret proprietors as their guarantors.

The number of foreign workers entering legally as industrial trainees has also risen. In 1987 there were 17,000, and by 1989 that number had grown to 29,489. While de facto labor is required as "practice," trainees need not be paid for their work—they are trainees, not laborers. This is an example of flagrant legalized exploitation and oppression. This trend of meeting domestic labor shortages by bringing in low-wage foreign workers with legitimate visas will probably expand in the foreseeable future, with educational institutions and corporations serving as recruiters.

Since the revised immigration controls have gone into effect, a new development known as the "Fujimori Phenomenon" has become conspicuous. Named after Peru's President Alberto Fujimori, who is of Japanese ancestry, second- and third-generation Japanese emigrants are used as workers to cover labor shortages in Japan. Such programs unmask a bias to favor workers of Japanese descent over other foreigners. Furthering Japanese ethnocentrism and racism, such a predilection does not contribute toward building respect for other peoples and cultures so that we may all "live together."

To summarize, Asian migrant workers were initially, and largely, women working in the entertainment/sex industry, but this narrow limit no longer applies. Today, both legal and illegal foreign migrant workers are filling a significant need in Japan's labor market and economic system. Futhermore, as they are absorbed in ever-increasing numbers into the lower reaches of Japanese society, they become a pervasive, if almost invisible, part of the social fabric.

CONTROL OF FOREIGN WORKERS

Two points sum up Japan's postwar immigration policy regarding foreign workers: denial of long-term residency, and denial of entry to unskilled laborers.

The Emigration and Immigration Control Law of 1951 not only disregarded basic civil rights but also gave broad discretionary powers to the Minister of Justice. Moreover, its actual implementation was routinely governed by shifting political and foreign policy considerations. For almost twenty years, the movements of all foreigners in Japan were governed by this law, but resident Koreans were its main targets.

As a result of Japan's thirty-five-year colonial rule of Korea, approximately 600,000 Koreans remained in Japan after World War II. Forced to take Japanese nationality during this period, the Koreans had been allowed only minimal participation in Japanese politics. When Japan regained its independence under the San Francisco Peace Treaty on April 28, 1952, Koreans were divested of their Japanese nationality by the Ministry of Justice.

Denied the right to choose nationality, they were thenceforth treated as foreigners. Their residence status, no longer a legal right, became a bestowed favor. Koreans in Japan now faced such problems as the threat of forcible deportation, thus restricting political activity to protest; insecure resident status if fingerprinting regulations were not fully complied with; and a re-entry permit system unfairly limiting freedom to travel abroad. Various movements have since sought to rectify the vulnerable legal position of resident-Koreans, and some exceptions to strict enforcement of these regulations have been made. But the basic stance of offering only "Japanization" or possible deportation has not changed, and resident-Koreans remain the target of administrative scrutiny. (Cf. II-11)

The 1951 Emigration and Immigration Control Law was thoroughly revised in 1982, as was the Alien Registration Law requiring the fingerprinting of foreigners. Renamed the Immigration Control Act and Law in Recognition of Refugee Status, the revisions were prompted by Japan's 1979 ratification of the UN International Covenant on Civil and Political Rights, and from 1975 by the mass exodus of Indochinese in the aftermath of the Vietnam War. The revisions pertained to the legal status and civil rights guarantees of foreigners, standards for certifying refugees, and provision of social welfare services to foreigners. The new law was also designed to cope with increasing numbers of migrant workers arriving in the late seventies.

This immigration control law underwent yet another, more retrogressive revision in 1989 (effective from June 1, 1990). Its principal points are: (a) greater differentiation of resident categories, from eighteen to twenty-eight, and further clarification of activity categories to include legal work, accounting, and job transfers within a company; (b) clarification of criteria for immigration investigation and simplifying procedures; and (c) strengthening of countermeasures to cope with problems of illegal workers.

However progressive the revisions may seem, the primary aim is to strengthen the regulation and control of increasing numbers of Asian migrant workers. Review of visa-issuing standards and short-term visa-waiver agreements with certain nations had already been reached even before the new revision. The new law strengthens punitive measures against undocumented workers by imposing penalties on their employers and job brokers. Furthermore, to prevent well-meaning employers from "mistakenly" hiring undocumented workers, the new law requires work qualification certificates. Clearly, shutting out unskilled foreign labor is the focus of these revisions.

By mid-July, barely a month after the new law had gone into effect, there was pressure from industry and business circles to ease the limitations on visa sponsors of industrial trainees so as to include small- and medium-sized firms. This indicates how strong the demand for unskilled labor is, and why the influx of migrants to meet this demand continues.

A significant crackdown on the 100,000 to 200,000 undocumented workers already working in Japan is a practical impossibility, and the new law makes no provision for any kind of amnesty. Because of the penalties, conscientious employers will stop hiring migrants, while unscrupulous employers will take advantage of the migrants' illegal status, making them vulnerable to further exploitation.

Since tightened immigration controls instill in migrant workers fear that they will be unable to reenter the country, many will opt to go underground and prolong their current stay, even under oppressive conditions. Fear of discovery and deportation will surely increase the incidence of improper medical care and inadequate or no compensation for work-related injuries. Denial of rights guaranteed under Japan's Labor Standards Law and of the basic right to social welfare services for foreign workers will also increase. It is no exaggeration to charge the government with promoting the violation of certain workers' basic human rights.

Japan's system of immigration control, including the new revised law, has consistently focused on rigorous law enforcement and exclusion of undesirables, while failing to safeguard human rights. It is essential to change this focus to one that will promote foreigners' rights. Reforms should include an impartial agency to hear appeals and take issue with administrative decisions regarding residence status, amnesty to migrants denied their basic rights, repeal of deportation regulations, and extension of reentry permits for long-term foreign residents.

So long as an overwhelming economic gap exists between Japan and other Asian nations, the pressure for Asian workers to seek work in Japan will continue. And so long as there is a serious shortage of young laborers in Japan, the pressure to use migrant laborers will persist. No official policy will keep them out. Current legislative actions ignore these basic realities, responding merely to immediate short-term interests. Hence, derivative problems develop and divert attention away from the basic issues.

THE PLIGHT OF ASIAN MIGRANT WORKERS

All foreigners must, within ninety days of arrival in Japan, register as aliens in the city or ward where they reside. When fingerprinted and issued an Alien Registration Card, they are eligible to apply for medical and other social welfare services. A foreigner with an appropriate visa and working for a corporation is covered under that corporation's group insurance plan. But the unskilled laborer, as an undocumented worker outside the alien registration system, is ineligible for basic medical care, though oftentimes most in need of it.

Migrant workers also face housing problems. Besides high rent, one must pay key money, an advance on the rent, and a gratuity. Many landlords refuse to rent to foreigners, especially Asians. Or they capitalize on rent difficulties; one Japanese landlord put two bunk beds in a small, dilapidated room and rented it to four Bangladeshi at an exorbitant rate. Many migrants, fearing discovery and expulsion, stay close to their workplaces and lodgings, and thus make few friends.

Male Migrant Conditions

Men migrant workers come mostly from Pakistan, Bangladesh, the Philippines, and Sri Lanka. They gravitate to sectors with notable labor shortages — construction, agriculture, and fisheries, or small foundries, print shops, and dry cleaning shops. (Table 12.4) Housing arrangements are about evenly divided between employer-provided quarters and apartment-sharing with compatriots. The wages are 80 percent to 90 percent of what a Japanese worker receives — unless, of course, a middleman or broker siphons off even more. In some cases they receive decent wages and food, though that scarcely alters the fact that migrant workers are used as cheap labor. Many men change jobs frequently in search of better employment conditions.

Some problems faced by male migrant workers stem from cultural and language differences. Among these are: (a) exploitation by middlemen; (b) expendable jobs at the bottom of the multi-tiered subcontracting system; (c) unclear terms of employment and working conditions; (d) nonpayment of wages; and (e) frequent work-related accidents and injuries. In many cases, the undocumented men have no means of redress for unjust treatment.

Female Migrant Conditions

The women tend to be Thai, Filipino, Korean, or Taiwanese, and the number of Latin American women is increasing. By comparison with her male counterpart, the migrant woman's situation is generally more confining; some are under constant surveillance. A small army of recruiters and brokers who traffic in women are active in both the women's home countries and Japan. Not infrequently their own compatriots marry Japanese men and become collaborators. Figures show that 80 percent to 90 percent of all women migrants, including those with legal visas, work in the entertainment/sex industry. (Table 12.4) This is a phenomenon unique to Japan among nations with large numbers of women migrant workers.

Specifically, many of the women work as hostesses, singers, or strippers in bars, cabarets, and nightclubs. Forced prostitution under many guises is often part of the job. Since the new (1990) immigration law imposes penalties on club and bar owners who employ undocumented workers, there has been a noticeable increase in the numbers of foreign women walking the streets near hotels in big-city entertainment districts.

The ever-expanding sex industry is sustained by Japanese business customs and by ordinary pampered men seeking diversion. Their self-indulgent mindset is reflected in Japanese society's permissive attitude towards prostitution and in the commercialization of sex rooted in the traditional discrimination against women. "Buying" a woman seems perfectly natural. Many migrant women tell of Japanese men who spot an Asian woman and straightaway ask, "How much?"

Certain violations of basic rights are common among employers of women migrants. These include confiscation of passports and return-trip tickets, nonpayment of monthly wages to inhibit escape, lump-sum wages paid at departure with excessive withholding of fines and broker fees, physical violence, and long work hours.

Wages, when paid, average only 50,000 yen monthly (US$300–$400). In many cases, women live in cramped quarters arranged by the employer and are kept under surveillance. A daily food allowance of between 500 yen and 1,000 yen is usually provided, half of which will pay for a bowl of hot noodles or a hamburger. There are cases where women in rural areas have been provided with rice and vegetables. From such meager food allowances and occasional tips, migrant women manage to send an average of 15,000 yen (US$100-plus) to their families back home. Such remittances may be possible for the first few months, but as the women become increasingly burdened by Japan's high prices, fines levied by employers, and loans for clothing and accessories, there is less money to send, and many are driven into prostitution.

Most women incur debts to recruiters back home for passports, visas, travel fares, and initial living expenses, and they arrive in Japan with little knowledge of their actual job or payment terms. Except for the legitimate entertainer visa, written contracts are rare and verbal agreements usually worthless. On arrival, they are literally sold to club owners. Thai women are especially vulnerable because of virtually no understanding of English or Japanese, and little experience outside the hill-tribe villages where most are recruited.

In many cases, an employer will demand work without pay until the purchase price has been covered. Debts calculated at two or three times the actual amount owed are not uncommon. To prevent escape, the women are intimidated by thugs and forced to take drugs that make control easier.

Deals among bosses are widespread. Women have been resold to another club or bar after a few months' work. Some are shuttled back and forth among many linked establishments. With little or no language ability, the women rarely know where the clubs are located, making it very difficult to seek redress for unpaid wages or acts of violence against them.

Even women with valid visas and written contracts are taken advantage of by employers who deduct fees for "working companions" (used for surveillance over the women) and who require additional work without compensation. Wages are often paid in US dollars based on exchange rates determined by the employer, which often results in further reduction of salary. If a woman is willing and able to spend a year or more in litigation to prove that the terms of her contract were broken by an employer, she may eventually receive compensation, but there are no guarantees. Practically speaking, it is virtually impossible to stay in Japan to pursue one's legal rights while being denied the right to work. In most cases, there is little choice but to compromise and accept the terms of the employer or broker.

Efforts at Organizing

In 1990 organizing efforts by undocumented men migrant workers from the Philippines, Bangladesh, and Pakistan began to take shape and have now reached the stage of determining rules and fees. Concerned people hope that cooperation between these men and support groups will yield improved conditions for workers now deprived of their rights.

The undocumented workers' rights to medical care and education are currently hampered by nationality restrictions and resident status requirements. To secure these rights, migrants who try to organize will need the cooperation of support groups in Japan and in their home countries.

Women migrant workers need to develop contacts among themselves and with support groups, but consciousness-raising and education for themselves must be the first priority. Then come efforts to inform and educate the Japanese public. Movements to change working conditions in general will be a key factor in freeing Asian migrant women from the need to work in the entertainment and sex industries.

Asian women migrants are presently objects of slave-like human trafficking made possible by the general toleration of prostitution in Japan. Laws concerning prostitution and the sex industry do not penalize customers, and the general attitude is that money can buy anything.

In the entertainment/sex industry, the women are not recognized as "laborers" with rights. In this sense, it is not the women but Japanese society that needs reforming. The issue is less one of personal morals than of structural exploitation of the weak by the strong, of the poor by the rich. Perhaps the key to transforming Japan's relationship with other Asian nations lies in just such a recognition.

CHRISTIAN RESPONSES

The early 1970s saw a marked surge in overseas tours by prosperous Japanese. Particularly noticeable were tours organized by companies for their male employees' recreation—a reward for performance—with prostitution included in the tour package. These sex tours initially went to Taiwan and Korea where the Japanese language was widely understood, but soon spread to the Philippines and Thailand, thriving recreational outposts for American GIs during the Vietnam War.

Criticism of the brazen, shameless behavior of Japanese men on these tours first surfaced overseas when, in 1973, the Federation of Korean Church Women issued an appeal to its Japanese counterpart protesting this re-run of colonial invasion and abuse. The following year, Japanese church women visited Korea to see the situation for themselves, and afterward mounted demonstrations and distribution of leaflets at Tokyo's Haneda Airport, calling for an end to sex tours. They delivered appeals to travel agencies and governmental offices. In 1975, protest activities put pressure on the Japanese government, and efforts to establish international networks began.

In 1978, the Japan Woman's Christian Temperance Union (JWCTU), a long-time proponent of women's rights, produced a slide show titled "Do you know the meaning of shame?—An appeal against prostitution tours," which was widely used by church women's groups and others to educate and garner support.

A growing protest movement in Japan and elsewhere in Asia resulted in travel agencies curtailing their promotions somewhat, and group tours for Japanese men declined. As the numbers of men traveling to other Asian countries dropped, recruiting organizations and tour agents already in those places began sending Asian women to Japan to service a growing domestic entertainment/sex industry.

Working at night and resting by day, these women were largely invisible. Because their plight went unnoticed by the general public, an appropriate response was slow in coming. Once informed, however, Japanese Christian men and women responded in signignificant and meaningful ways. The Association to Consider the Problems of Asian Women in Japan, the first migrant worker support group, was formed in 1985 in Kumamoto, based at the Tetori Catholic Church.

The year before, at its national convention, the JWCTU had approved the establishment of an emergency shelter for Asian women as its centennial project. On April 1, 1986, the JWCTU's Asian Women's Shelter HELP (House in Emergency of Peace and Love) began its service, and since then more than thirty support organizations have been formed by churches, citizen groups, and labor unions across Japan.

In March 1987, the Forum on Asian Immigrant Workers held its first regular monthly meeting. Organized by the Pacific Asia Resource Center (partly supported by Christian groups), it produced *The Asian Worker's Handbook* in 1988. Now available in English, Tagalog, Korean, Chinese, Bengali, Thai, and Portuguese, the booklet explains migrant worker rights and where to seek help. The Forum has sent open letters of inquiry to the Justice and Labor ministries, and made attempts to negotiate better conditions for migrants. In March 1989 it co-sponsored with a resident Korean support group a rally to protest the newly revised Immigration Control Act.

In April 1989 the Christian Conference of Asia's Urban Rural Mission held a conference in Osaka, with representatives from several Asian organizations, to identify common concerns and plan concrete ways to address migrant worker issues.

In September that year, the National Christian Council in Japan formed the Christian Coalition on the Problems of Refugees and Migrant Foreign Workers, which appeals to the government and the public for guarantees of migrant workers' rights, and promotes church involvement in such activities. In an effort to put pressure on the government by making an appeal to the United Nations Human Rights Commission (UNHRC), a World Council of Churches' fact-finding team was invited to Japan in June 1990. The team conducted investigations in the greater Tokyo area and found gross discrimination and human rights violations among migrants and asylum-seekers, and these findings were presented to the UNHRC.

In March 1990, the Asian Women's Shelter HELP, along with three Tokyo support groups, conducted a three-day telephone hotline to monitor complaints regarding the Tokyo Immigration Bureau. Out of 221 calls, 75 percent (165) were from Asians. Complaints focused on officials' overbearing attitude, refusal to answer questions, arbitrary questioning procedures, racial discrimination, and contempt for women. These charges were reported to authorities along with demands for rectification.

Christianity has a universality transcending national borders and upholds the worth of each individual, especially the powerless. Thus, it is only right that the churches should take part in the human rights struggles of migrants whose battle for individual welfare conflicts with the state interests. The churches must be even more receptive to the urgent needs of migrant workers, and strengthen efforts at networking and proposing new guidelines.

NEEDED CHANGES

At the heart of the Asian migrant issue in Japan lies the question whether it is possible, much less desirable, for Japan to maintain itself as a "homogenous society." According to Gunnar Nielson, there are 589 ethnic groups in the world's 168 nations, and only thirteen of these nations have a single ethnic group constituting a majority of its inhabitants. All others have coexisting ethnic groups with differing customs and languages. Japan is one of the thirteen, yet it urgently needs to muster the resourcefulness to accord respect to the ethnic minorities and diverse cultural ways within its borders.

Prerequisite to a sound migrant worker policy, Japan must resolutely affirm its basic commitment to upholding universal human rights for all persons. The Japanese people must acknowledge that human rights transcend the state, and that it is vital to enact laws and mechanisms to prevent discrimination and human rights abuses at all levels — state, institutional, and individual.

This will require antidiscrimination laws and equal-opportunity laws. Fair policies affecting non-nationals must be devised. Restrictions on long-term residents should be relaxed, and their right to choose place of residence and occupation recognized. Foreigners' rights of political participation on the local level should be considered.

Existing forms of economic cooperation and current levels of benefits accompanying Japanese corporate expansion into Asia will not alleviate the pressure on Asians seeking employment here — not as long as domestic Japanese industries face severe labor shortages. The demand will continue to encourage the supply through migrant labor sources. Therefore, some sort of administrative framework must be put into place to issue work visas, regulate supply, and allow some latitude in choosing work places. Efforts to provide training in skills that migrants can take back home is a responsibility of Japan as a developed country. Japan should turn from penalizing unskilled men to helping them become skilled.

More government aid and private resources should be directed to basic education, occupational training, and job creation for women throughout Asia. Greater emphasis is needed domestically on creating more job opportunities for women, and new initiatives to counteract discrimination against women are needed.

Many churches in Japan, particularly their women's groups, have been active in supporting Asian migrant workers, but there is an urgent need for wider participation by all Christians and churches, other religious groups, and various movements and support groups to care for our Asian neighbors.

13

The Crisis in Rural Evangelism

An External Perspective

Hoshino Masaoki

RURAL EVANGELISM IN JAPAN faces an extreme crisis, though not one of its own making. It lies on the brink of extinction because the rural sector as such is being decimated. That is why this essay is termed "an external perspective." No one would claim that the rural churches, their clergy and lay workers, and their mission strategies are without fault. The point is, though, they are waging a losing battle against forces beyond their control. Thus the stress here is not on internal church performance or personnel, but on the external situation being imposed on the rural sector and therefore also on rural evangelism.

SACRIFICE OF THE RURAL SECTOR

In June 1961 the Japanese government enacted the Basic Agricultural Law (BAL), which was intended to raise backward aspects of Japanese agriculture quickly to world levels. This policy had three pillars: to increase farm size through the free choice of farm households; to encourage food imports other than basic foodstuffs (rice, wheat, etc.); and to modernize agricultural management.

The policy has had thirty years to achieve these goals. The actual results are also threefold. First, Japan's self-sufficiency in food has dropped significantly—in grains, from 60 percent in 1960 to 30 percent in 1989. No known example is comparable to this sharp decline. Second, Japan has, by political choice, been completely changed from an agricultural to an industrial nation. And third, so many agricultural workers have been absorbed by the industrial sector that rural villages have been radically altered, as the numbers of those abandoning farms or who farm only part-time have increased sharply.

Ironically, a policy aimed at reconstructing agriculture has caused an even greater crisis. This is not entirely surprising, since the most zealous promoters of this policy were the country's financial institutions; they could anticipate greater gains by expanding the export and consumer economies.

The new agricultural law had been introduced in the National Diet in 1960 when the nation was in turmoil over renewal of the Japan–US Security Treaty. Few people took note of the BAL, not even most church people. Some protests came from rural churches, and there was some concern in church headquarters. But the energy and awareness needed to block, or even alter, the bill were totally lacking.

The policy then took its course. Many small-scale farmers left for factory jobs in cities. As farm population declined, only the elderly and women remained. With fewer hands, farm households responded to sales campaigns to buy farm machinery—and their debts piled up rapidly. In time, lack of farm workers and high-cost mechanization completely destroyed multiple-crop agriculture. Single-crop farming became centered on rice, causing oversupply. Because Japan's soil is unsuited to large-scale one-crop farming, large amounts of chemical fertilizers and pesticides were used, with inevitable adverse effects on people and environment. Somewhat belatedly, a handful of churches began to see the mounting crisis, but such vision did not extend to the church at large.

Rice has long been the main crop of Japanese agriculture. Indeed, the physical layout and the culture of farm villages have grown up around rice production. Rice fields need a lot of water, which comes from a common source and is therefore obtained by communal work. Erosion of age-old cooperative patterns under the BAL appears to have gone beyond control. To check oversupply, the government since 1970 has imposed "production regulations" on rice farmers, while allowing imports of foreign grains. These measures, added to oversupply, have collapsed rice prices. Production regulation means, in effect, price reduction.

Denying its own responsibility for this fiasco, the government blames the producers—yet severely penalizes farmers who ignore regulations. To the physical exodus from farms and the social disintegration of farm villages is added, then, the breakdown of farm morale and identity. Farmers lose their desire to produce and their sense of worth in doing so. Meanwhile, the gap widens between rural desolation and urban prosperity, leaving the diminished rural scene with little hope.

THE RURAL CHURCH

The Christian population in Japan hovers around 0.9 percent of the total population. Ways of counting Christians in rural areas vary, but the reality is not far from 0.003 percent of Japan's population. And rural church growth is not encouraging. Even long-established rural churches have not reached the farm population.

Reasons for the seemingly impenetrable barrier to rural mission are many, but a few stand out in any analysis. One is that Buddhism and Shintoism have for centuries been firmly rooted in the rural villages and farm households. With many traditional communal patterns, such as procuring water for irrigation of rice fields, village rules and customs bind villagers tightly, and outsiders are not readily tolerated. Interdependent households naturally defend the traditional religious bonds that undergird their livelihood. In this sense, rural religious culture has much in common with the national imperial cult.

Christianity is not wholly denied entry at the individual level. Most rural churches operate day-care centers or kindergartens, as well as church schools. Families gladly send their children to these programs, but this is not the same as embracing the Christian faith. A church school pupil might, on reaching high school age, seek faith and even baptism. At that point, much pressure is applied to abort this new interest—especially if the youth is an eldest son, his household's heir. Churches in such places have great difficulty in growing; most barely manage to exist by virtue of their facilities for village children. Consequently, church members in rural areas are rarely farmers; they are usually public servants or school teachers, that is, persons with no direct connection to agricultural problems.

In 1968 the present writer graduated from seminary and took a rural church with no members. To cope with loneliness, I concentrated on visiting rural families, rather than on building up a congregation. I went to farm homes every day, helped with farm work, and came to know the burdens borne by farmers. From 1970, I could see how the regulation of rice production robbed farmers of their incentive. And I watched the rural sector disintegrate.

Among church professionals, I was one of the few who was close to the farm scene, but I could not easily convey my concerns to the church at large. Eventually some rural churches and pastors, along with Christian agriculturists and activist farmers, raised their voices in protest to rural society's erosion. Rural evangelism until now has concentrated on planting churches in areas which Christianity has not yet reached; there has been almost no consciousness of relating to the rural crisis. As rural breakdown continued, however, to take its toll in the human alienation of individual farmers, more church people became concerned.

They were few in number, but enough to get something started. In summer 1978 the Rural Evangelism Conference was held at Tsurukawa Rural Seminary on the outskirts of Tokyo, with the support of the United Church of Christ in Japan (UCCJ). Such a conference at the national level had not been held for some time. It was an occasion for sharing ways of coping with rural problems; but, on the whole, discussion focused on how to promote evangelism in untouched farm areas. Even so, *who* was struggling with *what* became clear. Individual dots became linked to make lines, and lines coalesced to form a two-dimensional field. The conference and its follow-up efforts inspired other conferences on rural evangelism in other places in Japan.

TRAINING FOR RURAL MISSION

Tsurukawa Rural Seminary

In 1948 the United Church of Christ in Japan established the Research Center for the Christianization of Rural Areas, with generous contributions from overseas churches. The center developed into a seminary for preparing UCCJ ministers, and later also lay evangelists, for rural service. Because many rural churches had day-care centers and kindergartens, partly as a source of self-support, the school opened a department to train teachers for preschool education. Next it added a department to train rural lay leaders. A later addition was the Southeast Asian Rural Christian Leaders Training Course, opened at the request of the Christian Conference of Asia. The seminary then had five areas of research and education, making it a unique and effective institution. In 1956 it moved from its original site in Hino to Tsurukawa, both suburbs of Tokyo, and thus it became known in English as the Tsurukawa Rural Seminary.[1]

In 1968 the United Church of Christ in Japan, to which the seminary is officially related, undertook a reorganization that included plans to reduce and eventually eliminate overseas financial help for its regular programs. The UCCJ embarked on the road to self-support, leaving the rural seminary to assume its own financial responsibility. The seminary was forced to cut back on some programs. In 1972 it closed the research center and the training course for preschool teachers. In the next year the Southeast Asian Rural Christian Leaders Training Course was separated from the seminary, being reconstituted independently as the Asian Rural Institute (cf. I-4), located north of Tokyo in Tochigi Prefecture. It is especially regrettable that the sem-

---

[1] The formal Japanese name is Nōson Dendō Shingakkō (Rural Evangelism Seminary).

inary abandoned in midstream its mission to train lay leaders for rural evangelism, as well as its research center.

Still, the seminary has been able to send forth many able workers to serve churches on the frontiers of mission. It is these workers who have witnessed the suffering of farmers being sacrificed to Japan's industrial advance. They have faithfully performed their duty to be aware of and to care about those caught in the rural crisis.

The seminary is still located at Tsurukawa and has about forty students, all living together in dormitories and diligently pursuing theological studies from an "agricultural point of view." This means they share the burdens of people cut off from and marginalized in a prospering society. A small seminary still bears a great mission.

Asian Rural Institute

The purpose, educational philosophy, and achievements of Asian Rural Institute (ARI) are explained elsewhere in this book (I-4), especially its emphasis on food self-sufficiency and the essential relation of food and life.

Here we stress that the Christian Conference of Asia's request for an Asian leadership program was related to the great damage inflicted by Japan's armies on the Southeast Asian countries. The request and the response both assumed that the Japanese churches, having supported the war, now had a great responsibility to help with reconstruction in Asia. The Southeast Asian Rural Christian Leaders Training Course was a natural outcome of this mutual understanding. It is most unfortunate that the Japanese churches' strength, and the Rural Seminary's resources as well, were too limited to keep this fine program at Tsurukawa. Under the circumstances, of course, it is a blessing that ARI could go independent and manage its own affairs, though even today its support from overseas far exceeds that from within Japan. And the question of how the seminary and ARI can cooperate remains for future consideration.

THE FARMER'S VIEWPOINT

Opposition by the rice farmers to production regulations was sporadic during the 1970s, but by the early 1980s regulation was firmly established. Once proud of their high yield, farmers gradually lost their incentive, and in time domestic rice production was surpassed in volume by wheat imports from the Western countries. Yet farmers hung on doggedly, hoping for a policy change that would reward their persistence.

Instead, the farmers suffered a second external blow—this time from world trade negotiations. While Japan had accumulated a huge trade surplus, the

United States sought to overcome its recessionary trend (continuing since the Vietnam War) by pressing Japan to liberalize imports of agricultural products. Actually, Japan had begun lifting import restrictions on farm products one by one in response to American demands; indeed, it had already become the world's number one food importer. But rice had been carefully protected by law. The four-year-long Uruguay Round of global trade talks under the General Agreement on Tariffs and Trade (GATT), continued through 1990, have threatened this "last stronghold of Japanese agriculture."

Japanese farmers feel they have gone without fair rewards for many years.[2] Now they are pressed once more to foot the bill for industrial expansion. Production costs of domestic rice are too high for it to compete with imported rice; only a few large farms could survive liberalization. If the majority of farmers are forced to give up, the two-thousand-year-old physical and cultural topography of rural Japan will be irreversibly altered. In the farmers' view, once the rice fields are gone, Japan will no longer be Japan.

The price of Southeast Asian rice is said to be one-tenth that of Japanese rice. If this rice comes into the Japanese market, consumers will be as happy as the Southeast Asian suppliers. But the latter will be tempted to produce solely for the Japanese market, neglecting their own needs. Moreover, severe drought or other disasters could wreck the arrangement for suppliers and consumers alike — as attested by the history of Ethiopia and some other countries. In any case, those who benefit most from export-import relations are neither farmers nor consumers, but the dealers and financiers in between.

The Japanese farmers are closely watching the GATT talks. To them it seems clear that the ultimate US aim is to break down the protectionism of the European Community (EC). Japan's population is only 123.5 million; the European market is much larger. If Japan is but a tool for battering the EC citadel, then Japanese farmers are once more being sacrificed. In a time of unprecedented prosperity in Japan, the Japanese farmers face what may well be the greatest crisis in their long history — the loss of land and legacy for the foreseeable future.

At such a time as this I feel acutely the weakness of the Japanese churches. Now is the time, I believe, to seek cooperative relations with world Christendom. Only a limited number of Christians in Japan have had opportunities for fellowship with other Christians around the world. They know the World

---

[2] This attitude has deep, and justified, roots in centuries of exploitation. Taxes on agricultural production ran between 40 percent and 60 percent throughout the era of Tokugawa rule (1603–1868), with most peasants living in poverty; famines were not uncommon. Farm taxes have constituted a principal financial base for the modern industrialization of Japan since 1868. — Ed.

Council of Churches exists and, in ecumenical circles, that their own denomination is related to the WCC. But this is usually only incidental information, not part of their practical church life. Least of all do rural church members have access to churches and Christians in distant lands. Yet those lands, too, have rural areas and rural churches — which may well face similar problems. Rural churches in Japan need to hear the cries of their counterparts elsewhere, especially in small rural churches. Perhaps the crisis in rural evangelism in Japan would be understood well by those struggling in other corners of the world. Does not the shared vocation of mission move forward through mutual appealing and mutual listening, and finding ways to bear each other's burdens?

14

The Christian Churches and Heretical Movements

Jan Swyngedouw

IN THIS AGE OF ECUMENICAL encounters among the various Christian churches, it might seem inappropriate to deal with a theme that seemingly contradicts this spirit. Indeed, in Japan most Christians have dropped the word "heretical" from their vocabulary and try to look upon those who do not share a completely similar understanding of the Christian message as sisters and brothers in the faith, as siblings with opinions to be respected, as partners in the task of evangelizing this non-Christian nation. Church priorities in the past twenty years have been directed largely toward a common witness focused mostly on issues of justice and peace in a society which, driven by its economic success, has manifested some quite alarming national and international shortcomings.

Even so, there have been instances when a clear stance had to be taken, and attention all of a sudden turned to indicting groups of people who, using the name of Christianity, engaged in activities thought to be a counter-witness to the spread of the gospel. This has not involved light-hearted judgments, and church leaders making those judgments have not always had the general agreement of all strata of Japan's Christian population.

This article on heretical movements attempts to be as objective as possible by simply describing what has happened, but also recognizing how delicate and important the issue is for the image of Christianity in a country where most people are unfamiliar with distinctions that are normal in a proper faith perspective.

Christianity in Japan constitutes a very small numerical minority — roughly one percent of the total population. But through its many educational and welfare institutions and other public activities, its voice is often heard and sometimes heeded. So, when one group claiming to be Christian makes the news, for whatever reason, it naturally reflects upon the overall Christian image in a positive or negative way.

Japan is known as a "department store" or "laboratory" of religions, where one can find the most diverse expressions of religious faith. It is no wonder, then, that not a few religious groups — both indigenous and imported — give themselves a Christian label. Consequently, it is next to impossible to keep track of all of them, since most are active only on a limited local level and seldom are considered a challenge or threat to the main Christian bodies, even if their Christian identity is dubious.

Attention here, therefore, is given mainly to those groups which, because of their numerical strength and high social profile, are relatively well known in Japan: the Church of Jesus Christ of Latter-Day Saints (Mormon Church), the Watchtower Bible and Tract Society (Jehovah's Witnesses), and the Holy Spirit Association for the Unification of World Christianity (colloquially, the "Moonies," after founder Moon Sung-myung).[1] These three groups are generally viewed by most historic Christian churches as marginal to the orthodox Christian tradition; more specifically, they are at least heterodox, and not infrequently heretical.[2]

SOME STATISTICS

Statistics show that the Mormon, Jehovah's Witnesses, and Unification Association organizations have experienced extraordinary numerical growth in the past twenty years.

The Mormons in Japan

The Church of Jesus Christ of Latter-Day Saints, or popularly Mormon Church, was introduced to Japan in 1901 (immediately running into trouble because of its alleged advocacy of polygamy), and it continued missionary work until 1925. It was reintroduced after the Pacific War and in 1954 became a "religious juridical person," or incorporated religious organization recognized by the Japanese government. At the 1970 World Exposition in Osaka it had its own pavilion, clearly manifesting thereby its separateness from the mainline Christian bodies.

While in the early 1970s its membership hovered between ten and fifteen

---

[1] The Chinese characters for "association" (*kyōkai* 協会) are different from the similarly pronounced word for church (*kyōkai* 教会), but this organization sometimes refers to itself in English as "Unification Church." — Ed.

[2] In the dictionary senses of these two terms: heterodox because they hold beliefs quite different from orthodox Christian tradition; or heretical in that they deny or, as the case may be, corrupt traditional Christian beliefs. — Ed.

thousand, it suddenly jumped to about thirty thousand, reaching 37,587 by 1980. A few years later this figure doubled again, with the 1990 *Kirisutokyō nenkan* (Christian yearbook) giving the figure of 92,267 members (all statistics submitted by the church). No doubt this spectacular development is due in part to the highly visible activities of young American missionaries who, usually in pairs and conspicuous in their conservative attire, have become a familiar sight in Japanese cities and towns.

Since the Mormons do not seem to present themselves as part of traditional Christianity, there have been relatively few instances of conflict with mainline Christian bodies. Consequently, in Christian circles very little mention is made of them, except in a few evangelical publications that condemn them outright as heretical. The "Christian yearbook" for a long time listed Mormon claims, along with those of the Jehovah's Witnesses; but since 1979, their numbers have not been added into the total Christian population of Japan. The reason given is simple: the faith of these groups differs from historic Christian tradition.

Jehovah's Witnesses

The Watchtower Bible and Tract Society, commonly known as Jehovah's Witnesses, began its missionary activities in Japan in 1927. Suppressed in 1939 because three members refused military conscription (for which 130 members of the Society were jailed), their work was resumed soon after the Pacific War by American Watchtower evangelists, and the Society became an incorporated religious organization in 1953. Growth in the last twenty years has equalled that of the Mormon Church, and this is surely due in part to aggressive propaganda methods.

Statistics for the Society in the "Christian yearbook" remained fixed at 9,478 for several years (updated data presumably was not made available), then suddenly swelled to 41,695 in 1977, and then again to more than 80,000 in the early 1980s. Although the organization's name is still listed among Christian groups in the vernacular "Christian yearbook," from the latter half of the 1980s its membership claims have not been included. The mainline Christian bodies have shown more animosity toward the Jehovah's Witnesses than toward the Mormon Church (possibly because of the latter's "church" label). As we shall see later, there have been instances when the Jehovah's Witnesses' actions have caused social problems that aroused reactions from the mainline bodies.

The Unification Association

The Holy Spirit Association for the Unification of World Christianity began its activities in Japan in 1958, but October 2 of the following year—the day its first place of worship in Tokyo was opened — is usually given as the founding date of the Unification Association in Japan. The Association became an incorporated religious organization in 1964 and ever since has conducted highly publicized and well-financed missionary activities, especially among university students.

From 1974 the organization was listed in the "Christian yearbook" as a Protestant group, and its membership statistics were published, though not added into the total number of Christians in Japan (on the premise that its statistical methods were unclear). In the 1975 "Christian yearbook" the Association's membership is given as 170,000, dropping to 147,538 the following year, and then suddenly rising to 260,000 in 1978, where it remained until the mid-1980s. For reasons explained below, both the Unification Association membership figure and the name itself have been dropped from the yearbook's list of Christian groups since the 1989 edition.

Even if the reported number of adherents does not exactly reflect reality, the Association's apparent numerical success — including the fact that many members formerly belonged to mainline Christian bodies — is one factor behind the reactions of Christian churches to its competition in evangelistic endeavors. Since the Unification Association is the religious group whose Christian identity is the most questionable, the next section treats the challenge it poses.

THE CHALLENGE OF THE UNIFICATION ASSOCIATION

In the history of Christian churches in Japan during the past twenty years, the mid-1970s and the mid-1980s stand out as culmination points in the difficult relationship between mainline Christian bodies and the Unification Association. Public attention was drawn to the Association's activities by a series of articles published in the *Kirisuto shinbun* (The Christ Weekly) in 1974 that focused on its theology, recruitment methods, finances, and political implications. At the time, the Christian churches and the Japanese public were deluged with the Association's own publicity. This naturally raised questions about the organization's true nature, which, along with other warnings, led to a statement issued by the Faith and Order Commission of the National Christian Council in Japan on September 18, 1975, that "the Unification Association does not accord with the NCCJ's definition of Christian" — a position already taken by a number of Christian organizations in other countries.

Many Japanese Christian churches initiated study groups to consider the challenge of the Unification Association and to explore ways for coping with the many cases of young Christian believers who had become ardent followers of the Association, causing great distress to their families. On January 18, 1979, the NCCJ was moved to reaffirm publicly its earlier statement, once again rejecting as Christian the organization's views of the Bible, Christology, salvation, and the trinity.

A delicate point in this controversy was the fact that not a few well-known Christian theologians and other leading figures seemed to disregard these warnings by actively participating in conferences and meetings organized by the Unification Association or its subsidiary groups. One prominent example of such cooperation is the late Matsushita Masatoshi (1901–86), former president of St. Paul's (Rikkyō) University in Tokyo, who openly endorsed the Unification Association's activities and became one of its prime advocates in Japan.

Besides the broad spectrum of Association-sponsored international conferences attended by many Japanese Christian (and non-Christian) scholars and religionists, one principal means of mobilizing people for its cause was the International Christian Professors Association (IPCA), established in July 1981. The ICPA has since organized regular academic meetings, whose high standards cannot be denied. Even so, the continuing participation of some of Japan's most respected theologians and intellectuals created a sharp division in Christian circles and elicited severe criticisms from both church leaders and Christian workers who felt their efforts were being undermined by the Unification Association's offensive.

The second culmination point came in 1985 when the Roman Catholic Bishops' Conference of Japan issued, on June 22, a statement declaring its wish "to clarify the fact that the Unification Association cannot be considered a Christian church; even less can it be considered to be in accord with the Catholic Church. For these reasons it does not fall within the scope of the ecumenical movement." The statement also called on all Catholics "to avoid any contact with any movement or meeting sponsored by the Unification Association."

This declaration was apparently prompted by a letter from the Apostolic Nunciature in Tokyo, which, on instruction from the Vatican, issued a special warning for those engaged in education to be careful about the sect's activities. This was in line with a worldwide Catholic trend to take a clearer stand against the spread of sectarian movements and cults. The Unification Association's reaction came swiftly, requesting retraction of the bishops' statement. But on October 9, the bishops reaffirmed their theological reasons for declaring the Unification Association "non-Christian," citing various points similar to those already made by fellow Christians in Protestant circles.

Many Protestant churches, strengthened by this Catholic support, put new effort into their actions against the Unification Association. Among ini-

tiatives taken, the United Church of Christ in Japan at its Twenty-fourth
General Assembly in November 1986 issued a statement disclaiming any relationship with the Unification Association and declaring all mission cooperation with it "impossible." The UCCJ organized a liaison conference to hear
reports on harm done by the Association to UCCJ members and to organize
programs for enlightening and counseling "victims" of Association practices.

Since then, various churches have used publications, seminars, and other
means to inform their members about the dangers inherent in the Unification
Association. In this effort the churches have been helped by public opinion,
which in recent years has been increasingly aroused against the Association
by court cases probing its dubious business practices.

It must be said, however, that this issue of "heretical movements" remains
largely overshadowed by other major problems faced by Christians in Japan,
especially those related to the emperor system and its perceived revival at the
end of the 1980s with the succession from the late Emperor Shōwa (Hirohito) to the present emperor (Akihito). As is the case for nearly every issue
raised nowadays, no real consensus among the Christian faithful has been
reached on what concrete position should be taken toward the Unification
Association, and the problem will very likely continue to haunt the churches
for many years to come.

JEHOVAH'S WITNESSES IN THE NEWS

While the Unification Association has posed a continual problem during the
past two decades, other religious groups which could be expected to prompt
questions of heresy have only sporadically aroused overt reactions. One instance with serious implications for the Christian image in society at large was
a June 1985 incident involving the Jehovah's Witnesses. A young schoolboy
met with a traffic accident in Kawasaki City and was taken to a Catholic hospital, where he died a few hours later from excessive bleeding because his parents refused to let him receive a blood transfusion, saying it was against their
religious principles. Although such cases are not exceptional in Japan, this
case, for reasons yet unclear, was widely publicized in the mass media, creating the impression among the public that Christianity and its biblical faith are
quite backward, if not downright inhumane.

Both the Protestant "Christ Weekly" and the "Catholic News" devoted ample
front-page space to the incident, at least to inform their own Christian readers — even if they could not reach the general public — about the churches'
position on this matter. The tone of their coverage, however, was marked by
a moderation not seen in their treatment of Unification Association issues
causing concern at that very time. Noting clearly that the parents' action was

based on the heterodox biblical interpretation of Jehovah's Witnesses, care was taken not to condemn forthrightly but to understand, rather, the depths of faith and pain involved in the parents' decision. The incident was used, in other words, not as an opportunity for attacking heresy but for reexamining one's own tradition of biblical interpretation relative to the concrete problems involved.

The Catholic periodical stressed reverence for life as the primary guiding principle, giving it priority over religious freedom in this case, while the Protestant weekly said this case could serve as a brake on totalitarian tendencies of the state, which increasingly tries to take life-and-death decisions away from the individual. Neither these views nor the more strident ones against the Unification Association were necessarily shared by all Christian believers; but the relative differences in treatment suggest that attitudes toward suspected heretical movements might be greatly influenced also by factors outside the strictly doctrinal domain.

SOME OTHER CASES

As noted earlier, Japan is known as a fertile ground for new forms of religion. The Christian tradition is no exception, and there exist in fact many indigenous groups that claim a Christian label.[3] It is, however, somewhat surprising that these groups, even when their numerical growth or some other factor gains public attention, are seldom viewed by mainline Christian bodies in terms of orthodoxy versus heterodoxy. It is as though the new groups hardly merit any notice.

One reason for this curious situation might be that the new indigenous Christian groups, in self-understanding, propagation methods, and general perception, are readily grouped among Japan's "new religions" and thus are not so easily confused with established Christianity. They seem to pose little threat to Christianity in Japan. After all, most Japanese think of Christianity as a "Western" religion, and the new Christian groups by the very fact of their Japanese origin do not fit this description. (The Unification Association is neither Western nor Japanese, but Korean in origin; but the self-image it projects does impact Christianity's image directly.)

The Spirit of Jesus Church

The best example of a "Christian new religion" born in Japan that is seldom felt to be a threat (except in some local instances) is the Spirit of Jesus Church

[3] Cf. Richard Fox Young, "The 'Christ' of the Japanese New Religions," *The Japan Christian Quarterly* 57/1, Winter 1991.

(Iesu no Mitama Kyōkai Kyōdan). Organized before the Pacific War by Murai Jun, and named in accordance with a heavenly vision he reportedly received in 1941, this church became an incorporated religious organization in 1953. It is one of the fastest-growing Christian bodies in Japan, having increased its membership from 37,477 in 1970 (according to other sources, 62,080) to 433,108 at the end of the 1980s.

Taken at face value, this latest figure makes it the largest Christian denomination in Japan at present. Even so, discussions of Christianity in Japan usually disregard its existence; at the outset of the 1980s the vernacular "Christian yearbook" ceased adding its membership figures to the total Christian population. Moreover, whether or not it is heretical is seldom publicly asked, although it rejects the trinitarian doctrine and claims to be the only true Christian church in this country.

The Ark of Jesus

Among the many smaller Christian new religions, some have attracted public attention because of alleged wrongdoings. In most cases little or no reaction has come from mainline bodies, preoccupied as they seem to be with other issues. To cite one example: in the early 1980s a group called Iesu no Hakobune (Ark of Jesus), consisting of one male founder and about twenty female adherents, gained nationwide notoriety—including questions in the national parliament—when the founder was accused of having actually kidnapped the girls and exercised absolute control over them, against their families' wishes. (This resembled some cases of young people taken in by the Unification Association.) For the scandal sheets it was a welcome bone to gnaw on. But how much this and similar events actually affect the general image of Christianity is hard to gauge. The minimal reaction of the mainline churches might be the best indication of the relative importance of such events.

CONCLUDING REMARKS

General statistics on Christian believers in Japan currently put the figure at slightly less than one million, with a 500,000+ aggregate for the various Protestant churches, and 400,000+ Roman Catholics (plus a small number of Orthodox Christians), which together amount to slightly less than one percent of the total Japanese population. In public surveys, however, about two percent of respondents invariably name "Christianity" when asked their religious preference. Sociologists tend to explain this discrepancy by pointing out that quite a number of Japanese consider themselves Christian without holding membership in any specific church. They seem to esteem Christ and

Christian principles, but do not wish to be personally bound by organizational rules and doctrines.

Were we to add to the almost one million Christians in yearbook-listed churches all the currently unlisted adherents claimed by the Spirit of Jesus Church, the Unification Association, the Mormons, and the Jehovah's Witnesses, then the total easily reaches the two-million mark—a figure that calls into question the sociologists' judgment. Of course, it is the unlisted numbers that are most probably inflated.[4] But even after discounting unreliable figures, the successes of indigenous Christian groups cannot be ignored. And this fact offers us an opportunity for questioning our reasons for regarding those groups as being outside the Christian mainstream, and also whether they pose any real threat or challenge.

Judging from the above examples, we can only acknowledge the great difficulty in drawing general conclusions. To be sure, a genuine ecumenical spirit has spread in recent decades; yet certain evangelical or fundamentalist groups still indict others as heretical. Also, events occur in the mainline bodies that spoil the prevailing irenic atmosphere. Does this not contradict the priorities given to other issues, so that orthodoxy versus heterodoxy is rarely accorded more than secondary significance?

Not including membership data of the Spirit of Jesus Church and other churches in the yearbook is one way of distancing oneself from these groups, and care is taken not to fall into confrontational postures. The one big exception is, of course, the Unification Association, and this calls for further explanation. While doctrinal deviation is the stated reason for condemning this organization, other factors are clearly and preponderantly involved. Some problematic aspects have already been noted, especially recruitment practices and dubious financial deals, with serious negative implications for Christianity's image. Still worse, the Association has made serious inroads among mainline church members.

Yet another element may be added to this picture. In recent years the mainline Christian bodies have increasingly adopted bold stances on issues of justice and peace, and this has precipitated confrontations with social and political forces of a rightist nature. The Unification Association's open connections with right-wing causes has deepened the mistrust felt toward it.

While these non-doctrinal factors might not have determined church attitudes toward the Unification Association, they have heavily influenced the decisive stands taken toward movements that can only be called heretical

---

[4] In mainline denominations, local churches are often assessed "apportionments" to be paid into national church budgets, and this inhibits the temptation to inflate membership claims. Cf. Harry Burton-Lewis, "Statistics never lie—not much anyway," *Japan Christian Quarterly* 56/1, Winter 1990.—Ed.

in some sense. Yet, as already noted, there is no clear consensus among all the Christian faithful on this score, and this might seem to weaken our work and witness. It also signals to all concerned that the question of heretical movements is increasingly complex and will require continuous reflection and revision.

III

Caring and Communicative Ministries

15

Christian Work in the Yoseba

Kamagasaki, Sanya, Kotobuki, Sasajima

Koyanagi Nobuaki

IT IS DAY LABORERS who support the Japanese economy at its very base by building the infrastructures it needs. These laborers live in neighborhoods called *yoseba* ("gathering places"), where employers come daily to hire men looking for a day's work. These places are not what are ordinarily called slums.

In present-day Japan there are four major yoseba, each in a major metropolitan area. These are Kamagasaki in Osaka, Sanya in Tokyo, Kotobuki in Yokohama, and Sasajima in Nagoya. In addition there are smaller yoseba in other cities such as Kobe, Hiroshima, Hakata (central Fukuoka), and Naha in Okinawa Prefecture.

Day laborers are indispensable to Japan's ongoing processes of urbanization and industrialization, and the history of the yoseba is but the story of their role in these processes. The yoseba have expanded as the Japanese economy has grown. At the beginning of the 1960s, this growth was related to the energy revolution — the changeover from coal to petroleum — and to the mechanization of agriculture pursuant to the 1961 Basic Agriculture Law (cf. II-13). These changes resulted in a major population shift to the big cities. As coal mines closed, many unemployed miners headed for the cities to become factory workers or longshoremen. As farms became more mechanized, younger sons were no longer needed as farm hands; they too streamed into the cities. Thousands of jobless miners and farmers began city life in the yoseba where they could manage to live from the day of their arrival.

Since the 1960s, the yoseba have each experienced population fluctuations while continuing to serve as daily labor markets. Currently there are 25,000 in Kamagasaki, 6,000 in Sanya, 5,000 in Kotobuki, and 1,000 in Sasajima. New engineering and construction projects in these metropolitan areas usually trigger new influxes of laborers. During the 1963–64 construction for the 1964 Olympic Games in Tokyo, Sanya's population exceeded 10,000. In the 1969–70 preparatory period for the 1970 World Exposition in Osaka, nearly 30,000 laborers lived in Kamagasaki. Although Kamagasaki's number had once dropped to 18,000, it has recently swelled to 35,000 because of construction projects such as the Kansai Airport and the Kansai Science City.[1] One factor behind this increase is the large number of jobless workers from the restructured steel, shipbuilding, and railroad industries who have gathered in this yoseba to find work.

The yoseba first received public attention with the labor riots of summer 1960 in Sanya. The laborers rose up in revolt against society's propensity to value them only for their labor, refusing to recognize them as individual persons. In June of the following year, there was a week of rioting in Kamagasaki, arising from a traffic accident involving a day laborer. Though still alive, he was treated as if dead, greatly delaying police and ambulance service. The laborers who witnessed the incident shouted angrily, "Day laborers are people, too!" Their cries echoed through the yoseba for a week.

These riots evoked from government officials promises, made to the National Diet and prefectural legislatures, that they would assume more direct responsibility for day laborers. The actual result, however, was not greater concern for the laborers' human rights, only a tougher policy for maintaining public order. This policy was evident in increased police patrols and television cameras installed to monitor the yoseba neighborhoods. The laborers continued, as before, to work like slaves under poor working conditions and low wages. Gangster organizations that controlled the day-labor market were able to exploit them at will. When laborers showed resistance, they were silenced with violence. Nor did living conditions improve. Problems such as a high incidence of tuberculosis, poor housing, and a high truancy rate among neighborhood school children indicate neglect of the basic rights of city residents. In 1968 the laborers themselves formed a labor union and began fighting for their rights.

Japanese people in general perceived the yoseba as "dangerous, filthy places where lazy, good-for-nothing people live." There was no recognition that these laborers, whose rights as citizens and working people were being trampled on, were in fact supporting the Japanese economy. Few realized that these laborers, working in poor conditions for low wages, were laying

---

[1] This project includes a number of research and education facilties in the Kyoto–Osaka–Nara area, as well as new housing complexes. – Ed.

the foundation for Japanese economic growth by constructing countless roads, railroads, and buildings.

Christians have only recently become involved in the yoseba. The history of that involvement varies with the yoseba in question. Furthermore, each yoseba has its own particular prior history. What follows is a brief introduction of each, with a survey of the Christian work in it.

KAMAGASAKI – MISSIONARIES TAKE THE LEAD

Kamagasaki has the longest history, dating from before World War II. Its historical antecedents go back to the Fifth National Industrial Exposition of 1903. Residents along the road to the Exposition Park were forcibly removed to what was then the Kamagasaki district of Imamiya village, on the premise that it would upset the Meiji Emperor to have to pass through the Nagamachi slum on his way. Residents who resisted were forced to move by the police and army. Thus, Kamagasaki began as a slum.

The first to begin activities in this Kamagasaki slum was a Catholic group. In 1933 three sisters of the Daughters of Charity arrived from France and began settlement work, particularly medical care and child care. During World War II they were viewed as spies and even detained for a time by police. They continued their work until Kamagasaki was burned to the ground, and lost their convent as well. They resumed their work there in 1970.

Postwar Christian work in Kamagasaki began in 1964 with the arrival of German Lutheran missionary Elisabeth Strohm. Next came Tani Yasurō of the Catholic group called Gyōkōkai in 1965. The Gyōkōkai is a community founded in Kobe by the French priest Fr. Robert Vallade, which supports itself by recycling materials. Tani's activity led to the opening of its Osaka branch. In 1967, Pastor Kanai Aimei of the United Church of Christ in Japan (UCCJ) began working as a day laborer himself, in order to share in the suffering of the workers. In 1968, Koyanagi Nobuaki (a UCCJ pastor assigned to the Kansai Labor Evangelism Fellowship) began working as a case worker for truant school children in Kamagasaki. In 1970, Franciscan priest Fr. Heinrich Schnusenberg also began work. Thus Christians groped for new ways to provide Christian ministries in Kamagasaki.

In November 1970 the above five persons formed the Kamagasaki Support Group (Kamagasaki Kyōyūkai; herein KSG), an ecumenical Christian group for coordinating their work in Kamagasaki. The KSG agreed upon the following areas of cooperation: (a) Education, health, counseling; providing a dining hall or a place to stay temporarily for free was considered. (b) Care for children of the district and child-rearing guidance; though Kamagasaki is a day laborers' district, in 1970 a considerable number of children were also living there; this work was for the protection of their rights. (c) Relief and counseling for the old and sick; hospital visitation and an old peoples' club were planned. In these ways the group's aim was to concentrate on the people who are likely to be overlooked in the district.

The Kamagasaki Support Group's first joint project was a dining hall for laborers, called Shokudō Imamiya, which opened in 1971. The project soon expanded to include two more dining halls: Furusato Shokudō for old people, started by Fr. M. Heinrichs, and Ikoi Shokudō for laborers, begun by Pastor Kanai. Miss Strohm concentrated on child care and work with alcoholics. The Gyōkōkai continued its recycling activities, providing employment for sickly laborers. It also assisted in the rehabilitation of handicapped laborers.

The KSG's second phase of activity, begun in late 1975, was winter relief work from the end of December through February. In this phase there was a close tie-up with the labor movement. A day-laborers union had been formed in 1968 to work for laborers' rights. KSG operates the winter relief work in cooperation with the union and the Kansai Urban Industrial Movement (KUIM), which channels outside assistance to Kamagasaki. This relief project continues to offer food and shelter to out-of-work laborers during the winter months. Besides these services, it also engages in advocacy directed to government agencies.

Other joint activities at this stage included the Kamagasaki Seminar on Industry, Society, and Labor with its work/learning experience (sixteen seminars by 1990), the Children's Camp, and the Winter Relief Seminar, which promoted participation in the winter relief work. Since 1975, the "Kamagasaki Winter Relief Report" has been published to inform supporting churches and Christians about aspects of Kamagasaki laborers not covered by the mass media. During this phase the work in Kamagasaki became widely known among Protestant and Catholic churches, with many people from all over the country coming to walk through and observe Kamagasaki in order to deepen their awareness of its realities.

From 1976 to 1980, a group of Christian youth called the Kamagasaki Problems Study Group was active in providing literacy classes, a laborers' night school, and medical care. The House of Hope (Kibō no Ie), purchased by Miss Strohm, served as the base of their activities. The laborers' particularly appreciated the tearoom/reading room at the House of Hope. The medical emphasis of this phase — reduction of TB — later led to the hiring of two women staff members with KSG support from 1980 to 1984.

The third phase of Christian work in Kamagasaki began in 1984. In order to reorganize the various projects and to strengthen their cooperative relations, eleven groups formed the Kamagasaki Christian Association (Kamagasaki Kirisutokyō Kyōyūkai; herein, KCA). The spiritual foundation of its activities is virtually the same as that of the original Kyōyūkai (KSG) begun in 1970, but KCA has perhaps more fully implemented it. The eleven groups were: Furusato no Ie (Catholic; visitation of the elderly, dining hall, recreation room), Gyōkōkai (Catholic; recycling, community life), Ikoi no Ie (United Church of Christ; dining hall for laborers), Kibō no Ie (Japan Evangelical Lutheran Church; day center for alcoholics), Daughters of Charity (Catholic; hospital visitation, clothing repair), Guardian Angels Convent Kodomo no Sato (Catholic; children's club), KUIM Kamagasaki Committee (Protestant; labor problems, medical problems), Tabiji no Sato (Catholic; Jesuit pastoral care center, Kyōyūkai center, seminars, care for the sick and aged), Kamagasaki Counseling Room (Christian Medical Association; consultation on health and daily problems; closed in 1989), Deai no Ie (Catholic, Franciscan; rehabilitation residence), Elisabeth Strohm Sannō Children's Center (formerly Japan Evangelical Lutheran Church, now independent; children's club).

The activities of the Kamagasaki Christian Association during its twenty years since 1970 are recorded in the newsletters of its member groups, as well as in the following publications:

Elisabeth Strohm, *Kamagasaki wa watashi no kokyō* (Kamagasaki is my hometown), 1972;

———, *Kibō no machi — Kamagasaki ni ikite 20-nen* (Town of hope — Twenty years in Kamagasaki), 1988;

Kosugi Kunio, *Shashinshū — taihei no tanima no sei to shi, 1973–78* (Life and death in the tranquil slum, 1973–78 — A photo collection), 1978;

Koyanagi Nobuaki, *Kyōiku izen — Airin Shōchō Gakkō monogatari* (Before education — Stories from Airin District Schools), 1978;

Fr. Heinrichs, *Fukuin no chōsen — Kamagasaki kara 25-nen no fukuin senkyō no hansei* (Challenge of the gospel from Kamagasaki — Reflections on 25 years of evangelism), 1986;

Susukida Noboru, *Watakushi no seisho — Kamagasaki no hitobito ni oshierareta* (My Bible — Taught by the people of Kamagasaki), 1988;

Irisa Akemi, *Neechan gokurōsan — Kamagasaki de deatta hitobito* (Thank you, Sister — People I met in Kamagasaki), 1987;

———, *Itsumo no machi kado de — hiyatoi rōdōsha ni oshieraretsutsu* (On the usual street corner — Learning from day laborers), 1990.

KCA is planning to publish a book introducing its various activities to commemorate its first twenty years. In addition, since 1984, *Kamagasaki hakusho* (Kamagasaki white paper) covering work in Kamagasaki, and since 1986, *Kodomo no Sato tayori* (News from Kodomo no Sato) covering winter relief work for children, have been published annually.

In 1988, with the cooperation of district laborers, the Asian Friends Society was formed to assist migrant laborers from Asia.

SANYA — THE FIRST MAY DAY

Christians began work in Tokyo's Sanya district in spring 1966 when three pastors from the United Church of Christ opened the Sumidagawa Pioneer Church[2]: Nakamori Ikunoshin (1904–81), Itō Yukio (1924–80), and Tomura Masahiro (1923–). These three raised the flag of human liberation in Sanya. In the May Day march of 1967, a group of Christians carried the banner of the Sumidagawa Pioneer Church. Pastor Itō recorded the event: "This participation in the May Day demonstration by a small ragged band of laborers is the fruit of many years of a common bloody struggle by Christians and Marxists. There is one hope: human liberation." (*Kami naki jidai* [A godless age]; 1967.) Itō's desire bore fruit with the establishment twenty years later of the Sanya Laborers' Welfare Center (dedicated September 16, 1990; more about this later).

After Pastor Itō's death (January 23, 1980), Pastor Nakamori took over responsibility for the Sumidagawa Pioneer Church. After Nakamori died in 1981, it became the Sanya Pioneer Church, and UCCJ Pastor Ichinose Shinsuke took over. Tomura, who was then pastor of the nearby UCCJ Asakusa Hokubu Church, opened his church as a base of operations for Sanya laborers. With the dedication of the new Sanya Laborers' Welfare Center in 1990, Tomura has been called as pastor of Nihonzutsumi Church, which is part of the Center.[3] Pastor Nakamori's work is recorded in his autobiographical *Shita e noboru uta* (A song of ascending to the depths; 1973), which shows that mission in Sanya is anything but easy.

These are the main forms of ministry attempted by Christians in their early years at Sanya. Itō writes about the Sumidagawa Pioneer Church: "This church has Bible study and discussion groups, but we do not consider them our most important work. Since the need for our participation, as clergy and laity, in the labor movement and day-laborer movement is just as great, our church meetings lift up the meaning and goals of this social participation. In

---

[2] The Japanese term *dendōsho* is variously rendered "evangelism point," "preaching point," and "pioneer church" (from "pioneer evangelism"); the intention in all cases is fruition as a full-fledged church, so the last term is used herein. — Ed.

[3] Tomura is also a leading student and critic of Japan's emperor system. — Ed.

our meetings we simply learn of the depths of life and faith." (*Kami naki jidai*.)

Folk singer Okabayashi Nobuyasu and his friend Tagashira Michito gathered at Sumidagawa Pioneer Church and also raised questions about the form of the church. The circumstances of this questioning are recorded in Tagashira's *Sanya fōku Kyūba* (Sanya Folk Cuba; 1979). For example, inspiration for the well-known song "Sanya Blues" came from a poem by Dōshisha University professor Hiraga Hisahiro, entitled "Sanya Blues," which appeared in the journal *Sanya no Kirisutosha* (Christians in Sanya; issued since November 1967), edited and published by Tagashira. Okabayashi rewrote this poem and set it to music.

In Sanya of the 1970s, though the laborers movement was vigorous, Christian activity was rather subdued. The 1980s saw a resurgence of Christian work. The promotion of the documentary movie *Sanya—yararetara yarikaese* (Sanya—an eye for an eye!) provided the incentive. *Sanya* was filmed and produced by laborer Yamaoka Kyōichi and Satō Michio of the film movement, beginning in November 1984. But during the first month of filming, rightist gangsters, fearing the movie would expose too much about the yoseba, stabbed director Satō to death on December 22, 1984. Yamaoka then continued the production and completed the movie. He was killed by gunfire in the street on January 16, 1986, by rightists determined to keep the film from the public. Despite this assault, *Sanya* was shown at over three hundred locations throughout Japan and viewed by some thirty thousand people. Christians and churches in each area cooperated in promotion of the movie, and this effort laid the foundation for the movement to build the Sanya Laborers' Welfare Center.

It was Yamaoka who had first thought of building a base of operations for laborers in Sanya. After his death, laborers and Christians went to work on his dream in summer 1986. The following summer laborers from the yoseba and Christians began appealing for contributions. The UCCJ Social Concerns Committee endorsed the project. Pastor Tomura assumed leadership of the project and appealed for the cooperation of local churches.

Response to the appeal was good. Construction was begun in September 1989 and completed one year later. A special feature of this project was the effort to use the power of laborers to the fullest. The architect donated the plans, and the work was done by laborers, not only of Sanya but also from Hakata, Sasajima, and Kamagasaki. The Sanya Laborers Welfare Center's three-story building includes space for the UCCJ Nihonzutsumi Church as well as rooms for reading, consultation (on labor, legal, and medical problems), recreation, dining, and general meetings. The center is a very serviceable base of operations for the human liberation of Sanya laborers.

This center has given birth to an ecumenical activity—the Sanya Christian Council, begun in 1989. The background of this event goes back to 1978, when Indian brothers of the Missionaries of Charity began work in Sanya. About that time Pastor Kikuchi Mamoru of the UCCJ Brothers' House began evangelism while working as a day laborer. Ten years later, in May 1988, Pastor Kikuchi opened a dining hall for laborers called Maria, where Protestant volunteers and Catholic sisters worked together. Since 1988, the UCCJ Sanya Pioneer Church has provided a place for the youth volunteer movement called the Society for Thinking About Sanya Medical Care. In 1985 the Friends of Sanya (Sanyūkai), supported by a group of Catholics, initiated activities such as a free clinic, a recreation center for old people, and an elderly persons' club. Other groups include the Catholic Sanya MAC[4] and Minowa MAC devoted to alcoholic rehabilitation and the Franciscan Yamazato,[5] and Protestant groups such as the Seigawa Gospel Church and the Old Peoples' Society. These nine groups formed the Sanya Christian Council for mutual consultation and joint action. They also cooperate with the Nihonzutsumi Church. The 1990s should prove to be a springboard for Christian work in Sanya.

KOTOBUKI—A NEIGHBORHOOD CHURCH

The history of the Kotobuki district is intertwined with the history of wartime Japan. When the floating hotel once used as lodging for Yokohama port laborers became decrepit, they were relocated in Kotobuki. In the first post-World War II decade, Kotobuki was requisitioned by the U.S. Army and used as a supply depot. Upon its return in 1955, the construction of lodgings began. When the district acquired both a public employment office and a nearby yoseba, Kotobuki soon became a day laborers' neighborhood, particularly for longshoremen. By 1965 there were about seventy rooming houses, nearly all of them operated by Koreans.

The unique feature of the Kotobuki district is the strength of its neighborhood movement. The municipal Seikatsukan (Livelihood Center), which offers advice to laborers, can be appreciated only in the context of the neighborhood movement. Even local public workers supported this movement. Nomoto Sankichi, who worked at the Kotobuki Seikatsukan, left a record of this support in his *Kotobuki Seikatsukan nōto* (Kotobuki Seikatsukan notebook; 1977). In short, facilities needed by the district were obtained by

[4] Maryknoll Alcoholic Center
[5] An intentional presence among the poor.

virtue of the neighborhood movement. Christians became involved in Kotobuki only after 1970.

The Japan Baptist Yokohama Church, a century-old church founded in
1873 in the Kotobuki district, became involved with Kotobuki laborers from
1970 when Masu Iwao became pastor. Part of his activity is introduced in *Inochi to inochi to no deai — hiyatoi rōdōsha no machi, Yokohama Kotobuki ni te*
(Life-to-life encounters in the day laborers' town of Kotobuki, Yokohama;
1988).

Initially he related to the laborers simply as pastor of the neighborhood
church. In 1975 there was a falling out between district laborers and the Yokohama city government. To repair the relationship, the Kotobuki District
Citizens' Consultation was formed by eleven groups, including labor unions,
self-governing associations, and old people's associations. Pastor Masu functioned as its representative, helping forge neighborhood consensus and undertaking negotiations with the city. In addition, he organized a support
group called Nobana Kai (Wildflower group) in 1983, and a workshop for
the mentally disabled, Hadashi no Mura (Barefoot village), in 1985. About
that time the liaison committee of Christians working in Kotobuki increased
its activity.

The United Church of Christ in Japan begame involved in Kotobuki in
February 1974 when its Kanagawa District formed the Kotobuki Cooperative Project Committee for the support of work in Kotobuki — in particular,
to support Nonomura Yo of the Kotobuki Fukushi Sagyōjo (Kotobuki Welfare Workshop), a workplace for the disabled. District involvement deepened
when the district women began providing meals for the workshop. The district next undertook its own independent work: the Kanagawa Kotobuki
Center, opened in May 1988. Kanagawa District supports the Center's director, Mimori Isako, as well as another workshop for the disabled, Roba no
Ie (Donkey's house). The Kotobuki center is unique in the UCCJ's relations
with yoseba.

It would not do to forget the private welfare center for alcoholics,
Kotobuki Fukushi Sentā. The center has set aside one room for consultation
concerning alcoholism, where there is always a Catholic sister available.
This small project is the base for the work of Alcoholics Anonymous in
Kotobuki.

Another project in which Christians are leaders is the Thursday Patrol,
which offers assistance to laborers who sleep on the streets, especially during
the winter months from December through February. Since 1985 the
"Mokuyō Patorōru Hōkoku" (Thursday Patrol Report) has chronicled the
this work. The impetus for the patrol was a February 1983 incident in which
a group of youth clubbed to death three elderly and infirm unemployed

laborers who lived on the streets. Christians involved in Kotobuki could not ignore this incident. The patrol project and its opportunities for conversation with laborers living on the street throw much light on Japanese society, which treats day laborers as a disposable commodity.

A project undertaken jointly by laborers and Christians is the Karabao no Kai (Water buffalo society) to assist Asian migrant workers. In winter 1987 a Filipino laborer came to the Kotobuki Day Labor Union looking for work, and conversation with him revealed the conditions and abuse of human rights that Filipino and other Asian workers suffer. UCCJ pastor Watanabe Hidetoshi, newly returned from study in the Philippines, formed the Karabao no Kai and began work in June 1987.

Another not-to-be-forgotten episode is the production of a documentary movie featuring a Kotobuki laborer. Director Watanabe Haruaki of Yokohama Documentary Films had previously produced *Dokkoi! Ningen bushi* (All together now! The human dance; 1975) in cooperation with Ogawa Productions. He then made two films focusing on the people of Kotobuki: *Ikiru* (To live; 1981) and *Ikiru Paato 2* (To live, part 2), which may be considered sequels to *Dokkoi! Ningen bushi*.

SASAJIMA—LAUNCHED BY A FILM SHOWING

The showing of *Dokkoi! Ningen bushi* in December 1975 was the starting point for work in Sasajima. The Film Group that arranged its showing found the Kotobuki reality was also present in Nagoya: late that month eleven men died of starvation near Nagoya Station. Until then it was commonly believed that Nagoya had no yoseba. But right in front of Nagoya station—in Sasajima—existed a yoseba where day laborers gathered from five to eight in the morning. The eleven who died of cold or hunger were laborers who had secured work through this yoseba, but during the year-end holiday season they found no work, and so they died.

The Film Group, deeply moved by the seriousness of the situation, in January 1976 opened a soup kitchen and, through May, served rice balls and *miso* (fermented soybean) soup to laborers living on the street. Supporters included church members, students, and other citizens. The Catholic Diocese Center and the UCCJ Nagoya Church each offered a room for the soup kitchen work. This was the first winter relief work in Sasajima.

In 1976, the Nagoya Winter Relief Soup Kitchen Committee was formed. The Nippon Sei Kō Kai (Anglican) now began active participation. For their part, the day laborers themselves formed the Sasajima Yoseba Rōdōsha Yūshi no Kai (Sasajima Yoseba Laborers Volunteers' Group) to deal with their own labor problems. This in turn gave birth to the preparatory committee

(1981) that laid the foundation for the Sasajima Day Laborers' Union (formed in June 1982). In 1982, the unions representing the four big yoseba—Sanya, Kotobuki, Sasajima, and Kamagasaki—convened the National Day Laborers Union Conference, ushering in a new stage in the yoseba labor movement.

Among the Christians, the Catholics built a new building, the Fukushinkan, and offered it as the operational base for the soup kitchen work (1978). They also began their own independent Fukushinkan Soup Kitchen Committee in March 1980. Bishop Sōma Nobuo was the prime mover behind these activities. Fukushinkan was some distance from Sasajima, so in 1989 a Dai-ni Fukushinkan Ikoi no Ie (No. 2 Fukushinkan Rest House) was built near Nagoya Station as a meeting place for day laborers.

Nagoya city officials wanted to suppress this activity by laborers, citizens, and Christians. On January 4, 1984, three men who were protesting at Nagoya City Hall were arrested on charges of refusing to disperse. They were demanding protection of the human rights of laborers who have no choice but to sleep in the streets. One of the three was Ōnishi Yutaka, chairman of the Sasajima Day Laborers Union; the other two were Matsumoto Susumu and Tsunose Sakae, lay members of the NSKK Chūbu Diocese's pioneer church. The authorities not only indicted these three but also detained them for seventy days.

Laborers called for nationwide support and opened a protest meeting in Nagoya. Christian groups—including the National Christian Council, the United Church of Christ, the Nippon Sei Kō Kai, the Nagoya Christian Council, and the Catholic Nagoya Diocese—sent letters of protest to the mayor of Nagoya. At the Chūbu Diocese's pioneer church, the NCCJ's Nagoya Strategy Committee on Suppression of Winter Relief was formed. On January 30 the first issue of *Kyūenkai nyūsu* (Relief Group news) was published. This group was the nucleus of support in the legal battle until Nagoya District Court issued its decision on December 23, 1987. The Strategy Committee appealed to churches nationwide on behalf of the "Yoseba Three." The three accused men were unjustly fined ten thousand yen, but the Strategy Committee formed because of this trial was of immeasurable value.

> During this four-year-long legal battle, we received the support of a wide spectrum of people in all regions from Hokkaido to Okinawa. In each area, movements began to consider the human rights problems of lower-class day laborers. This trial focused public attention on the problems of the oppressed not only in Nagoya but also nationwide, and thus gained support for our position. Furthermore, the enthusiastic support received within Japan and also from abroad, especially from the laborers and

peoples of Asian nations, clearly showed that our movement has much in common with Asian laborers who are oppressed by the major nations' economic invasion of their countries. (Relief Group news, No. 16, March 20, 1988.) It was precisely this activity that led to the formation in October 1987 of the Society for Solidarity with Asians Residing in Japan.

Parallel to relief work, the movement for building the Sasajima Laborers Center climaxed with dedication of the center in October 1985. The first floor has a dining hall; the second floor, labor union offices; the third floor, a medical clinic; and the fourth floor, a meeting room. Though it is only a small building, it is a strong ally of the day laborers. The Nagoya YWCA formed the nucleus for this construction project, with financial support from local citizens and churches. Today there is among laborers, Christians, and local citizens a depth and breath of cooperation undreamed of fifteen years ago. Along with the work of Catholics and the Anglicans, the efforts of former Christians now separated from the organized church should not be overlooked. The work in Sasajima is recorded in the newsletter *Sasajima* (now in its fourteenth issue) and the winter relief work report *Ettō* (Surviving winter).

SELF-DETERMINATION AND LIBERATION

It is, of course, the laborers themselves who are the nucleus of the yoseba movements. They must gain their own rights and bring about reform of the present situation. It is therefore significant that labor unions are active in each of the yoseba: the Sanya Strikers, the Kotobuki Day Laborers Union, the Sasajima Day Laborers Union, the Kamagasaki Day Laborers Union, as well as the Fukuoka Day Laborers Union in Hakata and the Okinawa Day Laborers Union in Naha. The National Day Laborers Union Council formed by these unions held its seventh rally in June 1990 in Osaka. One commitment of these unions is never to repeat the wartime mistake made by Japanese laborers who supported Japan's aggressive wars. Their goal is to build a labor movement that will not undertake military or economic aggression against other countries.

Christian work in the yoseba has focused largely on problems of discrimination and laborers' human rights. Now Christians must broaden their concerns to include problems of economic justice and international solidarity, as the laborer movement urges. At the same time, sustained involvement with the yoseba raises the question of how much Christians, churches, and the church as a whole have reformed themselves. Without such change, churches

and Christians will repeat their past mistakes, and movements in the yoseba
will pass them by.

Joint struggles between laborers and Christians in the yoseba are moving
forward, with potential for involving other religions, as in the Buddhist support of foreign laborers in Nagoya. While building solidarity with more and
more people, Christians who work in the yoseba will go forward step by step
along the road towards human liberation.

16

Disabled Persons and the Churches

Kumazawa Yoshinobu

AN ESTIMATED 4.2 MILLION people were counted as disabled persons in the latest national survey (1987). This figure includes 2.6 million physically disabled, 0.4 million mentally disabled, and 1.2 mentally ill persons. The national survey, generally conducted every five years, focuses on the physically disabled; those with mental disablities are estimated from national census figures.

These numbers, however, cover only persons with disabilities serious enough to entitle them to government services. If those with chronic or intractable diseases as well as elderly persons needing attendant care were included, the number of Japanese whose lives are burdened with some disability would exceed 5 million, or four percent of the total population.

GOVERNMENTAL PROVISIONS FOR THE DISABLED

Prior to 1970, legal measures for disabled persons were widely spread among thirteen ministries and agencies.[1] Lack of a comprehensive policy and of consistency among measures were impediments to the efficiency of all programs and services. Coordination of various programs within a particular ministry or agency was difficult. In short, the government needed a basic policy on disabled persons.

The Basic Law for Disabled Persons

To meet this need, the Basic Law for Measures Concerning Mentally and Physically Handicapped Persons was enacted in 1970. Because the definition

---

[1] Data in this section is adapted from *Social Welfare Services in Japan* (revised edition), 1990, compiled by the Japanese National Committee of the International Council on Social Welfare.

of "disabled person" varied in laws for education, employment, and rehabilitation services, the new law settled on a definition of "mentally and physically handicapped persons" as those whose daily life or social life is considerably inconvenienced for a long period of time on account of a disabled limb or trunk, a handicap in the visual function, a handicap in the auditory function, a dysfunction in equilibrium, voice, or speech, a permament functional disorder in internal organs such as heart and respiratory organs, or a mental deficiency such as mental retardation.

The Long-Term Plan for Disabled Persons

In January 1982 the Central Council on Measures for Disabled Persons, consisting of persons with expertise and experience, submitted to the Prime Minister a recommendation on "What Japan's Long-term Plan for Disabled Persons Should Be." Its measures were to assist disabled persons during the decade beginning with the International Year of Disabled Persons (1981). The government followed up in March 1982 with its Long-Term Plan for Disabled Persons. The 47 prefectures and 10 designated metropolitan governments also adopted long-term plans for the disabled. Among other municipalities, 340 local governments began carrying out long-term activities. The Headquarters for Promoting the Welfare of Disabled Persons was opened in March 1982 to coordinate operations among various administrative levels and organs.

To mark the International Year of Disabled Persons, the government declared December 9 — the day in 1975 when the United Nations General Assembly adopted the "Declaration of the Rights of Disabled Persons" — as Disabled Persons Day to deepen people's understanding of the problems of the disabled and to promote their welfare.

Specific Measures

Of the 2.6 million physically disabled reported in the 1987 national survey, those of age 18 or over and presumably living at homes in communities exceeded 2.4 million; those below age 18 numbered 93,000. The number in institutions was 94,000.

Mentally and physically disabled children. The major cause of physical disability is cerebral palsy. Since prenatal disruptions of metabolism and birth complications can be considerably reduced by better maternal and child health care, government agencies have carried out research and preventive measures. Recently, the incidence of disabilities due to accidents is increasing, and additional preventive measures are being considered.

Mentally retarded persons. In 1891, Ishii Ryōichi (1867–1937) founded Takinogawa Gakuen, the first private institution in Japan for mentally retarded children. By the time the Child Welfare Law was enacted in 1947 to establish residential care institutions for children with moderate mental retardation, twenty-seven charitable institutions were already in operation nationwide. The 1960 Law for the Welfare of Mentally Retarded Persons extended care to mentally retarded persons beyond childhood.

At present the Central Child Welfare Council, in accord with the March 1982 Long-term Plan, is promoting three welfare goals for the mentally retarded: (a) prevention, early detection, and treatment of disabilities, (b) home-based and community-based welfare services, and (c) institutional care. Other measures deal with medical security, income security, employment, education, and taxes.

Mentally ill persons. With enactment of the Mental Hygiene Law in 1950, mental health came to be seen as an indispensable part of public health administration. Mental hospitals became mandatory at the prefectural level, confining persons in private homes was prohibited, and mentally ill persons could now receive institutional care. After an initial period, however, changes in social conditions and progress in psychiatry led to less emphasis on hospital-centered care. Stress was put, rather, on outpatient treatment and aftercare services. Accordingly, the Mental Hygiene Law was partially revised in 1965 to subsidize outpatient care. Public health centers began providing mental hygiene services, and new mental health centers were established at the prefectural level.

The National Institute of Mental Health had been founded in 1952 (since renamed the National Mental and Neurological Center, Mental Health Research Institute) to do research in support of government programs. In line with trends outlined above, the Mental Hygiene Law was revised in 1987 and renamed the Mental Health Law, with a further revision in 1988. The aim of these revisions is, while protecting the human rights of mentally ill persons, to assure appropriate levels of psychiatric treatment and social rehabilitation.

Elderly persons. Institutional protection was for many years the major need of indigent elderly persons and those who had difficulty in living independently due to mental or physical disability. Accommodation in homes for the elderly and provision of financial support were the main measures.

The postwar demographic shift from "many births and many deaths" to "few births and few deaths" occurred in tandem with economic growth that produced a high standard of living, easing the situation of some elderly people. But the migration of young people to urban areas, formation of nuclear families, and changes in attitudes and capabilities to care for elderly parents left many elderly persons in need of alternate care. The problems of the elderly shifted from poverty involving a small group of people to welfare and nursing issues involving virtually all the elderly. This made care for the elderly all the more a national task. The Law for the Welfare of the Aged, enacted in 1963, set the direction of welfare policies: self-help measures, family and community cooperation, and social services provided by national and local governmental agencies.

CHRISTIAN SOCIAL WORK FOR THE DISABLED

With only a brief indication of the scope of Catholic and Protestant facilities for the disabled, the focus here is mainly on ecumenical activities.

Catholic Services

Institutional Catholic work with physically and mentally disabled persons is directed to three main groups: mentally retarded children, persons with disabled limbs, and special nursing homes for the elderly. The Catholic Liaison Committee for Disabled Persons coordinates the various projects. The scope of the work is suggested by data in table 16.1.

TABLE 16.1

CATHOLIC INSTITUTIONS FOR DISABLED PERSONS

Diocese	Institutions	Staff	Occupants
Sapporo	4	61	138
Sendai	1	61	46
Urawa	3	94	240
Tokyo	1	32	152
Yokohama	2	163	230
Kyoto	4	313	381
Osaka	2	90	120
Hiroshima	2	98	190
Fukuoka	1	42	70
Nagasaki	4	496	466
Oita	2	74	172
Kagoshima	2	68	144
Totals	28	1,592	2,349

Source: *Katorikku nenkan* (Catholic yearbook), 1985.

Protestant Services

Most social work agencies and institutions related to the United Church of Christ in Japan (UCCJ) belong to the Japan Christian Social Work League (JCSWL), which also includes a few non-UCCJ institutions. There are nine UCCJ-related institutions that are not presently JCSWL members, four of which provide services for the disabled. At present JCSWL has 78 member bodies (comprising 207 individual institutions), of which 43 serve disabled persons. Included among these groupings are a handful of UCCJ-related comprehensive care agencies such as the Seirei Welfare Centers in Hamamatsu and Kobe, the Airinkai in Tokyo, and the Ainotomo Association in Chiba Prefecture.

The UCCJ has in recent years become more active in helping disabled persons serve at different levels of church life, including participation in committees. In 1988 the UCCJ held a consultation on combatting discrimination against disabled persons.

Work related to the Nippon Sei Kō Kai (Japan Anglican Church) goes back to Takinogawa Gakuen, the pioneer facility for disabled persons founded by Ishii Ryōichi in 1891. Data on current NSSK services are given in table 16.2

TABLE 16.2

NIPPON SEI KŌ KAI INSTITUTIONS FOR DISABLED PERSONS

Region	Institutions	Staff	Occupants
North Kantō	2	142	240
Tokyo	2	89	130
Yokohama	4	126	285
Chūbu	2	13,	
Kyoto	6	131	360
Osaka	2	32	55
Totals	18	533	1,070

Source: *Gendai shakai fukushi no genryū: Nippon Sei Kō Kai shakai jigyō shi* (The origins of modern social welfare: The history of social work in the Japan Anglican Church), 1988.

THE NATIONAL CHRISTIAN COUNCIL IN JAPAN

Japan Christian Council for Evangelism Among the Blind.

On her second visit to Japan, in 1948, Helen Keller was accompanied by the director of the John Milton Society, who urged that funds be raised for the blind. In response, a national network of blind Christians and agencies for the blind – related to the UCCJ or the NCCJ – formed a cooperative ecumenical organization called the Japan Christian Council for Evangelism Among the Blind, or popularly Mōden from the words *mōjin* (blind) and *dendō* (evangelism). Mōden, an associate member of the NCCJ since 1951, will soon celebrate its fortieth anniversary.

As of 1990, the Mōden network includes 9 institutions and 25 Christian lay organizations for the blind, with about 500 members. One member institution, the Saffron Home, is the only one of its kind in Japan that provides education for sightless women and girls.

Mōden's main activities are:

1.Evangelical retreats and training of the blind at the national, regional, and local levels.

2.Publication of Bibles and other Christian works in braille. In May 1990 the braille edition of the New Common Bible (cf. IV-28) became available through cooperation of the Japan Bible Society, the National Catholic Committee, the NCCJ, and Mōden. Other braille publications include the monthly *Shinkō* (Faith), evangelistic tracts, and some sixty books on the Christian faith.

3.Production of tape recordings of Bible readings, children's stories, testimonies of faith, and the bimonthly tape magazine *Otozure* (Visit).

4.Counseling to introduce churches to blind and visually impaired persons who seek closer ties with a church.

5.Pioneer work and advocacy in areas of difficulty faced by the blind, such as integrated education, higher education, marriage, family life, employment, and fuller participation in democratic processes.

6.Service to improve the social status of visually impaired persons and to foster evangelism among the blind by sponsoring exchanges with counterparts in South Korea, Taiwan, the Philippines, Bangladesh, and other Asian countries.

NCCJ Task Force of Disabled Persons and the Churches

The NCCJ Twenty-seventh General Assembly in March 1979 appointed a Special Committee on Physically Disabled Persons, which in July was renamed the NCCJ Task Force of Disabled Persons and the Churches. In 1980 the Task Force produced for sale special commemorative stationery;

sponsored a study tour to the United States and Canada; and sent participants to the International Rehabilitation Cooperation Convention.

During 1981, the International Year of Disabled Persons, disabled persons
were among delegates to the Christian Conference of Asia (CCA) Assembly.
Other Task Force activities included guidelines for disabled-friendly church
architecture, review of Bible expressions referring to disabled persons, speakers
dispatched to educate others on problems faced by the disabled, and participation in an overseas survey as well as in the first International Convention
of Disabled Persons held by the CCA. Since 1981, national exchange seminars with disabled persons and related groups have been held every year in
conjunction with the annual Disabled Persons Week.

The NCCJ in 1982 published *Kami no kazoku* (God's family) and appealed
for churches to include Disabled Persons Week in their calendars. Theological schools were urged to include education on disabled persons in their cur-
ricula. At this time Tokyo Union Theological Seminary (TUTS) introduced
the subject of disabled persons in its general lectures on practical theology,
and lectures are still being given at TUTS by Shimazaki Mitsumasa, former
chairperson of the NCCJ Task Force.

Disabled persons from the Catholic Church in Japan accompanied other delegates to the World Council of Churches' Sixth Assembly in Vancouver, July
1983. Since May 1984 the Task Force has issued the regular newsletter
Shōgaisha to kyōkai mondai nyūsu (News of disabled persons and the
church), and in 1985 it published the booklet *Mizawa no arawareru tame ni*
(May God's will be done). The current chairperson, Matsunaga Sadako, attended the Asia-Pacific Regional Convention of Disabled Persons in March
1989. The Task Force in December 1989 conducted a survey of disabled
persons' situations.

National Exchange Seminars

The International Year of Disabled Persons provided the impetus for the first
of the National Exchange Seminars for groups of disabled persons, held annually since with a wide variety of groups participating.[2]

Among the various seminar topics, one that gets regular attention is "theology of disabled persons," with lectures by the present writer (1986), UCCJ
pastor Kanekiyo Akira (1987), and Luthern Seminary professor Tokuzen

---

[2] Some examples are: Japan Mission to Lepers, Mōden, Lutheran Church Group for Co-
operative Evangelism with the Deaf, Association for Cooperative Evangelism with Phys-
ically Disabled Persons, Chūgoku Regional Group for Christian Evangelism with
Physically Disabled Persons, Hyogo Prefecture Group for Mutual Encouragement,
Kyoto/Shiga Council of Disabled Persons, UCCJ Hokkai District Committee for Church
Development with Disabled Persons, Catholic Liaison Committee for Disabled Persons.

Yoshikazu (1988). A symposium in 1990 heard presentations by UCCJ pastor Aoki Suguru, Japan Reformed Church pastor Ihara Makio, and UCCJ layman Shimazaki Mitsumasa.[3]

Three important trends have emerged from these seminars. One is a move away from the more elementary questions of disabled persons' situations to the deeper questions of a theology of disabled persons. The second is a shift by disabled persons from seeing themselves as the objects of mission to taking a more active role as the subjects (or agents) of mission. Third, what began as a theology *of* disabled persons gradually evolved into theology *by* disabled persons. This process has potential for giving birth to new theological insights within the church in Japan.

Exchanges have also taken place in regional settings, as in the western Japan (Chūgoku) "Gatherings to consider disabled persons and the church" held since 1981. The regional gatherings have had wide ecumenical participation, with the Alliance, Assemblies, Baptist, Catholic, Nonchurch, Reformed, and other traditions represented, along with the UCCJ. Participation by the Hiroshima Christian Social Center, Seikei Vocational Aid Center, Shikoku Christian College, and the Church of Christ's Volunteer Center have added significance to these gatherings.

NEW FRONTIERS

Growing Concern For the Mentally Ill

In Japanese churches the term "disabled persons" has meant almost exclusively *physically* disabled persons. This was evident in the NCCJ's first effort to deal with the issue in 1979 in setting up its Special Committee on Physically Disabled Persons. Even after the committee was renamed the Task Force of Disabled Persons and the Church, it dealt exclusively with issues of disability.

A change in this approach came after the fifth exchange seminar in 1985 when Sugawara Petero, author of *Daichi ni fusu* (Falling prostrate on the earth), spoke compellingly of the spiritual pain of mentally ill persons. After he accepted an invitation to join the NCCJ Task Force, the churches for the first time began to seek out the mentally ill. There followed a gradual awakening that the circle of disability embraces not only physical impairments but mental illness as well. The evolving trend opened up the possibility of mentally ill persons receiving formal theological education and ministerial

---

[3] On this symposium, see my article, "Theology of holism and the human body from the perspective of a theology of disabled persons," in *Shintaisei no shingaku* (Theology of holism), compiled by the Japan Society of Systematic Theology, 1990.

ordination. Some pastors have dedicated themselves to serving the mentally ill.

And yet, the mentally ill are still looked upon in a cold, judgmental way, even in the churches. Among those who have learned to help the physically disabled it is all too common to regard mental illness as scary and strange. Despite these odds, growing numbers of persons suffering mental illness are seeking salvation in the church. With the many strains of contemporary society, there is an increase in persons on the borderline of normal/abnormal, if not clearly ill mentally. It has never been more important than now for the church to update its attitudes toward mental distress. The Lord Jesus was always surrounded by troubled people. His attitude toward them was one of complete and loving acceptance. He always saw them as lovable persons on whom God poured his overflowing love.

Back in 1978 a low-key approach to this issue began in the Sharing Group on Theology and Mental Health. Since the death of the first chairperson, Kishi Chitose, in 1989, the well-known Christian psychiatrist Akaboshi Susumu has chaired the group. Using interdisciplinary exchange to gain a fuller understanding of people, the group held its twenty-third gathering in autumn 1990. The group is now planning to open Christian mental care clinics in Tokyo and Yokohama. Groundwork for this practical venture included a two-part lectures series in 1990 (eight lectures in summer, twelve in autumn) on the theme "Christianity and mental health." Cassette tapes of these lectures are to be made available through the cooperation of the Far East Broadcasting Corporation, a Christian broadcasting network. These are among the signs of hope for new developments in the Japanese churches as they relate to disabled persons.

Facing an Aging Society

Declining birth and death rates propel Japan along the path of becoming an aging society, one demographically shaped like an inverse pyramid. It is predicted that by the year 2020 one of every five Japanese will be over age 65. One significant aspect of an expanded elderly sector will be an increase in disabled persons. The pace at which this is happening in Japan is not yet seen in other countries (cf. III-17).

Faced with this prospect, the churches can ill afford to hold to their present course of concentrating efforts on those considered normal, healthy persons. With the twenty-first century just around the corner, the church's mission is inescapably broader than middle-class, middle-aged normalcy.

Indeed, its mission is no smaller than "God's family," which includes all age levels and all human conditions — the aged, youth and children, the healthy and the infirm. The church can be faithfully built when all these members of God's family are included. True worship in this spirit cannot be exclusively for one age or condition. How can our churches become true families of God? The answer to this question opens the gateway to the twenty-first century.

17

Hospices and Terminal Care

Saitō Takeshi

THE JOYS AND SORROWS of individual persons as well as the interactions of human beings must be understood in the context of the culture, society, and age we live in. One inescapable fact of Japan today is this: The ratio of elderly people to the total population is growing at a faster rate than in any other country in the world. Yet even long lives come to an end. So here I want to reflect on the issues of death and dying, on some related attitudinal changes, and on the roles that Christians and churches have in dealing with death and dying.

I spent fifteen years in the United States as a seminary student and then as a chaplain in a university hospital, where I ministered to dying patients. My experiences with such patients and their families and with health care professionals, both in the United States and later in Japan, have led me to ask what can be specifically expected of Christians in such situations. And the Christian's role in death and dying, of course, needs to be seen in the wider sociocultural context.

The atmosphere that surrounds death and dying in Japanese society, with its expanding elderly population, has much in common with the United States and other developed societies. With improved medical technology and public hygiene, Japan's death rate has gradually declined, giving the Japanese people the highest average life-expectancy in the world. In 1971 the average life span of men was 70 years; of women, 74. By 1987 the life span of men was 75; of women, 81. As the death rate drops, the ratio of elderly persons to the total population naturally rises (though sickness is more prevalent among the aged). In 1970 the elderly were 7.1 percent of Japan's population; in 1990, 11 percent. It is clear that this demographic trend will continue.

THE HOSPITAL: WHERE PEOPLE FACE DEATH

With rapid growth of the elderly population has come a remarkable increase in the number of hospitals and other health care facilities during the past decade. Under the banner of "welfare for the aged," many hospitals and facilities were built away from city and town centers. In the Japanese context this reminds us of the feudal-age *ubasuteyama* — mountains where old folks were once taken to die. Owing to the remote and inconvenient locations of facilities for the elderly, the frequency of visits by families and friends declines as time passes. The emotional distance between parent and child, and also among friends, becomes greater. More and more, old people are dying in loneliness.

But not only old people — most Japanese die in hospitals nowadays. Surveys of morticians show that almost always they are called to hospitals to pick up the bodies. Doctors devote themselves to making proper diagnoses of illnesses and giving appropriate treatment; nurses also try to help patients recover quickly and return to normal life. Other professional hospital staff are trained to assist in these health-restoring goals. They all tend to concentrate so completely on faithful execution of their professional responsibilities that they rarely ask the opinion of "outsiders" or "amateur" family members. It is only natural, then, that people feel some coldness or insensitivity in the closed systems of hospitals and their professional staffs.

Even though hospitals seem closed and unfeeling, patients with hope of returning to normal life can tolerate the seeming indifference as only a temporary condition. After all, they can focus on the primary benefit of a hospital stay: proper diagnosis and treatment leading to an early release. Patients with little or no hope of recovery, however, seldom feel that a hospital is the right place to spend their last days. Nor do families and friends consider hospitals appropriate for bidding loved ones a final farewell.

There is, moreover, an enormous gap between the amount of time medical professionals allocate to performing their duties toward individual patients and the long lapses of time experienced by dying patients and their family members. This time gap contributes to the feeling that hospitals are cold and inhuman.

In the late 1970s, concerned citizens began a movement to make medical care "warm" and "more human." They pointed out how sad it is for terminally ill patients to face death in a hospital — cut off from family and friends, hooked up to machines, and often unable even to utter a word. Some medical professionals themselves are concerned with treatment of the terminally ill. Although they seem to be lacking in concrete proposals, at least they have recommended that medical care be more human, warm, and considerate than present practices using the instruments of high technology that place advanced scientific knowledge above human concerns.

THE HOSPICE MOVEMENT IN JAPAN

To help deal with the above circumstances, two important books were translated and published in Japanese. One is *Care of the Dying* (Japanese version: *Shi no kango,* 1977), by Dr. Richard Lamerton, then at St. Joseph's Hospice in England. The other is *Hospice* (Japanese: *Hosupisu,* 1982), by Dr. Kenneth P. Cohen, which introduces St. Christopher's Hospice founded in London by Dr. Cecily Saunders. These books presented for the first time in Japan the basic ideas of helping terminally ill patients and their families.

Wakabayashi Kazumi, a journalist, visited hospices in both the United States and England, interviewing their founders and working teams. She then wrote a book titled *Yasuraka na shi no tame ni* (To die peacefully), and this book made many people aware of the existence of hospices, which previously were known to only a few medical professionals.

The purpose of a hospice is to take care of dying patients and their loved ones. The staff members not only control patients' physical pain medically but also listen to their problems, which increase as the time of death approaches. They give support as patients express fear, anxiety, sadness, and loneliness. Hospice treatment is based on the understanding that in the process of dying, people suffer not only physical pain but also emotional, social, and spiritual pain. At a hospice, therefore, a patient is not treated merely as a failing patient but as a still living person. There is, after all, no greater pain for a patient than separation by death from loved ones. Hospice teams extend a helping hand to all those facing the grief of this final separation.

Care in a hospice begins with specific questions: What are the needs of the patient and family, and what help are they seeking? Answering these questions takes a lot of listening to complaints of physical pain from the patient, and to expressions of emotional distress from family members. Hospice staff do their best to alleviate all pain and distress. They also lend positive support to help patient and family fulfill desires in the limited time they have left together.

The helping hand is not withdrawn when the patient dies; it remains extended to the bereaved family to give continued care. Doctors, nurses, case workers, chaplains, and volunteer workers at the hospice compose a team that seeks to meet the varied needs of patients and families.

Difficulties Faced in Japan

For Japanese doctors whose hospitals have never had chaplains, counselors, or case workers, it was rather shocking to hear about the "team medical care" so important to the hospice idea and practice in England. Many of them responded by saying, "Japan is not a Christian country," "Japanese patients do not like to be told the name or nature of their disease," and "Japanese patients do not have the self-confidence and strength to face death squarely." Thus they saw no need for hospices in Japan.

Even so, many old people and their families have expressed a desire for hospice care. Taking St. Christopher's Hospice as a model, some pro-hospice citizens mounted a campaign to start a hospice at Yodogawa Christian Hospital in Osaka and at Seirei Welfare Institute in Hamamatsu of Shizuoka Prefecture. I was still working as a hospital chaplain in the United States when this movement began, and I was asked to make preparations for the Seirei hospice. Dr. Kashiwagi Tetsuo of Yodogawa Christian Hospital planned to start one there.

In summer 1979 we went together to England to visit St. Christopher's Hospice and St. Joseph Hospice, and we learned much about running such a facility. In 1980 both Kashiwagi and I were invited to attend the first National Hospice Conference in England, and we were able to visit St. Christopher's again. On this trip we acquired much information from hospice directors about their situations. Because we made our new information available to newspapers, people's interest in hospices mounted rapidly. But it took a long time before our own hospices came into existence and began functioning. One inhibiting reason was the negative attitude noted earlier, especially "the Japanese are not Christian" or ". . . are not religious." This view stemmed from the fact that our two prime examples of hospices in England were both Christian institutions, and we often met resistance in comments such as "it smells like Christianity."

The difficulty in starting and operating a hospice stems not only from the lack of understanding or ignorance among doctors, who wield much power in the field of medicine. Our own attitude toward death also makes the task much harder. As I mentioned earlier, the death rate in Japan has dropped remarkably due to improved health care and medical technology; and nowadays most people meet their deaths in a hospital bed. Hence, death usually occurs somewhere far away from us and our daily lives. This appears to be the way we want it, for we tend to push death away from us, and would "kill" death were it only possible.

Terminal Care in a Society That Denies Death

Japanese airline carriers—proud symbols of modern technology—have no seat numbered "4" in their planes, as the Japanese pronunciation *shi* for "four" is the same as that for "death." No one wants to be reminded of death while in flight 30,000 feet above the earth. Likewise, there is no room numbered "4" in our hospitals, for that numeral is felt to be a bad omen. So we exclude it wherever possible, or use the alternate pronunciation *yon*. Also, in Japan even a small child does not want to be between two others when photographed, owing to the superstition that the middle one will die before the other two. Modern-day Japanese do not consciously admit to holding such beliefs, yet they avoid all suggestions of death as much as possible. Thus we live in a society that eschews all mention of death, indeed, abhors it and wants to eliminate it. We try to live as if we will never die.

We think of death as something ugly and unclean. After attending a funeral, for example, we seek purification by sprinkling salt on ourselves to get rid of the "dust of death" that might yet cling to us. In a word, our society denies the very fact of death and seeks to transmute it into something else. To repeat, we would "kill" death if we could.

Consequently, those who cannot reject dying — the terminally ill and their families — are themselves rejected by others while the dying is in process. The solemnity of one's once-in-a-lifetime death is not treated appropriately, and many die in anger and loneliness.

The Japanese people's denial of death, however, does not change the fact that we are born and we die without exception. Taking into account Japan's declining death rate, about 750,000 die annually. Most die in hospitals, which generally avoid death and dying. For example, when a patient dies in a hospital, the body is removed in such a way that other patients in that room do not even notice the removal. Not only is the death hidden from others; Buddhist priests and clergy of other religions are not welcome in hospitals. They are ill omens that remind people of death.

As noted above, the mass media have often taken up the subject of hospices ever since Dr. Kashiwagi and I attended the 1980 international hospice conference. They have publicized hospices as "warm, human medical care," and in doing so have idealized hospices. They created their own image of "hospices" before any actually existed in our country! And they made this image popular by using such terms as "human" and "the dignity of life." Moreover, besides our hospices in Osaka and Hamamatsu, many other hospices went into business before Kashiwagi and I could make clear the purpose of a hospice, the treatment given patients and families, what it means to be terminally ill, the basic problems of separation by death, and how a hospice team works. So we now have a variety of hospices, variously touted as "Japanese-style hospices," "Buddhist hospices," and "hospices without religious affiliation."

In the original hospice tradition, medical control of pain is used so that emotional, social, and spiritual needs can receive more attention. Some of the new Japanese hospices, however, take a different approach. They view pain control as a defeat of medicine's own original purpose, and say doctors should persist to the very end in efforts to improve the patient's health. At such hospices, like in any hospital, death is a taboo subject for patients and families alike, and they are not allowed to express the many emotions that well up in the face of impending death. These, then, are death-denying Japanese-style hospices where the numeral "4" is banned and people behave as if death never happens. It is not clear to me whether it is patients, families, or medical professionals—or all three—who most prefer this kind of hospice.

Most Japanese doctors do not, as a matter of principle, tell their patients the true nature of their illness when it is terminal, as in some cancer cases. They advise the families, who do know, not to tell patients the truth, and most families comply. The family members are usually afraid of telling the truth, partly out of deference to the doctor and partly out of consideration for the patient, whom they do not wish to shock. They want to protect the patient from emotional suffering.

I have not yet reached a conclusion on whether it is helpful or harmful to tell patients the truth. Still, the paternalism of doctors and families definitely makes communication very unnatural between patients and families as well as between patients and doctors and nurses. This makes it very hard for terminally ill patients to express their true feelings and to be understood.

WHAT CAN CHRISTIANS DO?

The Christian churches have, I am sad to report, been largely indifferent to the problems of the terminally ill and their families. Ministers have shown concern and given help to such people on a personal basis, but these concerns have as yet found no place in formal church policies and programs. I feel strongly that death and dying, along with separation by death, need serious consideration beyond the framework of medicine. Death, after all, not infrequently comes from causes other than sickness. As a hospital chaplain I have often been asked probing questions about the meaning of human existence, such as "Why me?" and "I have never done anything really bad, so why has this fate befallen me?"

There are no differences among races or nationalities when it comes to suffering and tears. Pain is the lot of every human being. And support for those afflicted by pain and suffering has to go beyond the realm and reach of medicine.

The number one cause of death in Japan is cancer—reportedly one out of four. Terminally ill patients increasingly know the truth about their illness, and they look with scorn upon the doctors' debate about whether to tell patients the truth. Indeed, to know the truth often arouses the will and energy to live. But whether the truth is known or not, the terminally ill patient experiences intense anxiety and loneliness as physical pain increases and physical functions decline.

One critical point of view says there is little difference among hospitals, homes, and hospices as places where people end their lives. So long as a doctor is in charge, the patient remains in the patient role. But a patient also remains a person, a father or a mother, a lover or a child. Life is more than physical existence, so death and the final separation it brings must be considered in more than medical terms. Because death and separation involve human life in a full sense, the churches and Christians need to offer helping hands to all those desperately wishing to be treated as a whole persons.

Little by little we have seen the emergence of various kinds of support groups. Some are formed by those suffering from the same illness; others by persons sharing the same grief and pain. In this society so oriented to production it is an uncomfortable role to assume, so these groups carry on their activities with inconspicuous seriousness. Persons helping with these groups — for cancer patients, alcoholics, mentally disturbed children, and so on — work on a volunteer basis, and they generally have difficulty in finding a place to meet.

The churches have tended to leave death and dying to the hospitals. Since death and separation from family are not just physical but emotional and spiritual problems as well, the churches should be with and support those who are most vulnerable and distressed. Cecily Saunders, founder of St. Christopher's Hospice, after years of dealing with dying patients, pointed out that the essence of terminal care is summarized in what Jesus said to his disciples at Gethsemane: "Stay here and keep watch with me" (Mt 26:36). It is not just a matter of skill or sharing something you have learned. Care for the dying transcends these things. It is impossible, she said, to understand other persons fully and perfectly; we do best just to be there and be still. And the most important of these is "be there."

This attitude has implications beyond care for the terminally ill. The "be there" emphasis came from the English hospice movement, but it is difficult to implement in Japan, not least because most hospitals have no chaplains. This account must end, then, with a query: Can the Christian churches in Japan find ways to "be there" with those facing death and to share the grief of their loved ones suffering the pain of separation? If so, can it be done in sustained institutional programs, not just personal ministries? And will Japanese society be receptive to innovative support and care for the terminally ill and other extreme situations?

18

Inochi no Denwa — Telephone Counseling

Saitō Yukio

UPHEAVAL IN EASTERN EUROPE since fall 1989 was not something that just suddenly happened — grass-roots movements for democratization were long under way. One small beginning in the larger process was the first telephone counseling service in East Germany, started in 1986 by Dr. Harmut Kirschner, a Lutheran living in Dresden. The government had persistently refused to authorize the service, which it saw as a threat to government control. When the authorities finally yielded, telephone counseling advocates felt the first first cracks had appeared in the Berlin Wall.

In 1989, Estonians opened a similar service; a recent visitor reports that the suicide rate there is an extremely high 25–30 per 100,000 population.

Volunteers in Beijing started telephone counseling services just before the June 1989 events in Tiananmen Square. Reports from the Beijing service indicate that some calls came from dissidents, and some came from soldiers and policemen; but the majority of calls involve marriage and family problems, and mental disorders.

The problems encountered by telephone counselors in Eastern Europe and China are much the same as those that motivated the beginning of telephone counseling in the West. They are problems that transcend systems and ideologies. Telephone counseling is a humane, democratic way of dealing with what amounts to a global crisis of the human spirit.

INOCHI NO DENWA AND ECUMENISM

"Inochi no Denwa" means, literally, "life telephone." Its relevance to the mission of the church in Japan and its potential for service to Japanese society are central concerns for Inochi no Denwa as it nears its twentieth anniversary.

Open and Impartial

When one hundred concerned Christians gathered in 1969 in response to the appeals of German missionary Ruth Hetcamp and formed the nucleus of what in 1971 became Inochi no Denwa, it was intended to be a Christian movement. The nature of its task, however, led some to feel the need for a wider range of participation. After much discussion, the choice was to be a citizens' movement open to Christians and non-Christians. It was more than an ecumenical movement, so we called it *puro-kato-non* (from the Japanese pronunciation of the first syllables of Protestant, Catholic, and non-Christian). Nowadays even that designation is avoided, as we do not inquire into anyone's beliefs.

In this sense, Japan's Inochi no Denwa is similar to England's Samaritans, which takes no religious position. Australia's Life Line, founded by Alan Walker, does have a clear Christian policy and participation is limited to Christians. Inochi no Denwa received much advice and aid from Walker and naturally absorbed much of Life Line's spirit and methodology. Inochi no Denwa maintains friendly relations but does not affiliate formally with Life Line; it has no formal relationship with the Samaritans.

Inochi no Denwa joined the International Federation of Telephonic Emergency Services (IFOTES), comprising the clearly Christian West German and Scandinavian telephone lifelines and the nonreligious French and Communist-bloc telephone lifelines and other groups. Life Line and the Samaritans, which have their own international federations, are not members of IFOTES. Inochi no Denwa's impartial stance is respected at home and abroad, inside and outside the church.

A Laypersons' Movement

As of July 1990, Inochi no Denwa centers number thirty-four (including two in the planning stage),[1] with over five thousand volunteers to staff them. Financial support is received from a wide variety of individuals and organizations — churches, ministers, and lay members, both Catholic and Protestant. Its funding possibly represents the most substantial ecumenical support in the history of the church in Japan. Moreover, Inochi no Denwa is a splendid lay movement; it offers people who are otherwise "frozen assets" an oppor-

---

[1] Center names, by region, are: Hokkaido: Asahikawa, Hokkaido; Hokuriku: Niigata; Tōhoku: Ashikaga, Miyagi, Morioka (planned), Sendai; Kantō: Chiba, Kawasaki, Ibaraki, Saitama (planned), Tokyo, Tokyo Tama, Yokohama; Chūbu: Hamamatsu, Nagoya; Kansai: Harimai, Kansai, Kobe, Kyoto, Nara, Wakayama; Western Honshu: Hiroshima, Okayama, Shimane; Shikoku: Ehime, Kagawa, Tokushima; Kyushu: Fukuoka, Kagoshima, Kitakyushu, Kumamoto, Oita; Okinawa: Naha. There is also the Tokyo English Life Line (TELL).

tunity to be helpfully involved. Surely there are few precedents where laypeople have been organized on a national level and become as passionately and continuously involved in a single sustained activity. The clergy support from the sidelines, while the laypersons become the nucleus in a field where they can perform a vital service. In a word, Inochi no Denwa has discovered a unique way to demonstrate the potential of lay activity.

Inochi no Denwa has also received attention from Japanese society in general. Previous examples of volunteer movements abound, but Inochi no Denwa has managed the balance between a high degree of training and a low dropout rate that makes for healthy continuity, while relying largely on volunteers. Also, its use of the telephone in a new system of counseling, open 24 hours a day, responding to suicide and other emotional crises, makes it more than just another volunteer movement for social welfare. It fulfills a pioneering role in preserving mental health at the local level. Accordingly, the Ministry of Health and Welfare has granted Inochi no Denwa the legal status of "juridical person" (*hōjin*), which is rare for organizations of this kind.

Cooperation with Non-Christians

There is admittedly some dispute as to whether Inochi no Denwa is truly ecumenical. For one thing, many Christians serve in Inochi no Denwa centers in the larger cities, but very few are found in centers in the smaller cities. Even in Tokyo, volunteers are careful not to ask each other whether they are Christians. In the beginning, all meetings began with prayer, but this was later dropped as inappropriate. In the day-to-day activities of Inochi no Denwa, neither Christianity nor any other specific belief system is imposed on trainees or active counselors.

In foreign telephone counseling agencies affiliated with Life Line, it is strictly forbidden in a telephone counseling situation to try to evangelize callers. Their basic policy is to support the person who is facing difficulty and respect his or her values, Christian or not.

Since Inochi no Denwa has this same policy, it may sound strange to call it "ecumenical." Some would say it is enough just to be a citizens' movement, or a volunteer movement in which many Christians participate. Having grown out of the church, its place in the ecumenical context might be called "anonymous ecumenism." The very fact that here the church and Christians have a place where they can work together with non-Christians is most important. Nationwide, many Christian clergy are involved in Inochi no Denwa, but not in their clerical capacity. For precisely that reason, Inochi no Denwa is a place where Christians, lay and clergy alike, are made humble. In a non-Christian country such as Japan, the church needs the kind of interface with society that Inochi no Denwa provides.

The positive meaning of Christian participation in Inochi no Denwa lies in the organization's primary task—counseling. Or to put it more plainly, it is found in the complaints that the callers want to talk about.

We used to think that anonymity and the non-visible nature of telephone counseling was one of the limitations of the telephone, but we have increasingly come to realize that, on the contrary, these very aspects facilitate self-disclosure and positive transference, enhancing the telephone's value as a means of treatment. For someone feeling emotional unease, the telephone is very "user-friendly."

A Special Role in Suicide Prevention

The suicidal problems and other mental disorders that people call to talk about represent what might well be called a microcosm of the mental condition of our times. From its inception, Inochi no Denwa has grappled with adolescent problems such as teenage suicide and family violence, and with problems related to mid-life crisis and so on—that is, with the typical pathological problems of each age group—and when needed, psychiatric care has been provided. Sometimes psychiatric treatment is not always locally available, however, so Inochi no Denwa has tried to evolve methods for dealing with emergency situations.

While community care with citizen participation is a current topic in social welfare, the participation of volunteers is also vital for dealing with socio-pathological problems such as suicide. This assessment is based not on the conventional notion that volunteers "provide cheap labor" or "fill a gap in government services," but on the idea that volunteers are truly necessary. In suicide prevention, especially, a psychiatrist's or clergy's professional status may sometimes be anti-therapeutic. Indeed, the sympathy and receptivity of the nonprofessional is in itself very important. Doublin's well-known saying is based on this understanding: "The use of nonprofessional volunteers is probably the single most important discovery in the history of suicide prevention. No progress was seen until they appeared on the scene." (The First Convention of the American Association for the Prevention of Suicide, 1969) This insight is also close to the Reformation concept of the priesthood of all believers.

Understanding the causes of suicide is definitely a matter for psychiatry, but suicide prevention by psychiatric treatment alone is impossible. The problem of suicide cannot be solved by the hasty imposition of values; neither is it simply a question of therapeutic techniques. The problem poses questions of the meaning and value of life on a deep level. At root, suicide is nothing less than a questioning of life itself, and thus is a challenge to the Christian faith. The Samaritans, which began in London, and Life Line, which began in Sydney, are the two bases from which telephone counseling has now spread throughout the world. By coincidence, the problem of suicide was the original impetus for both groups, and the founders of both were pastors.

Healing and Life's Meaning

In every age the church has had to deal with questions about the meaning of life. If Christians or other religionists do not deal with the pressing issues of our times, then who will? If the church is not aware of society's ills, and does not wrestle with them, then her ministry will be in vain. Yet these concerns must not be objectified as societal problems; we must see them, rather, as burdens shared by all humans and we must bear them together.

Inochi no Denwa functions as the ears of Christ's body, the church. It listens to the sorrows and troubles of our times. If the medical and social welfare institutions fail to perceive, or the church is not tuned in, to this suffering, then Inochi no Denwa must hear the callers' anxious and agonizing complaints on behalf of the church and welfare bodies. The church always has the task of looking squarely at the hardships of people and hearing their cries (Ex 3:7). As Jean Vanier expressed it so eloquently, the real tragedy of humanity is not that there are weak people, but that we do not incline our ears to hear their cries. In this sense, Inochi no Denwa's task is fundamentally different from giving advice to others out of pity. The dialogue of the telephone is essentially one between equals; it is a means of bearing our mutual burdens and weakness. From this is born true corporateness.

We often hear criticisms from within the churches that Inochi no Denwa fosters dependence (in Japanese, *amae*). Inochi no Denwa's aim is certainly not to foster dependence; on the contrary, it is to support the escape from dependence and the beginning of subjective [self-directed] living. The allegation of fostering dependence may stem from mere misunderstanding, or it may be an excuse to escape from sharing burdens, an excuse to discard the weak.

The experience of Inochi no Denwa is that the more people try to face serious problems, the more difficult it becomes to discuss those problems with the people closest to them. Children who call and tell us about being bullied at school or in their neighborhoods say they don't want their parents or teachers to think they are weaklings. Inochi no Denwa annually receives over four hundred calls from junior or senior high school girls who are pregnant and say they could never talk to their mothers about it. Middle-aged men suffering from depression show up at our psychiatric interview room, afraid to go to a company-provided clinic. Others come for advice on problems of personal relations within their church, because they cannot talk openly about these problems in church.

Dealing with emotional crises has traditionally been the province of education, religion, and psychiatric medicine; have they become incapable of performing this role adequately? That so many urgent social and personal needs are being brought to Inochi no Denwa compels us to question these traditional institutions. This does not mean that Inochi no Denwa takes the place of existing specialists; its role is, rather, to promote the use of many helping resources to support those hearts burdened by fear and torn by crisis.

Inochi no Denwa's attempts to give this support sometimes elicits from church circles this criticism: "It offers nothing more than psychological salvation." On the other hand, many people with no religious background believe that in the field of suicide and other crisis intervention, "religion is powerless." Both of these views are foolish and unproductive. What is actually at issue here is our understanding of "religion and health " and "the gospel and medicine." At Inochi no Denwa we must constantly deal with the old yet ever-new question of what constitutes "healing" in this age.

At Inochi no Denwa we simply come to know the depth of human pain and brokenness. And we feel helpless when confronted with some cases beyond our ability to give consolation or healing, and we know that we cannot save them. But we have learned to live with that, for we have also learned that the human condition is to be weak and broken, torn and full of wounds. It is a condition that cannot be hidden. And it is our own condition as well. So working with Inochi no Denwa inevitably and inescapably humbles us. Yet within the pain and perplexity of human existence we find comfort in Henri Nouwen's idea that the very one who is wounded can himself or herself be a healer.

19

Mass Communications

Yuguchi Takashi

POSTWAR TELECOMMUNICATIONS have been developed by both the government-sponsored Nihon Hōsō Kyōkai (Japan Broadcasting Corporation; popularly, NHK) and a number of private broadcast companies. NHK has a general and an educational TV channel, and a long-time feature of NHK's educational channel is the nonsectarian religious program first called "Shūkyō no Jikan" (The Religious Hour) and later renamed "Kokoro no Jidai" (The Spirit of the Times). This program features well-known guests and is broadcast nationwide.

Our discussion here, however, is confined to Christian programs sponsored by churches or other religious organizations and broadcast by commercial radio and television stations. The sponsors all face certain limitations. For example, most Christian programs have difficulty finding suitable talent. Funding influences the broadcast company's decision to cooperate, as does the sponsoring body's social standing. Moreover, the program code of the National Association of Commercial Broadcasters in Japan directly affects program content. The code's Section 7 on religion has four stipulations: (a) programs may not malign other religions or sects; (b) religious ceremonies and forms may not be treated with disrespect; (c) programs may not negate science; and (d) appeals may not be made for donations to specific religious groups.

SETTING THE STAGE: TILL 1975

The conditions for radio and television in the 1970s were set by developments in the late 1960s. In November 1967 operating licenses were given to eighteen new UHF television stations, heralding the licensing of a host of new UHF channels around 1970. Also, the years 1969–70 saw the opening of new FM radio stations in metropolitan areas, a foretaste of the proliferation of broadcast facilities in the 1980s.

Radio and TV Programming

Christian broadcasting had a much longer and larger history in radio than in television, and most Christian radio programs of the 1970s were holdovers from the 1960s. Representative examples and sponsors are: "Asa no Kotoba" (Morning Words), Christian Reformed Japan Mission; "Yo no Hikari" (Light of the World), Pacific Broadcasting Association; "Nazaren Awā" (Nazarene Hour), Japan Nazarene Church; "Kono Hito o Miyo" (Behold the Man) and "Kokoro ni Hikari o" (Light in Your Heart), the Lutheran Hour; "Famirī Awā" (Family Hour), Seventh Day Adventist; "Kokoro no Tomo" (Friend of the Heart), United Church of Christ in Japan and the NCCJ-related Audio Visual Activities Commission (AVACO) through their Joint Broadcasting Committee (JBC); and "Kokoro no Tomoshibi" (Lamp of the Heart) and "Taiyō no Hohoemi" (Smile of the Sun), Catholic Yoki Bokusha Undō (Good Shepherd Movement; popularly, YBU).

Most Christian radio broadcasting in these years had a similar format: a sermon-centered program broadcast on Sunday morning. In the 1960s, however, commercial radio programming, along with the listening patterns of the general public, shifted to late night hours. Midnight programs beamed at young people by Bunka Hōsō and Tokyo Broadcasting System (TBS) garnered large audiences, drawing attention to a new market potential. First among Christian groups to adjust to this trend were PBA's "Young Life Club" (1971) and the Lutheran Hour's "Image Capsule" (1972), which was later renamed "Capsule Mate."

One factor in the fairly smooth adjustment to late night youth-oriented programming was that Christian sponsors were quite at home with the kind of pop music so popular among young people. Non-Christian religious groups could not easily make the shift, as they did not have the cultural connections that Christian groups had to the rock and folk music preferred by the younger generation.

In television programming, Christian sponsors tended to use limited runs of once a week for three months (13 programs) or six months. An exception is the Catholic "Kokoro no Tomoshibi"; begun in November 1960 and aired on eleven stations by 1971, it is still running today nationwide. An early entry into the world of television was made by four Lutheran churches that formed a joint committee and from the late 1960s produced several series, such as "Sekai no Nihonjin" (Japanese of the World), "Ajia ni Ikiru" (Living in Asia), "Shin Warera Ichizoku" (We're a New People), and "Hitotsubu no Mugi" (A Grain of Wheat). This committee also sponsored special Christmas programs and the rebroadcasting of the film version of Miura Ayako's best-selling novel *Hyōten* (Freezing point).[1]

Evangelical groups sponsored the telecasting, from October 1973, of Billy Graham's "Hour of Decision" in three-month runs (13 programs) over seven stations in Hokkaido, Niigata, Sendai, Nagano, Hiroshima, and elsewhere, with Hatori Akira as host. The programs included Billy Graham's rallies in various parts of the world and his 1967 crusade in Tokyo's Budokan.[2] From October 1974 this three-month series was shown throughout Kyushu; in 1975, in four prefectures of western Honshu (Japan's main island); in 1976, in Tokyo, Osaka, Nagoya, and Sapporo; and in 1977, in six prefectures in the Tōhoku (northeastern) region and three prefectures in the Hokuriku (north-western) region. Earlier, in April 1970, evangelical groups had begun tele-casting Moody Science Films in Okinawa.

In connection with the scheduled 1972 return of Okinawa to Japan, ques-tions were raised in autumn 1971 about a possible connection between the Far East Broadcasting Corporation (FEBC) and an Okinawa-based psycho-logical warfare unit of the US Forces in Japan. But FEBC received its broad-casting license in December 1972 as a medium-wave station and began operations the following March. With headquarters in Los Angeles and an international network, FEBC had begun beaming short-wave Japanese-lan-guage programs from Manila in 1952. Due to an economic slump in 1973, Japanese manufacturers of electrical goods shifted from high-priced products to inexpensive short-wave receivers, prompting a short-wave boom in 1974 among middle school and high school youth. FEBC's Tokyo office is said to have received as many as ten thousand letters a month during this boom.

In January 1974, FEBC began tests with midnight broadcasts from its me-dium-wave station HLDA on South Korea's Cheju Island (south of Pusan). In July of that year, the Japan Evangelical Association sponsored ten-minute programs from 8:30 P.M. daily for five days, with messages by evangelists Izuta Akira and Hatori Akira. By the end of 1974 the current program (from 9:30 P.M.) was under way. From that time FEBC has had the unique role of providing medium-wave Christian radio programs reaching all of Japan from a nearby overseas broadcasting facility.

Short-wave radio evangelism in Latin America for persons of Japanese an-cestry was begun by PBA in 1963 from station HCJB in Quito, Ecuador.

---

[1] For more on this best-selling Christian novelist, see III-22.
[2] The Budokan ("martial arts hall"), a large facility next to the Imperial Palace in Tokyo, is used for large gatherings as diverse as sumo tournaments, rock concerts, and evangelistic crusades. — Ed.

The program "Voice of the Andes," hosted by Japanese missionary Ozaki Kazuo, continues to this day. FEBC also broadcast Japanese-language programs by short wave from Manila until 1980, and from station KTWR in Guam from 1978 to the present.

In the 1970s the Catholic-sponsored Radio Vatican presented a regular fifteen-minute (6:50–7:05 A.M.) program in Japanese on Tuesdays, Thursdays, and Saturdays over three short-wave frequencies.

Research, Support, and Other Activities

Among other notable ventures of this period was the establishment by the Lutheran World Federation of its LWF/Broadcasting Service Tokyo Office (George Olson, director), which undertook a number of research projects, such as how Christians relate to mass media, and a pioneer study of children and the mass media, especially TV and magazines (mostly comic books). At a time when theories of mass culture were prevalent, a vital finding was made that individuals are not necessarily automatons subject to mass media control, but can respond to media presentations as individuals.

This period also saw the emergence of grass-roots groups for the support of Christian media ventures, such as a council of evangelical churches for broadcast evangelism in the Osaka–Kobe area. A support group had first been formed in June 1972 by churches interested in children's TV programs, and in January 1973 it launched the Kansai TV Evangelism Council, with 148 churches participating. Soon this group also lent support to PBA's "Yo no Hikari" radio program and to telecasting of Moody Science Films. With this broadened scope, it changed its name to Kinki Fukuin Hōsō Dendō Kyōgikai (Kinpōden) and held an inaugural rally in Osaka. For three months (April–June) in 1973 it sponsored a morning program (7:15–7:30 A.M.) called "Hikari no Tantei Awā" (Lifeboat of Light Hour) on the Mainichi Broadcast System (MBS) station. Kinpōden became a major support group for "Yo no Hikari" and other radio and television evangelism in the region.

A similar group formed about this time in the Tokyo area to support a similar program titled "Tanoshii Sekai" (Happy World) to be broadcast on Fuji TV, 7:15–7:30 A.M. on Saturdays. Fuji TV, however, out of consideration for other religious groups, declined to have a church as sponsor, so this support group unavoidably used a pseudonym (Nichigan) as the program's sponsor. Support came from a wide spectrum in the greater Tokyo area — Holiness, Assemblies of God, Baptist, and Liebenzeller churches.

Another major event affecting not only Christian but other religious broadcasts as well was the decision by TBS, a major radio network, to cease all religious broadcasting. The gravity of this decision can be seen by looking at the example of the Lutheran Hour's "Behold the Man," the script for which was being written by the noted writer Sekiya Isoji.

Already the earliest scheduled religious program, at 6:25 A.M., the program was rescheduled by TBS in October 1970 for 5:30 A.M. The Lutheran sponsor left TBS in April 1972, shifting to FM Tokyo at 7:30 A.M., though this better time slot cost only half what TBS had been charging—a clear indication of TBS's effort to purge itself of religious broadcasting. At the TBS rate, the same program could have been run on several provincial stations at the prime morning time of 9:00 A.M.

The commercial stations had experienced steady growth in the postwar era, but in 1971 their annual profits fell below those of the previous year for the first time. A sudden rise in labor and production costs had forced them all to rationalize and diversify. Morning time slots had taken on new market potential, with commensurate rises in charges. In due course, what prompted the TBS decision was to affect broadcast rates at other networks throughout the nation.

RAPID CHANGE AND RECASTING: 1975–80

While some innovations had appeared in the early 1970s, most programs were carryovers from the preceding years. The latter half of the 1970s, however, was a time of rapid change in Christian broadcasting. Old forms were discarded, and new faces introduced in this five-year period would be in the spotlight in the 1980s. In that sense the late seventies recast the stage for Christian radio and TV programming in the eighties.

Radio

For the second time since 1971, earnings of all commercial stations in 1975 fell below the previous year's level. Radio stations sought to cope with this problem by raising rates, introducing greater variety in morning programming, and soliciting new program sponsors. This trend toward "wider programming" targeted a new market of automobile commuters by reporting news, weather, and traffic conditions. And it had a direct impact on Lutheran programs scheduled in morning time, such as "Kokoro no Uta" (Songs of the Heart).

Rising costs forced the Lutheran Hour sponsor to drop its 30-minute program "Behold the Man" in 1974, which it replaced with the 15-minute "Kokoro no Uta" program. Cost-cutting had, from the early 1970s to the late 1980s, shoved "Behold the Man" from prime times around 8:00 A.M. to times closer to 7:00 A.M. Likewise, "Kokoro no Uta" was moved to earlier times between its inception in May 1974 and the end of 1978. Such moves happened sooner and the new times were much earlier in large urban areas, where cost increases and program diversification were more marked than in town and country. PBA's "Yo no Hikari," which had starting times around 6:20 A.M. in the early seventies, also felt the pinch of commercial stations' new measures in 1977, adjusting to starting times around 6:10 A.M. from 1980. PBA expanded the program's weekly format in 1977, however, to two options, weekly and daily.

Catholic carryovers from the 1960s included "Taiyō no Hohoemi," an early morning program, and "Kokoro no Tomoshibi," which ran later in the morning or in late night time. The former generally held to its 6:20 A.M. starting time despite the new policies of commercial stations, partly because of its short length (five minutes), partly because Catholic funding was stronger, and perhaps also because long-time contracts were honored by station management.

The above Lutheran, evangelical, and Catholic examples formed the mainstream of Christian radio broadcasting in Japan, but some ventures prospered also in less urbanized regions. One example is the "Makoto no Sukui" (True Salvation) program broadcast nationally from Matsuyama City on Shikoku.[3] Started in 1968 by the Nihon Fukuin Senkyōkai (Japan Gospel Mission), this early morning program with messages by Mandai Tsuneo was by 1975 featured on fourteen stations. No regionally produced program had heretofore gained a nationwide audience, and much credit for this growth goes to Mandai's talents in opening up new evangelistic avenues in crusades as well as print, visual, and audio media.

Hokkaido Radio Evangelism and Mass Communications (HOREMCO), started in 1959, had built a solid regional base before its funding by the United Methodist Church in the United States ended in 1979. With indigenous support from believers throughout Hokkaido, HOREMCO continues its regional ministry as an independent venture.

Television

In 1975 television advertising income for the first time surpassed that of newspaper advertising to take top place among all the media. Even so, for several years beginning in 1975, revenues for the mass media as a whole were down. Meantime, the proliferation of UHF stations from around 1970 was accompanied by reorganization of the television industry into five major networks — a business strategy necessitated by rising costs related to the "oil shock" of the early 1970s. The impact on broadcast ethics resulting from "program requirements imposed from the outside" was another offspring of this time.

[3] The smallest of Japan's four major islands, located south of the Osaka–Kobe area.

Catholic programs. "Kokoro no Tomoshibi" up to 1975 was telecast on more than ten stations connected with the Nihon Television (NTV) network. After this network acquired many more VHF and UHF stations, the Catholic program was by August 1976 being run on thirty-one stations. The sudden growth was also due in part to an aggressive fund campaign mounted by Fr. James F. Hyatt of the sponsoring body and perhaps also because a slump in commercial broadcasting made rates for air time cheaper. This venture has since maintained its place with about fifteen each among VHF and UHF stations.

Support for Catholic radio and TV programs has come principally from the Good Shepherd Movement, which has supplied 50 percent of needed funds. Another 30 percent has come from religious orders, and the remaining 20 percent from overseas sources.

Evangelical programs. The rapid growth of the "electronic church" in the United States naturally had repercussions on Japan, and from the late 1970s evangelical use of television's potential expanded quickly.

The first venture was presentation of evangelist Rex Humbard's "Cathedral of Tomorrow" (Japanese title, "Asu e no Kibō") from April 20, 1975, on Television Kanagawa (TVK). In autumn of that year a full-page ad in the *Kurisuchan shinbun* (Christian newspaper) issued the invitation "You too can join in TV worship!" Then in January 1976, Humbard came to Japan to be on the program, as he did again in March 1977 for an evangelistic rally, and again in March 1980 for broadcasts on a seven-station hookup.

Following the July 1977 visit to Japan of Pat Robertson of the Christian Broadcasting Network (CBN), his "700 Club" program was presented from June 12, 1977, on TVK in an evening slot (10:00–10:30 P.M.). Robertson again visited in Japan in February 1978 and appeared on his program in a test run for receiving live telephone calls, though this venture was short-lived.

Another representative TV evangelist of the time was Jim Bakker, whose "PTL Club" was started in 1975 on only one station. It was five years before this program was introduced in Japan, but with an innovative twist: the American version was not dubbed in for use in Japan; the program was produced by Japanese persons. From April 1980 the program began telecasting over four stations in the Kantō region and two in the Kansai area, with Arai Kōji as host and Nakagawa Ken'ichi as producer. Another who contributed to this venture was Assemblies of God missionary Robert W. Houlihan (PTL Japan producer), who in 1978 had met Bakker in South Korea and proposed use of the program in Japan.

Adding strength to these evangelical efforts were a Japan visit by Robert H. Schuller, publication of the Japanese translation of Charles Colson's *Born*

Again (Word of Life Press, 1979), and installation of Jimmy Carter as president of the United States in January 1977.

Outside input was not limited to Americans. From South Korea came Cho Yong-gi, pastor of Yoido Full Gospel Church in Seoul (the world's largest church, with half a million members),[4] who conducted crusades in Tokyo and Osaka in 1978. Cho led additional charismatic meetings in various places in Japan until 1980. In response to Cho's crusades a nucleus of Assemblies of God churches formed the Japan Full Gospel Mission, which arranged for an hour-long program featuring Cho's messages. Called "Kōfuku e no Shōtai" (Invitation to Happiness), it was telecast on Kinki Hōsō Television (KBS) in July 1980, and on SUN Television (JOUH-TV) in October of that year. The Japan viewing was only slightly later than the April opening of this program on Korean television.

Lutheran programs. In 1974 the Lutheran World Federation and four cooperating Lutheran Denominations in Japan launched an all-Lutheran multimedia evangelism project lasting five years and costing 300 million yen. This venture included a survey of what motivates Japanese to become Christians, evangelism seminars, and strategies for multiple use of the mass media. Notable among projects ventured was the "Sekai no Okāsan" (Mothers of the World) program, which was telecast nationwide over the TV Asahi network. This program's production staff were inspired by encounters with Mother Theresa, who had been portrayed in the award-winning film "Mazā Teresa to Sono Sekai" (Mother Theresa and Her World) produced by the Daughters of St. Paul. The telecasting station was reluctant to list a church as sponsor in this case too, so the sponsor had to settle for "with the cooperation of the Lutheran Church."

Seventh-Day Adventist. With long experience in radio broadcasting, the Seventh-Day Adventist Church sponsored a television program called "Dr. Mason" for broadcast by Ryukyu Hōsō in Okinawa for three months beginning October 1979. In 1980 the same program later ran in Hokkaido (January–March), Tokyo (April–June), Osaka (October–December), and subsequently elsewhere in Japan.

Local church initiatives. One more noteworthy activity begun in the late 1970s was the initiative taken by local churches to organize a nationwide TV evangelism support group in September 1977. Inspired by TV evangelism

---

[4] See Daniel J. Adams, "Reflections on an Indigenous Christian Movement: The Yoido Full Gospel Church," *The Japan Christian Quarterly*, 57/1, Winter 1991, pp. 36–45. Adams notes that Japanese colonialism left Cho with bitter feelings that had to be overcome before he would go to Japan. — Ed.

in the United States, this group first sponsored the thirteen-part series "Ikiru" (Living) in Tokyo in January 1977, with later showings in Nagoya, Kansai, and elsewhere. In 1981 they brought out "Ikiru II" (Living, 2), which the Kinpōden organization then supported. The locally supported nationwide group was in fact a rather loosely knit organization.

DOLLAR–YEN AND ROLE REVERSALS: THE 1980s

Earnings by commercial broadcasting firms in the 1980s levelled off and held steady in line with the general shift of the economy from high to low growth. Provincial cities had three or four stations; metropolitan areas usually had five. With a peak of twenty-two newly licensed FM radio stations in 1982, the public enjoyed a widening range of choice in this field. One impact of the FM expansion was reduced revenues for medium-wave radio stations from 1982 on. Trends in early morning radio scheduling had stabilized since 1976, and many Christian programs retained their early time slots throughout the eighties.

Of course the Christian sponsors were not totally submissive to the commercial networks. The most persistent resistance to upgraded costs and diversified morning programming was the Lutheran support group (headed by Masaki Shigeru) for the program "Kokoro ni Hikari o" (Light in Your Heart). Till the bitter end (yielding finally in spring 1981) they fought for a fair balance between the roles of broadcast enterprises and religious sponsors, and public access to the air waves.

The Catholic "Kokoro no Tomoshibi" program from 1981 was run by more than thirty stations, and "Taiyō no Hohoemi" was featured by over twenty. Meanwhile, the new program "Sono Ayako no Kyō o Ikiru" (Living Today with Sono Ayako)[5] had been started on two stations in 1977; by April 1981 it had a network of eight stations; and by December 1986, twelve. The program was changed to "Muramatsu Eiko no Kyō o Ikiru" (Living Today with Muramatsu Eiko) in October 1987, and then in April 1989 to "Muramatsu Eiko no Anata to Tomo ni" (Muramatsu Eiko Joins You). By October 1989 this program had a network of twenty-one stations. Still, "Kokoro no Tomoshibi" stands out as the strongest Catholic program with a steady hold on its network of thirty-one stations.

American evangelistic programs were introduced one after another in the early 1980s and made impressive gains in cooperating stations. The PTL television program, starting with six stations in 1980, had ten in 1982, and with the help of increases in UHF stations, thirteen in 1983. In 1984 a ten-minute

[5] For more on this noted Catholic writer, see III-22.

late-hour radio program called "PTL Gospel Time" was started. And considerable energy was invested in nurturing supporters as "friends" and "partners" through rallies, crusades, and meetings with listeners. By 1984 its aggressive approach had yielded 30 percent support from indigenous sources. But from spring 1985 support from the United States dropped drastically, and PTL in Japan was forced to reduce the number of station contracts while appealing for increased Japanese contributions.

In late 1985 Nakagawa Ken'ichi resigned as host of "PTL Club," a role he had played for six years, to hold a timely consultation on the post-PTL prospects for TV evangelism in Japan. By the end of 1986 PTL support from the United States had dried up, and "PTL Club" reembarked in January 1987 solely on domestic support. Just at that time the sex scandal involving Jim Bakker made the news. Accordingly, PTL Japan was promptly renamed Christian Television Ministry (CTM), and the program was retitled "Lifeline" in July 1987. Then in April 1989, CTM was incorporated into the TV section of PBA.

In less than a year the Jim Bakker scandal was followed by one involving Jimmy Swaggart, who also disappeared from Japan's TV screens. For financial reasons, the Rex Humbard program had been cancelled in Japan in October 1986. The scandals, however, were by no means the only, or even the main, problem faced by TV evangelism in Japan. The radical reversal in dollar-yen values between 1985 and mid-1987 undercut US support for many ambitious mass media projects not only among evangelical but for ecumenical organizations such as the Lutheran Hour as well.

The Korea-based evangelical program "Kōfuku e no Shōtai" (Invitation to Happiness), however, added six stations to its network in October 1981, and renamed its sponsoring body the Zen Nippon Fukuin Senkyōkai (All–Japan Gospel Mission). It added another station in 1987. From June 1990 it began a radio program with the same title on station RKB Mainichi.

After scandal exploded PTL in mid-air and it was succeeded by "Lifeline," there was yet another new venture: "Harvest time," produced by Nakagawa Ken'ichi and launched from the outset (April 1986) with indigenous support. By November 1987 it was on ten stations, and from April 1988 began broadcasting in Japanese on Channel 18 in Los Angeles. By 1989 it had a twelve-station network in Japan, and overseas had added two stations in Hawaii and one in Chicago.[6] Undoubtedly, Nakagawa's approach to supporters and his administrative talents are key factors in this impressive record.

Not to be forgotten in this review of the eighties are the animated programs commissioned by Word of Life Press for professional production by

[6] All of these US cities have sizable communities of Japanese citizens.

Tatsu no Ko Production. The 26-part "Oyako Gekijo" (Parent–Child Theater) opened in October 1981 on twenty-two stations; the 26-part "Tondera
Hausu no Daibōken" (Great Adventure at Tondera House) was featured by
twenty-four stations from October 1982. Both were Bible-based stories pro-
fessionally produced for Japanese children.

Early FM radio programs of proven durability include the Lutheran
Hour's "Yoru no Meikyoku" (Classical Music for Night Listening; 1974)
and "Capsule Mate" (1972). Notable FM music programs of the 1980s include Iwai Daizō's "Gospel Music Inn" broadcast on FM-Mie. It went off the
air in 1987, but its format lives on in "Shalom Music Present," which has
been broadcast by ten FM stations since 1988. These recent programs have
pioneered a new approach to FM broadcasting.

Operating over the longest time, the Lutheran Hour has introduced a
great variety of Christian radio programming. Yet it has been seriously hurt
by the reversal in dollar-yen values, undercutting its US support lines, as well
as by conditions within the International Lutheran Laymen's League. Consequently the Lutheran Hour has had to cut back on both programs and station contracts, leaving it in a weakened condition for facing the future.

THE CHALLENGE TO CHRISTIAN COMMUNICATIONS

The above review of the past twenty years clearly shows that the late 1970s
were the watershed years of change in the Christian use of mass media. All
of the main trends — energetic evangelical activity, stalemated efforts among
ecumenical churches, and the stable but steady growth of Catholic work —
were already visible in the late 1970s.

Christian ventures into mass media have carved out a crucial arena for the
churches' involvement in, and contribution to, society as a whole. But if current trends in Japan's mass media continue, the market principle will unavoidably expose the churches' economic vulnerability and gradually reduce
their access to the increasingly costly media industry.

It can be expected that the massive flow of information from today's media
will eventually eclipse Christian communications on anything beyond a very
localized level. Unable to affect the course of the communications-transmit-
ting agencies, the question is, then, whether the churches will have a role to
play in nurturing a constructive, critical stance among the public, the intended receivers of so much communication.

In April 1987 one of Japan's newer religions, called Agonshū,[7] took the

---

[7] For more on this religion, see Leroy Seat, "Japan's Fastest Growing Religions," *The
Japan Christian Quarterly*, 57/1, Winter 1991. — Ed.

lead in utilizing satellite transmission; the Buddhist lay movement Sōka Gak-
kai and the Unification Association (popularly, Moonies) followed suit in
1989. Regular use of satellite facilities by a Christian group did not emerge
in the 1980s. Given the rapid proliferation of radio and TV stations throughout Japan, the communications industry can be expected to make fuller use
of a wider variety of new media as the whole of society settles into a full-
blown media age.

Thus far, the radio and television media have served well Japanese society's
vertical pattern of information dissemination from the top down, and Christian programming has on the whole adapted to this pattern. Utilization of
the various new media, however, may help create an attractive low-cost potential in less urbanized provincial regions. If so, the churches should aggressively engage in the decentralizing processes of communications conducted
in and for local communities. The basic questions facing Christian efforts in
local communities will be how to foster the local culture and communications so as truly to serve those communities; self-serving strategies will not do.

It is certain enough that the 1990s will be dominated by the wider range
of new media. But the simple proliferation of "hardware" (transmitting facilities) includes no guarantee that adequate "software" (programs) will be
forthcoming. In a word, the more facilities there are, the greater will be the
demand for suitable programs. A growing deficiency in software supply already exists. Whether the churches have the capability, or the potential, to
be good suppliers is an urgent question. At root this is a question of what
kind of relationship Christian communicators seek to foster with audiences
of both Christian believers and non-believers in the 1990s and beyond.

And this is a matter of developing communications founded on the love
of Christ in ways that relate effectively to our society. That calls for communications undergirded by love so as to speak the truth about today's world,
to listen to the voices of the voiceless, and to instill integrity and decency in
our communicating with each other. For this, it is imperative that our communications build relations of mutual trust—and this is true, of course, not
only in mass communications but in all our communicating at any level.
Trust must always be stressed as the companion of truth. For communications that lack trust are, after all, communications without reliable content.

20

The Task of Christian Publications

Akiyama Norie

EVERY SECTOR OF SOCIETY in Japan has experienced rapid change in the past twenty years, and the Christian churches could not escape the many currents of change. The nuclear arms race and peace, Yasukuni Shrine and the emperor system, and human rights and discrimination were some of the tougher issues the churches faced.

Within the Christian community itself, many critical problems demanded attention: student protests at universities and theological schools, serious dispute in the United Church of Christ in Japan (UCCJ) over the 1970 World Exposition in Osaka, the anti-Yasukuni Shrine movement, and the campaign for solidarity with the democratization movement in South Korea. Confronted from without and within by this host of issues, the churches were further challenged to reconsider their own confession of faith and understanding of the gospel.

In this welter of interrelated issues, Christian publications have performed a sustained and significant role. Christian publishers have always taken "evangelism through literature" as their first priority. Accordingly, they have in this turbulent period produced a wide variety of publications serving the Christian community's many needs — biblical, theological, philosophical, educational, devotional, and literary. Indeed, the variety and number of publications belie the Japanese Christian community's small size. These publishing ventures have undoubtedly made a major contribution not only to the churches' missional tasks but also to the spiritual and theological formation of the people of God in this land.

Christian publications have not been limited, however, to a narrow definition of Christian mission. They have also addressed the major issues of our time at home and abroad, seeking to comprehend the realities of contemporary society and expose them to the searching light of Christ's gospel.

Christian publications have provided an arena for interpreting the events, trends, and statements of the churches—a forum in which writers could express their grasp of truth with that freedom which is subject only to the sovereignty of God. The following account, while incomplete, reflects the efforts of Christian publishers to fulfill their collective journalistic task during the the past two stormy decades.

TRENDS IN CHRISTIAN PUBLISHING

The processes of bookmaking and marketing provide ample evidence of how socioeconomic forces have affected the work of Christian publishers. In an effort to touch on six areas, explanations will be necessarily brief and selective.

Distribution Channels

In the Japanese publishing world, distribution is monopolistically controlled by two large distribution agencies, Tōhan and Nippan.[1] These two agencies, in cooperation with the major publishing houses, exercise enormous control over the publications market, which is based on mass production and mass sales. The nationwide distribution system is so structured as to exclude the small-scale specialized publisher.

Consequently, Christian publishers laid plans in the 1960s to form their own distribution agency. The Christian Literature Center[2] and the Christian Publishers Distribution Association[3] cooperated in the establishment in September 1968 of the Japan Christian Publications Distribution Company, or Nikkihan.[4] This venture had the cooperation also of the Committee on Literature and Literacy of the National Council of Churches of Christ in the USA and the Christian Literature Fund[5] of the World Council of Churches. Nikkihan sales totalled 450 million yen in 1970, 2.06 billion yen in 1980, and 2.51 billion yen in 1989. Adding the sales of the Word of Life Press, the Christian Literature Crusade, and other Christian agencies yields a 1989 gross of over 5 billion yen (approx. US$38.5 million) in sales of Christian publications in Japan.

[1] Tōkyō Shuppan Hanbai (Tōhan), Nihon Shuppan Hanbai (Nippan).
[2] Kirisutokyō Bunsho Sentā.
[3] Kirisutokyō Shuppan Hanbai Kyōkai.
[4] Nihon Kirisutokyōsho Hanbai Kaisha.
[5] The Christian Literature Fund in 1975 merged with the Coordinating Committee for Christian Broadcasting (which had previously merged in 1965 with the World Association for Christian Broadcasting) to form the present World Association for Christian Communications.—Ed.

Christian Publishers

As of 1990, 109 publishers utilize Nikkihan's services. Of these, 9 belong to the NCCJ-related Christian Publishers Distribution Association, 8 belong to the Evangelical Bookstore Association (EBA), 8 are Catholic publishers, 25 are under independent management (some are managed by Mukyōkai, or Nonchurch, persons), for a total of 50 firms specializing in Christian publications.

Of these, the major firms in the NCCJ-related group are the Japan Bible Society, the United Church of Christ in Japan's Board of Publications, Kyo Bun Kwan (Christian Literature Society), Shinkyō Shuppansha (Protestant Publishing Company), Yorudansha (Jordan Press), Seibunsha (formerly Lutheran Literature Society), Kirisuto Shinbunsha (Christ Weekly Publishers), Sei Kō Kai Shuppan (Anglican Church Publishers) and the YMCA Press. The principal publishers in evangelical circles are Word of Life Press, Yamamoto Shoten (Yamamoto Publishers), and Shinchi Shobō (New World Books). The two main Catholic publishers are Chūō Shuppansha (Central Publishing Company) and the Daughters of St. Paul Press.

According to data from Nikkihan, 571 new titles were issued in 1985, 590 in 1986, 572 in 1987, 610 in 1988, and 586 in 1989, for an annual average of 580 titles. NCCJ-related publishers averaged 180 titles; EBA-related firms, 80; and Catholic publishers, 40. Together these three groups produced over half the total number of titles.

Christian Bookstores

By 1990, bookstores served by Nikkihan numbered 101, of which 30 are NCCJ-related, 38 are EBA-related, and 7 are Catholic bookstores. The NCCJ-related bookstores handle half of the total sales volume.

Except for the Kyo Bun Kwan bookstore located in the downtown Ginza district, Christian bookstores in Japan are small ventures with only three to five employees. All struggle to stay in business, especially under the economic difficulties induced by the 1973 "oil shock." Management hardships have forced some bookstores to scale down, merge with others, or close. To encourage healthy growth among the bookstores, the Christian Publishers Distribution Association instituted a system of advancing operating funds and sales based on consignment. In 1985 the Association established the Christian Literature Fund (50 million yen) to stabilize bookstores through financial assistance, and thereby promote the distribution of Christian books in Japan.

Besides serving Christian bookstores, Nikkihan also supplies Christian publications to book dealers nationwide through the major distributors. Cooperation among Christian publishers makes "sets" of Christian publications available to some 400 major bookstores throughout Japan. This arrangement is coordinated by a special committee of the Christian Literature Center. The Center also issues the 32-page monthly booklet *Hon no hiroba* (Book forum) to publicize new titles issued by NCCJ-related publishers. Each month 14,000 copies of this booklet are distributed nationwide to churches, Christian schools, public and university libraries, bookstores (Christian and general), and other agencies related to publishing.

Technological Progress and Book Costs

The 1980s have witnessed enormous change in the whole communications industry — word processors, computers, electronic photo-composition, electronic editing and transmission, and offset printing. These new technologies have brought revolutionary changes to publishing in all its editorial, production, and printing phases. In particular, the shift from time-consuming typesetting of hard type to the much faster computer typesetting system (CTS) that produces "camera-ready copy" for offset printing has been especially beneficial for small-scale, specialized publishers who produce a wide variety of materials but only in small numbers of copies. In short, the new computer-composition process can rescue small speciality publishers from the doomsday of high-cost production and high-price sales.

A general labor shortage in Japan has in recent years caused a sharp drop in printing and bookbinding efficiency. Efforts to secure competent workers by offering higher wages have run up production costs, driving the retail prices of Christian books well above those mass-produced by major firms. The inevitable drop in sales has put many specialized publishers in great jeopardy.

General Catalogue of Christian Publications

For some time the Christian Literature Center has produced a general catalogue of Christian titles every few years. Recently the Tōhan distributing agency added a Christian catalogue to its list of specialized catalogues, and Christian publishers are now cooperating with Tōhan. The 1990 catalogue of Christian publications (issued in November 1990) lists 120 publishers and 500 titles. Of a total of 40,000 copies of this catalogue, 30,000 have been sent through Nikkihan to churches and other Christian institutions throughout Japan. This catalogue will be issued annually.

Japan–Korea Exchange

Many churches in Japan have, through their support of the democratization movement in South Korea, entered into a deeper relationship with Korean churches. One fruit of new relations is the Christian Publishing Seminar organized cooperatively by the Korean National Council of Churches (KNCC), of which the Christian Literature Society of Korea (CLSK) is the principal publishing venture, and in Japan, the Christian Literature Center and the Christian Publications Distribution Association. The first of these seminars was held in Seoul in October 1988; the second, in Japan in October 1989. Presentations and discussions at the seminars have yielded joint publishing plans for the future. Another level of exchange is the Northeast Asia Christian Writers Conference, held in Japan in 1986 and in Korea in 1989.

CHRISTIAN PUBLICATIONS

Newly issued Christian publications in the past twenty years have probably exceeded 1,000 titles. It is impossible to survey the entire list, nor can every field be mentioned. Here we shall look only at those with special relevance to our times.

The New Common Bible

This new interconfessional translation of the Bible, a joint Protestant-Catholic effort, deserves special mention. Previous discussions between the Japan Bible Society and the Catholic Bishops' Conference led to formation of the Japan Bible Translation Research Council in 1969, and in the following year the Committee for Translation got under way (cf. IV-28). The first trial portion, Luke's Gospel, was issued in 1975, with the full New Testament appearing in 1978. Subsequent partial issues to test readers' reactions included Psalms and the books of Ruth, Jonah, and Job. After seventeen years of labor, the New Common Bible was issued in September 1987, along with a separate volume of the Old Testament including the Apocrypha. It happens that 1987 was the centennial anniversary of the Japan Bible Society, a propitious time for this epochal event in the history of Bible publication in Japan.

Distribution figures for the New Common Bible (NCB) from September 1987 to July 1990 are as follows:

Full Bible (OT and NT):	108,741
Old Testament with Apocrypha:	182,688
New Testament:	238,457
Total:	529,886

Growing numbers of churches and Christian schools are using this new Bible. Plans are also under way for commentaries and concordances based on the new translation,[6] and the Japan Bible Society is presently compiling a reference Bible version scheduled for publication in 1991.

Dictionaries, Complete Works, Selected Works

During the two-decade period, a number of important dictionaries were issued.

1971   *Shin Seisho daijiten* (New Bible dictionary). 1,806 pp. Kirisuto Shinbunsha.

1982   *Heburugo daijiten* (Dictionary of the Hebrew language). 1,504 pp. Seibunsha.

1986   *Kirisutokyō jinmei jiten* (Biographical dictionary of Christianity). 2,114 pp. UCCJ Board of Publications.
        Sekai Kirisutokyō hyakka daijiten (Encyclopedia of world Christianity). 1,036 pp. Kyo Bun Kwan.

1988   *Nihon Kirisutokyō rekishi daijiten* (Historical dictionary of Christianity in Japan). 1,736 pp. Kyo Bun Kwan.

1989   *Kyūyaku Shinyaku Seisho daijiten* (Bible dictionary of the Old and New Testaments). 1,456 pp. Kyo Bun Kwan.

Publication of complete and selected works of Japanese Christian authors in the 1971–90 period was as follows (publishers with an asterisk are not specifically Christian firms):

1971   *Ōsaka Motokichirō zenshū* (Complete works of Ōsaka Motokichirō [1880–1945]). 3 vols. Shinkyō Shuppansha.

1972   *Kurosaki Kōkichi chosakushū* (Selected works of Kurosaki Kōkichi [1886–1970]). 7 vols. Shinkyō Shuppansha.
        Gendai Nihon Kirisutokyō bungaku zenshū (Anthology of contemporary Japanese Christian literature). 18 vols. Kyo Bun Kwan.

1974   *Kuwada Hidenobu zenshū* (Complete works of Kuwada Hidenobu [1895–1976]). 7 vols. Kirisuto Shinbunsha.
        Kindai Nihon Kirisutokyō bungaku zenshū (Anthology of modern Japanese Christian literature). 15 vols. Kyo Bun Kwan.

1976   *Kanda Tateo chosakushū* (Selected works of Kanda Tateo [1897–1986]). 5 vols. *Misuzu Shobō.

1977   *Shiina Rinzō shinkō chosakushū* (Selected works on faith by Shiina Rinzō [1911–73]). 13 vols. Kyo Bun Kwan.
        Kumano Yoshitaka zenshū (Complete works of Kumano Yoshitaka [1899–1981]). 12 vols. Shinkyō Shuppansha.

---

[6] The UCCJ Board of Publications issued the second of its two-volume commentary on the NCB New Testament on February 20, 1991. — Ed.

1978   *Ishijima Saburō chosakushū* (Selected works of Ishijima Saburō [1904–75]). 4 vols. Kyo Bun Kwan.
       Ishihara Ken chosakushū (Selected works of Ishihara Ken [1882–1976]). 11 vols. *Iwanami Shoten.

1979   *Onomura Rinzō zenshū* (Complete works of Onomura Rinzō [1883–1961]). 3 vols. Shinkyō Shuppansha.
       Sekine Masao chosakushū (Selected works of Sekine Masao [1912–]). 20 vols. Shinchi Shobō.

1980   *Suzuki Masahisa chosakushū* (Selected works of Suzuki Masahisa [1912–69]). 4 vols. Shinkyō Shuppansha.
       Uchimura Kanzō chosakushū (Selected works of Uchimura Kanzō [1861–1930]). 20 vols. *Iwanami Shoten.

1982   *Nihon Kirisutokyō jidō bungaku zenshū* (Anthology of Japanese Christian children's literature). 15 vols. (plus 2 supplementary vols.) Kyo Bun Kwan.
       Asano Jun'ichi chosakushū (Selected works of Asano Jun'ichi [1899–1981]). 11 vols. *Sōbunsha.

1989   *Zoku: Kurosaki Kōkichi chosakushū* (More selected works of Kurosaki Kōkichi [1886–1970]). 3 vols. Shinkyō Shuppansha.
       Kinoshita Naoe zenshū (Complete works of Kinoshita Naoe [1869–1981]). 15 vols. Kyo Bun Kwan.

A large number of translated works also appeared in the period. Among better-known authors whose works were translated are Augustine, Pascal, Karl Barth, E. Thurneysen, Paul Tournier, C. S. Lewis, Ernst Troeltsch, and Rudolph Bultmann.

Theological Works

In this field, doctrinal works were at a low ebb, and there was little of note in indigenous theological research. Notable works by Japanese theologians included: Ueda Mitsumasa, *Kāru Baruto no ningenron* (Karl Barth's anthropology); Satō Toshio, *Kyūsai no shingaku* (Theology of salvation); Yoshinaga Masayoshi, *Kami no kotoba to shingaku* (Theology and the Word of God); Ōsaki Setsurō, *Kāru Baruto no Romasho kenkyū* (Karl Barth's study of Romans); Shige'izumi Teruo, *Augusutinusu kenkyū* (Studies in Augustine); Aono Tashio, *Jūjika no shingaku* (Theology of the cross).

During this period, a number of new theologies appeared in the West, such as the "death of God" theology, liberation theology, and feminist theology, and these were introduced to Japan through translations. Acceptance and advocacy of these new theologies was limited among Japanese churches, which generally maintained their preference for the theological approach represented by works of Karl Barth and Dietrich Bonhoeffer. (For example, the

UCCJ Board of Publications has recently published a 12-volume set of Barth's "Selected Sermons.")

The deepening relationship with Korean churches, however, did bring new theological input into Japan, particularly works on Minjung theology (Theology of the people) with its penetrating analysis of Korean history. Notable among Korean Christian works introduced to the Japanese are Ham Suk-hon's "Theology of the suffering Korean people," So Nam-dong's "Studies in Minjung theology," Min Kyong-bae's "History of Korean Christianity," Yu Tong-sik's "An intellectual history of Korean Christian theology," as well as works by Kim Dae-jung, Moon Ik-hwan, and Chi Myong-kwan. An English-language compilation of materials on Japan–Korea relations also appeared.

Biblical Research and Commentaries

Many works were published in the field of biblical studies. Notable works include Matsuki Saburō, *Shinyaku shingaku* (New Testament theology) and *Iesu to Shinyaku Seisho no kankei* (Jesus and the New Testament); Arai Sasagu, *Shinyaku Seisho seiten no seiritsu* (Establishment of the New Testament canon); Suzuki Yoshihide, *Shinmeiki no bunkengaku kenkyū* (Philological research on Deuteronomy); and Sekita Hirō, *Seisho kaishaku to sekkyō* (Biblical interpretation and preaching).

A number of biblical commentaries published in the period have received critical acclaim: Satake Akira, on Galatians and the Revelation to John; Tagawa Kenzō, on the Gospel of Mark; Arai Sasagu, on the Book of Acts; Yamauchi Makoto, on Philippians; and Tsuchiya Hiroshi, on the Pastoral Letters. Takemori Masaichi, Katō Tsuneaki, and Hasumi Kazuo compiled several volumes of selected expository sermons.

Yagiu Naoyuki's translation of the New Testament and Sekine Masao's translation of the Old Testament, both published in the period under review, were also well received.

Bible study is taken seriously in the Japanese churches, creating a sustained market for biblical commentaries, including extended series. Not a few well-known foreign series have been, or are in process of being, translated: A. Schlatter's New Testament Commentary (13 vols.); The Cambridge Commentary on the New English Bible, Old Testament (13 vols.); The Daily Study Bible (8 vols.); The Wesleyan Commentary (8 vols.); all from Shinkyō Shuppansha. The Kyo Bun Kwan published the Evangelisch-Katholischer Kommentar zum Neue Testament (3 vols.), and the UCCJ Board of Publications has published 7 volumes of The Interpreter's Bible.

Christian History in Japan

Here too there have appeared a number of outstanding works, particularly Ōuchi Saburo and Ebisawa Arimichi, *Nihon Kirisutokyō shi* (History of Japanese Christianity), and Dohi Akio, *Nihon Kirisuto Purotesutanto shi* (History of Protestant Christianity in Japan). Various historical materials have been recovered and preserved in recent publications. Some examples are reissues of early Christian periodicals such as *Shichi-ichi zappō* (Weekly miscellany), the first Christian weekly in Japan, published from 1875 in Kobe; *Jōmō Kyōkai geppō*, a Christian monthly produced from 1898 to 1936 (459 issues) by Congregational pastor Kashiwagi Gien (1869–1938); and *Rikugo zasshi* (Cosmos magazine), a highly influential Christian journal begun under the editorship of Kozaki Hiromichi (1856–1938) at the new Tokyo YMCA in 1880. The last was intended for Christian enlightenment relative to general issues of the day, but it changed over the next decades to a socialist journal and finally became the organ of the Unitarian movement in Japan, before its cessation in 1921.

Other reissues of historical sources include records of the Chinzei, Sanyō, and Hokkaidō presbyteries of the Church of Christ (Presbyterian). And it was a time of centennial histories: Dōshisha, Tōhoku Gakuin, Meiji Gakuin, and other Christian schools; Reinanzaka, Kōchi, Kyoto, Annaka, and other churches; and the Woman's Christian Temperance Union. Two excellent series of collected research articles also appeared: *Nihon Kirisutokyō shi sōsho* (History of Japanese Christianity series) and *Chihō no senkyō sōsho* (Mission in local areas series).

Devotional and Biographical Works

Among books for lay people, the works of Miura Ayako are loved by Christians and non-Christians alike, and her evangelistic impact has been considerable. Most of her books are issued by general publishers, but the UCCJ Board of Publications issued her *Izumi e no shōtai* (Invitation to the wellspring) and *Ikasarete aru hi* (A day of revival) in the period here reviewed. Mizutani Akio's critical review, *Moeru hana naredo — Miura Ayako's shōgai to bungaku* (Even if the flower burns — the life and literature of Miura Ayako) came out in this period, as did Harazaki Momoko's (1934–78) best-selling memoir of faith during her battle with cancer, *Waga namida, waga uta to nare* (My tears have become my song; 1979). Inoue Yoshio's biography of Johann Christoph Blumhardt (1805–80) and his son was published. E. Busch's biography of Karl Barth (in Japanese, *Kāru Baruto no shōgai*, translated by Ogawa Keiji) provided us with new insights into Barth's theology.

Social Issues

The primary focus of Christian publications in the two decades were the related issues of Yasukuni Shrine and state power, as exemplified by Tomura Masahiro's *Yasukuni tōsō* (The Yasukuni struggle), Iinuma Jirō's *Kokka kenryoku to Kirisutokyō* (State power and Christianity) and his *Tsu chijinsai iken soshō* (Lawsuit against Tsu City's unconstitutional groundbreaking ceremony). Along with the resurgence of rightist forces, problems of the imperial succession took center stage (cf. II-5). Sasakawa Norikatsu's *Tennō no sōgi* (The emperor's funeral), Tomura Masahiro's *Shinwa to saigi — Yasukuni kara Daijōsai e* (Myth and ritual — from Yasukuni to Daijōsai), and the collection of essays titled *Kirisutokyō to Daijōsai* (Christianity and the Daijōsai) are representative of many works that address issues of the imperial ideology and practices from a Christian standpoint. The imperial question is, of course, deeply related to issues of human rights, minorities, women's rights, rights of disabled persons, discrimination, and many books on these issues also came from Christian presses during the period.

Our brief survey of Christian publications in the 1971–90 period has left out vital areas such as education, literature, art, illustrated children's books, and many more. Specific Christian concerns such as wartime responsibility of the churches (in World War II), continuing problems in the United Church of Christ in Japan, and others were reluctantly omitted. The tasks of Christian writers and publishers extend far beyond these to include the swing to rightist ideology as a sign of our time, and the state of the churches in Japan, Asia, and the world.

Christian publishers may well find the twenty-first century even more trying and troubled than the past twenty years. We must constantly keep our eyes open, stand firmly on our faith, take the measure of the present age, and maintain our determination to carry on faithfully the tasks of evangelism and mission through Christian literature.

21

Christian Art and Artists

Takenaka Masao

SIGNS OF RENEWAL in Christian art in Japan appeared in the mid-1960s. The inaugural exhibition of Contemporary Japanese Christian Art held at the Waseda Hoshien university center in 1965 provided an occasion for artists and their audiences to share mutual concerns and encouragement. The print media offered an avenue for these interests to reach a wider audience: publication of *Seisho no kotoba*[1] in the same year presented to the public for the first time 100 contemporary art works that dealt with biblical themes. This book also served to stimulate discussions of the meaning and direction of Christian art in Japan.

DEVELOPMENTS AT HOME AND ABROAD

Christian art has come to life in the period under review partly because exhibitions have linked artists to appreciative audiences. But it has also been enlivened by new encounters with art and artists throughout Asia. One further stimulus has come from artistic recovery of Japan's Christian past. Brief accounts of these three trends follow.

Exhibitions

Expanding on the initial impetus of the 1960s, Christian art achieved greater depth and scope in the 1971–90 period. Exhibits at the local, national, and international levels gave steady stimulus to the visual arts, which are meant to be seen, not talked about. The artist's struggle to express a divine

[1] Literally "The biblical word," but more aptly rendered as "Creation and redemption manifested in Japanese art" by its editor, Takenaka Masao. Published by Sōgensha in 1965, the book is now in its sixth printing. — Ed.

message through a concrete image can only be appreciated by actually viewing the result.

Organizing an exhibition involves an enormous expenditure of time and energy to coordinate artists, prepare a catalogue, arrange for gallery space and publicity, transport art works, and so on. Art exhibitions are occasions for encounters among artists themselves and between artists and audiences. Religious art, however, is the fruit of a divine-human encounter; thus an exhibit of such art seeks to draw an audience into an appreciative sharing in the inspiration of this prior encounter. Some exhibitions succeed in attaining this sense of artistic excitement, often yielding a community of people who echo the original inspiration. Other exhibitions fail in this effort, usually because of inadequate attention to atmosphere.

During the 1971–90 period, Catholic and Protestant artists have cooperated in holding a national exhibition almost annually, numbering fourteen by 1990. This ecumenical effort is outstanding in a country with a Christian population of less than one percent.

The Exhibition of Contemporary Christian Art begun at Waseda Hoshien in 1965 continued there for six years to 1970. In 1973 the exhibition moved to the Nichido Gallery, one of the nation's most prestigious, located at the heart of Tokyo's downtown Ginza district. The shift involved a distinct change from the more informal Waseda setting, which was more or less open to entry by all interested artists, to the more regulated Nichido exhibition of artists belonging to the major art associations.

The Ginza setting was also more costly, and to obtain ecumenical support, the artists sought support from the Catholic Church, the United Church of Christ in Japan (UCCJ), and the Nippon Sei Kō Kai (NSKK). Two senior artists, the Protestant painter Tanaka Tadao and the Catholic sculptor Funakoshi Yasutake, were named to represent the participating artists. The invitation card for the third exhibition (1975) carried this message:

> Two years ago we began holding an annual exhibition of Christian art in Japan as one part of the ecumenical movement's search for the unity of the church. This year we invite you to the third exhibition. Due to the success of previous exhibitions, we were able this year to double the number of participating artists and the gallery space. Along with this quantitative expansion we seek to deepen the experience in terms of our witness to faith and our prayer for Christian unity. This year (as last year) we have included works by non-Christian artists, and we also welcome the works of two Catholic sisters. We extend this invitation in the belief that your presence will be an encouragement to all of us. – The Christian Art Association, May 1975.

The exhibition was held annually at the Nichido Gallery until 1984 when renovation of the gallery forced a move. It next opened in 1988 at the Ginza Art Center and, at the end of that year, appeared also at the Kyoto Art Center. In 1989 the works exhibited in Tokyo were also shown at the Kanazawa Art Center and the Kyoto Art Center to extend the circle of interest. Emphasis on selection standards limited the number of participating artists in these exhibitions to between eighteen and twenty-five, including painters, sculptors, and printmakers.

Asian Encounters

Perhaps the most distinctive development among Japanese Christian artists in the past two decades was the emergence of a strong desire for relations with other Asian artists. The stimulation felt by Japanese artists who turned to Asia for insight and perspective is partially conveyed in the book *Christian Art in Asia* published in 1975 by the Kyo Bun Kwan with the cooperation of the Christian Conference of Asia (CCA).[2]

At the first consultation on Christian art in Asia, sponsored by the CCA, August 24–30, 1978, Watanabe Sadao (printmaking), Ueno Yasuo (painting), Kamiya Kōhō (flower arrangement), and Ichikawa Katsuhiko (tea ceremony) attended from Japan. The writer serves as chairperson of the Asian Christian Art Association (ACAA); Tanaka Tadao has served on its executive committee (1978–84). Yoshida Tsutomu (calligraphy) and Nara Shin (architecture) attended the second ACAA conference held at Mt. Makling in the Philippines in 1984, when Ueno Yasuo was made a member of the executive committee.[3]

The seventh Exhibition of Christian Art in Japan, held on the occasion of the ACAA executive committee in Kyoto in 1979, included for the first time works of other Asian artists (four): Hong Chong-myung (South Korea), Nalini Jayasuriya (Sri Lanka), Jyoti Sahi (India), and Bagong Kussudiardja (Indonesia). Japanese artists have responded enthusiastically to invitations to participate in international exhibitions of Christian art at, for example, the World Council of Churches Sixth General Assembly (Vancouver) in 1983 and the CCA Eighth General Assembly (Seoul) in 1985. Twelve Japanese artists[4] participated in the International Art Exhibition Commemorating the Centennial of the Korean Church, organized by the Korean

[2] This work too was edited by Takenaka Masao. — Ed.

[3] See *The Magnificat in Asia Today*, the report of the Second All-Asia Consultation of the Asian Christian Art Association, March 1984.

[4] Horie Masaru, Horino Takako, Kawakami Yoshie, Matsuoka Yūko, Mikami Mariko, Nakayama Masami, Nishizaka Osamu, Ōta Hisashi, Tanaka Tadao, Tomiyama Taeko, Ueno Yasuo, and Watanabe Sadao.

Christian Artists Association at Seoul's National Museum of Modern Art in December 1985.[5]

At the Twenty-fifth Anniversary Exhibition of the Korean Christian Artists Association in May 1990, chairperson Youn Young-ja expressed a desire for regular exchanges between the Christian artists associations of Korea and Japan. Plans are now under way to have art works exchanged at each association's annual exhibition.

The Asian Christian Art Association has arranged for five Asian Christian artists to come to Japan for four-week visits: Nalini Jayasuriya (Sri Lanka), 1977; Edgar Fernandez (Philippines), 1978; A. Alphonso (India), 1983; Victor Thomas (India), 1988; and Paul Koli (India), 1989. He Qi, art teacher at Nanjing Theological Seminary, was scheduled (at time of writing) to spend four weeks in Japan in autumn 1990. The individual programs vary according to each artist's background and interests, as do their respective contributions to Japanese circles. While here, they can study Japan's artistic traditions and specific Christian art developments.

One of the most significant Christian art exhibitions was that held at Kyoto's Daimaru Department Store in October 1986, at which 85 art works by 43 artists from ten Asian countries were exhibited.[6] This was perhaps the most extensive exhibition of artistic works based on the Christian faith ever presented in Japan — a fact that helps explain the substantial interest shown by the 5,126 people who viewed the exhibition.

The International Exhibition of Christian Art in Asia, entitled "That All May Be One" and including forty selected art works (eight by Japanese), embarked on a European tour in February 1987. Starting in Switzerland and continuing to Sweden, Norway, and Finland, the exhibit then visited a number of cities in the United States before returning to Japan in May 1989. This extended tour was very fruitful in demonstrating the creative use of images and symbols by Asian Christians to convey the Christian message.

Memorial Witnesses to Martyrdom

In recent years several Japanese artists have memorialized the martyrs of Japan's "Christian century" (1549–1639).[7]

---

[5] "The Catalogue of the International Art Exhibition," commemorating the 100th Anniversary of the Korean Church, 1985.

[6] "The Catalogue of the Asian Christian Art Exhibition," held at Kyoto Daimaru (text in Japanese), 1985.

[7] Jesuit missionaries first arrived in Japan in 1549, with smaller numbers of Franciscans and others following; by the early 1600s, the Catholic population of Japan (mostly in Kyushu) numbered over 300,000. As Japan's rulers moved toward a period of national seclusion (1639–1854), the Christian community was suppressed, with some going under-

Nakayama Masami has depicted the 1619 incident of a family burned at the stake in Kyoto.[8] The chapel memorializing twenty-six martyrs in Nagasaki, designed by Imai Kenji and built in 1964, has powerful sculptures of the martyrs done by Funakoshi Yasutake.[9] These martyrs were forced to endure a long march from Kyoto to Nagasaki, where they were executed on February 5, 1597. Hasegawa Luka's painting of the tortuous scene of the trek to Nagasaki hangs in the memorial chapel. Hasegawa later went to Italy and in the years 1951–54 painted a series of murals on the walls of the Twenty-six Martyrs Memorial Church in the port town of Civitavecchia near Rome. This Franciscan church testifies in a quiet and moving way to the faith and hope of the twenty-six martyrs.[10]

In 1980 two Protestant artists, Ueno Yasuo and Mori Takehiko, exhibited works on the Ezo Kirishitan at the Eighth Exhibition of Christian Art in Japan. "Ezo" is an old term for part of Hokkaido where a group of Christians took refuge during the early seventeenth-century persecutions; "Kirishitan" was the term for Christians in those days. Ueno and Mori both belong to the Soga Kai, one of the leading national art associations, and participate in a group devoted to tracing the historical steps of Christians martyrs, who are said to number 106.[11] Ueno has adapted the double-door style of altar to his paintings, while Mori does bronze etching.

It is noteworthy that the history of martyrdom in the Christian century is being recaptured and movingly presented in contemporary Japan.

PROFILES OF LEADING CHRISTIAN ARTISTS

As all active Christian artists cannot be introduced here, profiles of five or six leading artists in several fields, with brief comments on some of their recent works, must suffice.

Painters

Tanaka Tadao. Generally regarded as the father of Christian art in Japan, Tanaka is one of the founders of the Kodo Art Association. He specializes in biblical images, often with a critical, ironic style. Tanaka received the Mainichi

---

ground, and foreign missionaries were expelled from Japanese shores. The martyrs referred to here were victims of this suppression. — Ed.

[8] See the special issue of *Gekkan Kyoto* (Kyoto monthly), December 1980, on Christian culture in Japan.

[9] "Nijūroku seijin" (Twenty-six martyrs), sculptures by Funakoshi Yasutake. Bijutsu Shuppansha, 1963.

[10] Adalberto Sisti, O.F.M., *I Martiri del Giappone e la Loro Chiesa in Civitavecchia*, 1974.

[11] "Ezo Kirishitan," in *Shinto no tomo* (Friend of the laity), November 1980.

Art Award in 1984. A collection of his biblical paintings was published in 1977, with 32 pictures in color, 16 in black and white.[12] Tanaka's works were exhibited in 1984 at the Hokkaido Museum of Modern Art in Sapporo and the Central Art Museum in Tokyo.

Koiso Ryōhei (1903–88). Koiso was a middle school classmate of Tanaka. Raised in a church family, he painted 32 series of biblical scenes (which he dedicated to the Japan Bible Society), and a Bible illustrated with his paintings was published in 1971. The Koiso family, following his will, contributed 2,470 of his works to the Kobe City Museum and the Hyogo Museum of Modern Art.

Watanabe Sadao. Watanabe's folk-art prints have made him perhaps the best-known Christian artist in Japan, and his biblical prints have been widely exhibited at home and abroad. Watanabe's major book, containing 48 color prints,[13] was made into a one-hour documentary by Japan Broadcasting Corporation (NHK). An English version of this film was scheduled for production in autumn 1990, with a dialogue between Watanabe and the present writer.

Ueno Yasuo. Among Japanese Christian artists, Ueno has perhaps shown the most vitality in the past twenty years. A teacher at Tama Art College, he specializes in Japanese-style painting and has gained popularity by his bold use of natural red, green, and gold. Besides depicting Ezo martyrs, in 1987 he painted two six-panel folding screens with the title "Time Engraving, 1945-8-6" to commemorate the atomic devastation of Hiroshima on August 6, 1945. (He dedicated the screens to the Hiroshima Museum of Modern Art.)

Nakayama Masami (1898–1979). A Catholic artist who worked well with oil and color etchings, he did oil paintings on such themes as "Resurrection Morning," "Tokyo Under Judgment," and "The Book of Revelation," besides the depictions of martyrdom mentioned above.

Miya Yoshihei (1893–1971). Miya studied at Tokyo Academy of Art and taught art at the Girls' High School in Kamisuwa, Nagano Prefecture until 1958. After joining a group pilgrimage to Palestine, he painted a series of biblical pictures, such as Ruth and Naomi, The Last Supper, and Golgotha.

---

[12] *Tanaka Tadao seisho gashū* (Tanaka Tadao's biblical paintings), with an introductory essay on the life and work of Tanaka Tadao (in Japanese and English) by Takenaka Masao. Kyo Bun Kwan, 1977.
[13] *Watanabe Sadao seisho hangashū* (Biblical prints by Watanabe Sadao), with 48 color prints, and an essay, "Watanabe Sadao: the man and his work" (in Japanese and English), by Takenaka Masao. Kyo Bun Kwan, 1988.

Miya was little known until his life and works were introduced in the present writer's book, *Tenchō no tabito* (Heavenly sojourner), published in 1979.

Sculptors

Funakoshi Yasutake. Funakoshi, a second-generation Catholic, is indisputably the leading Christian sculptor in Japan. As professor of sculpture at Tokyo College of Fine Arts, he has influenced many aspiring sculptors, including some Christians. Besides the twenty-six martyrs, he has done distinctive works of Hara no Jō, Father Damian, and Luis de Almeida (late sixteenth-century Jesuit priest and medical practitioner in Japan). Funakoshi's collection of essays titled *Kyogan to hanabira* (Gigantic rock and flower petal; Chikuma Shobō, 1982) won national acclaim.

Yamamoto Masahiko. An elder among sculptors, Yamamoto has chaired the Japan Artists Association (1974–78) and encouraged artists to make contact with artists in other Asian lands. One of his lasting works, called "Job," stresses the impact of suffering on Job's body—a point of empathy, since Yamamoto suffered exile in Siberia for two years after World War II.

Kōsaka Keiji. Kōsaka studied sculpture at Tokyo College of Fine Arts, receiving the strong influence of Takamura Kōtarō, and later taught at Aoyama Gakuin. His painting "Christ Bearing a Broken World" was displayed in the Christian Pavilion at the 1970 World Exposition in Osaka, accompanied by these words he penned:

> God himself died. What is the Cross?
> Who can see the Cross?
> Who dares lightly to call the name of God?
> Now the earth is split asunder,
> People languish in the depths of its dark cavity
> . . . find yourself at this point of origin.
> Believing that even a tiny seed will sprout at the feet of Christ,
> I take up my work with fear and trembling.

Each year Kōsaka exhibits his works such as "Trinity" (1973), "Eloi, eloi, sabachtani" (1979), and "Eve" (1983).

Kakei Gorō. A teacher at Aoyama Gakuin, Kakei was influenced by Asano Jun'ichi, pastor and Old Testament scholar, and has produced works on figures such as Noah and Job. Departing more recently from his earlier style, he expresses the agony and hope of people in a weighty style such as is found in his works "Rise up!" and "Asian woman."

Shinozaki Akio. In an accident while a student at Tokyo College of Fine Arts, Shinozaki lost one of his feet. He consistently expresses beauty in a simple style, like a pilgrim in search of eternal life. A recent example is his "Samarian woman."

Tomura Issaku (1909–79). A unique combination of sculptor and social activist, Tomura started out as a blacksmith making tools for farmers near Narita in Chiba Prefecture. When farmers in the area rose up to protest the confiscation of their land for the new international airport, he supported and eventually led their movement. He exhibited his work "Saku" (Split) in 1970 to express vividly the violent disruption of unity and harmony.

Women Artists

It is encouraging to see increasing numbers of women making contributions to the development of Christian art in Japan. Five are introduced here.

Yamashita Rin (1857–1939). Recent years have witnessed a revival of interest in the life and work of Yamashita Rin, the first Japanese iconographist as well as the first modern artist among Japanese women. Born in a rural village, she left home at age 15 to study art in Tokyo, where she entered the national academy of arts in 1877 as one of its first woman students. Coming under the influence of Bishop Nicolai of the Russian Orthodox Church, she was baptized in 1878 and, with the bishop's recommendation, went to study iconography at a monastery in Saint Petersburg (now Leningrad). Returning to Japan in 1883, she painted icons in Orthodox churches. Today we find 155 of her works in 22 churches throughout Japan. Two recent books tell her fascinating life story and reproduce some of her works in color: Ume Kajima, ed., *Yamashita Rin: reimeiki no seizōgaka* (Yamashita Rin: pioneer iconographer), with 29 color plates and 9 black-and-white pictures; and Kawamata Kazuhide, *Warera shōgai no ketsui* (Our life's determination [Bishop Nicolai and Yamashita Rin]).

Araki Ayako. A member of the UCCJ Kyoto Church, Araki was an active member of the Independent Art Association (Dokuritsu Bijutsu Kyōkai). To celebrate her seventy-five years of life, in March 1988 she exhibited her works in Kyoto Municipal Gallery and published her collected works (color reproductions of 76 oil paintings and of 43 sketches (dessin works). She became a professional artist while busy as a housewife and mother. Her paintings are rarely overtly religious; her subjects are usually natural objects such as trees, birds, insects, ancient walls and stones, by which she discloses the stream of life beneath the surface of reality.

Kawakami Yoshie. Kawakami was a pharmacist until her husband's death, when she began studying Japanese-style painting. She found comfort and hope in the Bible and expressed her faith and joy in her paintings. Once a year she invited friends and disciples to her home to view her works. She was particularly fond of depicting biblical stories about women — Lot's wife, the ten virgins, Mary Magdalen, and the Virgin Mary. In 1980 she published her collected paintings and poems under the title *Hana tagitsu* (Seething flowers).[14]

Matsuoka Yūko. Schooling at Wooster College in Ohio and her mother's influence made Matsuoka an avid advocate of international understanding through art exchanges. She exhibited her works in 1988 at Gallery Okabe with the theme "Heaven, Earth, and Poetry." A regular member of the Japan Christian Art Association, she works in a semi-abstract style that uses contrasting blues and reds as if musical lines ran through the images.

Horino Takako. Horino began studying art — while managing a small stationary shop — at Musashino College of Fine Arts where she specialized in etching. Plagued by prolonged bouts of illness, she perseveres in making prints with biblical themes cast in contemporary settings to express her prophetic concerns for justice and peace. Examples are her works on the Tower of Babel and the Flood.

New Artists

As in many other cultural areas, the bearers of current traditions in Christian art in Japan are soon to be succeeded by a new generation. Distinguished leaders are watching the horizon for their young replacements to appear. Certainly many would agree that Horie Suguru has met the expected standards; his debut won the Yasui Prize for new artists in 1980. A minister's son, he earns his living as a primary school teacher in Kobe. A careful student of the Bible, he presents its messages in striking water colors.

The latest annual exhibition of Christian art included three new artists: Hōjō Masayasu, who works with urban images, and two women artists, Ebina Kyōko and Hayashi Motoko, who express themselves in spirited forms and styles.

RELATED ARTISTIC FIELDS

Flower Arranging

Among efforts to express Christian faith through traditional forms, the art of flower arrangement (ikebana) stands out. The pioneer in this field is Ōta

---

[14] This collection includes an introduction in Japanese by Takenaka. — Ed.

Gakō, followed by Kamiya Kōhō and Yamanouchi Kyōko. All three have formal training and experience in teaching this art, which enhance their efforts to express biblical themes. Their selected works were compiled in the book *Consider the Flowers* (edited by Masao Takenaka; Kyo Bun Kwan, 1990), which was issued simultaneously in Japanese, English, and Swedish — an indication of the universality of the medium and the message.

Church Architecture

This field deserves a separate, lengthy treatment; here we can touch only on the current situation. Many Japanese church buildings are old and in need of renovation or replacement. The need for a comprehensive and critical guide to church architecture led to the 1985 publication of *Kyōkai kenchiku* (Church architecture) by the UCCJ Board of Publications. Behind the everyday title lies a wealth of historical, theological, and practical treatment of the theme as related to Japan.

The signs of renewal and lines of development noted in this essay have been ecumenically developed through close Catholic and Protestant cooperation. There is much healthy variety in the common quest for forms and styles suited to expressing Christian faith and mission in today's world. The deeper sense shared by Christian artists can be summed up in the words of a senior colleague, Tanaka Tadao:

> Christian arts were once used to decorate sanctuary walls in the early church. They were used to illustrate the Bible and to inspire a worshipful atmosphere in the medieval church. In the modern church they have served as a medium for confessing one's faith. Now we must, I believe, go a step further. Religion today is challenged to find a way to offer salvation to coming generations. Our calling as Christian artists is to respond to this challenge through our creative works.[15]

---

[15] Tanaka Tadao, "Shūkyō bijutsu ni tsuite" (Thoughts on religious art), *Sanyō shinbun*, November 10, 1970.

22

Japanese Christian Writers

Takado Kaname

WHEN THE SECOND WORLD WAR ended in 1945, there was not a single active Christian writer in Japan. By 1970, a quarter of a century later, there were over twenty. In 1972 the Kyo Bun Kwan (Christian Literature Society) began publishing its 18-volume series titled *Gendai Nihon Kirisutokyō bungaku zenshū* (Anthology of contemporary Japanese Christian literature). The series editors were novelists Shiina Rinzō and Endō Shūsaku, respectively representing Protestants and Catholics. The series comprises approximately 60 novels, 15 plays, and 30 critical essays. Of the twelve novelists included, there are seven Catholics and five Protestants; of the five playwrights, three Catholics and two Protestants.

The publisher introduced this anthology as follows: "In the chaotic postwar period marked by doomsday fears and existential crises, Christian writers brought forth a unique message that sprang from their inner core. In those critical times, their writings were a wellspring of the power needed for renewal."

In the fall 1972 issue of *The Japan Christian Quarterly*, with the theme "Contemporary Japanese Christian Writers," I contributed an article on postwar Christian writers.[1] At that time I spoke of a Japanese Christian writer's life and work, in a "heathen" land where Christians are less than one percent of the population, as a threefold struggle: (a) to be a Christian, (b) to be a Japanese, and (c) to persevere as a writer. Then I observed that, despite the difficulties, the emergence of more than twenty Christian writers under these conditions was in itself a miracle.

Christian writers of the prewar generation, that is, during the whirlwind

---

[1] "Postwar Japanese Christian Writers," translated by Esther L. Hibbard, *The Japan Christian Quarterly*, XXXVIII/3, Fall 1972.

decades of Japan's modernization from the late nineteenth century to the 1940s, had all eventually lost their faith—a faith that can be described as a kind of humanism, I noted. Then I pointed out that Christian writers who appeared in the 1945–70 period had professed in their works a clear faith in the cross and resurrection. Now, two decades later, I am even more strongly convinced that what I wrote then is true, because none of these postwar Christian writers has renounced that faith.

At the end of my 1972 article I made, with some diffidence, a rather daring forecast:

> I predict that, whether for good or ill, the arena of activity for Christian writers will become larger and larger. I believe that, just as Christian writers rose from the ruins of defeated Japan to become "a voice crying in the wilderness," so countless Christian writers, filled with the hope of resurrection from the annihilation of death, will rise from the inferno which is so confused, so corrupt, and so degenerate that it can only be considered as signaling the end of the world.[2]

However rash this prediction may have seemed at the time, it proved to be not far off the mark. In the twenty years since then, eleven new Christian writers have appeared—just counting novelists—and the significance of the Christian writers' overall contribution to Japanese society is more widely recognized than ever before. Most of the postwar Christian writers had already had works published and gained some recognition before being baptized; some were unknown Christian writers who came into their own during the 1970s and 1980s.

FAREWELL TO SIX SENIORS

During these twenty years of expanding numbers among Christian writers, we have had to bid a final farewell to six of our senior colleagues, each of whom was a precious, unique writer with deep roots in Japanese soil. They all sustained their faith till the very end and, rare in Japan, their funerals were all conducted in Christian churches.

Shiina Rinzō (1911–73)

Shiina Rinzō was the standard-bearer for the first group of après guerre writers who rose from the rubble and ashes of the Second World War. Coming from the lower ranks of the laboring class, this former communist was warmly received by young people as Japan's first existentialist writer. When

---

[2] *Ibid.,* p. 192.

Shiina, back in the 1950s, found his espoused ideology too limited, he was led to Christian baptism through his reading of Dostoevsky. After his baptism he wrote of the joy of his encounter with Christianity in *Kaikō* (Encounter; 1952), and expressed his experience of release from the absoluteness of despair in his novel *Utsukushii onna* (Beautiful woman; 1955), for which he received the Minister of Education Award for Literature. In these and other works he witnessed through his art to the Good News of Christ.

Chōekinin no kokuhatsu (Confessions of a prisoner[3]), published in 1969, was his last full-length novel. It was written from a faith grounded in the cross of Christ who undergirds all people teetering on the brink of hopelessness or fallen into the depths of despair. This work has been called the most truly Christian of all his writings. From 1960 till his death in 1973, Shiina Rinzō led a Christian writers' group called Tane no Kai (Seed group), and he especially encouraged young writers. From this group have come Abe Mitsuko, Mori Reiko, and the present writer.

Ishihara Yoshirō (1915–77)

The postwar Protestant poet Ishihara Yoshirō echoed the groans of those sunk in despair. When World War II ended, Ishihara was captured by the Soviet army and sent to Siberia for forced labor lasting eight years. Upon his return to Japan he published his enigmatic poetry penned in a chaotic era, drawing on his experiences in Siberia and on his understanding of the Bible as guided by his reading of Karl Barth. He recognized the limitations of words, opting for poetry which, from his pen, cried out as if from silent stones.

For his 1964 collection titled *Sancho Panza no kikyō* (The homecoming of Sancho Panza) he was awarded the "Mr. H. Award," and for his volume of essays, *Bōkyō to umi* (Nostalgia and the ocean), he received the Award of Distinction (Rekiteishō). From 1977, Ishihara served as chairman of the Japan Contemporary Poets Society. The minister who officiated at his funeral said, "No matter how far down a person may fall — no, precisely *because* of his fall — God's overpowering Yes speaks to him and pronounces him forgiven. The deceased poet had trembled before this awesome truth. Perhaps he was a bit too conscientious."

Mori Arimasa (1912–76)

Born the son of a Protestant minister, Mori Arimasa was richly endowed with talent and training. He read Descartes, Pascal, and Dostoevsky; played Bach

---

[3] Rendered as "People, like trees walking" by Noah Brannen in an unpublished translation referred to by several writers in the *The Japan Christian Quarterly* XXXIV/4, Fall 1973 — Ed.

on the organ; and for twenty-three years discussed Japanese classical literature in Paris with such notables as Edmund Husserl (1859–1938), Jean Paul
Sartre (1905–80), and Maurice Merleau-Ponty (1908–61). He was widely
known as a thinker, critic, and essayist. In his collection of essays titled *Babi-
ron no nagare no hotori ni te* (On the banks of the River Babylon; 1957) and
another, *Haruka na Nōtoru Damu* (Faraway Notre Dame; 1967), he wrote
of his struggle with the essential differences between Japanese and European
intellectual life. In *Tsuchi no utsuwa ni* (In earthen vessels), *Hikari to kurayami*
(Light and darkness), and *Aburahamu no shōgai* (A life of Abraham) he portrayed his struggle with the Bible.

These struggles stemmed from the accumulated experiences of a man torn
between Europe and Japan, and between flesh and spirit. "Faith pressed upon
me from within and without." This faith is difficult to describe, but it was extremely real to Mori—without it, he said, "a man cannot go on living as a
man." To maintain this faith, which is the source and the core of life, is a task
one must work at daily. As Mori put it, everything else "flows from faith."

Fukunaga Takehiko (1918–79)

Because Fukunaga Takehiko's parents were Christians, he attended church as
a child, and while he had some sense of sin as defilement, he had no specific
religious convictions. Struggling as an adult with chronic pulmonary tuberculosis, he wrote several novels: *Kusa no hana* (Flowers; 1954), *Bōkyaku no
kawa* (River of oblivion; 1964), and *Shi no shima* (Island of death; 1971),
the last of which won for him the Japan Literature Award. Beset with sins of
the past and confronted with imminent death, lovesick and lonely, he depicted postwar life in fiction marked by great delicacy and sensitivity. On his
sickbed in 1977 he received baptism performed by an evangelical minister.
Two years later he died.

Shimao Toshio (1917–86)

In the Second World War, Shimao Toshio was commander of a suicide
squadron in which the pilots strapped torpedoes to their bodies, but Japan
surrendered before his time came. After the war he began writing surrealistic
and realistic works based on his wartime experiences. Meanwhile, his involvement in an extramarital affair was discovered, and his shocked wife became
neurotic. As penance for his sin, he wrote a series of novellas—*Ware fukaki
fuchi yori* (From the deep abyss; 1955), *Shi no tōge* (Thorn of death; 1960),
and *Gake no fuchi* (The cliff's edge; 1960)—to cope with the feeling of persistent censure imposed by the reality of his demented wife. His penitential
quest led him to baptism as a Catholic in 1956.

Even so, Shimao's writing continued in this vein for sixteen years, culminating in the 1977 publication of *Shi no tōge* as a full-length novel. This work is the incredible record of the "thorn in the flesh" tormenting him as he prayed for his wife's recovery from mental illness and for his own restoration from death. The novel won the Yomiuri Literature Award as well as the Japan Literature Award.

Ariyoshi Sawako (1931–84)

Baptized as a Catholic in 1947 while in high school, Ariyoshi Sawako then studied at Tokyo Women's Christian University, a Protestant institution. She made her literary debut in 1956 with the novel *Jiuta*[4] (Folksongs), which won her a nomination for the coveted Akutagawa Prize. Representative of her works is the historical novel *Hanaoka Seishū no tsuma* (The wife of Hanaoka Seishū; 1966[5]), the story of the world's first successful operation for breast cancer under general anesthesia, by a premodern surgeon.[6] The story depicts the plight of women in feudal times, centering on an ugly battle between mother-in-law and daughter-in-law.

Several of Ariyoshi's novels treat problems of social justice in the light of Catholic faith. *Hishoku* (Without color; 1964) tackles racial problems in a story of a Japanese woman married to a black person. *Kōkotsu no hito* (An enchanted man; 1972) deals with problems of senility. The theme of *Fukugō osen* (Compounded pollution; 1973) is the threat of manifold forms of pollution. *Kōkotsu no hito*[7] portrays a woman who, in the course of caring for her husband's senile father, finds in the old person whom she at first detested what it means to be a human being, and she decides to spend the rest of her life serving God. Through this novel she spoke out against inadequate governmental care for the aged. The novel sold over a million copies.

However senseless their deaths may seem, the above six writers all died of some debility over which they had no ultimate control, unlike the deaths of writers Mishima Yukio (1970) and Kawabata Yasunari (1972), which were by their own hands. These Christian colleagues all realized their calling as writers and ended their lives surrounded by God's grace.

---

[4] English translation under title *Jiuta*, by Yukio Sawa and Herbert Glazer, in *The Japan Quarterly*, 2/1, 1975.

[5] English translation by Hironaka Wakako and Ann Siller Konstant, *The Doctor's Wife* (Tokyo: Kodansha International, 1978).

[6] On the role of Hanaoka Seishū (1760–1835) in Japanese medical history, see Masayoshi Sugimoto and David L. Swain, *Science and Culture in Traditional Japan* (Cambridge, Mass.: The M.I.T. Press, 1978; reprinted by Charles E. Tuttle Co., 1989), pp. 387–90. — Ed.

[7] English translation by F. Uyttendaele, in *The Japan Missionary Bulletin*, 26/10, 1972.

FOUR CATHOLIC ELDERS

Four outstanding Catholic writers who were most prolific in the 1950s and 1960s are recognized today as respected elders of the literary world.

Endō Shūsaku (1923–)

In his novel *Chinmoku* (Silence; 1966), a representative work of the 1960s, Endō asks whether it is possible for Christians to continue their hopeless battle in a pagan land like Japan, which he calls a "bottomless swamp." Several years later he published *Shikai no hotori* (Beside the Dead Sea; 1973), in which he took an original approach to the life of Jesus by tracing two different strains—the first concerns a nameless people living in the land where Jesus lived and died, people who bore in their bodies the imprint of that life. The other strain involves Japanese pilgrims to the Holy Land. Endō conjures up an encounter between Jesus of Judea, who lived and died almost 2,000 years ago, and the Japanese people of today.

If one reads this novel alongside another of his works, a commentary titled *Iesu no shōgai* (A life of Jesus; 1973), which takes the form of notes the author prepared while writing the Dead Sea novel, it becomes clear that Endō pictures Jesus in a form that appeals to the sensitivities of the "pagan" Japanese—he is a "weakling" who sides with other weaklings as their friend and comrade. Of course this weakling Jesus is powerless; he can do nothing to help those whom he loves. Yet, this same Jesus has the power to support us in some fundamental sense. This paradox suggests the metaphysical underpinnings of Endō's portrayal of Jesus.

Endō's range is fairly wide: straightforward literary works such as *Samurai* (Samurai; 1980) and *Sukyandaru* (Scandal; 1986[8]), critical biographies of Christian feudal lords (Kirishitan daimyō), and novels with popular appeal. All this has made him one of Japan's best-known novelists today. He is also president of the Japan Pen Club.

Ogawa Kunio (1927–)

In the 1960s, Ogawa Kunio produced three novellas based on his experiences in Europe and in his hometown of Shizuoka, and on his Christian faith. They brought the light of eternity to people whose hearts were darkened by suffering and anxiety. In the 1970s he began writing longer novels. *Aru Seisho* (A certain Bible; 1973) has one character who is obviously Judas, a young boy who stands for John, and one called simply "Ano Hito" (That Man). Through this fictional account, the reader can relive the experiences

[8] Translated by Van C. Gessel, *Scandal* (Charles E. Tuttle Co., 1988).

of Jesus and his disciples. The young boy is captivated by the words of Ano Hito — "My words will live forever," "People are vessels for light, and I am the one who can fill your hearts with light" — but the Judas character betrays him. Ogawa also uses biblical material in later works, as in *Ōka* (Songs of the king; 1988), in which young David is the main character.

Sono Ayako (1931–)

The story of her own life was a best-seller and made Sono Ayako widely known. Her fictional work *Mumeihi* (Nameless monument; 1969) stems from her understanding of the Book of Job and reflects her own life of suffering without reward. *Chi o uruosu mono* (Showers for the earth; 1976) takes the same line. *Kami no kegareta te* (God's defiled hand; 1979) is an indictment of the abortionist's "defiled hand," a literary echo of the countless cries of innocent babies entombed forever in darkness. In the serialized magazine story, *Sono hito no na wa Yoshua* (His name is Joshua; 1977–80), she pursues the historical Jesus. This story, however, was never completed, nor has it appeared in book form.

Miura Shumon (1926–)

Miura Shumon, husband of Sono Ayako, is the author of *Baberu no tō* (The Tower of Babel; 1971), *Gisei* (Sacrifice; 1972), and *Musashino Indean* (Indians of the Musashino plain; 1982), and other novels that are unpretentious yet have a sharp, penetrating grasp of human nature. These works are the fruits of a mature Christian life. From 1985 to 1987 he was director of the government's Cultural Agency and is at present board chairman of Nihon Bungeika Kyōkai (Association of Japanese Writers).

SEVEN LEADING CONTEMPORARIES

Sakata Hirō (1924–)

A Protestant writer whose vigorous writing career began in the 1970s, Sakata Hirō was born and raised in a Christian home. He was baptized while in middle school but later drifted away from the church. In 1974 he published *Tsuchi no utsuwa* (Earthen vessel), taking his mother's death from cancer as the novel's story line. His mother was organist for her church and had lived a life of service and involvement in various social projects. This novel won Sakata the Akutagawa Prize. With Christians as his main characters, he wrote the novella *Ashifumi orugan* (Pedal organ; 1975) as well as several full-length novels: *Haikyō* (Apostasy; 1976), *Karyō* (Flower mound; 1977), and *Madosan* ("Mr. Mado"; 1985). In these works his characters are different from ordinary Japanese living in pagan Japan; they are well-mannered persons reared in Christian homes who are embarrassed because they never really put down roots in Japanese soil, yet they press on in their quest for truth and love. Through these characters Sakata provides a close-up of Christian life in Japan in all its humorous ordinariness.

Ohara Tomie (1912–)

The 1970s also saw the emergence of two women writers who, under the influence of Endō Shūsaku, were baptized as Catholics and whose writings reflected greater depth after their baptism. They also began producing significant novels dealing with religious themes. One of them is Ohara Tomie, who made her literary debut with *Sutomai tsumbo* (Deafness from streptomycin; 1956). For her novel *En to iu onna* (A woman called En; 1960), the story of the loneliness and resignation of the daughter of a samurai held in confinement for forty years, she received both the Mainichi Publisher's Cultural Award and the Noma Literary Prize and reaped acclaim as a writer. She was baptized in 1976 at age 61.

Using material gathered on her pilgrimage to the Holy Land, she published a collection of essays, titled *Erusaremu no tabi* (Journey to Jerusalem; 1976), on the worlds of the Old and New Testaments. In a succession of novels beginning with *Shinjū no umi* (Ocean of faith; 1977), she pursued the new life of freedom her characters find in acquiescence as they survive nature's cruelties and the inscrutable whims of fate. In *Aburahamu no makuya* (Abraham's tent; 1981), inspired by events involving a heterodox group calling themselves Iesu no Hakobune (The Ark of Jesus; cf. II-14), she depicts a prayer commune formed by dropouts from society. In *Hagaru no arano* (The desert of Hagar; 1986), persons alienated from human society and its futility seek to weave a new life of fellowship.

Takahashi Takako (1932–)

In graduate school Takahashi Takako wrote her master's thesis on François Mauriac (1885–1970) and did a critical study of Endō Shūsaku's works. Her husband Takahashi Kazumi was also a writer, and near the time of his death she began to write novels dealing with the evil hidden in a woman's heart. In 1975, at age 43, she was baptized in the Catholic Church. After writing on the theme of provoking a woman friend to commit suicide, in *Yūwakusha* (The tempter; 1976), and developing a metaphysical vision in *Ten no mizuumi* (The lake of heaven; 1977), she produced several long novels dealing directly with the Catholic faith, such as *Arano* (Wilderness; 1980), *Yosoi se yo, waga tamashii yo* (Prepare thyself, my soul; 1982), and *Ikari no ko* (Child of wrath; 1985). In 1986 she lay down her pen and entered a nunnery. The overall theme of her novels is the weight of sin and guilt that burdens women possessed of a satanic sexual passion and their deliverance from eros to a life of agape.

Moriuchi Toshio (1936–)

Baptized in the Catholic Church during his high school days, Moriuchi Toshio drifted over to a Protestant church for a while, then returned to the Catholic fold. He made his debut in literary circles in 1969. Possessed of a delicate, nervous disposition, he sought salvation from anxiety and the fear of death through the writing of a brief work that won him the new author's literary award. In 1985 he produced *Hone no hi* (Bones of fire), a long novel reminiscent of Dostoevsky. Its hero, by wounding another, opens his own wounds and is tormented by a consciousness of sin and despair. Moriuchi displays a sure existential grasp of reality in his portrayal of this experience in all its inescapable superhuman and supernatural aspects.

Kaga Otohiko (1929–)

Kaga Otohiko's mother was a Catholic, and he is a professor at Sophia University (Catholic) in Tokyo. Prompted by his mother's death, his writing reflects his spiritual development toward receiving baptism at age 58. His metaphysical novel *Senkoku* (The verdict; 1982), about a psychiatrist's experience with a condemned prisoner, probes his discovery that the darker the darkness encountered, the brighter is the light of redemption. *Shitsugen* (The moor; 1985) tells of love between a mentally disturbed Catholic student in a women's university and a middle-aged automobile mechanic with a criminal record. Through a false accusation they are both sent to prison, but they overcome this and their disparate ages to find a life of true love.

Tanaka Komimasa (1925–)

Tanaka Komimasa was born and raised in a Protestant minister's home, studied philosophy, led a prodigal's life, and eventually settled down to do translation work and write popular fiction. At age 54, in 1979, he wrote of his father for the first time in a work called *Poroporo*, for which he was awarded the coveted Tanizaki Prize. This work, in the style of Samuel Becket and the theater of the absurd, portrays his father's prayers as incomprehensible nonsense (represented by the book's title). Another work drawing on the same experiential background is *Amen chichi* (My amen father; 1989). A humorous though difficult metaphysical work is his *Kanto bushi* (A song of Kant; 1985).

Mori Reiko (1928–)

Upon graduation from a girls' high school, Mori Reiko was baptized in a Baptist church related to a mission school, but gradually she drifted away from the church. Later she joined Shiina Rinzō's Tane no Kai and, under his influence, recovered her faith. Her first work was *Mikan no karute* (An incomplete medical chart; 1963). For her novel *Mokkingu-bādo no iru machi* (Town with a mockingbird; 1980[9]) she was awarded the Akutagawa Prize and won a place in literary circles. The novel depicts women approaching middle age — ugly and lonely, uprooted from native lands — and asks how such people whose lives are darkened by sin and despair can lift their eyes up to the light. Since then, she has written *Ten no ryōken* (Hound of heaven; 1980), *Kaminchu* (Sorceress; 1989), and other works of a religious nature.

NOTABLE OTHERS

Owing to limited space, a number of noted writers must simply be listed without elaboration.

Shigekane Yoshiko (1927–), a Protestant, in 1980 received the Akutagawa Prize for her *Yama'ai no kemuri* (Smoke amidst the mountains).

Kizaki Satako (1939–), a Catholic, received the Akutagawa Prize in 1985 for her *Aogiri* (Green paulownia[10]).

Abe Mitsuko (1912–), a Protestant, won the women writers' award in 1964; and while serving as a pastor in the United Church of Christ in Japan, she produced *Oitaru Shinderera* (Cinderella grown old; 1981) and other works.

Playwright Tanaka Sumie (1908–), a Catholic, published her novel *Tsuwano no no* (The plain of Tsuwano) in 1972.

Miura Ayako (1922–), a best-selling Protestant author, had her first success when her novel *Hyōten* (Freezing point; 1964) won the Asahi Newspaper's award. She has since produced *Shiokari tōge* (Shiokari pass; 1968), *Hosokawa Gurashia Fujin* (Madame Gracia Hosokawa; 1975), *Kairei* (Ocean peaks; 1978), and many other novels with Christians as main characters. Her fame extends beyond Japan to Taiwan, South Korea, and elsewhere.

Inoue Hisashi (1934–), a prolific Catholic writer, won the Naoki Prize for his novel *Tekusari shinjū* (A love-suicide with handcuffs; 1972).

Konaka Yōtarō (1934–), who became known for his involvement in the anti-Vietnam War movement, wrote *Nada kōkō* (Nada high school).

[9] Translated by Noah Brannen as "Desert song" in *The Japan Christian Quarterly* LI/4–52/1, Fall 1985–Winter 1986.

[10] English translation by Carol A. Flath, *The Pheonix Tree and Other Stories* (Tokyo: Kodansha International, 1990).

Besides novelists, Christian writers presently active include: playwrights Tanaka Chikao, Yashiro Seiichi, Kitamura Sō, and the present writer; literary critics Sako Jun'ichirō, Takeda Tomoju, and Kazusa Hideo; and poets Anzai Hitoshi and Shimazaki Mitsumasa.

A PERSONAL RECKONING

Reflections on the Past Two Decades

The 1970s were a time of ideological battles and schisms, and the church could not escape this maelstrom. Confrontation erupted everywhere, and this was not conducive to fruitful dialogue. Amid all the confusion, writers avoided being swept into the conflict, sticking instead to their own literary circles and concentrating on their writing. Their literary works transcended ideological and theological conflict, surmounted denominational lines and distinctions between Christian and non-Christian, and thereby provided an open forum where, through reading, dialogue could still take place.

Japan has yet to give birth to a distinctive Christian theology. But Japanese Christian writers have produced a wealth of literature that articulates Christian faith and thought in the indigenous idiom of the Japanese people and their daily life. How was this possible?

Perhaps, from a global perspective, it can be said that the threat of nuclear annihilation and environmental erosion of our common planetary habitat made people feel the need for an eschatological vision, and Christian writers were able, intentionally or not, to answer this need.

Or it could be that, whereas writing from a clear Christian standpoint is declining in Europe and North America, in Japan it is Christian writers who, because they have no choice but to work amid the tensions of a pagan society, see the issues of life in starker contrast, and thus their writing casts their distinctive standpoint into sharper relief.

From the perspective of Christian civilization in the West, it might be said that committed Christian writers have a role to play in Japan—hardly even a hinterland in that distant perspective—because Christian standards enable them to see the distortions arising from the new consumer society and empower them to correct those distortions, or at least to point the ethical and philosophical way toward reform.

Prospects for the Coming Decade

What do the 1990s hold in store for Christian writers in Japan? It is next to impossible to imagine the course ahead for individual writers, each with a personal spiritual life, as they face a bewildering, rapidly changing world situation.

If permitted to express my own personal hope, I would urge them to portray ever more deeply and starkly the reality of human sin, of the demonic forces in the world that outstrip our common perception, and to persist in probing why sin and evil exist and how they continue to affect our lives.

I would like them, as well, to search for new answers regarding Japan's proper relations with our Asian neighbors, and in this context, to continue dealing with Japan's guilt in war and its invasion of other Asian lands.

I would encourage them, in their literature, to present the Good News as the ground of hope and courage for all — the prosperous and well-fed, the hungry and poor, the sick in body and spirit, those whose lives have lost all meaning.

Even so, I would remind them that in the 1990s and on into the twenty-first century Japanese Christian literature will definitely face such hard times as to permit little optimism for all our hopes and dreams.

IV
Churches, Councils, and Movements

23

Profiles of Member Churches of the National Christian Council in Japan

Compiled by Douglas P. Mikell

THE PROFILES PRESENTED here were provided by persons who have served for extended periods the churches they report on. They are: William F. Honaman, the Anglican Church of Japan; Henry French, the Japan Evangelical Lutheran Church; Leroy Seat, the Japan Baptist Convention; Glenn Gano, the Japan Baptist Union; and John McIntosh, the Korean Christian Church in Japan. Douglas P. Mikell did the profile of the United Church of Christ in Japan, drawing on the *Kyodan Newsletter* and chronological material provided by Igarashi Yoshinobu; he was also responsible for the overall compilation of this chapter.

THE UNITED CHURCH OF CHRIST IN JAPAN
(Nihon Kirisuto Kyōdan)

The United Church of Christ in Japan (UCCJ), the largest Protestant denomination in Japan, entered the 1970s embroiled in controversy. The transitional social climate, characterized by unrest and a sense of alienation, especially among youth, greatly affected the church's witness and functioning. The dispute over the 1970 World Exposition (Expo 70), aggravated by related problems, became the catalyst for questioning the church's structures and affiliated educational institutions as well as the nature and witness of the church itself.

The Dilemma of the Early 1970s

The controversy had both theological and nontheological roots, some extending back into an earlier period. The union's wartime origin and the church's self-acknowledged complicity in the war were called into question.[1] While the 1954 Confession of Faith, a doctrinal statement, clarified the post-war church's identity, many cite the 1967 Confession of Responsibility During World War II as recovering the church's integrity, by openly dealing with the church's wartime role. The dilemma was basically a question of whether one confession or the other, or both, would have priority in defining the church's contemporary mission.

Factors such as the renewal of the Japan–US Security Treaty, the Vietnam War, and Japan's growing economic prowess amidst Asian poverty coalesced to call forth images of Japan's militaristic past. Fears that the church could once again be drawn into an unsavory supportive role prompted searching questions. Moreover, the UCCJ's great diversity and its multifaceted presence throughout society made it all the more vulnerable to suspected complicities. Again, the essential question was the extent to which these factors of its historical context and conduct should determine the nature and scope of its message and mission, as against missiological parameters drawn from biblical and theological traditions.

This dilemma cropped up repeatedly, denying a quorum to assemblies at the national and district levels. The UCCJ general assembly was paralyzed from 1969 to 1973, as were, for varying periods, the following district assemblies: Kanagawa (1969–71), Kyoto (1969–74), Hyōgo (1969–76), Osaka (1969–81), and Tokyo (1969–90). In all these cases, the focal point of dialogue was the Expo 70 dispute (cf. II-8). The UCCJ General Assembly of 1974 officially acknowledged its error in approving UCCJ participation as a co-sponsor of the Christian Pavilion at Expo 70. It also asserted that Tokyo Union Theological Seminary, founded by the UCCJ, had erred in calling in riot police to resolve its campus conflict in 1969 (cf. II-7).

The "path of dialogue" was initiated by the UCCJ moderator to accommodate persons wishing to pose critical questions but lacking representative status in church councils, in hopes of resolving an impasse and promoting organizational reform. Considerable tension had arisen over what was regarded as failure to maintain the Confession of Faith as the essential component of ministerial examinations. Persons and congregations of more conservative evangelical leaning protested this omission, and some critics of the "path of dialogue" gathered in 1977 to form the Federation of Evangelical Churches in the UCCJ, organizational successor to the earlier Alliance of Evangelicals.[2]

During this same period, the Japan–North American Commission on Co-

---

[1] The UCCJ was formally established in June 1941.
[2] This organization itself came under criticism in 1979 when it held its own ministerial examinations and administered ordination and licensure.

operative Mission (JNAC) was reorganized (1973), replacing the former Interboard Committee for Christian Work in Japan. The commission links the UCCJ with church partners in North America. This organizational change fully recognized the self-reliant status of the UCCJ (initiated in the 1960s) and signaled a new era in church-to-church relationships.

Constructive Engagement, 1978–87

With a deepened commitment to its mission in the world, the UCCJ looked outward to the struggles of minorities. The 1978 General Assembly voted to commit the church itself to combatting discrimination against the Buraku people both in the church and in society. This commitment took on concrete form in the Buraku Liberation Center opened in 1981 in Osaka. The UCCJ in 1984 also acknowledged that Kagawa Toyohiko (1888–1960), noted evangelist, social reformer, and author had on occasion used discriminatory language characteristic of his times.

Looking into issues of church and society also required a reassessment of the 1969 union of the "Japan and Okinawa kyōdans."[3] Since 1978 the issue has been discussed in both ecclesial and socio-historical terms, with an eye to avoiding the appearance of a larger church gobbling up a smaller one.

Reconsideration of the church's responsibility prompted a growing awareness of Japan's Asian neighbors and a desire to forge church partnerships. In the early 1970s the UCCJ entered into covenant relations of cooperative mission with the Presbyterian Church in the Republic of Korea, the Presbyterian Church of Korea, and the Korean Methodist Church. Later, a covenant relationship with the Presbyterian Church in Taiwan was established in 1984.

With like actions by general assemblies on both sides, the UCCJ and the Korean Christian Church in Japan (KCCJ) entered into another covenant agreement in 1984. Recognizing Japan's oppression of Koreans during the period of Japan's colonial domination (1910–45) as well as continuing discrimination against Koreans in Japan, the two churches pledged to respond to God's call to mutual mission. One concrete expression of this commitment is joint action to protect the human rights of resident Koreans.

Concern for reconciliation within the church led to a formal apology to persons of the Holiness bloc in the original wartime UCCJ. The 1986 General Assembly acknowledged that the UCCJ had not supported, as it should have during and following the war, the faithful resistance of Holiness groups against state authority and power.

---

[3] Both the Japan united church and the Okinawa united church used the term *kyōdan*, meaning "religious organization." The Japanese term is handy shorthand for in-house communication; but it is also widely used by non-Christian religious organizations as well, for which reason we use it here only when necessary. — Ed.

Resistance and Renewal, 1988–1990

Encouraged by the courageous wartime witness of Christians who resisted government suppression, the UCCJ has increasingly spoken out prophetically against abuses of Japan's emperor system and its rising militarism since the mid-1960s, when the neo-nationalistic trend emerged. Constitutional separation of religion and state has been seriously challenged by government manipulation of imperial symbols to promote nationalism and militarization in the period under review. This issue moved quickly to the forefront when Hirohito, the wartime emperor, fell ill and death seemed imminent in September 1988. The UCCJ General Assembly in November called for resistance to any overt activities threatening to stifle religious freedom. Official church statements also protested government support and funding of specifically Shinto funerary rites for the late emperor in 1989 and for the enthronement rites of his successor, Akihito, lasting till November 1990.

In cooperation with partner churches and the National Christian Council in Japan, the UCCJ continues its involvement in peace, justice, and human rights concerns, especially in the Japanese and Asian contexts. Mutual involvement with Asian colleagues and churches has enhanced the UCCJ's sense of its mission as an Asian church.

The past twenty years have tested what it means to be a united church. Energies are increasingly turning toward reconciliation and renewal. Two indicators illustrate this well: a modest growth in membership despite the duress of controversy in the early 1970s; and the church's overseas involvement in mission. Twenty-six UCCJ missionaries now serve in eleven overseas lands in a variety of ministries, a heritage begun when the first postwar missionary was sent to Brazil in 1957.

Through its congregations, districts, and numerous church-related institutions, as well as its extensive ecumenical ties, the UCCJ witnesses to fellowship and unity in Jesus Christ. Continued commitment to renewal and reconciliation of the whole church is its agenda for the 1990s.

THE ANGLICAN CHURCH OF JAPAN
(Nippon Sei Kō Kai)

The past twenty years have produced some remarkable points of growth and change in the Anglican Church of Japan.[4] One key point is the shift in the

---

[4] The Nippon Sei Kō Kai (NSKK), which might be rendered literally as the "Japan Holy Community," has no official English title. "The Anglican Church in Japan" is often used in international communications, while the acronym NSKK is common in domestic use; both are used herein. — Ed.

House of Bishops, since the 1970 death of Bishop Yashiro Michael Hinsuke, a strong leader from 1945, to an entirely postwar membership. Under their leadership, the following developments are noteworthy.

From Self-reliance to Partnership

Japanese economic growth in the early 1970s coincided with the church's decision to end financial support from abroad, enabling it to move from financial dependence to self-reliance. The NSKK has since developed partner relationships with the worldwide Anglican communion through the Anglican Consultative Council (ACC), of which it is a full member as a Province.

The NSKK's past slogan of "Mutual Responsibility and Interdependence in the Body of Christ" and the ACC's working principle of "Partners in Mission" have greatly contributed to the NSKK efforts to establish and cultivate new relationships with Anglican churches in Asia, Africa, Latin America, and the Pacific region. There are regular joint mission consultations and frequent personnel exchanges with the church in South Korea. Cooperation with churches in the Philippines has been very close in mission, education, and development. A few NSKK medical personnel are serving in Bangladesh. Scholarships are provided annually to bring African students to Japan.

These interactions have given new insight into missional cooperation with the NSKK's traditional church partners in the United Kingdom, the United States, and Canada.

A New Agenda

Social justice. The NSKK's agenda has historically concentrated largely on evangelism, mission, pastoral work, social service, and education. Influenced by a growing global, ecumenical consciousness, the church has increasingly realized the importance of Christians working to achieve a more just and participatory society. This understanding undoubtedly led the General Synod ten years ago to form five commissions for dealing directly with various justice issues. One notable achievement was the reopening of a church and community center for a Korean congregation in Osaka, which had been closed during the Pacific War and ignored since — an action symbolic of the church's repentance and its desire for solidarity with much-discriminated Koreans in Japan. Another significant move was the deletion from the Prayer Book of the prayer for the emperor and imperial family. Actions with such socio-political relevance were completely beyond the church's vision thirty years ago.

Okinawa Diocese. The Okinawa Diocese was transferred to the Anglican Church of Japan by the Episcopal Church in the USA in 1972, prior to the administrative reversion of Okinawa to Japan, giving the church a total of eleven dioceses. An Okinawan was elected as the diocese's first bishop. Inclusion of the diocese gave church members on Japan's main islands a new awareness of their wartime responsibility and their discrimination toward people of Okinawa. Participation by representatives of the new diocese in committees at all levels of the church provided impetus for actions to correct old inequities as well as for new missional opportunities.

The Book of Common Prayer. A rather thorough revision of the Book of Common Prayer was approved by the General Synod in 1990 — the first major revision since 1959. The new version embodies significant liturgical changes that make worship services more responsive, participatory, and collective, and less authoritative, triumphalistic, and dogmatic. Written in modern language, it includes entirely new translations of the Lord's Prayer, the Creeds, and the Psalms.

Canon Law. A complete revision of Canon Law yielded a new Provincial (national) structure that achieves greater consistency in regulations and actual operations. The streamlined structure provides for full representation of all bodies in a system that can function in ways more representative of the church's entire constituency.

Women's status. A major change in Canon Law in 1977 makes women eligible for ordination to the diaconate — a giant step toward inclusion of women in the priesthood. Four women were promptly ordained deacons, though none have since been added. A strong movement is currently advocating women's involvement at all levels of the church's life. The General Synod responded in 1990 by forming the Study Committee for the Realization of the Ordination of Women to the Orders of Priest and Bishop, an action that enhanced women's opportunities to be heard in church councils.

Urban mission ventures. Seven new mission stations in major urban areas — Sapporo, Tokyo, Yokohama, Nagoya, Osaka, and Fukuoka — have been developed through local initiatives without outside support.

Church-related institutions

Although the overall Anglican membership is relatively small, NSKK-related institutions are well known and rooted in society. They include five universities, four junior colleges for women, several secondary schools, a few major hospitals, and about fifty social welfare centers. Contemporary trends in government policy and political ethos make it difficult to maintain both a strong social standing and the clear Christian identity inherited from the past. Even so, these institutions will continue as the front line of the church's mission, where Christian values and integrity command respect.

THE JAPAN EVANGELICAL LUTHERAN CHURCH
(Nihon Fukuin Ruteru Kyōkai)

Toward Self-reliance

From the early 1970s the Japan Evangelical Lutheran Church (JELC) moved toward self-sufficiency, addressing internal structural concerns as well as relations with overseas church partners. At its 1970 General Assembly the JELC called for self-reliance in three areas: evangelism, finance, and administration. A five-year plan (1970–74) was undertaken, and the 1972 General Assembly approved significant changes to eliminate presupposed overseas financial assistance. When the five-year goals were met, church leader Nakajima Makoto led a delegation of Japanese Lutherans on a visit to the United States at the invitation of the American Lutheran Church for an act of mutual recognition of the JELC's new self-reliant status.

The policy of self-reliance led the JELC to reconsider its relations with partner churches. In 1974 the Joint Lutheran Committee for Cooperative Mission, of which JELC is a member, released a statement to confirm the following provisions as applicable to the JELC: (a) JELC would participate in world evangelism as a "responsible" church rather than merely a receiving one; (b) JELC would maintain active relations with partner churches; and (c) JELC would assume responsibility for itself.

Media Ministry

Japan's Lutheran Hour has produced an outstanding variety of radio and television programs. In a bold move to expand media ministries, the Tokyo branch of the Lutheran World Federation (LWF) Mass Media Research Office in 1974 launched a five-year multi-media project, with Okada Teruyoshi as director. One notable venture was the nationwide TV program called "Mothers of the World." Another was a survey of what motivates individual Japanese to become Christians (cf. III-19).

Institutional Ministries

The JELC has long been involved in promoting education and nurture of church members. The Seventh General Assembly in 1976 approved a program for training of laity and clergy to serve as "God's people who witness and serve."

The Japan Lutheran Theological College and Seminary in Tokyo provide undergraduate and graduate education for training future church leaders, both lay and clergy. The college and seminary are shared with the Japan Lutheran Church (Nihon Ruteru Kyōkai).

Two institutes, one for scholarly studies of Luther, the other for pastoral care, are located on the college/seminary campus. The Luther Studies Institute is a major Asian center for original Luther studies; it is also engaged in translating Luther's collected works into Japanese. Since 1982 the Pastoral Growth and Counseling Center has given leadership to training for ministries in these areas.

The JELC maintains five homes for the elderly, facilities for disabled persons, orphanages, and facilities for ministering to children subject to domestic abuse and those with school-related problems.

Peace and Justice Issues

Since 1982, the Hiroshima Peace Seminar has been jointly sponsored by the Peace and Nuclear Disarmament Committee of the JELC Western District and the Japan Lutheran Theological College and Seminary. Although the main focus of the seminars has been nuclear weapons, more recently the seminar has expanded its scope to include environmental problems related to nuclear power plants, the "justice, peace, and integrity of creation" themes promoted by the World Council of Churches, links between peace and problems of discrimination and the marginalization of minority groups, and the emperor system and its connections with war responsibility. Variations on the peace seminars include the International Peace Seminar, held in 1987 in cooperation with the LWF and the NCCJ, and peace seminars conducted for high school students in 1988 and 1990.

The Life Together movement, organized and led by the laity, works to raise the church's consciousness of problems faced by developing nations. It raises funds for projects addressing women's issues and for emergency aid to victims of famines or natural disasters.

As plans for the rites of imperial succession became known, the JELC General Assembly in 1990 issued a statement protesting the Shinto-based enthronement ceremonies. The protest appealed to constitutional separation of religion and state, and also stressed the emperor system's part in Japan's militaristic past.

Cooperative Ventures

The JELC began pioneer evangelism in the northernmost island of Hokkaido in 1981 with the establishment of the Hokkaido Special District, which today has eight congregations served by six Japanese pastors and two missionary pastors.

The church's mission and evangelism extend overseas. By agreement with the Evangelical Lutheran Church in America, a JELC pastor ministers to Japanese in California. Since the 1970s, JELC missionary pastors have worked with the Lutheran Church in Brazil to serve Japanese immigrants in the Sao Paulo area.

The JELC is involved in promoting dialogue with the Anglican and Roman Catholic churches in Japan. Conversations with the Anglicans, begun in 1990, seek mutual understanding and cooperation in both faith-and-order and life-and-work issues. Dialogue with the Roman Catholics has resulted in mutual recognition of baptism and a theological treatment of common understandings of Christian faith to be published in 1991.

Future Prospects

Plans are under way to celebrate the centennial year of the Japan Evangelical Lutheran Church in 1993 and make it an occasion for revitalizing the church. Earlier concerns with internal structures and self-sufficiency have enabled the church to turn more recently to evangelistic outreach and social witness. Now attention must be given to reversing the general trend toward decreased baptisms and youth involvement. It is hoped that the centenary celebration will give birth to programs and projects for growth and renewed commitment at the congregational, district, and national levels.

THE JAPAN BAPTIST CONVENTION
(Nihon Baputesuto Renmei)

The 1970s — A New Era

The Japan Baptist Convention (JBC) entered a new era in the 1970s. Baptist mission had been born and nurtured in Kyushu until World War II ended in 1945; the postwar JBC reached out to the whole nation with new vision and faith, aiming to establish churches in every prefecture. The church weathered the storms of student protest in the 1960s, while also overcoming the wartime legacy of Asian antagonism.

Surviving Controversy. The decade opened with controversy over JBC's joint sponsorship of the Baptist World Congress held in July 1970 at Tokyo's Budokan hall. Despite opposition by a disgruntled minority representing fifteen churches and organized as the Tokyo Joint Struggle Council, the congress went smoothly, drawing 8,672 participants (1,347 from Japan). The congress theme, "Reconciliation through Christ," symbolized new relationships with Christians around the world as well as a sense of responsibility for evangelism at home and abroad.

At the decade's outset the JBC faced a "seminary problem" at Seinan Gakuin University's Department of Theology, JBC's primary institution for training pastors. Students called a strike in September 1970, and classes were not resumed until the following January. From April 1971 the seminary began rebuilding a greatly reduced student body. Not until the next decade, however, had enrollment returned to the pre-strike level. By the late 1980s the number of ministerial students had reached a thirty-year peak.

Striving for self-reliance. The JBC meeting in 1976 passed a second five-year plan for self-support based on three pillars: advance of self-reliant Baptist churches, pioneer evangelism, and training of ministers. The Convention accepted a graded decrease in subsidy from the United States for the 1977–81 period, and from 1982 the seminary's operating budget would be entirely free of dependence on foreign funds. In accord with the denomination's plan for self-support, this goal was realized.

A nationwide Brotherhood Association was organized in 1978 with support of the seminary as one major objective. During "Seminary Week"—starting on the fourth Sunday of June each—each church was urged to remember the denominational seminary and pray for its adequacy; to pray for the present training and future ministry of seminarians; to pray that many persons would devote their lives to Christian ministry; and to include a "seminary offering" in its regular giving.

Women have made an outstanding contribution to the support and growth of Baptist work in Japan. On the fiftieth anniversary of the JBC women's department in 1970, a new Japan Baptist Women's Union was formed. Recognized as an "unofficial auxiliary" of the Convention, its annual Christmas offerings have played a major role in supporting home and foreign missions. The offering goal for 1990 was 51 million yen (US$400,000).

Leadership training. To provide more trained leaders for a growing number of churches, the Tokyo Association of Baptist churches in the 1970s opened Tokyo Baptist Seminary, a low-budget night school staffed by local pastors and teachers. In the mid-1980s a similar training school for church workers, called Kyushu Baptist Seminary, was started in Fukuoka by some pastors in Kyushu.

A new faith statement. The Convention's thirty-third annual meeting in August 1979 adopted a new "Statement of Faith of the Japan Baptist Convention" to replace the previous statement approved in 1947. The *Church Members' Handbook* (revised in 1989), however, still contains both statements.

The 1980s — A New Spirit

The 1980s opened with an expanded world mission program. The JBC already supported a missionary couple in Brazil; now it reached out to Asia. In

May 1981 representatives of JBC's Foreign Missions Committee signed an agreement with Baptists in Indonesia for exchanges of Christian witness. Later a similar arrangement opened doors for work in Thailand.

Recognizing common cause in the struggle for religious freedom, Baptists have cooperated with other Christians and groups in advocating separation of religion and state. The thirty-seventh JBC annual meeting in late August 1983 issued a statement protesting Prime Minister Nakasone Yasuhiro's "official visit" to Yasukuni Shrine on the fifteenth of that month. The annual meeting of the next year issued a strong protest against possible Yasukuni visits by the emperor, prime minister, and Cabinet members.

The JBC executive secretary and several other representatives visited South Korea in September 1984 to deliver to the Korean Baptist Convention and the Korean National Council of Churches a letter addressed to "Korean brothers and sisters in Christ." The letter conveyed an apology for sins committed against Koreans during Japan's colonization of Korea and an appeal for renewed cooperation in mission.

Throughout the two decades Baptists have been involved in ministries to the sick, disabled, and aged. They maintain the Baptist Hospital and Nursing School, as well as a home for the aged, in Kyoto. Hisayama Ryōikuen in Fukuoka provides a home with the most modern facilities for severely handicapped persons. This home has the enthusiastic cooperation of volunteers from churches and schools of other denominations as well as the sacrificial service of many Baptist pastors and lay people.

As in previous decades, one of the Baptists' greatest evangelistic opportunities is religious work among the nearly 10,000 students at Seinan Gakuin in Fukuoka City and some 3,000 women students at Seinan Jo Gakuin in Kitakyushu City in northern Kyushu. Many graduates of these schools carry with them into society a deep understanding of Christianity, and growing numbers of graduates can be found in Baptist and other denominational churches throughout Japan.

When JBC celebrated its fortieth anniversary in 1987, it had some 280 churches and mission points with an aggregate membership of 28,000. This represented a 17.5-fold increase in the number of churches and a 56-fold increase in church members for the four decades. The vision for growth in churches and members is alive and well, and JBC is working toward a church/member count of 500/50,000 in the year 2,000.

In 1988 the annual convention meeting issued a statement confessing the sin of compliance with Japan's World War II effort and asking forgiveness. The statement also related faith to a lifestyle of peacemaking. Among housekeeping affairs, the annual meeting (continued for forty-two consecutive years) was replaced by a biennial meeting.

The 1970s and 1980s were a time of struggle for the Japan Baptist Convention, as it was for most Christian groups in Japan. But as a new decade opened in 1990, the Convention enjoyed a greater spirit of unity and of cooperation in addressing the problems of Japanese society and in serving those in need of loving care. Indeed, it possessed even greater confidence and commitment to advancing together toward a future of growth and faithful witness. Out of the chaos of the early 1970s had come a sense of order, purpose, and hope for the JBC's future.

THE JAPAN BAPTIST UNION
(Nihon Baputesuto Dōmei)

In 1973 the centennial of the Baptist mission in Japan was celebrated at Yokohama Baptist Church (est. 1873), the first Baptist church in Japan. The Japan Baptist Union (JBU) was established in 1958 after a number of churches historically related to the American Baptist Foreign Mission Society withdrew from the United Church of Christ in Japan in order to carry out Christian work based on Baptist tradition and polity. Several five-year plans yielded new churches, and the centennial was marked by a new ten-year plan to promote pioneer evangelism, strengthen lay witness, achieve self-support, promote mutual cooperation between churches, and to participate in overseas mission. Top priority was given to the training of pastors.

Owing to student protests in the late 1960s, Kantō Gakuin College of Theology entered a time of confusion. The JBU established a program to recommend ministerial candidates to other seminaries and to supplement their training with courses on Baptist history and church polity. When the College of Theology was closed to new students in 1969, this alternate program was in place. In 1973 the JBU began a three-year training program on the Kantō Gakuin campus, but some students continue to attend other seminaries.

Throughout these twenty years, pioneer evangelism has been a major thrust, and a number of new preaching points were started. Most of them have become churches.

An overseas mission society was established in 1969, which sent a medical doctor to India for three years, and an agriculturist to the Philippines for two. In 1987 the doctor went to Bangladesh (where he could use the Bengali language he had learned in India). Contributions to this society have helped support a hospital in West Bengal, India, various projects in the Philippines, and scholarship programs for pastors from Thailand, India, and Burma who have studied at the Asian Rural Institute. Youth tours to study mission have visited India, Thailand, and Bangladesh.

Stewardship has shown remarkable growth in the past decade. A fifteen-year self-support plan was completed in 1988, and the Japan Baptist Union became independent of all outside financial assistance. To celebrate this achievement, a new church was planted in Sapporo, completely funded by the JBU. In 1990 a 100-million-yen campaign for the Pastors' Pension Fund was successfully completed. Many churches have rebuilt or extended their facilities with their own resources in the past decade.

Social concerns rank high on the JBU agenda, and churches have joined in the struggle for separation of religion and state and in other justice and peace causes. Annual appeals are sent to the government to protest visits to Yasukuni Shrine by the prime minister and his Cabinet members. In 1989 various JBU committees and local churches joined in active protest against the Shinto-related enthronement rites. Revision of the Alien Registration Law and appeals concerning discrimination against Buraku people are other concerns.

Students in JBU-related schools far outnumber church members. In the next several years, five of these schools will celebrate their centennials. Providing Bible teachers and chaplains and assigning missionaries to the institutions is a high priority for JBU; but as schools expand, secularization advances and relationships become increasingly formal. How to strengthen the relationships and enlarge the Christian presence on campuses continues to challenge the church and school leaders.

Pioneer evangelism, pastor training, and overseas mission stand foremost among the goals of the Japan Baptist Union as it enters the final decade of the century.

THE KOREAN CHRISTIAN CHURCH IN JAPAN
(Zainichi Daikan Kirisuto Kyōkai)

Witness and Struggle against Discrimination

At its twenty-sixth General Assembly in 1970 the Korean Christian Church in Japan (KCCJ) set forth its new stance on social responsibility: "It is the task of Christians to reform any kind of political or social discrimination." This was a clarion call to Korean Christians to combat the odious discrimination that plagues all Koreans living in Japan.

In a special session the same year, the General Assembly approved plans for the Korean Christian Center in Osaka's Ikuno district in a pointed affirmative action on a key social issue for resident Koreans. Completed in 1983, the center has played a major role in the struggle against discrimination.

The 1973 General Assembly approved a Basic Policy that placed high priority on regaining ". . . our ethnic identity that has become lost because of

Japanese society and the education it gives. The gospel of Christ is the power," it continued, "which makes possible our self-restoration" in that very society.[5]

The battle to remove the yoke of discrimination from the necks of Koreans and other minority groups is far from over, yet tremendous strides forward have been made, with many Japanese churches and lay organizations actively supporting the struggle (cf. II-11). Not least among supporting groups is the United Church of Christ in Japan, which entered into a covenant of co-operation with the KCCJ in 1983. On February 8, 1984, a ceremony celebrating this covenant was held at the KCCJ Osaka Church. The covenant targetted discrimination as a missional task. On June 10, 1984, KCCJ and UCCJ leaders mounted a campaign to collect 500,000 signatures to demand revision of the despised Alien Registration Law, an institutionalized form of discrimination.

In April 1988 the KCCJ moderator and six other KCCJ representatives visited Seoul to ask the South Korean government to assist in winning an improved legal status for Koreans in Japan.

Unification of Korea

The 1971 KCCJ General Assembly declared itself in support of Red Cross talks between North and South Korea—and the Assembly's moderator issued an endorsement the next July when government officials of North and South Korea made a statement on unification of the peninsula.

The 1973 Basic Policy also clearly stated the church's responsibility to work toward reconciliation of North and South Korea: "We are resolved to pray and make every effort toward the realization of a unified country with a national government committed to liberty and justice." This policy has been consistently pursued. In July 1988 the KCCJ released a statement clarifying its position in response to the "Declaration of the Christian Church in Korea Regarding National Unification and Peace," issued by the Seoul-based Korean National Council of Churches.

From July 29 to August 12, 1989, six KCCJ members visited North Korea and met with Christians there. Together they affirmed (a) the need for more exchange opportunities, (b) their mutual commitment to mission cooperation between churches on both sides, (c) their common calling to work for unification, and (d) a plan to hold an international symposium.

The KCCJ then took the initiative in sponsoring a Koreans' consultation in July 1990, with four delegates from the Korean Christian Federation

---

[5] Lee In-ha, "A sojourner's theology, part 3," *The Japan Christian Quarterly* 56/1, Winter 1990, p. 42.

(KCF) of North Korea joining Korean Christians from South Korea, Japan, and other lands. (Preparatory meetings had been held in Glion, Switzerland, in November 1988 and December 1990; cf. I-2.) This consultation discussed mutual responsibilities for mission and for the peaceful unification of Korea, and then issued a joint statement calling for continued encounter, dialogue, and commitment.

The Basis and Tasks of Mission

The struggle to eliminate discrimination and the movement for unification of Korea have both been grounded in faithfulness to the gospel of Jesus Christ. The Basic Policy of 1973 expressed this fundamental commitment in practical terms that called for the formation of house churches, increased funding for leadership training, and the founding of independent schools to foster ethnic identity and the Korean language.

The KCCJ General Assembly of 1977, looking toward the church's seventieth anniversary the next year and thus reflecting on the past decade, chose the slogan "Jesus Christ is our hope." It presented the denomination with three objectives: raising up a new church generation, mapping out a new life for Koreans in Japan, and defining the church's mission in the context of world history.

That this vision was gradually becoming more inclusive was evident when this assembly approved a revision in church rules to permit the ordination of female clergy and elders, an issue under debate for several years. To date, four women elders and two women clergy have been ordained, with the first Japan-born woman entering the ministry in 1989.

The 1978 General Assembly set forth a declaration of responsibilities, hopes, and outlook that upheld the tasks of evangelism under the one Lord and called the whole church to the work of church extension and the strengthening of its influence in home and community.

At a rally in Osaka in October 1988 to celebrate the eightieth anniversary of Korean Christian mission in Japan, the mission tasks of the new decade were affirmed as: (a) preserve the historical legacy of faith passed on by previous generations; (b) carry out mission as the servant of God and the people; (c) uphold the autonomy and integrity of the (north- and south-oriented) Korean community in Japan; (d) establish one hundred congregations by the ninetieth anniversary; (e) train workers for many Christian vocations; and (f) participate in ecumenical movements for justice and peace.

24

The National Christian Council in Japan

Yamaguchi Akiko

IN AUTUMN 1970 the National Christian Council in Japan[1] moved its offices from Tokyo's downtown Ginza district to the new Japan Christian Center in the Waseda University area in northwest Tokyo. Other churches and organizations moving into the new facility included the United Church of Christ in Japan, the Japan Baptist Union, the Korean Christian Church in Japan, the National Committee of YMCAs in Japan, the Japan Christian Federation of Childhood Education, and the Japan Christian Medical Association. The Audio Visual Activity Commission (AVACO) occupied an attached building. Next door was Waseda Hoshien (Baptist student center built in 1922), which had sold a portion of its land to the new Christian Center. From the 1970s the site became a major hub of ecumenical Christian activity and citizens' movements.

With the financial backing of its member bodies[2] the National Christian Council in Japan (NCCJ) was able, despite its small scale, to acquire the new office space and embark upon cooperative work among the churches during the 1970s, though the way ahead was not always smooth. The NCCJ in those years did not accept as a "joint project" just anything that groups could do together; the content and purpose of joint efforts were critically scrutinized as the NCCJ probed its way into the future.

Given its ecumenical mandate, the NCCJ plays a primary role in nurturing

[1] When organized in 1947, the organization's name was National Christian Council of Japan; the change to ". . . in Japan" was made in 1985. The later form is used herein. — Ed.

[2] The NCCJ includes both churches and other Christian organizations; some are full members, others affiliates. See the list appended to this chapter. — Ed.

relations with churches and projects outside Japan. A strong ecumenical base at home is essential to performing this role well.

THE ECUMENICAL HOME FRONT

A 1967 proposal to open a Christian pavilion at the World Exposition of 1970 (Expo 70), to be held in Osaka, provoked intense opposition that sent violent tremors throughout the Christian community in Japan, and some of the scars still remain (cf. II-8). Serious reflection on the NCCJ's initial approval of that proposal (1968) has spawned in NCCJ circles an attitude of great caution in reaching decisions. At the same time, the experience made it clear that the mission of the church is impossible without a discerning insight into, and active participation in, the realities of Japan and the world. Since then, both caution and commitment have been guidelines for NCCJ activities.

Practically speaking, the turmoil of the 1970s affected the finances of Christian churches and organizations in varying degrees, and the NCCJ particularly has suffered two decades of chronic financial difficulty.

Crafting New Structures

The NCCJ General Assembly in 1970 carried out structural reforms that yielded three divisions for mission, education, and service, as well as the Division of Christian Literature and the Division of Audio-Visual Aids. Five years later, in response to requests for simplifying structures to fit actual conditions, the general assembly combined mission and service into one division. The former mission division's International Affairs Committee now functioned on a broader mission-service scale for domestic and overseas emergency relief as well as long-term exchange and assistance programs. Also, AVACO dropped its status as an NCCJ project to become an independent corporate entity, related to the NCCJ as a member body.

Since 1959 the NCCJ Center for the Study of Japanese Religions, located in Kyoto, has engaged in dialogue with other religions. The March 1982 General Assembly established in Tokyo another center, the Christian Center for Response to Asian Issues (CCRAI), to build a network among the Asian churches for gathering information on grass-roots conditions throughout Asia and conveying the findings to citizens in Japan. CCRAI was charged with the heavy responsibility of promoting genuine involvement of Japanese churches in the lives of Asian peoples and churches.

While the NCCJ continued to feel the need for simpler structures, it was constantly confronted with pressing issues that resulted in the formation of various working committees, such as the Special Committee on Buraku

People and Discrimination, the Task Force for Disabled Persons and the Churches, the Special Committee on Nuclear Issues, the Peace Committee, and the Philippines Committee, as well as smaller committees on China, opposition to apartheid, and other issues. These committees have not had adequate funding, so all have had to share limited NCCJ staff time and depend heavily on volunteers and voluntary contributions.

Committee Activities

Buraku discrimination. The Special Committee on Buraku People and Discrimination was set up in 1976 by the Twenty-sixth General Assembly to deal with Buraku issues on behalf of the entire Christian community, especially the NCCJ member bodies. It conducted an extensive signature-collection campaign to support the appeal of Ishikawa Kazuo who, despite his compelling claims of innocence, was sentenced to death—a verdict widely considered discriminatory (cf. II-11). The committee produced a collateral reader entitled *Ibara no kanmuri* (Crown of thorns) for use in Christian schools, and in summer 1990 it sponsored the first seminar on liberation education for Christian school teachers.

Peace and nuclear issues. The 1976 General Assembly adopted resolutions opposing nuclear weapons and nuclear energy plants, and from this was born the Special Committee on Nuclear Issues, which has since sponsored lectures, developed slide sets and other resource materials, and held joint Catholic-Protestant prayer meetings. The Peace Committee was founded by the 1979 General Assembly to explore theological resources for peacemaking, and in time the committee developed a more practical range of seminars, field trips to nuclear sites and military bases, and network relations with overseas peace workers.

Disabled persons. Preparatory to the International Year of Disabled Persons scheduled for 1981, the 1979 General Assembly also established the Task Force on Disabled Persons and the Churches. Interaction among various church groups has been promoted through exchange programs with disabled persons' organizations, and the churches have been urged to fulfill their calling to be an inclusive "family of God" by eliminating all forms of discrimination, whether theological views or physical impediments in architecture and furnishings. It appealed for churches to observe "Disabled Persons' Week" in November (the week including the second Sunday), and this observance is gaining acceptance among NCCJ member churches.

Shinto and the state. The last of several attempts to pass a proposed bill for the "Nationalization of Yasukuni Shrine" in the Diet was defeated in 1974.

Even so, the ties between the state and Shinto have since grown closer as one critical Shinto-related event follows another: the Tsu City groundbreaking-ceremony trial (1977), the decision for official use of imperial era names (1979), the establishment of a memorial day for the war dead (1982), the final appeal against the enshrinement of a former Self-Defense Forces officer (1988), the death of the late Emperor Shōwa (1989), and the enthronement rites, including the controversial Daijōsai, for the new emperor Akihito in November 1990 (cf. II-5). The Special Committee for Yasukuni Shrine Problems has closely monitored these events and consistently opposed the emerging state-Shinto alliance evident in them.

Rights of foreigners. Things have been much the same for the Committee on Human Rights for Resident Foreigners, which opposed the 1973 revision of the Immigration-Emigration Control Law. The government next turned to revision of the Alien Registration Law, its instrument for control of foreigners, carrying out revisions in 1982 and 1985, which the committee also opposed. But the abolition of the required fingerprinting and the obligatory carrying of the Alien Registration Card at all times are regarded as still distant realities.

International affairs. Of committees with pre-1970 histories, the International Affairs Committee maintained its major focus on aid projects for Asia and Africa; but, going beyond traditional relief for victims of earthquakes, storms, floods, and hunger resulting from these, it has also developed long-range programs for promoting self-reliance in the target countries. While campaigns for the Indochina Hunger Relief Fund and the Asia–Africa Hunger Relief Fund were continued, other less dramatic long-range efforts were made to support Asia Rural Institute, and to send agricultural specialists to Bangladesh and Kenya as well as Japanese language teachers to China.

Migrant workers. During the 1970s the Urban Rural Mission Committee put special stress on strengthening ties with workers in various Asian lands. During the 1980s, however, growing numbers of Asian workers migrated to Japan in search of jobs. Accordingly, the committee took a special interest in the human rights of these workers in Japan. In 1990 this committee began working with CCRAI on problems of resident foreigners in Japan, both those brought here long ago under Japan's colonial policies and those more recently attracted by Japan's economic prosperity. The goal is to get more churches involved in the human rights problems of the migrant workers.

Mission consultations. In September 1971 the second Consultation on Mission in Japan was held at the Amagi Sansō retreat center, with participants from ten denominations and eight organizations. The theme of "Salvation today" helped set the course for NCCJ activities in the 1970s. The third Consultation on Mission, held in December 1980, took the theme "Mission in Japan, Asia's 'affluent' nation" as it sought to set specific missional priorities for the decade ahead. Subsequent mission consultation themes were: "A church that bears the pain of the times" (1981), "Today's crisis in education and the task of mission" (1983), and "Working together in the Lord" (1987).

Memorializing the war dead. The annual prayer service held at the National Tomb of the War Dead, located in the Chidorigafuchi Park in Tokyo, is among problems seriously discussed in NCCJ circles in recent years. Since 1960 the Christian Peace Prayer Meeting has been held each year at the Chidorigafuchi site early in the morning of August 15 (the day World War II ended in the Pacific theater). Initiated by concerned church members in the Tokyo District of the United Church of Christ in Japan, the prayer meeting gradually attracted Christians from other denominations. From 1970 the NCCJ Mission and Service Division assumed responsibility for the meeting. In the 1980s, however, questions arose about its nature.

The Christian memorial prayer meeting was originally conceived as an alternative to the Shinto memorials at nearby Yasukuni Shrine. Even if Yasukuni Shrine were not nationalized, the August 15 memorials to the war dead should take place not there, but at a nonreligious site. And one purpose of the Christian meeting was to inform the public that such a site already existed at Chidorigafuchi, Japan's collective "unknown soldiers' tomb." The service was held at an early hour so as to start the memorial day with a clear "anti-Yasukuni" witness. In time the criticism arose that this site too was established by the government to commemorate soldiers who died for Japan's imperial causes, and thus it is little more than a "secular Yasukuni." As such, said critics, it cannot be considered a proper place for a peace prayer meeting.

The Mission and Service Division's board of directors, central committee, and executive staff discussed this problem repeatedly from 1981 to 1983, but failed to reach a full consensus, though the problematic nature of NCCJ sponsorship of the prayer meeting was conceded. Since 1984 a committee of volunteers has assumed responsibility for continuing the peace prayer meeting. From these circumstances the lesson once more becomes clear: NCCJ planning and execution of a project always requires more than gathering and acting on a basis that is "ecumenical" only in the sense that denominational lines are crossed.

OVERSEAS RELATIONS

Asian Churches

The NCCJ has always served as a key link between churches in Japan and those overseas, but from the 1970s the challenge has been to go beyond simple fellowship to working together on specific problems (cf. I-4). Japanese Christians have been distressed to see church and ecumencal leaders in South Korea, Taiwan, and the Philippines repeatedly arrested for opposing dictatorial regimes in their countries. But the Japanese Christians have also realized that those regimes have Japan's economic backing. Indeed, affluent lifestyles in Japan depend in no small degree on the sacrifices of peoples in other Asian lands.

The NCCJ has issued statements of concern and protest, and even sent investigating teams to these countries, though its efforts are meager compared with the problems faced. These actions have drawn criticism from some church members who claim the church should not get involved in politics. But among nonchurch citizens concerned about Asia, many have been so impressed by Christian witnesses in these countries that they have shown new interest in Christianity, and the NCCJ name is a trusted one among these citizens.

South Korea. Relations with the church in South Korea took a great step forward in the summer of 1973 with the holding of the first Japan–Korea Church Consultation. It was a propitious time: the Korean churches were just getting involved in the popular democratization movement in Korea, and the Japanese churches were beginning to deal with human rights problems of Korean residents in Japan. Moreover, many consultation participants were for the first time made aware of the Japanese sex tours to Korea.

Six Japan–Korea Church Consultations were held through 1987, and several separate consultations have been held on the human rights of Korean residents in Japan. Another joint NCC consultation was held in November 1989 on textbook revision by Japan's Ministry of Education (obscuring the reality of Japan's wartime aggression in Korea and elsewhere). Problems of fingerprinting and the Alien Registration Law will come to a head in 1991 when the present law expires and the status of Koreans in Japan is to be redefined.

North Korea. In spring 1987, Sumiya Mikio, chair of the NCCJ-CCRAI board, led a three-person team on a visit to churches in the People's Republic of Korea, reopening fellowship with Christians in North Korea. In the following year, the NCCJ invited a delegation of North Korean Christians to Japan, and laid plans for a symposium on unification of the Korean peninsula. The

North Korean delegates were unable to come, but the symposium was held without them on the theme "Peace and unification of the Korean Peninsula and Japan's Responsibility." Prior to this, in May 1988, the NCCJ in Japan had sent a "Letter to the (South) Korean National Council of Churches" acknowledging Japan's historical responsibility for the division of the Korean peninsula and pledging to cooperate with Korean Christians north and south to realize unification.

In September 1989 a four-person delegation from the (North) Korean Christians Association, led by Kim Un-bong, arrived in Japan. Through this visit Japanese Christians could see how fervently Korean Christians hope and pray for unification.

The Philippines. Fellowship with the Philippine churches led to the first Japan–Philippines Church Consultation in November 1983, and in turn to the formation of the NCCJ's Philippine Committee. The second consultation was held in 1985, focusing on problems of militarization and the export of Japan's polluting industries to the Philippines.

China. Relations with churches in China received renewed attention in autumn 1983 when a Japanese delegation visited churches in China, and again in autumn 1984 when a Chinese delegation came to Japan and visited churches in various places.

Asian issues. A special feature of recent years is the expanded interaction with Asians on issues concerning education, women, and youth. For its annual Christian Education Week, the NCCJ Education Division has promoted knowledge of Asia by producing leaflets on the Philippines, South Korea, and Thailand, as well as slides on various Asian countries. Japan–Korea youth consultations were initiated in 1979, and a continuing joint theological seminar for women was started in 1988.

Crisis in the CCA

In December 1987 the government of Singapore suddenly ordered the Christian Conference of Asia (CCA) to cease all activities and forced its foreign staff to leave the country. The NCCJ in Japan protested this oppressive action and did its best to help the CCA continue its functions, especially from 1988 by hosting one of the dispersed CCA offices in Osaka (others were set up in Manila, Chengmai, and Hong Kong). This arrangement imposed great difficulties on the CCA, but having a CCA office in Japan has helped lessen the gap between the churches of Japan and Asia.

ONGOING TASKS

In 1990 the NCCJ maintained an Anti-Daijōsai Signature Campaign Center to enlist the support of NCCJ-related and other Christian organizations to oppose use of public funds for the Daijōsai (Great Food Offering Ceremony) that followed the public Enthronement Ceremony (Sokui-no-rei), as the Daijōsai is clearly a religious (Shinto) ceremony. Long after the Daijōsai, however, the relation of the churches and the emperor system will still be a major concern for the NCCJ, as will the problems of Asian migrant workers, human rights in Japan, and interactions with Asian peoples. Indeed, the scope and intensity of these problems will very likely increase, calling the NCCJ to a more comprehensive and integrated search for peace and justice.

Cooperation with the Roman Catholic Church has centered on the theological work of the Faith and Order Committee. The committee has worked out common translations of the Lord's Prayer and the Nicene Creed, as well as a joint translation of the study book "Baptism, Eucharist, and Ministry" produced by the Faith and Order Commission of the World Council of Churches. Dialogue and cooperation in such areas is expected to continue (cf. IV-28).

Each year the Sunday preceding Pentecost is designated "Asia Sunday." Observance of this special Sunday has spread widely since the late 1980s, yielding a new level of grass-roots ecumenism in Japan.

In spring 1989 a World Council of Churches delegation led by Frank Chikane, general secretary of the South African Council of Churches, came to explain to Japanese churches how Japanese economic power is supporting apartheid in South Africa. The NCCJ responded by forming its Anti-apartheid Committee under the Mission and Service Division. Representatives of East German churches visited Japan in spring 1990, and testimonies of the lay Christians left a deep impression in the minds of their Japanese hosts. These two examples indicate that Japan's global economic expansion is already projecting the Japanese Christian community into new areas of challenge in Africa and Europe, as in these cases, and the rest of the world as well.

NCCJ LEADERSHIP

Moderators of the NCCJ General Assembly during the 1970–90 period were as follows:

1970–73	Gotō Makoto (NSKK)
1973–76	Aikawa Takaaki (JBU)
1976–79	Yamada Jō (NSKK)

1979–82	Kishimoto Yōichi (UCCJ)
1982–85	Lee In-ha (KCCJ)
1985–88	Satō Kunihiro (JELC)
1988–91	Takeuchi Kentarō (NSKK)

Yamada (1976–79), initially elected vice-moderator, replaced moderator Shiozuki Kentarō (then general secretary of the National Committee of the YMCAs in Japan), who had to resign soon after his election. Lee In-ha, a Korean resident in Japan, was the first foreigner elected to serve as NCCJ moderator. Sekiya Ayako, then president of the Japan YWCA, was the first woman to be elected vice-moderator (1976); she served a second term in that office (1982–85) and was succeeded by two women successively, Isshiki Yoshiko (1985–88) and Yamaya Shinko (1988–91).

General secretaries during the 1970–90 period were:

1970–78	Nakajima John Masaaki (UCCJ)
1978–85	Shōji Tsutomu (UCCJ)
1985–present	Maejima Munetoshi (UCCJ)

APPENDED LIST OF NCCJ MEMBER BODIES

Full members

Anglican Church in Japan (Nippon Sei Kō Kai)
Church of Christ (Nihon Kirisuto Kyōkai) [Presbyterian]
Japan Baptist Convention (Nihon Baputesuto Renmei)
Japan Baptist Union (Nihon Baputesuto Dōmei)
Japan Evangelical Lutheran Church (Nihon Fukuin Ruteru Kyōkai)
Korean Christian Church in Japan (Zainichi Daikan Kirisuto Kyōkai)
United Church of Christ in Japan (Nihon Kirisuto Kyōdan)
Audio Visual Activity Commission (Kirisutokyō Shichōkaku Sentā)
Christian Childhood Education Association (Kirisutokyō Hoiku Renmei)
Christian Culture Association (Kirisutokyō Bunka Kyōkai)
Japan Bible Society (Nihon Seisho Kyōkai)
Japan Christian Medical Association (Nihon Kirisutosha Ika Renmei)
Japan Woman's Christian Temperance Union (Nihon Kirisutokyō
    Fujin Kyōfūkai)
National Committee of YMCAs in Japan (Nihon YMCA Dōmei)
YWCA of Japan (Nihon YWCA)

Affiliate members (partial list)

The nineteen affiliate bodies include other denominations (e.g., Christian Catholic Church, Japan Free Methodist Church), local union churches (e.g., Tokyo, Yokohama, Kobe), mission societies (e.g., German Midnight Mission, Swiss East Asian Mission), various educational centers (e.g., Keiyō Education and Culture Center, Christian Academy), and peace groups (Fellowship of Reconciliation). Cf. *Kirisutokyō nenkan* (Christian yearbook), 1990, p. 344.

25

Evangelical Churches

Izuta Akira

THE EVANGELICALS OF JAPAN comprise many denominations and evangelistic organizations. These bodies were able to make a new start after World War II, coming together in three general categories. The first consists of those groups that left the United Church of Christ in Japan (UCCJ), such as the Reformed Church in Japan, the Japan Holiness Church, and the Japan Assemblies of God. In the second category are those groups established after the war, such as the Immanuel General Mission, the Christian Brotherhood, and the Christian Holy Convention. Finally, the third category consists of mission-founded groups begun after the war, such as the Evangelical Free Church of Japan, the Presbyterian Church in Japan, and the Japan Baptist Church Association[1]. Altogether, there are probably over one hundred evangelical denominations. In addition there are numerous para-church organizations, each doing its own kind of work.

THE POSTWAR SITUATION

With so many groups of such varied backgrounds, it is only natural that the evangelicals of Japan have exhibited considerable diversity in theology and practice, and that early on there was a lack of unity among them. But as evangelicals reflected on this problem, there arose in the 1960s a strong tendency to seek unity, and several interdenominational associations were born.

The first, the Japan Evangelical Association (Nihon Fukuin Dōmei), or JEA, was established in 1968 as a result of the many prayers and much perseverance over a long period of time (member bodies of JEA are indicated by

[1] *The Evangelicals of Japan,* pp. 10–16.

an asterisk). The second, the Japan Christian Layman's League (Nihon Kuri-suchan Shinto Renmei), is a society formed in 1969 to assist lay people in their work of evangelism and service in the church. A third group, the Japan Evangelical Theological Society (Nihon Fukuin-shugi Shingakkai), was begun in 1970 with the goal of promoting cooperative theological research.

Through the establishment of these associations and organizations, the spirit of unity has born fruit, as evangelicals have been able to share their experiences and gain a wider perspective.

Calvinistic Denominations

Calvinism has of course had an influence on Japanese Christianity since the arrival in Japan of the first Presbyterian and Reformed missionaries in the mid-nineteenth century. Among Calvinistic denominations in Japan that are included in any listing of evangelical churches, the following may be mentioned here:

Reformed Church in Japan (Nihon Kirisuto Kaikakuha Kyōkai). Mission organizations of the Southern Presbyterian, Christian Reformed, and other mainline Presbyterian churches gave their cooperation to this group of churches that left the UCCJ in 1946.[2] The new denomination was formed on the basis of the Westminster Confession.

On its thirtieth anniversary in 1976, the denomination issued a "Statement of Faith Concerning Church and State," in which the prophetic role of the church toward the state was stressed. The church adopted a "Statement of Faith of the Reformed Church in Japan" on its fortieth anniversary in 1986, which made clear its position on specific issues such as biblical doctrine and the Holy Spirit.[3]

The Reformed Church has planted churches nationwide, and has six presbyteries in the northeast, east, and central regions of Japan's main island and on Shikoku island. It is a steadily growing denomination, going from 5,338 members in 1971 to 8,468 members in 1990.

*Presbyterian Church in Japan (Nihon Kirisuto Chōrō Kyōkai). This denomination was established in 1956 through the work of Presbyterian missionaries who began evangelizing after the war. They have made efforts in

---

[2] The United Church of Christ in Japan (Nihon Kirisuto Kyōdan) was formed in 1941 partly as the culmination of a quest for Christian unity that began in 1872 with formation of the first Protestant church in Japan, the Nihon Kirisuto Kōkai, in Yokohama; and partly in response to the wartime Japanese government's pressure on Christian and other religious groups to organize under a single national organizational headquarters. In the post-World War II period, various churches left the "Kyōdan" partly because of its "tainted" formation under government pressure, and partly to regain their own denominational identity. — Ed.

[3] See *Kaikakuha taikei kiroku* (General records of Reformed Churches), 1986.

education and evangelism through the establishment of Japan Christian Theological Seminary (Nihon Kirisuto Shingakkō). This school merged in 1980 with Tokyo Christian College (Tokyo Kirisutokyō Tanki Daigaku) and another school to become Tokyo Christian Institute (Tokyo Kirisutokyō Gakuen). Under Dr. Maruyama Tadataka, who had become president of the school when it was known as Tokyo Christian College, the school became a four-year college in 1990 under the name Tokyo Christian University (Tokyo Kirisutokyō Daigaku). (Cf. IV-26) The Presbyterian Church in Japan consists of two presbyteries, east and central. It has grown by a factor of four from 541 members in 1971 to 1,928 members in 1990.

*The Evangelical Presbyterian Church in Japan (Nihon Fukuin Chōrō Kyōkai). Five independent Presbyterian churches came together to form this denomination in 1979, and currently there are nine churches with about 500 members. These churches are making strides in growth by aggressively working together to plant new churches. It has made great contributions to JEA.

Cumberland Presbyterian Church (Kanbārando Chōrō Kirisuto Kyōkai). This group had been planting churches prior to the war, but was reorganized after the war in 1950. Focusing on the formation of healthy churches, the group has tripled in size from 466 members in 1971 to its present membership of 1,500 members in eight churches.

Biblical Church (Seisho Kirisuto Kyōkai). The Reverend Dr. Oyama Reiji founded this church in 1953. Centered in the Tokyo area, there are currently 42 churches and evangelistic points, with a current membership of about 1,000. Rev. Oyama is involved in training pastors at Tokyo Shingakkō, the denomination's seminary. He has produced a modern Japanese translation of the Bible called Gendaiyaku Seisho and has published many books.

Lutheran Denominations

Besides the mainline Lutheran bodies in Japan, evangelical Lutheran groups are the following:

Kinki Evangelical Lutheran Church (Kinki Fukuin Ruteru Kyōkai). Fourteen churches begun by a Norwegian mission group joined to form this denomination in 1961. It has planted churches mainly in the Kinki (Kyoto–Osaka–Kobe) region of Japan, and the number of churches has doubled to 28. Membership has also doubled, from 1,228 believers in 1971 to about 2,500 in 1990.

West Japan Evangelical Lutheran Church (Nishi Nihon Fukuin Rūteru Kyōkai). In 1962 this denomination was organized by eight churches started by the Norwegian Lutheran Church. It has focused mainly on church plant-ing in western Japan. The group's multifaceted ministry includes operation of the Kobe Lutheran Seminary (Kobe Rūteru Shingakkō) and "The Lu-theran Hour" radio program. In the 1980s the seminary was given accredit-ation by the Asian Theological Association. At present there are 36 churches, with growth from 1,123 members in 1971 to 2,600 in 1990.

*Japan Lutheran Brethren Church (Nihon Rūteru Dōhō Kyōdan. Churches born as a result of the evangelistic work of the Lutheran Brethren Church of America were the basis of this denomination when it was established in 1951. The work of this group has mostly been in the northeast part of Japan. In 1989 its seminary was moved from the city of Akita to Sendai. It has tripled in size from 349 members in 1971 to about 1,000 members in 1990.

Arminian Denominations

Holiness and Pentecostal denominations in Japan can be grouped into the following three categories: Holiness denominations that began before the war, denominations started by Japanese after the war, and Pentecostal de-nominations.

*Japan Holiness Church (Nihon Hōrinesu Kyōdan). This denomination was formed in 1949 by Holiness churches that withdrew from the UCCJ,[4] and Rev. Kurumada Akitsugu was chosen to be its chairman. In the 1970s lead-ership passed to a new generation, and the current chairman is Rev. Murakami Nobumichi. Dr. Kobayashi Kazuo serves as president of the denomination's school, Tokyo Biblical Seminary (Tokyo Seisho Gakuin), an accredited seminary and a member of the Asian Theological Association.

The denomination has eighteen districts actively engaged nationwide in church planting. Currently there are 157 churches. Membership has doubled from 5,032 in 1971 to 11,000 in 1990. The denomination, a member of JEA, also belongs to the Japan Evangelical Fellowship (Nihon Fukuin Renmei), or JEF, and provides leadership in interdenominational circles.

*Kirisuto Kyōdaidan (Christian Brotherhood). Established in 1946, this de-nomination has nine districts nationwide and is aggressively involved in planting churches. In 1976 a sense of renewed vision was reflected in a series of denominational slogans such as "Building a biblical faith," "Thoroughgo-ing sanctification," "Fullness in prayer," and "Redoubled soul-winning evan-gelism". With this sense of vision the denomination has been even more

---

[4] Some Holiness churches remained within the UCCJ, whose current moderator is Tsuji Nobumichi, a pastor of Holiness background. — Ed.

vigorously pursuing evangelism and church growth. Currently there are 3,364 members in 78 churches.

Christian Holy Convention (Kirisuto Seikyōdan). In 1958 various Holiness churches gathered to form this denomination, and chose Rev. Mori Gorō as its chairman. Carrying out church planting nationwide in five districts, it has about 1,500 members in 41 churches.

Immanuel General Mission (Imumanueru Sōgō Dendōdan). This denomination was founded in 1945 with Dr. Tsutada Tsugio as its president. Doctrinally the group belongs to the Wesleyan Methodist tradition, holds to a biblical faith, and is enthusiastically involved in evangelism. In 1971 Dr. Tsutada died quite suddenly, and Rev. Asahina Hiroshi has since provided leadership as president.

Planting churches in its nineteen districts throughout the country, the group has also sent many missionaries overseas. Dr. Tsutada Joshua of this denomination is president of the Evangelical Fellowship of Asia. In 1989 the group erected a seminary chapel and library on a budget of one billion yen. There are currently 115 churches. Membership has grown from 7,500 in 1971 to 12,000 in 1990.

Japan Gospel Church (Nihon Fukuin Kyōdan). At the organizing meeting of this denomination in 1952, Rev. Hoshino Eiichi was elected president. Although the group has in the past put much effort into church planting and missions to Asia, in the 1970s and 1980s there have been no notable developments. At present there are 32 churches, with membership having doubled from about 1,000 in 1971 to 2,000 in 1990.

Nihon Seisen Kirisuto Kyōkai Rengō.[5] Formed in 1969, this denomination was centered in the person of Rev. Yamamoto Iwajirō, who had left the Immanuel General Mission. In the 1970s the group was solidified as an organization, and in the 1980s focused on building up the local church. Currently there are 1,500 members in 10 churches.

The Free Methodist Church of Japan (Nihon Furii Mesojisuto Kyōdan). This denomination was reorganized in 1952 after leaving the UCCJ. Engaged in church planting in its three districts centered in the Kansai area, the group operates Osaka Christian Junior College (Osaka Kirisutokyō Tanki Daigaku). In 1984 the churches of this group separated from the Japan Free Methodist Church (see below) over what seems to have been matters of faith and theology. There are 2,500 members in 30 churches at present.

---

[5] An association of churches formed around Rev. Yamamoto's Seisen Church in Tokyo. — Ed.

Other Methodist denominations include the Japan Free Methodist Church (Nihon Jiyu Mesojisuto Kyōdan) and others, each vigorously involved in church planting.

Japan Assemblies of God (Nihon Asenburiizu obu Goddo). Separating from the UCCJ in 1949 to form a denomination, this group has planted churches in nine districts throughout the country. Active in missions, the denomination has sent many missionaries overseas. It has also made significant contributions as a member of JEA and the Japan Evangelical Theological Society. Membership in 1971 of about 5,000 has doubled to over 10,000 in 1990.

Besides the above groups, there are many other Arminian and Pentecostal denominations, each making use of its own distinctive gifts in active evangelism. Nationwide these groups have roughly doubled in membership, and there has been a growing spirit of cooperation among them.

Alliance Denominations

These are denominations made up of churches that come from a broad perspective to work together, yet do not necessarily adhere to the same theological point of view.

The Evangelical Alliance Mission (Nihon Dōmei Kirisuto Kyōdan). Originally begun through the mission work of the Scandinavian Alliance before the war, this denomination left the UCCJ after the war in 1948 and began church planting and the building up of the denomination chiefly through cooperation with the missionaries of TEAM (The Evangelical Alliance Mission).[6] It is vigorously planting churches throughout its sixteen blocs nationwide.

The denomination did have its own college, Tokyo Christian College, but as was mentioned above, the school in 1980 merged with Japan Christian Theological Seminary and another school, Kyōritsu Joshi Seisho Gakuin (Kyōritsu Women's Bible School), to form Tokyo Christian Institute. In 1989 the school moved from Kunitachi in Tokyo to Chiba New Town, and in 1990 it became a four-year college renamed Tokyo Christian University (cf. IV-26).

The group plays a leadership role in JEA. In 1971 there were 117 churches and about 4,000 members, and in 1990 there are 144 churches with about 7,000 members.

The Japan Alliance Church (Nihon Araiansu Kyōdan). This denomination left the UCCJ in 1949, and has planted churches in six districts located in the

---

[6] The English name of the Japanese denomination and the name of the mission organization are the same—Tr.

Chūgoku and Shikoku regions. In the 1980s, however, the group began work in Tokyo and the surrounding Kantō area. At present there are about 3,000 members in 39 churches.

Japan Church of Jesus Christ (Nihon Iesu Kirisuto Kyōdan). A group of churches launched this new denomination after leaving the UCCJ in 1951. In nine districts nationwide they have grown considerably through an active commitment to church planting and the building up of existing churches. The denomination has produced many talented pastors and evangelists who are active throughout the country, such as Sawamura Gorō, Nagashima Sachio, Nakajima Akira, Moriyama Satoshi, and Honda Kōji. Currently a younger generation is beginning to take active leadership. In 1971 there were about 8,000 members, and the 1990 membership is about 11,000. There are plans for the group to begin joint operation of a seminary, Kansai Seisho Shingakkō, with the Japan Evangelical Band (Nihon Dendōtai).

Fukuin Dendō Kyōdan (Gospel Evangelism Church). This group was begun by M. Burnett and others of the Central Japan Pioneer Mission, who did evangelism in Gunma, Tochigi, and Saitama prefectures. The denomination came to its present structure in 1947 after leaving the UCCJ. In 1970 services were started in many places in Tokyo. Currently there are 61 churches and 1,300 members.

Baptist Denominations

Following World War II, many Baptist mission groups came to Japan and began vigorous church planting in various parts of the country. In time many denominations were born, and these are continuing to build the church under Japanese leadership. These groups have experienced growth especially in the 1970s and 1980s, quadrupling in size on the average.

Japan Baptist Church Association (Nihon Baputesuto Kyōkai Rengō). This group, established in 1965, has planted churches primarily in the Kantō and Kansai regions. For the most part the denomination has concentrated on church planting in Japan, but in the 1980s it invested effort in foreign missions, sending three missionaries to the Philippines. In 1971 there were 700 members in 21 churches, and in 1990 there are about 2,000 members in 47 churches. (The present writer, a member of this denomination, serves as chairperson of JEA.)

Japan Conservative Baptist Association (Hoshu Baputesuto Dōmei). Through the evangelism of Conservative Baptist missionaries working chiefly in the northeast region, this denomination was founded in 1964. Church planting was also begun in the Kantō area in the 1970s. This group has put effort into theological education and evangelistic literature, through the establishment of a seminary, Seisho Shingakkō, and a Bible publishing organization, Seisho Tosho Kankōkai. It has tripled in size from 26 churches and 680 members in 1971 to 69 churches and 2,000 members in 1990.

Japan Baptist Bible Fellowship (Nihon Baputesuto Baiburu Feroshippu). Formed through missionary work that began in 1949, this group has planted churches in seven local associations throughout the country. It has doubled its membership from 930 members in 55 churches in 1971 to about 2,000 members in 69 churches in 1990.

Japan Baptist Conference (Nihon Baputesuto Senkyōdan). Established in 1961, this denomination has been evangelizing primarily in the Kinki and Tōkai regions. The group has also built a Christian Center in the city of Tsu, Mie Prefecture, and has put effort into student work. Currently there are 11 churches with about 400 members.

Japan Baptist Association (Nihon Baputesuto Rengō). This denomination was begun in 1964 through the efforts of Rev. Amari Misao and others, and it has planted churches chiefly in the Kantō area. At the present there are roughly 300 members in 10 churches.

Okinawa Baptist Convention (Okinawa Baputesuto Renmei). Begun in 1955, this group has been aggressively planting new churches in Okinawa, and has participated in such events as the Billy Graham Crusade. There are currently about 2,000 members in 33 churches.

There are many other evangelical Baptist denominations besides those mentioned here. Taken as a whole they have experienced comparatively favorable growth, but individually they are not large denominations, having no more than 2,000 members each.

Mennonite denominations

There are also a good many Mennonite denominations in Japan. The following are the main ones:

*Japan Mennonite Brethren Conference (Nihon Menonaito Burezaren Kyōdan). Evangelistic work in this denomination began in 1950, with churches planted mostly in the Kansai area. A seminary, Fukuin Seisho Shingakkō, was established in Osaka to train pastors. In the 1980s, church planting was begun in Hiroshima and other areas. At present there are 25 churches and 1,619 members.

Japan Mennonite Christian Church Conference (Nihon Menonaito Kirisuto Kyōkai Kyōgikai). Missionary work began in 1951, chiefly in Hokkaido, and the denomination was incorporated in 1982. In 1989 its Hokkaido Mennonite Education Center was started. Currently the group has 19 churches and about 500 members.

Japan Mennonite Christian Church Conference (Nihon Menonaito Kirisuto Kyōkai Kaigi).[7] This denomination began its church planting work mainly in Kyushu in 1951, and was formally organized in 1965. There are presently 17 churches and about 800 members.

Free Churches

Groups like the Evangelical Free Church and the Covenant Church draw upon the tradition of pietism and apply their unique faith stance and characteristics to active church planting.

*Japan Evangelical Free Church (Nihon Fukuin Jiyū Kyōkai). Started by missionaries working in the Kansai and Kantō regions, this denomination was formally established in 1956. Nationwide expansion has included church planting in the Tōkai area in the 1970s, and in Hiroshima and Sendai in the 1980s. The group's aggressiveness in evangelism has produced striking church growth, particularly in the Tōkai area. In 1989 a special meeting was held to commemorate forty years as a denomination, with representatives invited from sister denominations. In 1971 there were 34 churches with 643 members, but by 1990 there had been tremendous growth to 45 churches and over 3,000 members. Total offerings have exceeded the one-billion-yen level.

*Japan Covenant Christian Church (Nihon Seikei Kirisuto Kyōdan. Begun by missionaries of the Evangelical Covenant Church of America who planted churches primarily in Tokyo and the Kantō area, this denomination was established under its present name in 1967. The group operates Covenant Seminary (Seikei Shingakkō). At present there are 18 churches with about 800 members.

*Mission Covenant Church in Japan (Nihon Seiyaku Kirisuto Kyōdan). Church planting was begun after the war by missionaries of the Swedish Covenant working in Okayama and the Chūgoku region, and the denomination was organized under this name in 1964. There are currently 23 churches and about 800 members.

*German Alliance Mission (Dōmei Fukuin Kirisuto Kyōkai). Missionaries of the German Alliance began this denomination with work chiefly in the Tōkai

---

[7] While this and the previous denomination are separate organizations, as their Japanese names indicate, they have the same English name in the 1990 edition of the *Kirisutokyō nenkan*. — Tr.

area. In 1980 Tōkai Shingaku Juku was begun as a school for training pastors and lay leaders. Its growth and stability over the past twenty years are notable; in 1971 there were 17 churches and 139 members, and in 1990 there are 21 churches and about 900 members.

These four denominations have continued talks to promote closer fellowship and cooperation with each other.

Independent Churches

There are many churches that might not necessarily be called "independent," but they do not belong to any of the above categories. The following are representative groups.

Nihon Fukuin Kyōdan (Japan Gospel Church). Evangelism was begun by the Nihon Dendō Mission (Japan Evangelism Mission)[8] in 1950, mainly in Niigata Prefecture. The group maintains a school, Seisho Gakuin, in Kashiwazaki, for training church workers. Currently there are 600 members in 18 churches.

The Worldwide Evangelization for Christ International (Sekai Fukuin Dendōdan). In 1950 the British missionary R. Fulton began evangelistic work, and churches have since been started, predominantly in Shiga Prefecture. The denomination has close ties to the Christian Literature Crusade (Kurisuchan Bunsho Dendōdan). At present there are 12 churches and 400 members.

Japan Bible Evangelical Church (Nihon Seisho Fukuin Kyōdan). The Swedish Evangelical Mission Society began planting churches in 1951, working mainly in Hokkaido. Today leadership is in Japanese hands, and effort is being given to the building up of the local church. There are currently 400 members in 10 churches.

Zion Christian Church (Shion Kirisuto Kyōkai). In 1934 Rev. Kishida Aiji began work in Tokyo's Ōta ward, and since then church planting has spread to Kanagawa and Ibaraki prefectures. At present there are six churches with an aggregate membership of 1,700.

Church of God Renmei (Nihon Kami no Kyōkai Renmei).[9] This group left the UCCJ in 1949, and formed a fellowship under the leadership of Rev.

---

[8] Parenthetical English names of the church and the mission have been supplied by the editor, and are not official. — Ed.

[9] The Japanese term *renmei*, meaning "association" or "fellowship," is part of the English name of this organization as listed in the 1990 *Kirisutokyō nenkan*. — Tr.

Taniguchi Shigetoshi. The denomination operates a school, Tamagawa Seigakuin. Currently there are 600 members in 16 churches.

Church of God (Chāchi obu Goddo). In 1951 church planting was begun in Kawasaki by R. Sheldon. The number of Japanese pastors has increased and the church has grown. There are 15 churches and 620 members at present.

Besides these groups, there are others of an even more independent nature.

The Independent Christian Churches Fellowship (Tanritsu Kirisuto Kyōkai Renmei). Churches that for various reasons did not join any other denomination came together to form this fellowship in 1964. These churches are actively engaged in evangelism in locations throughout Japan. Currently there are about 50 churches and 3,200 members.

Evangelical Church Association in Hokkaido (Hokkaidō Fukuin Kyōkai Kyōgikai). This is an organization of churches, located mostly in Hokkaido, that were given birth through the efforts of the Overseas Missionary Fellowship. It operates a Bible school, Hokkaido Seisho Gakuin. Membership currently stands at 1,200 in 20 churches.

Japan Liebenzeller Church Association (Ribenzera Kirisuto Kyōkai Rengō). Begun by missionaries from Germany in 1927, this group was reorganized in 1961. It is active chiefly in Kanagawa and Saitama prefectures. There are presently 44 churches and 1,700 members.

Nihon Shinyaku Kyōdan. Churches started by the work of Ear Eastern Gospel Crusade became the core of this group, which was established in 1961. Evangelism has been centered in the Kantō area. Currently there are 29 churches and about 900 members.

The above four groups are eagerly pursuing talks toward a merger.

Beyond these, there are many others carrying on evangelism within the framework of their own traditions.

GENERAL TRENDS

As can be seen, there truly are many evangelical denominations in Japan. The following can be said to be general trends among evangelicals during the twenty years from 1971 to 1990.

Steady, solid growth. There has been a passing on of leadership from older generation to younger, and from missionary to Japanese. In addition, there have been emphases on lay evangelism and the building up of the local church. As a result of these factors, there has been growth of two to four times in these twenty years, giving the denominations a solid foundation. There has been extensive construction of new church buildings, and it can be said that churches are beginning to take root in their communities. There is enthusiasm in the churches for world missions, and in the aggregate, about 300 missionaries have been sent abroad.

Increased unity and cooperation. Churches in the pietistic and independent traditions, for example, have moved forward in talks leading toward cooperation or merger. In addition, most of the denominations listed above have membership in JEA. To be sure, this fact reflects the multiplicity of denominations, but it is also a sign that these groups are maturing and coming together. It is a sign of unity in the midst of diversity, and of cooperation in the proclamation of the gospel. These groups are also eagerly seeking solidarity with evangelical churches in the rest of Asia and the whole world.

Growing concern for social issues. Substantial work has been done in education through seminaries and universities, and there has been an increase in interest in Japanese culture. In particular, Japan Evangelical Theological Society has since 1988 held a yearly study seminar on the theme "The gospel and culture" to wrestle with this question. Also, many groups have taken up issues such as the Yasukuni Shrine and the status and enthronement of the emperor, especially the Daijōsai rite.[10] There has also been an eagerness to make apologies for the war waged in Asian countries, and to work with their peoples in the proclamation of the gospel.

---

[10] Daijōsai, or "Great Food Offering Ceremony," is the last of four main rites for the enthronement of a new emperor; with ancient roots in harvest festivals, it is traditionally regarded as the rite that confers alleged "divinity" on Japan's emperor. See also II-5. — Ed.

26

Evangelical Councils and Movements

Izuta Akira

A LARGE NUMBER OF EVANGELICAL denominations and para-church organizations in Japan are actively involved in the evangelistic task. While the result has been the strengthening of evangelistic outreach and church growth, confusion and a lack of unity have also been evident at times. Serious reflection on this problem by leaders in the evangelical community led to the birth of several interdenominational organizations: the Japan Evangelical Fellowship (Nihon Fukuin Renmei), the Japan Protestant Conference (Nihon Purotesutanto Seisho Shinkō Dōmei), the Japan Evangelical Mission Association (Zainichi Senkyōshi Dan), and others. None of these organizations, however, was truly representative of the evangelical community as a whole.

In 1968, following much prayer and patient discussion among evangelical leaders, the Japan Evangelical Association (Nihon Fukuin Dōmei) was formed. Following this, the Japan Christian Layman's League (Nihon Kurisuchan Shinto Renmei) and the Japan Evangelical Theological Society (Nihon Fukuin-shugi Shingakkai) came into being in 1969 and 1970 respectively. Thus, through the formation of these several organizations, the evangelical churches in Japan were able to realize a sense of unity and cooperation as they headed into the turbulent decade of the 1970s.

GROWING EVANGELICAL DENOMINATIONS

The various organizations making up the evangelical community in Japan have, on the average, grown between two and four times in size during the 1971–90 period (cf. II-25). Closer inspection shows that the growth rate was slightly higher during the 1970s than in the 1980s. The active evangelistic efforts of each organization, the training of strong leaders, and the Japan

Congresses on Evangelism can all be seen as important factors in these two decades of growth among evangelical organizations.

Church Growth

The growth of a church is, in certain respects, like the growth of a human being. While an infant may develop differently from an adult, it is nevertheless crucial that consistent growth occur in each stage of the overall growth process. For a church moving into a more mature stage of its life, this will entail the raising up of strong leaders and the training of believers in order that they too may take active roles in the total growth of the corporate body.

Many of the denominations that were reorganized following World War II are now approaching their thirtieth or later anniversaries. This of course implies that their respective organizational structures have solidified and that needed leaders have been trained. Also, various denominations started by mission organizations in the postwar years have begun to show a large measure of success and effectiveness as a result of both the training of national pastors and the implementation of bold evangelistic plans.

The blessing received from the Japan Congress on Evangelism held in Kyoto in 1974 played a large part in the growth of evangelical groups. That congress served as an important catalyst for a number of churches and denominations that subsequently experienced greater growth. An evangelism congress is like an evangelistic crusade in that immediately visible results cannot always be expected. Yet in the long term the great effect of such a congress becomes clearly evident.

Within the evangelical community there are many para-church organizations that specialize in student evangelism, literature, broadcasting, and other areas. It is clearly evident that great effectiveness has resulted when the efforts of these organizations were skillfully combined with the ongoing work of denominations and local churches. The many positive results indicate that while the decade of the 1970s was a period of upheaval and confusion, it was nevertheless a time when various evangelical churches experienced steady and consistent growth.

Active Church Planting

A primary factor in the growth of the evangelical churches during the 1970s and 1980s was aggressive church-planting programs. Most of the pioneer evangelism and church planting that took place right after World War II was the work of missionaries. In the 1970s that responsibility shifted more and more into the hands of Japanese pastors, and from the beginning of the 1980s, church planting was increasingly carried out through denominational-level planning. In any case, evangelical denominations are presently working together actively in the task of church planting. A typical growth rate of an evangelical denomination with no more than a dozen congregations at the time of its formation was a tripling of its number of churches in fifteen years.

White Fields in Japan (Kokunai Kaitaku Dendō Kai) is an interdenominational support organization committed to church planting. It provides financial and strategic support to new evangelistic efforts of many groups. This organization's experience so far has yielded much valuable data. According to Satake Tokio, its general manager, a clear pattern or trend is discernible in the pioneer evangelism and church planting of the past thirty years.

Church planting in the immediate postwar years was done primarily by foreign missionaries. In the next period the planting of churches was increasingly a cooperative effort between missionaries and Japanese pastors. Most recently, the evangelistic task has been under the direction of denominations, as these groups have developed strong and workable plans. The better the planning and the greater the spirit of cooperation within a denomination, the more effective the evangelism and church planting has been. Also, the character and quality of the evangelist, the particular characteristics of the targeted area, and the actual strategy being employed are all important factors in the end result of an evangelistic effort.

A troubling concern, however, remains. While church planting efforts continue to increase in large metropolitan areas that have proven more receptive, the number of new outreach efforts in unchurched rural areas — traditionally hard to reach — continues to decline. We should not lose sight of our primary goal of reaching all of Japan by being slavishly controlled by growth statistics and thus directing our strategies and plans exclusively toward the most receptive groups and areas.

Rising Seminary Enrollments

As the evangelical churches have grown in number and size, the number of persons dedicating their lives to Christian service has also grown so much that both denominational and interdenominational seminaries are now overflowing. Denominations that prefer to train prospective pastors along their own distinctive theological lines have formed their own seminaries, while comparatively smaller denominations or those more amenable to cooperative educational ventures have sent their students to interdenominational seminaries. Overall, several tendencies can be observed in seminary education during the past twenty years.

The first is the remarkable increase of students at interdenominational seminaries whose programs are based on a biblical faith. The second is the growing number of seminarians of comparatively older ages. Some of them quit their company jobs part way through their careers, while others have begun their seminary studies upon reaching mandatory retirement age. The older seminarians, usually more mature in faith and human relations, do excellent pastoral work soon after graduation.

The expanding number of seminarians makes clear the need for much closer coordination between the educational institutions and the denominations carrying out specific evangelistic plans. Without such coordination, the problem of graduating students not finding church placement will arise. Also, if seminary educational programs should lose touch with the actual needs of churches, and thus fail to match their ministerial demands, it will become impossible for the churches to carry on sound and viable work in the new era.

Meanwhile, discussions are presently in progress concerning accreditation through the Asian Theological Association so that the seminaries will be able to confer theological degrees.

UNITY AMONG EVANGELICALS

It is often noted that during the turbulent 1970s the evangelical churches in Japan experienced unity and cooperation. Though this phenomenon itself deserves closer attention, it is perhaps more important to focus on some of the results of this cooperation.

The First Japan Congress on Evangelism

In 1974 there were two congresses on evangelism that had great import for both Japan and the world. The first was the Japan Congress on Evangelism convened June 3–7 at the Kyoto Convention Center. Sponsored by the Japan Evangelical Association, this congress brought together 1,300 delegates from around the country. Shared research findings and fervent discussions touched upon all areas of the evangelistic task in Japan.

The opening worship was led by the executive committee chairman, Andō Nakaichi; the biblical message was brought by John Stott; and the present writer's keynote lecture addressed the main theme: "Japan for Christ." This theme was developed with four topics — gospel, church, Holy Spirit, and cooperation — as basic starting points. General sessions considered these topics, and special workshops treated different aspects of evangelism in more detail. Also, many actual case studies of church planting and church growth were introduced, and the experience and encouragement of these examples were shared. At its close the congress issued its Kyoto Declaration.

The second important congress was the International Congress on World Evangelization held July 16–25, 1974, in Lausanne, Switzerland. This gathering grew out of proposals and leadership by Billy Graham, Bishop Jack Dain, Leighton Ford, and others. It brought together 3,700 participants from around the world, including 53 from Japan. Building on the results of the recent Japan Congress on Evangelism, the Lausanne Congress further enhanced the Japanese delegates' sensitivity to the great challenge of world evangelization.

The Billy Graham Crusade

In 1967, Billy Graham held a crusade at the Budokan and at Korakuen Stadium in Tokyo, and this was followed by another evangelistic crusade in 1980 that took place at six different locations in Japan, beginning in Okinawa. Various evangelical churches cooperated in this 1980 crusade, with Andō Nakaichi, Funamoto Sakao, Shimamura Kikaku, and Horiuchi Akira serving as overall directors of the crusade. Nagashima Yukio chaired the national executive committee, and the following individuals chaired the six regional executive committees: Orita Masahiro, Okinawa; Nagashima Yukio, Osaka; Tanimoto Kiyoshi, Hiroshima; Kedo Kenji, Tōkai region; Kanō Shozen, Fukuoka; and Honda Kōji, Tokyo. A total of 334,848 people attended the crusade meetings, with 26,038 making decisions to become Christians.

This crusade served as a great challenge to the evangelical churches. It was made possible through the cooperation and initiative of many local congregations and by a mood of solidarity among evangelicals nationwide. Even so, a serious problem arose concerning how each church would elect to cooperate in this joint endeavor. A denominational decision to support the crusade did not necessarily translate into willing cooperation by each of its member churches. Local churches that felt stronger denominational ties tended to follow their denomination's decision. Churches that stressed local and regional priorities felt that any decision to support the crusade should be left to local congregations and individuals. At the time, this issue posed a serious problem of communication and cooperation among the evangelical churches.

The Second Japan Congress on Evangelism

Following the Billy Graham Crusade of 1980, the Second Japan Congress on Evangelism was held June 7–10, 1982, at the same Kyoto Convention Center. Although sponsored by the Japan Evangelical Association, participation was open to all groups, and approximately 4,000 people attended. An opening message was brought by Andō Nakaichi, with a keynote lecture given by Matsumura Etsuo. Following a Bible lecture by Phillip Teng, topical speeches were given by Hattori Yoshiaki, Hatori Akira, and the present writer. As in the first congress, the lectures were followed by various general sessions and special workshops. Beyond sharing personal opinions and examples of successful evangelism, this congress provided an excellent opportunity for thinking and strategizing together about the evangelistic mission.

Again a Kyoto Declaration was issued, but this time with a strong emphasis on the social responsibility of Christians. This was in keeping with the post-Lausanne movement among evangelicals worldwide to recognize anew that social responsibility and action are important and integral parts of the gospel. The declaration said in part:

> We are concerned about the resurgence of right-wing movements and the inclination toward militarism that can be observed in the Yasukuni Shrine problem as well as in other areas. As Christians of the only country to experience a nuclear bomb attack, we firmly oppose the use of military power in resolving conflict, and we further resolve to work for peace.

EVANGELICALS MOVING FORWARD

After the Second Japan Congress on Evangelism, the Japan Evangelical Association began a process of reorganization so that it might more adequately represent the various evangelical churches. This reorganization was in some ways the natural result of growth and change within the evangelical churches; it was also a necessary step in preparing for further growth and expansion.

The New Japan Evangelical Association (JEA)

Following a season of discussion and preparation, the new Japan Evangelical Association was established in 1986. In its revised structure, denominations can hold membership, while para-church organizations may join as associate members (in the former structure, individual congregations could apply for membership). The restructuring preserves the autonomy of churches in Japan, while making JEA more consonant with the Japanese organizational patterns.

At the time of JEA's reorganization there were 32 member denominations, comprising 900 churches and approximately 50,000 believers, and 17 organizations were associate members. As of 1990, JEA has roughly doubled in size, with 52 member denominations comprising 1,600 churches and 100,000 believers, and 31 associate member groups. JEA presently has six permanent commissions: Evangelistic Strategy, Theology, International Relations, Economic Concerns, Social Concerns, and Women's Concerns. Each of these commissions is engaged in ongoing work.

JEA is affiliated with the World Evangelical Association and with the Evangelical Fellowship of Asia for cooperation on international levels with other evangelical groups. JEA is also involved in disaster relief work, one recent example being the aid sent to Bangladesh after the great flooding there.

Social issues such as those surrounding the period of official mourning for the late emperor and the enthronement ceremonies for the present emperor, particularly the Daijōsai rite, are of concern to us (cf. IV-25, n. 8). This present focus on the emperor system concerns our Asian neighbors as well, and in solidarity with them we have expressed to the government our unified view of opposition to these imperial rites. JEA also seeks to disseminate ideas, information, and strategies concerning the evangelistic task.

The Third Japan Congress on Evangelism was planned on three different levels: regional (within Japan), national, and international (Asian). On the regional level, "mini-congresses" were scheduled throughout 1990 in seven different locations from Hokkaido in the north to Okinawa in the south, under the direction and initiative of local churches in each region. The international event was the Asian Missions Congress (AMC '90), convened August 27–31, 1990, in Seoul, Korea, with 2,500 participants, including 275 from Japan. A national congress is to be held in June 1991 in Shiobara, Tochigi Prefecture, with 1,200 delegates expected, to discuss evangelistic strategies from a national perspective.

It is the hope of JEA and the evangelical churches in Japan that through these conferences a further unity and spirit of cooperation will be realized in the task of mission and that the evangelical community will be able to double in size again by the year 2000.

Tokyo Christian Institute

Many leaders of the evangelical denominations had long desired and devoutly prayed for a truly interdenominational educational institute to be established, and to this end had held discussions with administrators involved in theological education. The outcome of these overtures was the merger in 1980 of three existing schools: Japan Christian Theological Seminary, of Presbyterian background; Tokyo Christian College, operated by the Japan Evangelical Alliance Church; and Kyōritsu Women's Bible Institute, an independent school.

The location chosen for the new venture was the Tokyo Christian College campus in Kunitachi, Tokyo. This newly integrated school, called the Tokyo Christian Institute, was composed of three departments: Tokyo Christian College (a two-year school), Tokyo Christian Theological Seminary, and Kyōritsu Christian Institute, to serve as a research department. Beyond this, the administrators envisioned, as part of the institution, an accredited four-year university to offer a more standard and complete education and also enable the school to make a greater contribution to the international community. For this to happen, however, the school needed a more adequate campus and facilities, a better equipped library, and a faculty strengthened by hiring additional professors.

The search for a larger, new campus site led to a move to Chiba New Town, where a new classroom building, library, gymnasium, and chapel were subsequently built. Also, additional teachers were hired to strengthen and enlarge the faculty. In December 1989 the fervent prayers and efforts of all involved came to fruition when the Ministry of Education granted approval for the institution to operate a formally recognized four-year university, and in April 1990 the school officially opened its doors as the Tokyo Christian University.

Yoshimochi Akira currently serves as president of the Tokyo Christian Institute and as the chairman of the board of directors; Maruyama Tadataka, as president of the Tokyo Christian University. Shimokawa Tomoya serves as dean of the Tokyo Christian Theological Seminary; Uda Susumu, as director of the Kyōritsu Christian Institute (research center). The research center is affiliated with the Asian Theological Association and offers a Master of Arts program.

Two Evangelistic Crusades

Two large Christian gatherings were held in fall 1990 in the Kantō (Tokyo) and Kansai (Osaka–Kobe) areas. On October 1, an evangelistic meeting called "Gospel '90," took place at the Budokan in Tokyo, with 11,000 people attending. Of these, 266 persons made first decisions to become Christians; 553 believers made commitments to enter full-time Christian service. The well-known American gospel singer Sandy Patti and her ministry team were special guests. Following an opening concert of music and praise, Honda Kōji, the well-known Japanese evangelist, brought a message. The meeting's success depended in large part on the cooperation of many evangelical churches and para-church groups.

Evangelical churches in the Kansai region invited the internationally known evangelist Luis Palau to Osaka for a crusade held October 17–21 at Osaka Castle Hall. An Argentine evangelist in the Billy Graham tradition, Palau has held crusades worldwide and has been powerfully used by God even in many communist-bloc countries. The crusade's slogan "From the churches to Osaka Castle Hall . . . and from Osaka Castle Hall to a revival in Japan" expressed the cooperating churches' fervent prayers for a spiritual awakening. The crusade included a special gathering for women on October 18 as well as a men's meeting on October 19. Special meetings for youth and children on October 20 were followed by a gathering on October 21 for new believers. The aggregate participation in all meetings was 52,700 people, of whom approximately 3,000 made first decisions to follow Christ. Prior to the Osaka crusade, a Luis Palau Crusade in Okinawa had 6,000 participants in six meetings.

The last crusade of this kind in Japan was the 1980 Billy Graham Crusade held just ten years ago. These two 1990 crusades have surely inspired a new vitality in the evangelical churches in Japan.

SUMMING UP

Looking back, we have seen that, through the complex and far-reaching changes of the 1970s and 1980s, evangelicals continued to make progress in both numerical growth and unity of spirit, and this was true not only of individual denominations but of interdenominational fellowship and activities as well. In interdenominational affairs, especially, the two-decade period saw a heightened sense of solidarity and cooperation in our ties with other countries. We have been able to send many missionaries to various Asian countries, and through international fellowship and conferences we have been able to begin cooperating in concrete ways in our common mission task.

The evangelical churches in Japan, started and nurtured by many mission organizations following World War II, gradually became spiritually and economically self-supporting during the 1950s and 1960s, and in the last twenty years have continued to grow larger, reaching the point where they are now able to send out missionaries to other countries throughout Asia and the world.

With only ten years remaining in this twentieth century, special strategies are being drawn up by many denominations in the evangelical community for carrying out the mission task. Some denominations are hoping to double the number of their congregations through an aggressive church-planting strategy. Still others hope to double their church memberships by more effectively training and activating the present believers, thus putting their energies into the growth of existing congregations.

The evangelical community plans to continue its efforts to cooperate with Asia and the rest of the world in the work of mission. Looking forward to the next historic milepost, the dawn of the twenty-first century, the evangelical churches in Japan are committed to moving ahead with zeal and courage in the mission to which God has called it.

27

The Roman Catholic Church in Japan

Matsumoto Saburō

THE SECOND VATICAN COUNCIL, concluded in 1965, resulted in major re-forms that have radically altered the shape of the Roman Catholic Church as known over the past four hundred years. The reforming influences were ex-tensive: from basic understandings of church and faith to more practical mat-ters of organizational structures, liturgy, and the church's relations to modern society and other faiths. Implementing the reforms mandated by the Second Vatican Council (or Vatican II) has been the primary task of the Catholic Church in Japan[1] from the mid-sixties to the present.

VATICAN II IN THE JAPANESE CONTEXT

Beginning with the translation and publication of official documents, litur-gical renewal, and restructuring of church organization, then going on to re-education of priests, religious, and laity, cooperation with other Christians and other religions, promotion of justice and peace, and other social involve-ment — the work of applying the spirit of Vatican II to the Japanese context was a big assignment, indeed.

Liturgical Renewal

Council-induced changes were first seen in the liturgy. Respect for the native genius of local cultures and societies led the Council to sanction use of local languages in the liturgy, which for many centuries had used only Latin. The Church in Japan, therefore, soon began putting the liturgy into the Japanese

---

[1] References in this chapter to "the Catholic Church" or even "the Church" are solely to the Roman Catholic Church, in Japan or worldwide, unless otherwise specified. — Ed.

language and adapting it to Japanese culture. With the publication of the rites for marriage and funerals (December 1971), for confirmation (February 1974), for the initiation of adults (March 1976), and then the liturgy of the Mass (December 1978), most rites came to be celebrated in Japanese. Moreover, new music was composed to suit the Japanese texts, replacing the Gregorian chant. The remaining task is to build on this translation into Japanese and initial adaptation so as to promote the inculturation of the Church in Japanese culture.

Progress in Ecumenism

On the ecumenical front, Vatican II was a historical turning point, and the Church in Japan undertook active involvement soon after the Council. On the local level, Catholic-Protestant observances of the Week of Prayer for Christian Unity as well as other joint meetings became common (cf. IV-28). At the denominational level, dialogues were initiated with, among others, the Nippon Sei Kō Kai (Anglican Church) in April 1972 and with the Lutheran Church in February 1985. In time, deeper mutual theological understanding made possible a mutual recognition of baptism with these two communions (Anglican, May 1977; Lutheran, December 1988).

Furthermore, joint Protestant-Catholic efforts to produce a new common Bible came to fruition first in September 1975 with publication of the interconfessional translation of the Gospel of Luke, and then of the New Testament in September 1978. After major revisions of the New Testament and the Old Testament, the *Shin Kyōdōyaku Seisho* (The New Common Bible) was published in September 1987.[2] The Catholic Church immediately adopted this as the official translation for use in public worship. In accordance with this decision, the Japanese form of Jesus' name — Iezusu — previously used in Catholic liturgical texts was now changed to Iesu, the form long used by other Christian bodies.[3] With this seemingly slight adjustment, a longstanding mark of disunity was removed. Unity in the "name of the Lord" had come one step closer.

The 1980s saw increased Catholic cooperation with the National Christian Council in Japan concerning such sociopolitical problems as the Yasukuni Shrine, imperial enthronement, release of Korean political prisoners, peace and nuclear disarmament. The Japanese Catholic Justice and Peace Council was the main vehicle for this joint activity.

---

[2] A separate edition of the Old Testament with the Apocrypha was also published at this time.

[3] The pronunciations vary by one syllable: "yeh-zu-su" for Iezusu, "yeh-su" for Iesu. — Ed.

Interreligious Dialogue

Dialogue with religions other than Christianity became common in the 1970s, when East-West tensions were still high. Sensing anew their common responsibility for peace, various religious groups sponsored the World Conference on Religion and Peace (1970) and the Asian Conference on Religion and Peace (1976), in which Japanese Catholics also participated. In 1976, Cardinal Pignedoli, head of the Pontifical Commission for Interreligious Dialogue, came to Japan to participate in the Japan Conference on Religion and Youth. Moreover, when Pope John Paul II invited religious leaders from around the world to pray for world peace at Assisi in Italy in October 1987, many Japanese representatives were among those who went.

In addition, interest in Zen has spread within the church, with many members introducing Zen meditation into their prayer life. Fellowship with Zen and other Buddhists has developed in many locations. These new ties led to East-West spiritual exchanges, begun in September 1979. In the first exchange, fifty-one Buddhist priests experienced a month of monastic life at Catholic contemplative monasteries in Germany, France, Belgium, and the Netherlands. In the second exchange, seventeen European contemplative monks (mostly Benedictine) visited Japan to experience life in Buddhist temples for a month. Alternating every four years, this project in shared experiences, mutual learning, and deepening understanding is still continuing.

Church Identity and Fellowship with Asian Churches

Following the Second Vatican Council, heightened awareness of the importance of local and regional churches issued in a greater sense of identity as the church in Japan and as an Asian church. In November 1970, Pope Paul VI convened and personally opened the first synod of Asian Bishops, which decided to form the Federation of Asian Bishops' Conferences (FABC) as a permanent organization. The FABC was established in November 1972 and held its first meeting in Taipei in April 1974. The Catholic Bishops' Conference of Japan, not yet officially a member, sent only observers, but five years later joined the Federation.

Contacts have since developed rapidly between the Japanese Church and other Asian Churches, especially with the Philippine Church, not only at the official level but at personal and parish levels as well. During the Mass at the fourth FABC meeting held in Tokyo in 1986, Archbishop Shirayanagi, head of the Catholic Bishops' Conference of Japan, expressed apologies to the Asian bishops for the wartime responsibilities of Japan and the Catholic Church in Japan. This was the Japanese Catholic Church's first public confession of its war responsibility.

The Japanese Church's sense of identity as a local church also increased, and from 1974 various groups formed organizations or conferences to link local work at the national level. Communication and cooperation between these groups has become increasingly close. The Bishops' Conference also became more active and vocal — a trend that was strengthened by Pope John Paul II's visit to Japan in 1981 — resulting in the "Basic Policy and Priorities of the Catholic Church in Japan" issued in 1984 and the convening of the first National Incentive Congress on Evangelization (NICE-I) in 1987 (treated later).

THE PAPAL VISIT AND ENLIVENED SOCIAL WITNESS

The Calling to Peacemaking

The papal visit gave encouragement and further direction to the new movements spurred by Vatican II. Pope John Paul II arrived in Japan on February 23, 1981, and during four days visited Tokyo, Hiroshima, and Nagasaki, meeting innumerable people both in and outside the Church. As the first pope to visit Japan, he received extensive coverage by the news media. His "Peace Appeal" made at Hiroshima made an especially strong impression. His visit had an enduring impact on the Church of the 1980s in terms of a livelier identity as a local church, a renewed enthusiasm for evangelization, and a strengthened sense of responsibility for peace.

In response to the Pope's "Peace Appeal," the Catholic Bishops' Conference of Japan issued a statement titled "Peace and the Japan Catholic Church Today" (May 1981), stressing the importance of peace education and participation by the whole church in peacemaking. In the following year, 429,690 signatures were collected on a nuclear disarmament petition for delivery by the Japanese Catholic Peace Mission to the Second United Nations Special Session on Disarmament (June–July 1982) in New York. In addition, a Peace Novena has been planned every August, with peace campaigns held in all areas of the country, but centering on Hiroshima and Nagasaki. Furthermore, a pastoral letter titled "Hope for Peace" was issued in July 1983, calling for development of grass-roots peace activities as a particular vocation of the Catholic Church. At the Third United Nations Special Session on Disarmament (May–June 1988), a petition for disarmament and the abolition of nuclear weapons, bearing the signatures of 206 Asian bishops, was presented to the UN General Assembly.

Catholic Social Action

Vatican Council II strongly stressed the social and political responsibilities of Christians and the Church. Furthermore, Pope Paul VI's Apostolic Exhortation *Evangelii Nuntiandi* (1975), which taught that evangelization is not only proclamation of salvation in the Kingdom of God but also involvement at the deepest levels of society and culture to help realize that Kingdom here on earth, made a big impact throughout the world, adding support to the development of liberation theology in Latin America. In Japan of the 1970s, the Council, the Apostolic Exhortation, and conflict over the Japan–US Security Treaty combined to increase awareness of issues such as human rights, social justice, and discrimination. Again, as Pope Paul VI urged in January 1967, Justice and Peace Commissions (or Councils) were formed throughout the world, resulting in a worldwide network.

Refugee relief. The Japanese Catholic Church's Justice and Peace Council held its first national meeting in 1975. With the end of the Vietnam War that year, the "boat people" refugee problem received worldwide attention. When the first refugees arrived in Japan in June 1975, the Catholic Church, through its relief agency, Caritas Japan, responded to requests from the United Nations and the Japanese foreign ministry and opened temporary quarters in five churches and convents. As the number of refugees increased, more quarters were provided; but a more systematic response to the problem was needed. Following an April 1977 conference of the directors of refugee relocation centers, nationwide efforts were begun to collect funds for the reception of refugees. The strategy was changed from receiving and sending refugees elsewhere to helping them settle in Japan. The Catholic National Strategy Committee for the Settlement of Refugees was formed in 1982 (renamed the Special Committee for the Settlement of Refugees in May 1985).

Migrant workers. An increasingly prominent problem of the 1980s was that of Asian migrant laborers. From around 1981, rising numbers of Asian women (particularly Filipinas) came to Japan for work in the tourist and entertainment trades, with major increases in 1983 and 1984. They were, and still are, sometimes forced into prostitution or otherwise exploited, with restriction of freedom and placement in wretched conditions being not uncommon. Local churches and convents assisted in such cases, but at the request of the Filipino bishops, persons who had been involved in such assistance formed the Committee to Help Asian Women Residing in Japan, in April 1983, with the backing of the Catholic Committee for International Cooperation (in 1984, renamed the Committee for Solidarity with Asian Women Residing in Japan). From about 1987, male laborers also increased, not only from Asia but also from Latin America. Among women, problems also arose from international marriages. With a wider variety of people assisted and problems faced, the above committee was renamed the Committee for Solidarity with Migrant and Foreign Workers. Helping persons were dispersed widely throughout the nation in an effort to meet expanding needs in various contexts.

Human rights. While the problem is multidimensional, the Church's primary concern is always for human rights. In 1983 the Catholic Committee for Human Rights and Social Welfare was formed in order to view social problems comprehensively. The Liaison Association for the Disabled, the National Liaison Association of Catholic Volunteers, the Braille Library, the Alcohol and Drug Dependency Strategy Committee, and the Federation of Prison Chaplains, for example, were placed under this committee's purview. In June 1984 the Japanese Catholic bishops' message "Life, a gift from God – A Catholic understanding of the dignity of the life of the fetus" was issued to stress the sinfulness of abortion and the need to protect the human rights of unborn children.

The disabled. The rights of the disabled and their welfare are also major concerns. In December 1980 the Catholic Bishops' Conference issued a message on the International Year of Disabled Persons (1981), setting a goal of equality and full social participation for the persons with disabilities and appealing for progress toward this goal particularly within the Church. During the 1980s the National Catholic Committee sought to publish all of its works simultaneously in both print and braille forms at the same price. From January 1985 its publications have carried a notice granting permission for braille translation, enlarged photocopying, and sound recording for the visually impaired. In addition, the Order for Mass in Sign Language was issued in April 1990, facilitating the participation of the hearing impaired in the liturgy.

Buraku discrimination. Among the major human rights issues of Japanese society is the discrimination suffered by the Buraku and Korean communities (cf. II-11). Discrimination against Buraku people was, in Catholic circles, first taken seriously by the Kyoto Justice and Peace Council. From there concern spread more widely, with this issue becoming the theme of the 1978 national gathering of the Catholic Justice and Peace Council. Deliberations of the 1979 World Conference on Religion and Peace provided an impetus for further awareness of the discriminatory nature of the Japanese religious world. The Religious Council for Solidarity in Dealing with the Dōwa [assimilation] Problem was formed in June 1981, and the Christian Council for Solidarity in Dealing with the Buraku Problem was formed in October 1983, both with Catholic participation.

Within the Catholic Church, criticism of the use of the discriminatory expression *tokushu buraku* ("special communities," i.e., segregated areas for former outcaste groups) led to formation in January 1984 of the Catholic

Committee for Buraku Liberation, under the Justice and Peace Council. In December 1987 the Church's requirement that those seeking marriage must provide copies of their family registries (to check possible bigamy or re-marriage) was dropped in order to protect human rights.[4] An affidavit that each partner is unmarried is now acceptable. Despite these measures, interest and action to eliminate discrimination have yet to reach all parts of the church.

Korean residents. Concern for the human rights of Koreans in Japan has intensified since around 1982, with special focus on the Alien Registration Law. In February 1984 the Episcopal Commission for Social Activities, under the Catholic Bishops' Conference, presented a memorial to the prime minister, the minister of justice, and the minister of home affairs, calling for repeal of the fingerprinting requirement of the Alien Registration Law. Appeals for support were made within and without the church, but the church as a whole was yet lacking in understanding and awareness. But when Fr. Edouard Brzostowski refused to be fingerprinted in October 1984, and other foreign missionaries soon followed suit, greater awareness arose within the Church and an antifingerprinting movement emerged. The Episcopal Commission for Social Activities sent many inquiries and requests to govern-ment offices concerning the Alien Registration Law and its fingerprinting re-quirement. With revision of portions of the registration law in 1987, the movement has subsided somewhat. Given the continuing treatment of fingerprinting refusers and of third- and fourth-generation alien residents, the movement must yet persevere in its long uphill struggle.

Separation of Religion and State

The most critical problem facing the Japanese Catholic Church in political affairs is the separation of religion and state. Since 1969, repeated introduc-tion in the Diet of bills proposing the nationalization of Yasukuni Shrine has aroused in the Catholic Church a deepening sense of crisis. In 1973 the Arch-bishop of Tokyo, Shirayanagi Seiichi, sent a message to the prime minister in opposition to a nationalization bill. In 1975 he joined representatives of thir-teen other Christian groups in signing a declaration opposing nationalization of Yasukuni Shrine. In August 1980 the Catholic Bishops' Conference of Japan issued a joint declaration, "In opposition to the Yasukuni Shrine na-tionalization bill." Although the bill was defeated each time in the Diet, the basic principle of separation of state and religion shows signs of break-ing down; cabinet ministers increasingly make public visits to Yasukuni

---

[4] Family registries are often used in general society to check on possible Buraku back-ground, hence checking family registries has a discriminatory connotation. — Ed.

Shrine,[5] and lawsuits against Shinto ceremonies for purifying public building sites have failed in many districts. The Japanese Catholic Church has therefore sustained its opposition, with the Justice and Peace Council taking the lead.

With the passing of Emperor Shōwa on January 7, 1989, the problem of separation of state and religion suddenly escalated. Accession of the new emperor to the throne was observed according to numerous prewar rites, many based on State Shinto, and at great cost to the national treasury.[6] The government was questioned by civic, religious, and political groups of all kinds. The Bishops' Conference on the day of the emperor's death made an appeal to the Catholic faithful, warning against State Shinto and ultranationalism: "Greatest care must be taken to avoid making any human being into a god, or any human system absolute, or any particular nationalism universal." On January 9 a message was sent to then Prime Minister Takeshita Noboru to request that the basic principle of separation of state and religion be adhered to rigorously in the funerary rites and observances for Emperor Shōwa.

Again in November, the standing committee of the Bishops' Conference sent a message to Prime Minister Kaifu Toshiki, calling for adherence to the basic principle of separation of state and religion in the accession rites of the new emperor and in particular that the Shinto ceremony called Daijōsai not be held as a state function nor receive state funding. Petitions to this effect were jointly circulated for signature by the Catholic Justice and Peace Council and the National Christian Council in Japan. The many issues involved in imperial succession have aroused much interest and debate both within the church and in society in general.

EVANGELIZATION: THE SHARED TASK OF THE WHOLE CHURCH

The local church's sense of identity, particularly as a Japanese church, grew stronger, as already noted, with the 1981 papal visit to Japan. To respond to the realities and changes of Japanese society and effectively carry out the mission of the church, however, working only at the diocese level is not enough. In the 1980s the Japanese church came to feel strongly the need to work as one for the common goal of evangelization. With a mounting sense among bishops, priests, religious orders, and laity that they bear together the

---

[5] The visits are made in official capacities as cabinet ministers, not as private citizens; this sometimes includes contributions made from public funds, another target of criticism as unconstitutional (cf. II-5). — Ed.

[6] The enthronement rites in November 1990 cost over 8 billion yen, with an additional 4 billion yen for nationwide police security; at the average 1990 US dollar/yen exchange rate of US$1/¥142, the bill was US$84.5 million. — Ed.

church's responsibility for evangelization, it became necessary to organize structures for this common task.

The Bishops' Conference first set out, in June 1984, to reform the central structures that support the work of the entire church in Japan as well as to establish a basic common policy for the whole Japanese church and to set the priorities for policy implementation. Within these priorities, provision was made for calling a National Incentive Congress on Evangelization as a visible sign of the common responsibility of the whole church for evangelization.

Basic Policy and Priorities

The basic policy can be summarized in two points:

1. Each and every member of the church is an evangelist, sharing the joy of one's faith with many people, leading them to baptism.

2. In solidarity with people forced into positions of powerlessness, all members of the church must work for a culture and society that acknowledges the worth and importance of all people.

The priorities can be summarized in three points:

1. The diocese and parish are to be nurtured as evangelistic communities.

2. Concrete cooperation is to be developed among religious orders, missionary societies, and various institutions.

3. In 1987, bishops, priests, religious, and laity are to be called together for a National Incentive Congress on Evangelization (NICE) to discuss long-range prospects and policy.

Accordingly, the First National Incentive Congress on Evangelization (NICE-I) was convened in Tokyo in November 1987. This congress provided the Roman Catholic Church in Japan with an operational focus.

First National Incentive Congress on Evangelization

The Second Vatican Council stressed the dignity, rights, and responsibility of the laity to counterbalance what had become an overly clerical church. After the Council, therefore, a variety of lay movements and organizations were encouraged. Still, the laity seldom had opportunities to participate publicly in the decision-making processes of the church, to discuss matters on a equal footing with bishops and priests, or to take up their common responsibility. In this respect, NICE-I was an epoch-making experiment, giving concrete expression in Japan to the spirit of Vatican II.

The Bishops' Conference decided that the basic character of NICE should be a process of "listening, digesting, implementing." Accordingly, public hearings for the laity were held in all areas of the three Archdiocesan Provinces (Tokyo, Osaka, Nagasaki), which were attended by some two thousand lay persons. With this broad input of lay opinion, the theme of NICE-I was set as "Creating an open church." Pursuant to this theme, three topics were discussed in each diocese and at the national level: a church involved in society, a faith nurtured in daily life, and parishes engaged in evangelization. For fifteen months from July 1986, conferences of various kinds were held at every level by groups, churches, districts, and dioceses.

Convened in Kyoto on November 20, 1987, NICE-I was attended by 276 people (17 bishops, 112 priests, 147 lay people) representing all sixteen dioceses, 127 secretaries, and 150 members of the local preparations committee. Debate lasted for four days, resulting in a fourteen-item summary report, which was turned over to the Bishops' Conference.

The Bishops' Conference called a special meeting in December to consider this report and responded with the statement "Tomo ni yorokobi o motte ikiyō" (Let us live together with joy). This positive evaluation of the congress and its report expressed determination to reexamine the church's attitudes and faith-lifestyle and to aim for a radical transformation. In order to implement the proposals of the report, it established the NICE Promotion Committee, as well as two project teams to tackle the two most important proposals: casting the light of the gospel on social issues, backed by problem-solving policies and structures; and building programs for lifelong growth in faith.

The NICE Promotion Committee and the two project teams began work from April 1988. Since the problems are basic and far-reaching, much time will be needed before concrete results can be seen. In December 1988 the Bishops' Conference, following a proposal by the NICE Promotion Committee and the two project teams, decided to establish a Japan Catholic Research and Training Center in Nagoya as one step in implementing the NICE-I suggestions. Ground was broken for its building in January 1989.

Parallel with the work of the NICE Promotion Committee, various other committees, such as the Episcopal Commission for Missionary Activities and the Catholic Committee for School Education, tackled the NICE-I proposals. Furthermore, each diocese, parish, and religious order is working to implement the goals of NICE-I. Since 1988 the Japan Catholic Church has begun to move in accordance with these goals.

At a special meeting of the Bishops' Conference in December 1988, it was decided to convene the Second National Incentive Congress on Evangelization (NICE-II) sometime between autumn 1992 and spring 1993. The theme is to be "The family."

28

Protestant–Catholic Cooperation

Maejima Munetoshi

THE WORK OF VATICAN II has stimulated and challenged the ecumenical movement in Japan, yielding fruit in the form of mutual understanding and cooperation among the churches and fellow Christians. When Pope John Paul II visited Japan in 1981, he observed that the small community of Christians in Japan had together grown into a vital force that is a continuing source of hope in Asia. His message reaffirmed the importance of ecumenical cooperation in Japan.

BUILDING A COOPERATIVE FRAMEWORK

The National Christian Council in Japan (NCCJ) invited two Roman Catholic representatives — Bishop Sōma Nobuo, of the Catholic Church's Ecumenism Committee, and Fr. Fujiwara Masanori, secretary of the committee — to its Twenty-third General Assembly held at Amagi Sansō, March 10–12, 1970. The assembly's primary focus was on mission policies of the churches in Japan, and on how the churches could become financially independent of foreign sources. The time had come for the Japanese churches to make a major policy shift from being heavily dependent on churches overseas to becoming financially autonomous institutions. This basic issue was triggered by the challenge of the student movement, which had questioned the validity of the participation by churches, both Protestant and Catholic, in the 1970 World Exposition (Expo 70) held in Osaka.

Two months later, on May 13, the Catholic Church held its Ecumenism National Assembly with the participation of eleven Protestant representatives, including the NCCJ's moderator, Gotō Makoto, and its general secretary, Nakajima Masaaki. While the assembly issued no resolution on cooperation, it served as a good forum for the exchange of opinions on intercommunion, urban issues, pollution problems, prayer meetings in local churches, and joint community-wide Christmas services. The NCCJ representatives expressed their appreciation for the invitation to participate and their commitment to cooperation for greater unity in mission.

In anticipation of increased cooperation, Catholic and Protestant representatives had established the Japan Ecumenical Association on May 24, 1969, with these objectives: (a) dialogue and cooperative action for unity among the churches; (b) research on tasks for ecumenical mission; (c) dialogue and cooperation with leaders of other religions and communities; and (d) exchange and cooperation with organizations in Japan and overseas that share similar goals.

The Week of Prayer for Christian Unity

Started in 1908 by the Rev. Paul Watson of the Episcopal Church in the United States, the Week of Prayer for Christian Unity has long been observed in countries throughout the world, with special focus on unity between Catholics and Protestants. In 1958 a joint preparation committee for the week of prayer was formed, and Vatican II in 1964 formally recognized the importance of the Week of Prayer for Christian Unity. From 1966 the World Council of Churches and the Vatican have cooperated in planning the event's theme and worship program.

In 1967 the National Christian Council in Japan and the Catholic Church produced a joint prayer book along with an explanatory booklet and posters to be distributed among the churches. Since 1969, preparatory work for the Week of Prayer for Christian Unity has been carried out by a joint committee of the NCCJ and the National Catholic Committee.

Each year in January the service for Christian unity week is prepared by local committees, and this effort strengthens ecumenical cooperation at the local level. Breakfast prayer meetings also involve lay people in ecumenical cooperation, as do community-wide Christmas programs.

The World Day of Prayer (WDP) movement, started in 1887, has also spread to Christian communities throughout the world. Japanese participation in this ecumenical event began in 1932. On the first Friday in March each year, more than ten thousand women in over two hundred communities in Japan come together in a circle of prayer that extends around the world. Offerings from the Japanese WDP services go toward support of various women's projects and endeavors in Asia.

Christian unity cannot be realized by merely studying creeds and church structures; it is gained, rather, through encounters of prayer and sincere dialogue, which afford opportunities to become liberated from fixed concepts and attitudes.

The New Japanese Common Bible Translation

The first committee meeting for the common Bible translation, a joint Protestant-Catholic venture, was held on August 27, 1970. Work was continued over the next seventeen years, yielding a new translation that was published in September 1987. Completion of this project was part of an ecumenical linkage of global scale based on the "Guiding Principles for Interconfessional Cooperation in Translating the Bible," issued in 1968 by the United Bible Society and the Vatican's Secretariat for Promotion of Christian Unity.

Initiative for the joint translation project was taken in the mid-1960s by the Japan Bible Society and the Catholic Bishops' Conference. The International Bible Translators Seminar was held in 1966, and the following year the possibility of joint translation work was examined. Strong appeals in support of the project had been made at the seminar, and it was decided to undertake research on unifying the translations of proper names and terminology in the Bible. From this meeting was born the Japan Bible Translation Research Council, which began work from its first session in July 1969. The committee for common translation was formed in May 1970 with five members each from the Japan Bible Society and the Catholic Bishops' Conference; this committee completed its translation work in 1987.

The joint translation project made a major contribution to ecumenism in Japan. Beyond unifying biblical names and terminology, it made available a common Bible, and using it has created greater unity in ecumenical worship services and prayer meetings. Of special importance is uniformity in the Japanese pronunciation of Jesus' name: in Catholic liturgy, it had been pronounced "Iezusu" (yeh-zu-su), whereas Protestants used the slightly different "Iesu" (yeh-su). The Protestant usage was chosen for the common translation.

The introduction to the newly published New Testament (1978) explains that Catholic and Protestant churches have traveled different roads since the sixteenth century, but they have a basis of unity in the Bible. "Through this project we have reaffirmed our responsibility to spread the truth of the Bible to all peoples in a common effort to bring unity among them all. The re-uniting movement among the churches is aimed not only at restoring unity to the divided Christian churches but also at creating a movement of hope for the peace and unity of all humanity. We affirm that Jesus Christ as revealed in the Bible is the Lord of Peace, removing the racial and cultural barriers that separate peoples of the earth."

Translating the WCC Statement on "Baptism, Eucharist, and Ministry"

Dialogue meetings to strengthen relations between the NCCJ's Faith and Order Commission and the Catholic Church's Ecumenism Committee were begun on July 12, 1981, and have been continued every year. Discussions center on the issues faced by Protestant and Catholic churches each year, followed by a question-and-answer period. These meetings have been a valuable forum for advancing ecumenism in Japan.

In July 1985 a joint Catholic-Protestant translation of the World Council of Churches' document "Baptism, Eucharist, and Ministry" was completed. The WCC Faith and Order Commission meeting in Accra, Ghana, in 1974 had issued its initial document, "One Baptism, One Eucharist, and a Mutually Recognized Ministry." Meeting in Lima, Peru, in 1982, the commission issued the "Baptism, Eucharist, and Ministry" document, which was adopted by the Sixth WCC Assembly in Vancouver, Canada, in 1983. It was an epochal event in ecumenical history.

Translation of the WCC document was undertaken by the NCCJ Faith and Order Committee, which also included Catholic and non-NCCJ Protestant members. Given the document's importance, it was agreed to seek wide ecumenical approval of the translation before publishing it. Meetings called for this purpose began in March 1984, and in July 1985 the Japanese version was published. The final translation also included views of an Orthodox Church representative. Protestants and Catholics sponsored a gathering in May 1986 to celebrate the book's publication, and various suggestions for Christian unity were made on this occasion.

It may be added that this same committee produced a common translation of the Lord's Prayer for use in ecumenical services. The trial translation was issued in November 1971, and the approved version was used in the 1972 services of the Week of Prayer for Christian Unity.

JUSTICE AND PEACE ISSUES

The devastation of World War II left Japan with little hope of rapid economic recovery, but the successive occurrence of two costly wars in nearby Asian lands — Korea and Vietnam — had by the 1970s propelled Japan to the threshold of unprecedented prosperity. Two international events had signaled a bright future: the 1964 Tokyo Olympics and the 1970 World Exposition (Expo 70) in Osaka.

The churches in Japan, however, were shaken and divided by the criticism of Expo 70 that erupted. The target of criticism was a pavilion sponsored cooperatively by the NCCJ and the Catholic Church in Japan. Controversy in the United Church of Christ in Japan became so intense that the UCCJ's largest district (Tokyo), for example, was unable to convene its district assembly from 1969 to 1990 (cf. II-8).

The crux of the criticism was not merely to oppose the celebration of Japan's new economic power as represented in Expo but to call for ethical scrutiny of Japan's postwar responsibility toward fellow Asians. The positive impact of all the furor was to stimulate the churches to reflect on "Asia and Japan," "Japan within Asia," and "Asia within Japan."

In 1972 the Catholic Bishops' Conference issued a pastoral letter calling the church, in the spirit of Vatican II, to "take the gospel to society" by tackling the problem of economic inequality. The church's evangelization, it urged, should embrace "the least of these brothers and sisters," especially those who represent "Asia within Japan."

The Japan SODEPAX (Society, Development, and Peace Committee, a joint Catholic-Protestant venture) had been started in January 1971 to deal with problems arising from the war in Indochina, to work for improved Sino-Japanese relations, and to respond to developmental needs in Asia.

Within Japan, establishment of the "lifeline" telephone counseling (cf. III-18) was an example of ecumenical cooperation to help people deal with the many personal dislocations attendant upon rapid economic growth. Many other joint ecumenical activities were undertaken and continued in the 1980s. Several examples follow.

The Christian Association in Kamagasaki

Rapid economic growth has spawned large day-laborers' communities in every metropolitan area: Sanya in Tokyo, Kotobuki in Yokohama, Sasajima in Nagoya, Kamagasaki in Osaka, and Hakata in Fukuoka, to note the larger ones (cf. III-15). Day laborers are at the bottom of the socioeconomic ladder; the social majority treats them contemptuously, referring to them stereotypically as "dirty," "dangerous and frightening," and "lazy."

In Osaka's Kamagasaki district some 40,000 people live in a tiny area of half a square kilometer. Each year, over a hundred die by the roadside; the name and origin of some are unknown. In 1969 a group of Christians began helping these marginalized persons, and in 1970 the Kamagasaki Christian Association (KCA) was formed by the German priest Fr. Heinrich Schnusenberg (Franciscan) and Tani Yasurō of the Catholic Church, the German missionary Elisabeth Strohm (JELC), and Rev. Kanai Aimei (UCCJ). In 1975 three pastors of the Kansai Urban Industrial Mission — Koyanagi Nobuaki, Arakawa Juntarō, and the present writer — cooperated with the KCA to provide overnight camp services to day laborers during winter months. Through such activities, mutual trust was developed among Christian workers and day laborers.

Ecumenical support for day laborers has since spread to day-laborer communities in other cities. But a growing concern at present is how to extend similar services to foreign immigrant workers in Japan.

Peace and antinuclear movements

On August 15, 1970, Catholics for the first time joined in holding the early morning prayer meeting for peace at the National Tomb of the War Dead in Chidorigafuchi Park, giving a stronger ecumenical basis to this annual activity first begun in 1960 by concerned Protestants (cf. IV-24). Chidorigafuchi is located across the street from Yasukuni Shrine, a prime symbol of Japanese militarism. For Christians who struggle against the "nationalization" of Yasukuni Shrine, the annual prayer service is a vital countervailing symbol. Later in the day each August 15, memorial services are held throughout the nation to affirm the necessity of opposing war, not as its victims but with an awareness of having been aggressors in war.

In the months before the United Nations Second Special Session on Disarmament scheduled for June 1982, the movement for general disarmament and abolition of nuclear weapons swelled worldwide. The joint Catholic-Protestant prayer service for peace and a nuclear-free world, held in St. Mary's Cathedral in Tokyo on May 30, 1982, gave voice not only to this global call but also to that of Pacific peoples opposing Japan's plan to dump nuclear wastes in the Pacific Ocean.

On May 3, Constitution Day, in 1984, over three hundred people gathered for a peace prayer meeting sponsored jointly by the Catholic Justice and Peace Council and the NCCJ Peace Committee. This meeting was held in Yokosuka, where both the US Navy and Japan's Maritime Self-Defense Force have large bases. The prayer service was followed by a march down Yokosuka's main street to testify publicly to the values of peace and human rights (cf. II-6).

Yokosuka was again the venue of ecumenical cooperation on April 11, 1988, when Catholic and Protestant clergy in the city petitioned the mayor to refuse port entry and homeporting rights to the US Navy's cruiser *Bunker Hill* and destroyer *Fife*, both of which are fitted for nuclear-capable Tomahawk cruise missiles. To support the UN Third Special Session on Disarmament (June 1988), Catholics and Protestants joined in a prayer meeting on June 12.

Solidarity with Korean Christians

A joint South–North Korean statement in favor of reunification of the Korean peninsula was issued in July 1972; but in October, South Korea's President Park Chung-hee imposed martial law. Those who worked for democracy in South Korea were suppressed, and in 1973 many Christian ministers and priests were arrested. Then on August 8, former presidential candidate Kim Dae-jung, a Catholic, was kidnapped in midday from a Tokyo hotel by agents of the Korean CIA.

In January 1974, the Japan Emergency Christian Conference on Korean Problems was organized, with Rev. Nakajima Masaaki as chairperson. In August of that year an emergency meeting on Korean issues was organized by the NCCJ and the Catholic Justice and Peace Council under the theme "Responding to the Korean people's conscience." Out of this came the Japan–Korea Christian Liaison Council formed by Inoue Yoshio, Masaike Hitoshi, Rev. Lee In-ha, and Bishop Sōma Nobuo.

The Emergency Conference's purpose was to gather information about South Korea's democratization movement and send documentation to supportive people throughout the world. When freedom of speech was stifled under martial law, the conference persevered in its work under very difficult conditions. The Japan–Korea Christian Liaison Council held prayer meetings and symposia to stress the link between the struggle for human rights and the churches' freedom in Korea. The years of continued cooperative struggle with the Koreans propelled the ecumenical effort from the mid-1980s into a movement toward peace and the reunification of South and North Korea, involving the Korean churches and the World Council of Churches (cf. I-2, IV-23).

Solidarity with Philippine Churches

Working in solidarity with Korean churches helped bring the question of Japan–Philippine relations to our attention, for relations with both countries are indicative of problems inherent in the wartime and postwar political and economic situation in Asia. Martial law was declared in the Philippines in September 1972, a month earlier than in South Korea. The Japanese government supported oppressive regimes in both countries with economic aid, and Japan's successful penetration of the Philippine and Korean economies was carried out with support of the dictatorships of both states. Thus Japan's advance into these economies is called "economic invasion." Two typical problems caused by this invasion follow.

Navotas Fishing Port. Due to faulty construction work done by a Japanese company in a project to modernize the Navotas fishing port, residents of the area suffered much in a resulting flood. Refusing to listen to the people's complaints and protests, the company went ahead with its construction work. The present writer visited the area in 1974 and then organized a Kansai

Urban Rural Mission group to work in solidarity with the people in Navotas. Following negotiations with company officials in both Japan and the Philippines, the company finally accepted the demands of the Navotas people.

Kawasaki Steel. Kawasaki Steel had a plant in Chiba (east of Tokyo) that caused serious pollution in the area. Vigorous protests led the company to move its operations to the Philippines, where it built a metal-working (sintering) plant on Mindanao Island. This made Kawasaki Steel a target of criticism for exporting its pollution to the Philippines. Fr. Yamada Keizō visited the area in 1975 and organized solidarity efforts among churches in Japan and the Philippines to increase opposition to the company's activities. From these two cases there developed an ecumenical network called the Japan Coalition for Philippine Concerns (JCPC).

These activities helped Japanese Christians discern their common responsibilities toward Korea and the Philippines. In November 1983 the NCCJ and the Catholic Justice and Peace Council held an international conference on human rights in Korea and the Philippines in the context of peace in Asia. In April 1989 the NCCJ and the NCCC-USA sponsored a Consultation on Peace in Asia and the Pacific, with the participation of Japanese Catholics as well as delegates from the NCCs in Korea and the Philippines.

To address the issue of severe hunger on Negros Island in the Philippines, the Negros Campaign got under way in February 1986 to support the people of Negros in their efforts to achieve economic and political self-reliance.

Human Rights of Korean Residents in Japan

The struggle against compulsory fingerprinting of foreign residents in Japan began in 1980 when a Korean who had lived in Japan for forty years challenged in court the Alien Registration Law's senseless oppression of the rights of habitation and lifestyle. This struggle brought Japanese Christians and foreign missionaries into a joint effort with Koreans in Japan to support fingerprint-refusers. In time, over two hundred support groups were formed nationwide, with Christians taking leading roles. The movement helped deepen our understanding of biblical terms such as "sojourners" and "the least of these brothers and sisters" in the ecumenical context. This new awareness guided the formation in 1987 of the National Christian Council for Dealing with the Alien Registration Law Problem, embracing thirteen churches and organizations, both Catholic and Protestant.

The Emperor System and Yasukuni Shrine

Japan's modernization began with the opening of the Meiji era (1868–1912), but this period also marked the launching of the nationalistic emperor system. In 1868 the Tokyo Shōkonsha, a shrine for the spirits of the war dead, was erected near the Imperial Palace. Its name was changed in 1879 to Yasukuni Shrine. This shrine is where the emperor (Tennō) worships those who died in battle for the Tennō (cf. II-5).[1]

Along with the expansion of the Self-Defense Forces following the end of the Allied Occupation in 1952, the ruling Liberal Democratic Party laid plans to "nationalize" the Yasukuni Shrine (i.e., return it to national government administration and funding, from which the Allied Occupation had separated it on the principle of separation of religion and state). In 1967 a bill calling for nationalization of the shrine was brought before the Bureau of Judicial Affairs of the national parliament's Lower House.

In December 1967 the NCCJ formed its Special Committee on Yasukuni Shrine, and Catholics as well as Protestants not related to the NCCJ were participating in this committee by the following year. The overall movement involves, of course, a much broader religious community embracing Buddhists and adherents of Japan's newer religions.

For the emperor to make visits to this shrine implies official approval of its status as the symbol of Japan's militarism and nationalism. These issues related to the emperor system are of great concern to those who have long struggled with, and at times suffered because of, the imperial ideology and structures.

From the late Shōwa Emperor's death in January 1989 to November 1990, there were four major rites for the accession of the new emperor to the throne. The last two were the public state ceremony of enthronement (Sokui-no-rei) and a private Shinto rite of the Imperial Household, the Daijōsai (Great Food Offering Ceremony), both held in November 1990. The Daijōsai is the rite in which the emperor is traditionally believed to assume his alleged divinity. Christians naturally view government promotion and funding of this Imperial Household rite as unacceptable regression to the past history of imperialism, militarism, and colonialism—all in the name of the emperor.

In November 1989 the Anti-Daijōsai Signature Campaign Center was organized through the cooperation of NCCJ-related, non-NCCJ, and Catholic churches. The center's goal was to take a prophetic role in countering the resurgent nationalism and the revival of the imperial ideology in Japan today.

Ecumenical cooperation in the 1970s and 1980s has presented us with many opportunities to work together on common issues related to the mission of the church. This ecumenical cooperation was not manufactured on

---

[1] Yasukuni is a Shinto shrine, and the "fallen heroes" of war, when enshrined here, are believed to become "gods" in the Shinto sense. — Ed.

some theological premise; rather, it has grown out of our common engagement in these issues and our listening to the voices of God's people, for it is
these shared ministries that have empowered us to enter into authentic ecumenical cooperation and action. May God continue to bless this work for his
Kingdom.

Appendix

Members, Churches, Clergy: 1970-90

Church / Mission	Members	1970 Churches	Clergy
Protestant: NCCJ-related			
United Church of Christ in Japan	204,064	1,652	2,037
Anglican Church in Japan	1,325	335	373
Japan Evangelical Lutheran Church	15,702	142	271
Japan Baptist Convention	21,260	249	319
Japan Baptist Union	4,617	60	105
Korean Christian Church in Japan	2,089	45	41
Protestant: non-NCCJ			
Church of Christ* (Presbyterian)	12,546	120	131
Reformed Church*	5,364	83	89
The Evangelical Alliance Mission (TEAM)	3,823	120	228
Immanuel General Mission	8,227	103	147
Japan Holiness Church	5,215	119	250
Japan Assemblies of God	7,063	104	220
The Salvation Army	10,160	119	265
Seventh-Day Adventist Church	6,699	131	468
Non-Church Group (Mukyōkai)	1,500	50	–
Others	93,186	2,029	2,648
Subtotals			
Protestant Churches/Missions	452,840	5,461	7,992
Roman Catholic Church	337,243	984	9,678†
Holy Orthodox Church	9,549	49	62
Grand totals	779,632	6,494	17,732

*Currently considering NCC membership.

† This figure (for all years) includes clergy as well as men and women in religous orders and societies.

Compiled by Takado Kaname from the *Kirisutokyō nenkan* (Christian Yearbook) for respective years. (Note: Each yearbook reports on the previous year.)

Members, Churches, Clergy — *Continued*

| | 1975 | | | | 1980 | |
Members	Churches	Clergy	Members	Churches	Clergy
Protestant:NCCJ-related					
194,059	1,653	2,270	189,480	1,670	2,188
52,143	334	406	55,252	275	339
17,913	139	161	19,330	141	192
23,113	246	305	25,485	256	327
4,273	61	106	4,114	66	102
2,650	45	40	3,196	48	53
Protestant: non-NCCJ					
12,750	131	147	13,191	130	149
5,798	82	106	6,875	104	103
4,867	109	284	5,735	143	305
8,552	133	159	10,103	150	209
5,966	127	249	7,563	133	276
5,318	108	251	6,722	116	274
9,876	96	249	9,510	89	233
7,771	111	485	9,372	122	825
1,510	45	—	1,557	47	—
100,995	2,078	2,885	108,784	2,367	3,156
Subtotals					
457,554	5,498	8,103	476,249	5,857	8,721
359,176	1,030	9,362	387,204	1,014	9,896
24,758	82	38	25,199	112	72
Grand totals					
841,488	6,610	17,503	888,652	6,983	18,689

Members, Churches, Clergy — *Continued*

Church / Mission	Members	1985 Churches	Clergy
Protestant: NCCJ-related			
United Church of Christ in Japan	196,148	1,697	1,977
Anglican Church in Japan	55,987	317	328
Japan Evangelical Lutheran Church	20,333	138	156
Japan Baptist Convention	26,845	268	364
Japan Baptist Union	4,271	71	104
Korean Christian Church in Japan	4,200	60	60
Protestant: non-NCCJ			
Church of Christ (Presbyterian)	13,213	136	156
Reformed Church	7,918	112	117
The Evangelical Alliance Mission (TEAM)	5,972	125	206
Immanuel General Mission	12,060	164	246
Japan Holiness Church	9,542	152	311
Japan Assemblies of God	8,560	139	272
The Salvation Army	7,894	84	228
Seventh-Day Adventist Church	10,885	137	909
Non-Church Group (Mukyōkai)	1,340	42	–
Others	117,786	3,058	3,381
Subtotals			
Protestant Churches/Missions	502,954	6,680	8,815
Roman Catholic Church	410,758	1,018	8,059
Holy Orthodox Church	25,498	87	78
Grand totals	939,210	7,785	16,952

Members, Churches, Clergy — *Continued*

| | 1990 | |
Members	Churches	Clergy
Protestant: NCCJ-related		
201,468	1,702	2,087
57,478	315	348
21,212	154	149
29,223	294	422
4,884	72	117
5,454	70	64
Protestant: non-NCCJ		
13,719	141	158
8,468	115	143
7,168	144	243
12,090	115	262
10,792	157	315
10,121	156	319
4,933	80	229
11,210	146	125
1,510	60	—
146,782	3,080	4,106
Subtotals		
546,512	6,801	9,087
412,023	1,026	10,281
25,803	86	68
Grand Totals		
984,338	7,913	19,436

Sales Of Bible Supplies in Japan, 1970-90

Year	Full Bibles	Old Testaments	New Testaments	Subtotals
1970	157,611	14,152	496,704	668,467
1971	163,912	11,624	495,083	670,619
1972	187,459	11,954	657,969	857,382
1973	234,160	13,463	1,031,370	1,278,993
1974	238,737	13,729	799,217	1,051,683
1975	228,845	15,188	1,056,274	1,300,307
1976	203,557	9,979	885,358	1,098,894
1977	227,670	12,410	974,562	1,214,642
1978	210,392	10,287	1,042,201	1,262,880
1979	222,009	12,323	927,293	1,161,625
1980	244,430	12,688	1,205,826	1,462,944
1981	251,181	13,755	924,084	1,189,020
1982	221,461	13,950	766,359	1,001,770
1983	174,657	11,305	907,059	1,093,021
1984	184,135	10,848	704,281	899,264
1985	182,276	9,527	831,135	1,022,938
1986	190,179	10,019	498,858	699,056
1987	250,142	8,661	835,075	1,093,878
1988	233,737	7,238	419,467	660,442
1989	218,156	5,357	565,409	788,922
1990	225,312	3,060	672,782	901,154
Totals	4,450,018	231,517	16,696,366	21,377,901

Source: Japan Bible Society

Sales Of Bible Supplies — *Continued*

Single Books[1]	Braille	Tapes	Tracts[2]	Maps	Totals
3,271,536	4,870	—	4,928,175	6,886	8,879,934
565,331	4,206	—	4,165,664	7,986	5,413,806
455,849	3,755	—	4,327,864	9,620	5,654,470
1,307,142	4,802	—	4,730,180	14,428	7,335,545
652,769	4,714	—	4,578,495	18,486	6,306,147
170,363	4,515	—	5,792,620	14,958	7,282,763
224,766	4,201	—	6,664,328	12,069	8,004,258
269,087	5,067	709	9,361,401	14,170	10,865,076
126,020	5,122	1,656	9,088,475	12,414	10,496,567
89,290	4,977	1,671	8,662,211	14,971	9,934,745
199,610	5,750	1,517	10,203,039	13,410	11,886,270
76,090	5,672	1,718	8,477,773	12,619	9,762,892
60,340	6,274	1,839	10,144,690	12,404	11,227,317
106,299	6,213	2,172	8,626,031	7,811	9,841,547
119,843	4,899	3,203	7,817,336	7,542	8,852,087
73,338	5,044	5,128	7,465,970	9,617	8,582,035
64,256	4,397	4,922	8,245,901	7,372	9,025,904
79,878	4,534	4,945	8,321,072	6,744	9,511,051
89,038	3,876	4,332	6,914,940	6,392	7,679,020
32,500	6,382	3,532	7,807,489	3,964	8,642,789
39,890	7,575	3,992	7,661,998	4,783	8,619,392
8,073,235	106,845	41,336	153,985,652	218,646	183,803,615

[1] E.g., Psalms, one of the four Gospels.
[2] Selected Bible sentences in leaflet form.

Chronology: 1945–90

ABBREVIATIONS USED:

CCA	Christian Conference of Asia
CCC	China Christian Council
JEA	Japan Evangelical Association
JELC	Japan Evangelical Lutheran Church
JBC	Japan Baptist Convention
JBU	Japan Baptist Union
KCCJ	Korean Christian Church in Japan
NCCC-USA	National Council of Churches of Christ in the USA
NCCJ	National Christian Council in Japan
NSKK	Nippon Sei Kō Kai (Anglican Church in Japan)
RCCJ	Roman Catholic Church in Japan
UCCJ	United Church of Christ in Japan
WCC	World Council of Churches

PREPARATORY PERIOD: 1945–70

1945

Aug. 15   World War II ends; Japan accepts terms of Postdam Declaration (emperor system remains intact).

1947

May 2   Alien Registration Law is issued as emperor's final imperial ordinance under old Constitution.

May 3   Japan's postwar Constitution (promulgated Nov. 30, 1946) becomes effective.

1948

Apr. 14   UCCJ founds Research Center for the Christianization of Rural Areas (forerunner of Tsurukawa Rural Seminary).

Aug. 22   World Council of Churches is founded at inaugural assembly (to Sept. 4).

1950

June 25	Korean War begins (truce is signed July 27, 1953).
July 8	Gen. Douglas MacArthur, Supreme Commander for the Allied Powers (SCAP), orders Japan to establish National Police Reserves (forerunner of today's tri-service Self-Defense Forces).

1951

Jan. 1	Gen. Douglas MacArthur calls for peace treaty and rearmament of Japan.
Apr. 13	Christian Peace Association is founded to oppose rearmament, preserve the Constitution, and promote peace activities in Christian churches.

1952

Apr. 28	San Francisco Peace Treaty and Japan–US Security Treaty (signed Sept. 8, 1951) become effective, ending Allied Occupation of Japan.
May 2	Alien Registration Law is revised, making fingerprinting mandatory.

1956

Dec. 18	Japan becomes member of United Nations.

1959

May 14–24	East Asia Christian Conference is founded.

1960

June 19	Japan–US Security Treaty is revised; 300,000 anti-treaty demonstrators surround National Diet building.
Mar. 18	Japan Overseas Christian Medical Cooperative Service (JOCS) is founded by Japan Christian Medical Association (est. 1946).

1962

Oct. 11	Vatican Council II begins (to Dec. 8, 1965).
Nov. 3	UCCJ issues declaration on preservation of Constitution; designates first Sunday in August as "Peace Sunday."

1965

Sept. 25   Japan and South Korea sign treaty for normalization of relations, leaving unresolved status issues for Koreans in Japan.

1967

Mar. 26   UCCJ Moderator Suzuki Masahisa issues "Confession of Responsibility During World War II."

July 28   UCCJ sets up Special Committee on Yasukuni Shrine Issue (NCCJ forms similar committee in December).

1968

Mar. 19–20   NCCJ General Assembly approves plan for Christian Pavilion at 1970 World Exposition in Osaka.

Mar. 20   NCCJ issues statement against bill to nationalize Yasukuni Shrine.

Apr. 29   Japan Evangelical Association (JEA) is founded.

Sept. 15   Japan Christian Publications Distribution Co. (Nikkihan) is founded.

1969

Feb. 25   UCCJ merges with United Church of Christ in Okinawa.

May 24   Catholic and Protestant representatives form Japan Ecumenical Association.

June 30   Liberal Democratic Party introduces bill for nationalization of Yasukuni Shrine (repeats annually through 1973).

July 31   To date, religious groups' nationwide campaign against state administration of Yasukuni Shrine garner 3,772,218 signatures.

Dec. 9–12   NCCJ and NCCC-USA hold joint peace conference; discuss Japan–US Security Treaty and Okinawa.

1970

Mar. 15   World Exposition (Expo 70) opens in Osaka (to Sept. 13).

Apr. 10   Japan Holy Orthodox Church's intention to become independent is recognized by Russian Orthodox Church headquarters in Moscow; Japan denomination holds first general assembly July 12.

Apr. 27   Japan Evangelical Theological Society is formed.

July 12–18   Baptist World Congress is held in Tokyo.

Aug. 27   First Catholic-Protestant committee convenes for inter-confessional translation project for a common Bible.

Nov. 5   Japan Christian Center building is completed (Tokyo).

Nov. 22–29   First conference of Asian Catholic Bishops convenes at St. Thomas University in the Philippines; Federation of Asian Bishops' Conferences (FABC) is formed.

1971–90 PERIOD

1971

Jan. 19   Japan SODEPAX (Society, Development, and Peace) Committee is formed by NCCJ International Affairs Committee and Catholic Justice and Peace Council; holds first conference Aug. 25–27 on "Asia and Japan."

July 18   Japan YWCA's "Pilgrimage to Hiroshima" annual program begins.

Oct. 1   Inochi no Denwa (Telephone Counseling) is founded (Inochi no Denwa Association is formed Aug. 16, 1977).

1972

Mar. 10   Centennial of first Protestant church in Japan.

Apr. 29   First meeting of RCCJ–NSKK joint dialogue committee.

May 15   Ryukyu Islands, including Okinawa, revert to Japan.

Oct. 17   President Park Chung-hee declares martial law in South Korea, followed by arrests of democratization advocates, including many Christians.

Oct. 20   Kyo Bun Kwan inaugurates 18-volume series, *Gendai Nihon Kirisutokyō bungaku zenshū* (Anthology of contemporary Japanese Christian literature).

Nov. 24   Japanese Diet confirms "Three Non-nuclear Principles" proposed in Jan. 1968 by Prime Minister Satō Eisaku.

1973

Jan. 1   Japan–North American Commission on Cooperative Mission (JNAC) replaces Interboard Committee for Christian Work in Japan (IBC).

              RCCJ establishes Naha Diocese, following May 1972 reversion of Okinawa to Japan.

Feb. 28   Japan Holy Orthodox Church opens Tokyo Orthodox Theo-
            logical Seminary.

May 14   Asian Rural Institute is founded (formerly Southeast Asia
            Rural Christian Leaders Training Course, now separated from
            Tsurukawa Rural Seminary).

July 2–6   First Japan–South Korea Church Consultation is held by
            NCCs of both countries (Seoul); Korean Church Women
            United appeal for action against Japanese sex tours to Korea.

Aug. 19   Centennial of Baptist mission in Japan is celebrated at the first
            Baptist church in Japan (Yokohama).

Nov. 20–23 UCCJ General Assembly convenes after four-year lapse due
            to Expo 70 dispute.

1974

Jan. 15   Japan Emergency Christian Conference on Korean Problems
            is formed; Liaison Christian Council between Korea and
            Japan is organized.

Apr. 22   Federation of Asian Bishops' Conferences (FABC) holds first
            convention in Taipei.

Apr. 26   Japan Holy Orthodox Church becomes member of World
            Council of Churches.

June 3–7   Japan Congress on Evangelism is held by JEA in Kyoto.

June 9   KCCJ Research–Action Institute for Koreans in Japan
            (RAIK) is founded in Tokyo.

July 16–25 International Congress on World Evangelization is held in
            Lausanne.

Sept. 3–5   All-Lutheran Multimedia Evangelism Conference in Kyoto
            launches five-year, ¥300-million multimedia project.

Oct. 10   Kyo Bun Kwan inaugurates 15-volume series *Kindai Nihon
            Kirisutokyō bungaku zenshū* (Anthology of modern Japanese
            Christian literature).

Dec. 10–13 UCCJ General Assembly acknowledges error in approving
            UCCJ participation as co-sponsor of Christian Pavilion at
            Expo 70.

1975

Apr. 22   National Catholic Women's League is founded in Tokyo.

June 27   First Vietnamese refugees reach Japan; Caritas Japan provides
            five temporary shelters in churches and convents.

July 7	RCCJ founds Federation of Catholic Colleges (Hiroshima)
Aug. 15	Prime Minister Miki Takeo makes first official postwar visit to Yasukuni Shrine, though as a "private citizen"; helps redefine this day as occasion for memorializing war's end to one for honoring the nation's "fallen heroes."

Association of Bereaved Christian Families issue denunciation of imperial and official government visits to Yasukuni Shrine, of unilateral state memorializing of Christians, and of claim that Yasukuni Shrine is a sacred place for all of Japan's war dead.

Sept. 15	Japan Bible Society celebrates centennial.
Sept. 18	NCCJ Faith and Order Commission issues statement that "the Unification Association does not accord with NCCJ's definition of Christian" (reaffirms statement Jan. 18, 1979).
Nov. 1	Catholic Justice and Peace Council holds first nationwide convention (Tokyo).

1976

Mar. 25–26	NCCJ adopts resolution opposing nuclear weapons and nuclear energy plants (later forms study group, May 12, 1978).
May 1	RCCJ forms Federation of Catholic Junior Colleges.
Oct. 16	Catholic Bishops' Conference founds Japan Missionary and Pastoral Center (renamed Japan Catholic Missionary Research Center, Sept. 14, 1984).

1977

Apr. 13	Caritas Japan sponsors first liaison conference of Vietnam refugee center directors (22 persons from 9 institutions).
Apr. 28–29	Federation of Evangelical Churches in the UCCJ is formed.
May 16–18	NSKK canon law change makes women eligible for ordination as deacons (first women ordained to diaconate in 1978).
June 8	Ministry of Education urges singing of *Kimigayo* imperial anthem in elementary and middle schools.
Oct. 11–13	KCCJ approves ordination of female clergy and elders.
Nov. 3	Japanese representatives attend first meeting of the Pontifical Council for Laity (at the Vatican)

1978

Feb. 11   800 participants join Christian rally in Tokyo on theme of "Yasukuni Shrine — assessing wartime responsibility."

Apr. 6–12   Okinawa Christian Council (OCC) and NCCC-USA hold church consultation on problems of US military bases in Naha.

May 12   NCCJ Executive Committee forms Nuclear Issue Study Group proposed by Sekiya Ayako (NCCJ vice-moderator) and others.

Aug. 24–30   CCA sponsors first consultation on Christian art in Asia (Indonesia).

Sept. 15   Interconfessional translation of New Testament is published (New Common Bible, Sept. 5, 1987).

Oct. 7–10   Fourth national convention of the Catholic Justice and Peace Council takes up Buraku problem.

Dec. 25   RCCJ publishes Japanese Missal, vernacular translation of the liturgy inspired by Vatican II.

1979

Mar. 26–27   NCCJ appoints Special Committee on Physically Disabled Persons (in July renamed NCCJ Task Force of Disabled Persons and the Church).

June 15   Japan Missionary and Pastoral Center (RCCJ) issues document "Toward the evangelization of Japanese society."

Aug. 8–10   JBC adopts new "Statement of Faith" (replaces 1947 Statement).

Sept. 3–30   First East-West Spiritual Exchange sends fifty-one Buddhist priests (mostly Zen) to experience monastic life in eleven European monasteries; exchanges continue every four years, with Japanese Buddhists and European Christians alternating.

Sept. 24–28   CCA and NCCJ hold joint conference in Tokyo on human rights issues of the Philippines.

Oct. 16   NCCJ forms Peace Study Committee (later, Peace Committee).

1980

Apr. 1   Merger of Japan Christian Theological Seminary, Tokyo Christian College, and Kyōritsu Women's Bible Institute (from Apr. 1, 1990, Tokyo Christian University).

June	Catholic Justice and Peace Council begins circulating petition demanding immediate withdrawal of Japan's plan to dispose radioactive waste in the ocean (76,000 signatures collected by March 1981).
Aug. 23	National Catholic Youth Gathering (Nagasaki) draws 1,300 young people.
Nov. 23–24	Japan YMCA celebrates centennial.

1981

Feb. 23	Pope John Paul II visits Japan; makes peace appeals in Hiroshima (25) and Nagasaki (26).
June 12	RCCJ Committee for Ecumenism and NCCJ Faith and Order Commission hold first annual meeting for dialogue.
June 29	JBC, NCCJ, RCCJ, and UCCJ join other religious organizations to form Religious Council for Solidarity in Dealing with Dōwa [Assimilation] Problem.
Sept. 1	UCCJ opens Buraku Liberation Center in Osaka (dedicated Nov. 8).

1982

Mar. 17–18	NCCJ establishes Center for Christian Response to Asian Issues (CCRAI) in Tokyo; dedicated June 5.
	RCCJ forms National Liaison Association of Catholic Volunteers.
May 22	RCCJ peace mission, represented by Archbishop Shirayanagi Seiichi, presents nuclear disarmament petition with 429,690 signatures to UN Second Special Session on Disarmament.
May 30	Joint Catholic-Protestant prayer meeting for peace at St. Mary's Cathedral in Tokyo draws over 2,000 participants.
June 5	Catholic Bishops' Conference proclaims Aug. 6–15 annual Peace Week (first is observed this year).
June 7	NCCJ Vice-moderator Sekiya Ayako leads religious delegation to deliver 300,000 signatures to UN Second Special Session on Disarmament, in New York City (to July 10).
July 17	Catholic Liaison Association for the Disabled holds founding convention in Kyoto.
Aug. 25–27	JELC adopts new Book of Worship.

1983

Jan 10   Catholic National Strategy Committee for Settlement of Refugees holds first national meeting.

Apr. 13   RCCJ forms Committee to Help Asian Women Residing in Japan, in response to request of Bishops' Conference of the Philippines.

May 3–5   JELC holds first Hiroshima Peace Seminar (also Nagasaki Peace Seminar, Aug. 7–9).

May 21   CCA Urban Rural Mission founds Asian Women Workers Center (Tokyo).

June 1   Korean Christian Center (KCCJ) is completed in Osaka.

July 18   Okinawa Christian Center (Ginowan City, Okinawa) founds Peace Center.

Sept. 1   KCCJ ordains first women minister.

Sept. 22   Ten NCCJ representatives visit restored churches in China at invitation of China Christian Council (CCC) (to Oct. 22).

Oct. 3   Christian Council for Solidarity in Dealing with Buraku Problems is formed by Catholics and Protestants.

Nov. 1–2   Catholic Justice and Peace Council and Protestant NCCJ hold international consultation on "Peace in Asia: human rights in Korea and the Philippines."

1984

Jan. 12   Catholic Justice and Peace Council forms Committee for Buraku Liberation.

Apr. 7   Yodogawa Christian Hospital opens 23-bed hospice.

May 3   Over 300 people attend prayer meeting for peace, sponsored by NCCJ and Catholic Justice and Peace Council.

June 23   RCCJ adopts "Basic Policy and Priorities of the Japan Catholic Church," making first National Incentive Congress for Evangelization (NICE-I) focus of the church's work.

Sept. 22   NCCJ hosts ten CCC leaders on visit to Japanese churches (to Oct. 2).

Oct. 29   WCC sponsors ecumenical consultation on "Peace and justice in Northeast Asia" at Tōzansō, Japan (to Nov. 2).

Nov. 12–14   UCCJ issues "Basic Understanding of Mission in the World," placing missional priority on Asian context.

1985

Jan. 10   RCCJ decides to issue braille editions of all National Catholic Committee publications, and grants permission for enlarged copying and sound recording.

Jan. 20   RCCJ Committee for Other Faiths issues "Handbook for Catholic faithful concerning ancestors and the departed."

Mar. 28–30   NCCJ Peace Committee holds first peace conference, near Tokyo.

May 13–14   RCCJ holds first study seminar on problems of Asian women residing in Japan; publishes handbook.

June 22   Catholic Bishops' Conference of Japan issues statement "to clarify the fact that the Unification association cannot be considered a Christian church, even less . . . in accord with the Catholic Church, (and) does not fall within the scope of the ecumenical movement."

Aug. 15   Prime Minister breaks all precedents by taking entire Cabinet on "official visit" to Yasukuni Shrine.

Sept. 2–4   Christian Publishers Association founds Christian Literature Fund (50 million yen) to stabilize Christian bookstores.

1986

Feb–July   RCCJ holds open hearings in major cities to prepare for first National Incentive Congress on Evangelization.

Apr. 1   Asian Women's Shelter HELP is founded by Japan Woman's Christian Temperance Union to commemorate centennial.

Apr. 26   Chernobyl nuclear accident spreads radioactive plume over Eastern and Western Europe, stirring nuclear anxiety worldwide.

Aug. 29   NCCJ Peace Committee holds second peace conference in Yokohama, conducts observations of US and Japanese military facilities (to Sept. 1).

Sept. 2–5   Christians from North and South Korea meet for first time since division, in Glion, Switzerland.

Sept. 17   At fourth convention of Federation of Asian Bishops' Conferences (FABC), Archbishop Shirayanagi Seiichi confesses war responsibility of Japan and Japanese church, apologizes to Asian bishops (first formal RCCJ statement on this matter).

Nov. 11–13   UCCJ General Assembly issues statement disclaiming any relationship with the Unification Association and declares mission cooperation with it "impossible."

1987

Jan. 15   National Christian Council for Dealing with the Alien Registration Law Problem is formed by thirteen churches and organizations, both Catholic and Protestant.

Feb. 23   International Exhibition of Christian Art in Asia embarks on European and USA tour (to Mar. 7).

Mar. 31   JELC, with NCCJ cooperation, holds Hiroshima International Peace Seminar on "Our Christian mission for reconciliation today" (to Apr. 3).

May 5–12   NCCJ three-person group visits Christians in North Korea.

July 27–30   NCCJ Peace Caravan (16 participants, 2,000 km) visits churches and nuclear sites in northeastern Japan.

Aug. 1–3   NCCJ Peace Committee holds third peace conference (Sendai) on "Peace as today's mission priority."

Sept. 5   New Common Bible is published (dedicated Sept. 15).

Nov. 20–23   RCCJ convenes first National Incentive Congress on Evangelization (NICE-I) in Kyoto.

Dec. 30   Singapore government abruptly closes CCA office and expels CCA staff from country; NCCJ hosts CCA head office in Osaka (other units dispersed to Manila, Hong Kong, and Chiengmai).

1988

Jan. 15–17   Seven women from Japan attend first Japan–Korean Women's Theological Consultation in Seoul (second in 1989, in Tokyo).

Apr. 4   International Christian Consultation on Peace and Justice in Korea, in Inchon, South Korea.

Apr. 11   Catholic and Protestant clergy in Yokosuka petition mayor to deny port entry and homeporting to two nuclear-capable US Navy vessels.

May 25   Delegation takes petition for disarmament and abolition of nuclear weapons, bearing signatures of 206 Roman Catholic bishops in Asia, to UN Third Special Session on Disarmament.

July 24–27   NCCJ Peace Caravan conducts study of ten military sites of US and Japan along circular perimeter of metropolitan Tokyo.

Oct. 17–19   NCCJ sponsors symposium on "Japan and peaceful reunification of the Korean Peninsula" (Tokyo).

Nov. 11   RCCJ celebrates 400th anniversary of Funai Diocese (Oita) in Kyushu.

Nov. 15–17   UCCJ forms Special Committee on Gender Discrimination (active from Mar. 27, 1989).

Dec. 16   Catholic Bishops' Conference follows up NICE-I proposals by founding Japan Catholic Formation Center (later named Japan Catholic Study Center) in Nagoya; plans second National Incentive Congress on Evangelization (NICE-II).

1989

Jan. 7   Shōwa Emperor (Hirohito) dies.

Mar. 29   NCCJ and NCCC-USA hold Consultation on Peace in Asia and the Pacific, near Tokyo (to Apr. 1), with participants from Japan, USA, Canada, Korea, Philippines.

July 11–20   Second Lausanne World Evangelism Congress is convened in Manila.

Sept. 21   NCCJ approves Anti-Daijōsai Signature Campaign Center, with support of non-NCCJ and Catholic churches; center opens Nov. 1.

Sept. 28   Twenty church representatives from North and South Korea join Japanese colleagues in Tokyo consultation on peaceful reunification of Korean peninsula (to Oct. 5).

1990

Mar. 5–12   WCC sponsors conference on "Justice, peace, and the integrity of creation" in Seoul, Korea.

May 20–24   NSKK approves new Book of Common Prayer (provisional revision issued May 1986); passes resolution for "committee to study ordination of women to the orders of priest and bishop."

June 13–18   NCCJ hosts WCC fact-finding team on discrimination against foreigners in Japan.

July 10–13   Five North Korean Christians visit Japan at KCCJ invitation for meetings on peaceful reunification of Korean peninsula.

July 14–21	NCCJ's Center for Christian Response to ASIAN Issues (CCRAI) sends group to China.
Aug. 26	Catholics and Protestants hold joint assembly to oppose homeporting of two US Navy nuclear-capable vessels in Yokosuka.
Aug. 27–31	Asian Missions Congress is held in Seoul.
Oct. 1	Gospel '90 meeting is held in Tokyo.
Oct. 17–21	Luis Palau Crusade is held in Osaka.
Nov. 12	Enthronement ceremony (Sokui-no-rei) is held for Emperor Akihito.
Nov. 22–23	"Great Food Offering Ceremony" (Daijōsai), a Shinto rite, completes imperial succession.

Index

Index

Christianity in Japan, 1971-90

定価3,500 円
（本体3,398 円）

1991 年 5 月 20 日　初版発行

編　者　熊沢義宣・D. スウェイン　　　　　装　幀　熊谷博人
発行者　中村義治
発行所　株式会社　教文館
　　　　東京都中央区銀座 4—5—1　振替・東京 2—11357　電話 03(3561)5549
印刷所　壮光舎印刷株式会社
製本所　渡辺製本株式会社

配給元　日キ販　東京都新宿区新小川町 9—1　振替・東京 3—60976
電話 03(3260)5670　　　　ISBN 4-7642-7133-8

© 1991　落丁・乱丁本はお取り替えいたします．　　Printed in Japan